Life Experiences, Development and Childhood Psychopathology

Ian M. Goodyer

University of Cambridge and Addenbrookes Hospital

JOHN WILEY & SONS

Chichester · New York · Brisbane · Toronto · Singapore

Other Wiley Editorial Offices

John Wiley & Sons, Inc., 605 Third Avenue,
New York, NY 10158-0012, USA

Jacaranda Wiley Ltd, G.P.O. Box 859, Brisbane,
Queensland 4001, Australia

John Wiley & Sons (Canada) Ltd, 22 Worcester Road,
Rexdale, Ontario M9W 1L1, Canada

John Wiley & Sons (SEA) Pte Ltd, 37 Jalan Pemimpin #05-04,
Block B, Union Industrial Building, Singapore 2057

Library of Congress Cataloging-in-Publication Data:

Goodyer, Ian M.
    Life experiences, development, and childhood psychopathology / Ian
M. Goodyer.
        p.   cm. – (Wiley series on studies in child psychiatry)
    Includes bibliographical references.
    ISBN 0-471-91602-1
    1. Life change events—Psychological aspects. 2. Child
development. 3. Child psychopathology. I. Title. II. Series.
    [DNLM: 1. Child Development. 2. Life Change Events—in infancy &
childhood. 3. Mental Disorders—in infancy & childhood.
4. Personality Development. 5. Socialization. WS 105 G658L]
RJ507.L53G66 1989
155.4—dc20
DNLM/DLC
for Library of Congress   89–16630
                                                            CIP

British Library Cataloguing in Publication Data:

Goodyer, Ian M.
    Life experiences, development and childhood
psychopathology.
    1. Children. Psychopathology
    I. Title
    618.92 8907

    ISBN 0-471-91602-1

ISBN 0 471 91602 1 (ppc)
ISBN 0 471 93132 2 (pbk)

For Jane, Adam and Sarah

Contents

Series Preface

During recent years there has been a tremendous growth of research in both child development and child psychiatry. Research findings are beginning to modify clinical practice but, to a considerable extent, the fields of child development and of child psychiatry have remained surprisingly separate, with regrettably little cross-fertilization. Not much developmental research has concerned itself with clinical issues. Studies of clinical syndromes have all too often been made within the narrow confines of a pathological condition approach with scant regard to developmental matters. The situation is rapidly changing but the results of clinical–developmental studies are often only reported by means of scattered papers in scientific journals. The *Wiley Series on Studies in Child Psychiatry* aims to bridge the gap between child development and clinical psychiatry by presenting reports of new findings, new ideas, and new approaches in a book form that will make them available to a wider readership.

The series includes reviews of specific topics, multi-authored volumes on a common theme, and accounts of specific pieces of research. However, in all cases the aim is to provide a clear, readable and interesting account of scientific findings in a way that makes explicit their relevance to clinical practice or social policy. It is hoped that the Series will be of interest to both clinicians and researchers in the fields of child psychiatry, child psychology, psychiatric social work, social paediatrics and education—in short all concerned with the growing child and his problems.

This seventh volume focuses on the role of acute life events and chronic life experiences in the genesis of child psychiatric disorder. The general topic of 'stress' has been the subject of much research and there is a large literature on life events and adult disorder. However, it is only in the last few years that much serious attention has been paid to the issue as it applies to children. In this highly topical book, Ian Goodyer reviews the field in terms of concepts, empirical findings and clinical implications. Attention is drawn to the need to consider the links between acute happenings and the longstanding adversities that often precede or follow them. Do psychiatric risks derive from the *event* of parental divorce or from the discord and conflict that precede the breakup or from the many changes in family life that tend to follow? Is bereavement a risk factor mainly as a consequence of the feelings of loss or are the subsequent changed patterns of child care the more relevant factor? In order to seek answers to questions such as these, Ian Goodyer brings together a complex literature on chronic adversities and on acute life events—two topics that have tended to remain surprisingly separate from each other.

His approach differs from that usually followed in the adult field in terms of a strong concern for developmental issues. The book tackles a range of developmental questions of theoretical and practical importance. For example, it asks whether the risks to children from unpleasant 'stress' experiences mainly stem from *parental* reactions or from their own direct responses. In what ways, for example, do the responses of adolescents to bereavement, or hospital admission, or war, differ from those of pre-school children? In tackling these questions, Ian Goodyer succinctly summarizes some of the relevant key features of childhood psychological development.

Psychosocial researchers and clinicians generally think about peoples' responses to psychological stress in terms of the emotions and thought processes that are evoked. That is, of course, a crucial part of the story. However, laboratory researchers concerned with stress effects have mostly focused on physiological reactions to physical stressors with a special emphasis on neuroendocrine and autonomic processes. In recent times, attention has also been paid to possible effects on the immune system. The book reviews what is known in these fields and considers its application to the psychosocial arena.

Clinicians have to be concerned with the practical implications of research findings. Accordingly, the final chapters of the book turn to questions on what should be done to prepare children to cope with stress experiences and what types of treatment are required to help those who have experienced bereavement or disasters.

Much remains to be learned on the types of children's reactions to stress and adversity, but already much knowledge has accumulated. This book admirably brings together concepts and findings in its appraisal of the policy and practice implications of research findings and in its evaluation of the questions that remain to be tackled.

Michael Rutter

Preface

The last decade has seen a substantial increase in the literature on stress in childhood and adolescence. We have had scientific confirmation of the importance
of family and social adversities in the onset, and maintenance, of emotional and
behavioural disorders in childhood and adolescence and researchers have begun
to look for factors in the environment that protect children from such disorders.
While there are still many questions to be answered concerning the role of social
experiences in children's lives, recent research has improved our understanding
of the mechanisms through which social factors exert their influences on the
maintenance of well-being and the development of psychopathology.

The findings of social psychiatric research in young people has demonstrated
that the processes involved in the child's appraisal of desirable and undesirable social experiences are important mediators in determining an individuals
response to the environment. Physiological as well as psychological factors contribute to this appraisal process and highlight the complex relationships that
exist between neural and hormonal networks, emotions and cognitions.

The clinical significance of social adversity has resulted in considerable debate about how children should be treated following severe life events such as
divorce, death and personal injury. The importance of formulating social policy, to prevent or ameliorate the effects of chronic social adversities, has also
received considerable attention.

These three broad themes—social causation, personal disposition and practical implications of life experience—are brought together in this volume. A
developmental view is taken throughout; showing how similar life experiences
can exert different effects at different ages and stages of a child's life. It is apparent, for example, that mental disorder in young people is more likely to be
caused by configurations of social factors rather than by any single experience
from the child's past or, indeed, present. It is also becoming apparent that the
effects caused by such configurations of social experience derive from different
physiological and psychological pathways. Thus, no single theory of stress can
account for an individual's response, in either the short or long term, to recent
life events or ongoing difficulties.

It is clear that our knowledge of the links between social psychological and
physiological factors is limited and many questions remain to be answered. Fu-

ture research requires closer co-operation between developmental scientists and clinical practitioners in the field of child mental health. A theory of developmental psychopathology will then continue to unfold—informing clinicians, assisting treatment and policy decisions, and clarifying the origins and consequences of life experiences in young people.

Finally, I should like to thank Michael Rutter for his invitation to write this book and for his advice on earlier drafts of the manuscript. Thanks are also due to my former teachers and colleagues in the Departments of Psychiatry and Child Psychiatry at the Universities of Oxford, Newcastle and Manchester in the UK and Brown University, in the USA. The efforts of Maureen Noble and Eileen Richardson in the preparation of this book are gratefully acknowledged.

Part One

Social Conditions

Chapter 1

Social Events, Experiences and Development

STRESS AND PSYCHIATRIC DISORDER—HISTORICAL INTRODUCTION

The word stress can be found in the *Oxford English Dictionary* and has acquired a diversity of meanings over many years. The word itself has continued to enjoy a widespread use in biology and medicine despite an almost chaotic disagreement over its definition (Mason, 1975). From a scientific point of view the word stress is used to mean many things by many different people and may refer to:

1. A form of stimulus or stressor;
2. An inferred inner state;
3. An observable response or reaction.

Much research on stress has concentrated on a class of stimuli or situations to which everyone is exposed to a greater or lesser extent in the natural course of life. These phenomena have been called life events and are components of the first definition of stress given above, i.e. a stimulus or stressor.

The notion that such events can be considered as stressors was postulated by physiologists who became interested in the relationship between bodily changes and certain factors containing an emotional component, such as pain and hunger. Cannon (1929) made a detailed observation of bodily changes related to pain and hunger and the major emotions; his experimental work provided the necessary link in the argument that stressful life events can prove harmful and he cited a number of striking clinical cases. For example, a case of persistent vomiting which started when an income tax collector threatened punishment if a discrepancy in a tax statement was not explained, and which ceased as soon as the clinician went to the collector as a therapeutic measure and straightened out the difficulty.

Through both further experimental studies and clinical examples such as these he showed that external stimuli associated with emotional arousal caused changes in basic physiological processes. In this manner Cannon laid the groundwork for psychophysiological research (Cannon, 1928, 1929).

A further influence came from the studies made by Selye (1956) who concluded that stress is a part of life and that the ordinary everyday activities of living, e.g. eating or not eating, breathing or not breathing, muscular activity or no muscular activity, sleeping or not sleeping, all effect the dynamic steady state. He stated that the effects of these activities are not qualitatively different from those stressors that are used in the laboratory and that 'to be alive is to be under stress'. Selye's idea formed the basis of research on relationships between stressors and physiochemical responses. In recent times these studies have included the examination of relationships between specific stressful experiences that can be considered fear-provoking, and biological changes in the subject, in particular effects on cortisol secretion (Cox, 1978; Rose, 1980). The foundations of this work also included the influence of Harold Wolff, who investigated the relationships between emotional factors and bodily changes (Wolff et al., 1950).

Studies on patients with physical disease suggested that clusters of life events occurred prior to the development of symptoms and a number of authors suggested that events requiring a change in life circumstances were intimately associated with physical disease (Weiss et al., 1957; Greene and Miller, 1958; Graham and Stevenson, 1963; Rahe and Holmes, 1965). The physical illnesses studied included coronary disease, pulmonary disease, reticuloendothelial disease and inguinal hernias. From these studies researchers had suggested that clustering of life events achieved aetiological significance as a necessary but insufficient cause of these illnesses. However, these studies had no systematic method for collecting life event information and lacked specificity concerning the types and numbers of events recorded.

Within psychiatry the aetiological importance of life events was first suggested by Adolph Meyer. Meyer, a physician and psychiatrist, placed great emphasis on the use of the life event chart as a tool in diagnosis, and he described important aspects of this part of his practice in his writings (Meyer, 1951). He considered it important to document the patient's date of birth, periods of disorders of various organs, and data concerning the situations and reactions of the patient. Situations he considered important were: the change of habitat; school entrance; school graduation; school change or failure; various jobs; dates of potentially important births and deaths in the family and other fundamentally environmental incidents.

A crucial conceptual issue that Meyer advocated was that life events played a part in the aetiology of psychiatric disorder. Meyer suggested that life events need not be bizarre or catastrophic to be pathogenic and even the most normal necessary life events are potential contributors to the development of psychiatric conditions. His teaching was reflected in a conference held in 1949 in the United States by the Association of Research into Nervous and Mental Diseases; Life Stress and Bodily Disease. By this time there was already extensive research attempting to examine the effects of stress on a variety of symptoms affecting different physical structures, such as the intestinal tract, the respiratory system, muscles and joints, the cardiovascular system, skin diseases, genito-urinary disorders and growth development.

Following Meyer's work, researchers have attempted to answer the question as to whether or not there is a relationship between stressful life events of any type and the development of psychiatric disorder. If Selye's observations about the general adaptation of stress were correct, then any event which effects the dynamic steady state can be construed as having some stressful component. The key question then is, 'What are the properties or conditions that distinguish more stressful life events from less stressful life events?' If such properties can be identified then what are the pathological effects on such events?

Since the observations of Meyer, a number of approaches to the study of stressful life events have occurred, some researchers have studied clinical syndromes whilst others have been concerned with epidemiological approaches. Some have focused on the issues of what properties or conditions distinguishes more stressful life events from less stressful events, whereas others have examined the effects of such events. Most of this work has been carried out with adults and relatively little has looked at the importance of these key factors in children and adolescents.

THE MEANING OF LIFE EVENTS AND DIFFICULTIES

From the discussion so far a 'life event' may be defined as:

> Any event or circumstance occurring in the life of an individual that may have the potential of altering an individual's present state of mental or physical health.

This definition makes no assumptions about the direction or effect of events on health change.

The above definition of an event, however, will not tell us the meaning of this social experience, for example, if it is desirable or undesirable. Thus marriage and divorce, birth and death, all constitute life events. Before deciding the meaning of any single event we are likely to want to know a great deal about it and to whom it has occurred. Take the example an 8-year-old boy witnessing the death of a stranger; whilst this would be unpleasant it is likely to be less so than witnessing the death of a grandparent and we are not likely to assume he will be adversely affected by these two events to the same degree.

If it is further discovered that the 8-year-old was particularly fond of his grandparent, the degree of undesirable impact this event will have upon him will be greater than if he had hardly known them. In other words, the social and personal context within which an event occurs may determine its meaning for any given individual.

Finally we need to know something about the person who experiences an event to make a judgement about its impact. To use the above example a little further, supposing the 8-year-old boy had previous similar experiences, i.e. he had observed death in strangers or grandparents before, then we may need to modify our judgements about the impact of the event because the appraisal of the experience may be influenced by the child's personal knowledge of similar past events. The personal characteristics of an individual will influence the impact of events by determining the meaning of events that occur to him or her. The understanding of a social event requires an understanding of its social conditions and the personal characteristics of the child who is the focus of the event.

However, events need not always be considered as undesirable or as causal factors for psychiatric disorder. There may be advantages to experiencing stressful events at different times in development and life is made up of important and everyday events that are desirable and provide meaning in people's daily lives. Certain types of events are unavoidable and necessary. For example, separations from parents, attending school and having vaccinations all represent different types of necessary stressful events. Furthermore, there are many everyday events in life that represent important and useful experiences with a tolerable degree of stress, perhaps minor illnesses and a visit to the family doctor, learning to swim or riding a bike, or perhaps failing simple tasks like jigsaws or a classroom examination may be a few of many possible examples. The context and type of a life event may therefore influence its impact on an individual for better as well as worse. This illustrates that an event implies a change in an individual's circumstances, but not the type of effect (desirable or undesirable), temporal quality (the duration of response) or its salience (the personal meaning to any individual).

It follows from this description that, in order to evaluate the meaning and likely effect of any given event, we need to know substantially more than just its general characteristics in a few words. The widely differing and complex social circumstances in which events occur, and by which individuals experience them, require substantial description before they can be evaluated for their effects on normal development and their contribution for psychopathology.

TOWARDS A TYPOLOGY OF EVENTS AND DIFFICULTIES

A descriptive model of events and difficulties substantially improves the range of classification of these social experiences. Classification will clearly be dependent on both the quantity and quality of information obtained. Categorisation of events can take into account differing degrees of psychological and social complexity. Thus the simplest category will be to distinguish the events themselves from other social factors.

Clearly events and difficulties may be considered in numerous ways depending on their social characteristics, psychological meaning and potential effects on people's lives. Both clinicians and researchers will need to consider how best to assess social adversities in their work. The present purpose is to suggest a framework by which adversities in children's lives may be classified and evaluated. A broad taxonomy of recent events and ongoing experiences pertinent to childhood is described in an effort to promote further thoughts in this area of child mental health.

THE PURPOSE OF CATEGORISING EVENTS

Throughout this book there is an implicit statement that social experiences, with all their richness and variation, may contain commonalities, shared characteristics, that allow us to make general statements concerning their similarities to, and differences from, each other. We can group or classify social experiences according to a set of given criteria, such as their shared social characteristics, their type of effect, or their frequency.

We need first, however, to ask the question why should events be categorised? The simplest answer is that the strength of the association between *events and another variable*, e.g. *psychiatric disorder*, may vary according to the type of event and the *form of psychiatric disorder*. By attempting to improve the *specificity* of the relationship between the two variables, there may be a greater association and consequently a better explanatory fit between events and disorder. Similarly, we may show a lack of association between *events and disorder*. Of equal importance would be the discovery of associations between *events and health*, rather than disorder. Our understanding of *normal psychological development* may be improved by specifying clearly any associations between *events and personal development*. *Classifying* phenomenon is a central rule in scientific study.

Classification occurs throughout medicine and occupies an important role in psychology and psychiatry. Often schemes of classification are incomplete or inaccessible. In general, however, this is because knowledge about the things to be classified is limited and this results in judgements, or sometimes educated guesses, as to where things should be placed in the scheme. In such classification, reviews and reclassifications of phenomenon are inevitable as knowledge improves.

Perhaps the most powerful classifications are those which are *natural* such as those occurring in biology resulting in classes of flora and fauna, found as a result of differences and similarities between anatomy, physiology and chemistry.

However, natural classifications lead to propositions about the subject matter other than those which resulted in the classification itself. This may lead to more and important similarities (and perhaps differences) than those originally recognised. When concepts are developed to describe a set of phenomena that are considered related to each other and different from other phenomena, they give rise to classes of objects. In the present circumstances we have conceptualised life events as a class of social experiences and this general class may (and surely does) contain further classes of events which may be further classified by other factors. The important *philosophical* issues of classification and concept are beyond the scope of this book but cannot be ignored in scientific enquiry. Kaplan (1964) provides a useful introduction into this area. Some of the most influential philosophers such as Plato, Mill, Kant and others have shaped modern thinking in this area.

For example, Macintyre (1976) notes that the philosopher Kant observed more than a century ago that concept and theory formation go hand in hand. In modern times this interdependence and somewhat paradoxical position (i.e. proper concepts are needed for good theory and good theory is needed for proper concepts) has been the subject of continuing debate amongst philosophers of science (e.g. Popper, 1962).

Some of the classes of events will be defined because they fall naturally together, for example, achievements or accidents. Others will depend on concepts derived from less observable phenomena and may depend on judgement, for example, the desirability of divorce. These more psychological concepts are important because by using them we hope to improve our understanding of the contribution of life events and social difficulties in psychiatric disorders of childhood and adolescence.

EVENTS AS INDIVIDUAL EXPERIENCES

Events may be considered individually, i.e. each as a class on its own. In this way quantitative estimates of life events can be made by simple counts of event occurrence. Individual counts of events are likely to be the least sensitive method of event analysis. They may suggest at best that events are associated with disorder but will not provide the clues to the mechanisms for the association. When events have been used in this way it is not possible to determine if they have other properties (e.g. desirable/undesirable, controllable/uncontrollable) which may help in interpreting their meaning and influence on disorder or wellbeing.

The assumption for counting events is that they possess equivalence in their effects (Selye, 1956; Holmes and Rahe, 1967) and the mechanism through which they exert effects is that of life change. The stress induced by life change is taken as the most important characteristic that a life event has. Therefore events as disparate as marriage, change of employment, starting school or leaving home are likely to evoke stress through the mechanism of life change. The degree of life change attributed to each event can be determined through assigning a score of life change units to indicate that divorce, for example, is likely to be more stressful than, say, passing an exam (Coddington, 1972a, b). (For further details see Chapter 8.)

The major criticism of this approach is that events are not likely to exert equivalent effects and life change units may not reflect the many other qualities that a life event may possess. Life change is likely, therefore, to be an insensitive measure of the psychological effect of a recent life event. Marriage and examinations may both contain *quantities* of life change but the *qualities* of these social events are not equivalent and their effects will not be clear without a fuller understanding of their nature and circumstances.

TRANSITIVE NATURE OF EVENTS

Some events, such as divorce, irrevocably alter a child's life circumstances, whereas others, such as a minor accident, once over, return the child to the previous status quo. Furthermore, divorce will always be a transitive event by definition. Separation of parents, however, may not be truly transitive as they may reunite, sometimes rapidly. The effects of separations such as these would not be classified as transitive because they do not result in permanent alterations of the status quo in the child's life. The significance of separation should not be undervalued but correct classification may help to understand the role of different forms of separation for different types of psychopathology at different ages and perhaps for different sexes.

THE SOCIAL CHARACTER OF EVENTS

Events may be classified according to some *general characteristic* apparent in their definition. For example, events may occur to family members and be classified as family events. Accidents may be classed together, as may events related solely to marriage or school.

This social descriptive classification is unlikely to achieve greater specificity on its own for a number of reasons, e.g.

1. The classes of events may not be mutually exclusive, e.g. accident to a family member may be classed in at least two ways accident/family.
2. The classification has no prior psychological assumptions, i.e. we cannot tell anything about the qualities of any single event or class of event from these descriptive classifications.

Using the *social characteristics* of events may have utility in combination with other conditions associated with the event. For example, *undesirable* events occur with significantly greater frequency in a *family context* than in a *school context* in school-age children (Goodyer, Kolvin and Gatzanis, 1985).

These findings suggest that the strength of the association between life events and developmental psychopathology will be best determined by evaluating the range of characteristics in any one life event.

In all three classifications discussed so far the lack of psychological concepts results in potential weaknesses for measuring events. Until the meaning of events is accounted for it is not at all clear how events may influence the onset of disorder on distress. In the above example it is the combination of the psychological concept of undesirability and the social concept of family that confers greater meaning to the life event and strengthens the association with psychopathology. Equally important, it is not clear how children may *comprehend or cope* with stressful events to prevent themselves from becoming disordered.

THE PSYCHOLOGICAL CHARACTER OF EVENTS

Desirability of events

Events may be judged as having different degrees of desirability. Consequently, events may range from being perceived as markedly desirable to markedly or severely undesirable. In general, studies investigating the relationship between events and psychiatric disorder are concerned with the presence of undesirable events. Furthermore, it is not undesirability in some general social sense (e.g. nuclear war can be seen as undesirable to all) but in a particular sense (e.g. the death of a person can be seen as undesirable only to those who were associated with that person through family or friendship ties). Undesirable events can therefore be conceptualised as exerting a particular undesirable impact on a person. Brown and Harris (1978) referred to this potential as threat and Paykel and colleagues (1980) as negative impact.

Of course, there may be important questions to ask concerning desirable events, particularly in developmental terms where we are concerned with investigating factors that promote normal development. Thus the quantity and quality of desirable events requires consideration and may provide important clues concerning children's individual *competence* and *resilience* (Garmezy, 1985; Masten *et al.*, 1988).

Controllability of events

Events can be viewed as being within the *potential control* of a person or being clearly outside of his or her control. For example, a death of a relative or accident to a friend or relative are events outside the control of a child (of course, the conditions of the event are crucial to this assertion, i.e. we assume the child is not a cause of the event). By contrast exam failure or loss of friendships may be within the child's control (again the sense of this assumes that the controllability of the event has a causal connection to the event occurrence). Events can be judged as being within or outside the person's control according to the context of the event.

Perceived outcome of events

Some events may carry markedly undesirable qualities that are undesirable because the event has to occur, e.g. a necessary operation involving general anaesthesia. In certain events, however, the expected outcome can be foreseen with a reasonable and acceptable degree of continuity. However, in some events the outcome is not clear, e.g. a child's view of parental argument. The perceived outcome may clearly vary according to what is known about the event and what is believed by the child. The future is seen differently at different ages and this requires consideration. Overall *perceived outcome* may be viewed as the degree to which the outcome of an event can be considered as clear. It will be important to determine over what time period this clarity can reasonably be expected, i.e. days or weeks rather than years.

Loss and separation

Perhaps two of the most psychological components within events are the degree of loss and/or separation an event may carry. This concept is, of course, a particular form of the consequences of a stressful event. Loss has been an important life event measure in adult studies on depression (Finlay-Jones and Brown, 1981; Paykel, 1983; Brown, Harris and Bifulco, 1986). Loss may reflect a physical loss or exit from a child's life. This may be a person, animal or object. Loss may also reflect the permanent alteration of an idea or belief as a consequence, for example, of new information. These different psychological qualities of loss, i.e. real loss and symbolic loss, can be reliably measured from life events interviews and significantly improve the specificity of loss events to depression in young women (Brown, Harris, and Bifulco, 1986). As yet the symbolic notion of loss has not been used in studies in evaluating events in childhood or adolescence. Separation is a central theme in developmental research (Ainsworth *et al.*, 1978; Wolkind and Rutter, 1985a) and may constitute loss but in many cases as a transitive event. Short-term separations may of course be highly stressful. Knowledge concerning the frequency, duration and social context of separations events will be important in determining their effects as loss events.

Additions or gains

Events that reflect permanent gain to a person's social field have been referred to as entrance events (e.g. birth of a sibling, relative permanently staying in the household). These events are likely to have important connotations for some children because of the alterations in family relations (Dunn and Kendrick, 1982). The birth of a sibling provides a good example of the possible range of meaning in an entrance event. A new baby is likely to be seen as desirable by the adults in most families (clearly in some cases birth can be undesirable, such as in unwanted pregnancies). The event may have an undesirable effect on siblings however. Older siblings may react adversely with increased aggression and an alteration of their relationship with mother. A series of complex effects, some desirable others less so, can arise as result of this entrance event. The effects measured will depend on who is considered the focus of the event, mother or sibling. Thus entrance events may carry different forms of meanings (desirable and undesirable) according to the focus (i.e. who the impact is being considered for) of the event.

Choice of action

How individuals might cope with events may depend on what psychological choices they perceive or may be perceived as given to them. Divorce leading to custody directed by the courts may be an example of leaving a child with no or little choice in an undesirable event. Other events may result in a number of choices of action for a child. For example, choosing between parents by indicating with whom the child wishes to live may carry a risk to well-being.

Dangerousness and events

Some events may be construed as carrying a degree of personal danger to the physical self. Finlay-Jones and Brown (1981) showed, for example, that such events were more likely to occur prior to onset of anxiety disorders in adults. In childhood and adolescence, dangerousness of events may also be important when they carry physical threat. For example, accident and illness events are significantly associated with psychiatric disorder in school-age children (Goodyer, Kolvin and Gatzanis, 1985). However, there appears to be no specificity with diagnosis. A refinement of the measurement of danger has recently been reported. Events were classified according to the degree of real danger to the self and to the degree that danger may occur to the self (Brown, Bifulco and Harris, 1987). Improving the sensitivity of the measurement of danger significantly improved the association between events that carried symbolic danger and depression in young women. This refinement is an example of improving concept formation and classification in life events research.

Expectation and events

Perceived occurrence of events may be important in determining an event's impact on well-being. For example, unexpected events may be particularly relevant in acute distress reactions. Thus events may carry one or more *psychological dimensions* according to the social context of the event. The qualities that may be assigned and rated will clearly depend on the amount and type of information.

The potential for multidimensional psychological concepts in life events suggests that there may be many ways in which events could be evaluated and that choice of concepts might depend on the questions being asked (Do events cause psychiatric disorders? Do events protect against psychiatric disorders? Do events differentiate between distress and disorders?) and the population studied (psychiatric cases, well community subjects, community subjects who have experienced some adversity, e.g. disaster, earthquake or war) whose social adjustment is being evaluated.

TIMING, INTENSITY AND DURATION OF EVENTS

An adequate evaluation of the meaning of events cannot be made without a clear description of three other factors. Firstly, when exactly did the event occur? The *timing* of an event may be significant if the question under consideration is whether an event is responsible in some way for change, adverse or otherwise. Life event studies in both adults and children indicate that events are likely to cluster in the 16 weeks closest to onset of disorder, suggesting timing is of some importance, at least for some psychiatric conditions (Brown and Harris, 1978; Paykel, 1983; Goodyer, Kolvin and Gatzanis, 1987). This theme is discussed in more detail in Chapter 9 when we examine the mechanisms by which life events may exert their effects.

The *intensity* of an event is also of considerable importance. How undesirable, for example, does an event have to be to exert an effect on psychiatric disorder? Again, in both adults and children the answer seems to be that it is events with at least moderate to severe degrees of threat or negative impact that are important for the majority of anxious and depressive disorders (Brown and Harris, 1978; Paykel *et al.*, 1980; Goodyer, Kolvin and Gatzanis, 1985).

Finally, the *duration* of an event is crucial and will influence how an event is described and subsequently evaluated. For example, continuous marital disharmony over many months may end in divorce. To consider them as independent adverse experiences may be unreasonable as the former leads to the latter. In this respect divorce in some cases or a surgical procedure may represent the *end stage* of an adverse process. In most cases the end stage represents the nodal point of an event and the descriptive stage is the context in which the event occurred.

DEVELOPMENT AND EVENTS

Social characteristics, psychological meaning, timing, intensity and duration constitute the core principles of life events. There are, however, some further points that can influence the understanding of events; in particular, the significance of events during development. For childhood and adolescence, events may have different impacts at different times. For example, Ferguson (1979) has shown that experience of hospitalisation may reduce fears of hospitals in school-age children but not in pre-schoolers.

Thus the impact of social events and circumstances will in part be dependent on a child's cognitive and perhaps emotional development. This indicates that the evaluation of events must take into account developmental features before a judgement about impact can be arrived at.

PROVIDING A DEVELOPMENTAL BIOGRAPHY

The provision of adequate developmental information is a prerequisite to understanding the potential meaning of a life event. In the Newcastle life events study on children and adolescents each event description included a subject description (Goodyer, Kolvin and Gatzanis, 1985). As with adult studies social family circumstances were provided, including a full description of house environment, family size, employment states and illness histories of family members. In addition, however, a child's age, developmental history (motor and language milestones), education progress, school environment, intellectual studies and illness history are essential for a judgement of event impact. In addition to the developmental biography two developmental concepts require consideration.

TRANSITIONAL EVENTS

Some events will be expected and constitute necessary major adaptations to a child's life because they introduce or represent a new sequence in the chain of social development. Such events can be termed transitional. Such life events represent a discontinuity in social experience because they introduce a new environment. The child's lifestyle is interrupted. Psychological consequences of interruptions of this nature have been poorly studied. What evidence there is suggests that in adults at least there is a reduced sense of control and expectancy over one's surroundings (Mandler, 1975; Fisher 1986). For example, attending play group or school, leaving home either through attending residential education (boarding school, university) or starting a home of one's own, are all examples of transitional events. Transfers from one social group to another, such as primary to secondary school or secondary school to university, are also transitions. Transitions of leaving home for boarding school or university are known to be associated with mental and physical distress in some cases (Fisher and Hood, 1988). We know little about transitions in younger people, such as primary to secondary school. We do know that starting school is a major adaptation and can result in significant distress for some children, which may herald the beginnings of a school refusal syndrome (Hersov and Berg, 1980).

These events are normative experiences for many children but may constitute important sources of events whose hedonic qualities and individual effects may not be in the same direction, e.g. going to university may be socially desirable but personally distressing.

NON-NORMATIVE EVENTS

That certain events are inescapable in development is self-evident. The matter is discussed in detail in Chapters 6 and 7 but examples can be found in biological, psychological and social phenomena. Thus attaining developmental milestones are events, the development of reason and the first day at school are all events of one kind or another. Furthermore and importantly, they occur at certain expected chronological ages. In some children, however, expected normative events occur at the wrong chronological age, i.e. they are non-normative in time, although not in content. For example, death of a parent in early childhood, sexual intercourse in the pre-pubertal child and pregnancy in the early teenage years can all be viewed as non-normative.

LATENT EFFECTS OF EVENTS

A third developmental concept is the suggestion that events can have different effects on the *future* even if their *immediate* impact carries a degree of adversity. Two forms of effect are possible. Firstly a beneficial *steeling effect*, suggesting that there are learning experiences to be gained from adversity which can be utilised at a later point in time. Secondly an adverse *sensitising effect*, suggesting that there are negative learning experiences from previous adversity that may contribute to the development of later psychiatric disorder.

What conditions determine whether an event carries steeling or sensitising effects is not clear. For example, children may learn coping strategies from stressful events for later adversities. Alternatively earlier stresses may result in a failure to learn coping skills when faced with later adversities.

Steeling effects also highlight the question of how *intense* an event needs to be. Thus, it may be that relatively minor events, perhaps the everyday hassle of life, constitute sufficient steeling effect (Patterson, 1983; Lazarus, 1984), as well as more obviously stressful events such as hospitalisation, where we have already noted that older children may benefit from hospitalisation experiences. Minor illnesses may also have beneficial effects for later coping (Parmalee, 1984). For example, children may learn adaptive behaviours for coping with illnesses through early contact with the health care services, perhaps in the pre-school years. Perhaps early exposure combined with successful managing of everyday ailments and the experience of painful but short-lived events such as vaccination provide important social learning. What we do not know is how these latent experiences manifest themselves at later points in time. Firstly, what triggers are needed to evoke recall of such early experiences? Secondly, what effects might past experiences have in the presence of recent events? Thirdly, do past experiences matter only for similar experiences in the present or do they exert a more general effect on how social adversity in the present may be dealt with? These issues concerning the potential mechanisms through which events may exert their effects are discussed in detail in Chapter 8. Early experiences may be sensitising for later difficulties.

FOCUS AND AMPLIFICATION

As we have seen in many examples, events may not exert their effects directly on a child but through their parents. It may be that other individuals, such as teachers and friends, are the recipients of the direct effect of an event but indirect effects do occur to the child. The *focus* of an event refers to those for whom the event has a *direct* effect. The *amplification* of an event refers to those *indirectly* affected as a consequence. For example, a psychiatric disorder in a mother is a life event for the family. A direct focus may occur for the child if as a consequence of a delusional state the parent attacks the child (Anthony, 1986). More likely, and more frequently, an indirect focus on the child occurs and the consequences of parental psychiatric disorder are expressed through parenting deficits and difficulties in parent–child relations (Rutter, 1988b). Under these circumstances the effects of parental psychiatric disorder have been amplified to disrupt social relations as well as causing a direct effect on the mother's well-being. Amplification effects may be more frequent in children and young adolescents where life events may focus more directly on parents, siblings or others, such as teachers (Monck and Dobbs, 1985). In contrast, older adolescents may have more direct and focused effects of life events, perhaps related to the increased social flexibility with increasing psychosexual development.

A TAXONOMY OF LIFE EVENTS

The preceding discussion suggests that further research may benefit from a classification of life events that provides an opportunity to examine the role of events in child development and developmental psychopathology.

Because of the potentially important role different types of events may play at different ages, and because events may be important in promoting health as well as mental disorder, this taxonomy attempts to include classes reflecting these issues.

Multiaxial taxonomy of events

1. Temporal—Past–recent, immediate or distant in terms of days, weeks/months or years.
2. Quantitative—Single, multiple.
3. General Social Class—Marriage, family, accidents, illness, legal, school.

4. Antecedent Psychological Class—Perceived expectancy of occurrence, perceived controllability of occurrence.
5. Descriptive Psychological Classes—Loss, danger, threat, desirability, disappointment.
6. Consequential Psychological Classes—Perceived outcome, controllability, separation (exit), entrance, choice of action, altered circumstances.
7. Developmental Classes—Transitional (adaptive), non-normative steeling/sensitising.

All classes of events can be subject to further classification describing:

(a) Quality of impact rated on a scale (i.e. degree of severity, success or pleasure).
(b) Independence of event from other phenomenon, e.g. as a cause rather than consequence of mental disorder.
(c) Focus of event, i.e. the subject of the event classification should be identified, e.g. child only, parent, marriage.

This tentative model is a multiaxial scheme whereby events may be rated on all axes and all classes. This approach to the rating of events has been taken by researchers testing hypotheses about the origins of adult psychiatric disorder and suggests that a multidimensional approach may be more sensitive than an individual one and provide a greater specificity both in terms of variance explained and specificity between events and disorder (Brown, Bifulco and Harris, 1987; Miller *et al.*, 1987).

LONGER-TERM SOCIAL EXPERIENCES

Many social experiences that influence development and have a causal effect on psychopathology are not circumscribed events but more ongoing processes, where delineation of a beginning and an end stage is not possible (Rutter, 1985a; Goodyer, Wright and Altham, 1988). These experiences may be adverse and carry a variable degree of undesirable impact, e.g. marital disharmony over weeks, months or years, or financial hardship or long-term illness in a parent, are examples of longer-term difficulties.

Not all long-term social experiences will be difficult. Indeed some will be socially required for normal development and for protection against undesirable experiences. A supportive relationship with one parent, peer group relationships, and adequate financial support for food, clothing, socialisation, are some examples.

Like events, ongoing experiences can be described in relatively factual terms as well as from a person's point of view (subjective appraisal). Also like events, such descriptions will lead themselves to a classification scheme.

In contrast to discrete recent life events, ongoing difficulties in a child's life which may have an influence on psychiatric disorder have been studied relatively extensively, as have ongoing desirable experiences that may protect children at times of stress (Rutter, 1966, 1979; Garmezy and Rutter 1985).

Thus substantially more is known about these longer-term experiences than events. However, the interaction between events and difficulties and between events, achievements and socially desirable experiences has received relatively little attention. The importance of contextual descriptions of the circumstances in longer-term social experiences is as relevant as it is for events. Thus to know that a mother of a child is depressed is important, but it is difficult to comprehend its impact without further information. For example, the duration and frequency of depression, the number of episodes, the need for hospitalisation in the past, responses to treatments, impact on family life when in hospital can all be enquired after.

Similarly, poor housing conditions can be carefully calculated to include an inventory of household effects (including the facility for toys and play) as well as attention to the number of rooms, their condition, the geographical area and the family's duration of stay in the house.

These descriptive contexts provide information for judgements and classifications of the types of ongoing social experiences.

SOCIAL TYPOLOGY OF ONGOING EXPERIENCES

Clearly, long-term experiences can be classified according to their general social characteristics, as can events, thus difficulties may be family, marital, school, social, financial, employment, legal.

DURATION AND FREQUENCY

Long-term experiences may wax and wane over time; the exposure to such experiences may therefore vary. The amount of exposure could be an important judgement if the experience is being considered as a *putative cause* of some factor, health or illness. This may be firstly considered by the duration of the experience and the frequency of occurrence if applicable, e.g. marital arguments/violence. In some cases, however, the exposure may be continuous, e.g. poor housing conditions.

A rating of the quality of the experience may be made according to severity of the context. Thus severe marital disharmony which has been continuous for more than two years, and during which the child has witnessed several violent episodes between parents, is qualitatively different from marital disharmony of less than a year's duration with no violence.

The importance of assessing the quality of marriage is crucial in investigating the associations between marital adversities and psychopathology in children.

Present evidence indicates that it is children chronically exposed to violent marriages who are at significant risk (Rutter, 1988b). Whether the mechanism for this risk relates to deficits in ongoing parenting or exposure to other types of adversity, e.g. the impact of violence on social and emotional devlopment, is not yet fully understood.

Thus a descriptive account of experiences provides for two judgements:

1. The quantity of exposure to the experience;
2. The quality (undesirability or desirability) of the experience.

TEMPORAL IMPACT OF EXPERIENCES

The point at which children are exposed to undesirable and desirable experiences in their development may be critical. As with life events, establishing the timing of past and recent experiences may be important when considering continuities and discontinuities of social influences on development and psychopathology.

THE FOCUS OF LONG-TERM EXPERIENCES

The involvement of a child may be important in considering longer-term social experiences. Thus the focus of marital difficulties is between adults, and effects on other family members, whilst varying in severity, will be *indirect*. Similarly, a successful career for a parent is immediately desirable for him or her and may have indirect benefits for the child, such as a better standard of living, but may carry with it indirect difficulties, e.g. frequent moves of house or school.

Alternatively, experiences may have the opposite focus, for example, chronic illness in the child will have clear direct undesirable effects for that child and potentially undesirable effects indirectly for other family members. Similarly, a regular success and interest in some activity (sport, drama, hobbies, etc.) may have direct benefits for the child and indirect benefits for the parents, as their own sense of worth may be enhanced and they may take some credit for their child's success.

PSYCHOLOGICAL ASPECTS OF LONGER-TERM EXPERIENCES

The theme has been developed that longer-term experiences may have costs and benefits for different persons, depending on their personal involvement, focus, exposure to the experience and the intensity of the social experience. The psychological components of these experiences are also important and may be considered in the same format as for events.

Thus social experiences may have had antecedent expectations, they may carry degrees of threat, loss, danger or degrees of comfort and safety, according to their descriptive content. Finally, they may carry consequences such as the perception of their outcome, the degree of control for the child on the potential choice of action, the experience of permanent separation.

DEVELOPMENTAL INFLUENCE OF SOCIAL EXPERIENCE

Similarly, the normative, steeling and transitional concepts can be applied to experiences. Perhaps of considerable importance in developmental terms is the absence of beneficial experiences, in particular, the role of social experiences in promoting normal development, including the intrinsic features of emotional and cognitive development that may promote protective or coping responses to later stresses. Perhaps the presence and absence of positive experiences in early development, such as positive emotional relations with care-givers, stimulation and interaction with peers and mastery of tasks, are influential in promoting resilience to stress through the intrinsic development of self-esteem (Harter, 1983; Garmezy, 1985; Masten *et al.*, 1988).

STRUCTURE, PROCESS AND LONGER-TERM SOCIAL EXPERIENCES

The role of adverse environmental factors has been highlighted by much research in childhood and adolescence. Perhaps the main thrust of the last 20 years' research has been toward understanding those environmental conditions that are involved in causing or increasing the risk of psychiatric disorder in childhood and adolescence.

Thus poverty, unemployment, psychiatric disorder in parents, physical and emotional neglect and criminality have been shown repeatedly to exert adverse influences on child development and increase the risks of psychiatric (particularly conduct) disorder (Rutter, 1979, 1987a). Furthermore, the powerful influences of these social factors have been shown to repeat themselves in many (although not all) families from one generation to the next (Kolvin *et al.*, 1983; Madge, 1983).

However, far less is known about the *mechanisms* by which these social factors exert their effects in psychological terms. From the point of view of long-term social experiences it is important to discriminate between the *structure of social conditions* such as poor housing, and the *process of social experiences* such as marital arguments and misery in the child.

THE RELATIONSHIP BETWEEN EVENTS AND LONGER-TERM EXPERIENCES

It is important to identify where possible the temporal association between events and experiences. This may refer to a short time period of days, weeks or months, such as the duration between a bereavement and the onset of grief, or it may refer to a substantive period of years, such as the effects of events in one developmental period over another.

Within-time relations

A narrative of late pregnancy and early infancy serves as an illustration of within-time associations between ongoing experiences and events. Pregnancy which has been 'uneventful' gives rise to the event of birth and the experience of care-giving for mother and care-receiving for the child. Events may occur at any time throughout this normal process. Pregnancy may be eventful and mothers may be ill, foetuses abnormal, birth may be traumatic for mother or infant and result in illness or disability.

Similarly, in middle childhood the experience of family-based socialisation is altered by the event of going to school and the subsequent reorganisation of the ongoing social conditions for the child.

Finally, as an example in adolescence, the biology of puberty results in physical (permanent) alterations to the individual which may result in widening the scope for life events and concurrently further reorganise social conditions.

Between-time associations

This concerns the influence that life events and experiences of infancy have on the events and experiences of other developmental periods, such as middle childhood and adolescence. Present knowledge indicates that both continuities and discontinuities occur between social experiences in different time periods, but what social factors are involved and how they exert their influences is less than clear (Rutter, 1983b). The use of social inquiry methods to obtain life histories including early experiences has had some success in adults (Parker, 1979, 1983; Brown, 1988). The methodological advances in these studies is the reliable and valid collection retrospectively of life history information that includes social experiences and events from earlier time periods. These social inquiry techniques can be adapted for use in younger populations to measure and evaluate social events and experiences across different time periods.

Interactions between social factors

Life events may be occurring within the same time period as ongoing social experiences because of psychological processes exerting effects between social factors. Some recent findings suggest, for example, that in anxious and depressed children mothers are significantly more likely to report poor confiding relations in their own lives and indicate they are feeling distressed (Goodyer, Wright and Altham, 1988). In the absence of a recent undesirable life event these two maternal factors are independent of each other, suggesting that the origins for both are different. In the presence of a recent undesirable life event that has had a direct impact on the child, the three factors (maternal adversities, life events and emotional disorder) are dependent on each other, suggesting a potentially causal relationship between ongoing maternal adversities and life events focused on children (Goodyer, Wright and Altham, 1988). Two possible mechanisms can be outlined here and are discussed in more detail in Chapter 9:

1. Specific connections exist between events and difficulties, for example, a divorce as a consequence of continuous marital disharmony or exam failure as a result of continuous poor educational achievement.
2. The general effects of social experiences may allow events to occur, for example, depressed mothers may not caretake adequately and children may wander, be neglected, play truant from school. These events are not specifically connected to maternal depression but are generally occurring as a result of lack of care.

Finally, there may be no clear relationship between events and experiences, for example, exam failure in the child may occur in the presence of adequate maternal caretaking.

SUMMARY

1. Life experiences are one form of stress and can be considered as discrete life events or ongoing experiences.
2. Classification of events and experiences can be made according to their general, social, and psychological characteristics.
3. Developmental characteristics of the child will influence the impact of events and experiences.
4. The same events and experiences may have different effects at different points in a child's life. Events may be undesirable at one point in time but carry advantages at another.
5. Some events and experiences may be causes of psychopathology. Other events will occur as a consequence of psychopathology. Life experiences may relate to each other in their origins or their effects.
6. Evaluating the psychological effect of life experiences requires a knowledge of the antecedent circumstances, the social context, and likely outcome of the event or experience considered.

Chapter 2

Adaptation, Adjustment and the Family

INTRODUCTION

As we have discussed in Chapter 1, life events and difficulties do not occur as mechanical experiences in time. They have both antecedents and consequences for children. In addition, both the *origins* and *effects* of stressful life events and difficulties need to be considered in the context of development. In other words, the significance of events and difficulties for developmental processes are as much a legitimate concern of child mental health professionals as are social stresses which may cause psychiatric disorder.

In this chapter on family adversity both the costs and benefits of events and difficulties will be examined. The effects of family adversities at different points in development and the role of past experiences in shaping coping processes for dealing with future social stresses will be discussed.

As well as looking at major life experiences, such as divorce, permanent separations and leaving home, we will examine how everyday experiences can influence relationships between parents and children. These daily hassles and their influence on interpersonal relationships are considered by some to be at least as significant in their impact on well-being as major events and ongoing difficulties. They may be the core stresses exerting an adverse influence on everyday family life and on parent–child relations (Patterson, 1983; Patterson and Dishion, 1988; Murray, 1988).

EVOLUTIONARY ASPECTS OF PARENTING

Higley and Suomi (1986) in their review of parental behaviour in non-human primates point to the paradoxes for researchers who study human development. The paradox may be summed up in the dichotomy between neurological senso-rimotor development in the human infant, which is advanced and sophisticated compared with other species, and the profound dependence on their parent for nutrition and protection many months longer than their other mammalian species. The period of infancy and the duration of parental care is especially protracted. This makes the experience of early maternal care a special factor in the experience of stress, because infants are tied to their mothers for nutrition, thermoregulation, protection and transportation in the first few days or weeks of life and continue to be so for their social and emotional needs in succeeding months or years. Furthermore as Harlow (1959) points out, human infants are dependent in this fashion because it takes years for their physical, cognitive and social capabilities to mature fully.

This extended period of parental involvement in primates may have evolved to increase behavioural flexibility of the individual and to decrease the relative degree of 'hardwiring' of behavioural patterns to permit the extensive environmental adaptability that human beings are capable of (Mason, 1979). Thus in primates maternal care goes beyond basic provision of food and protection.

Within this long-term nurturing experience are many life events. As Lipsitt (1983) indicates, there are many risks and hazards in infancy. The process of being born, experiencing hunger, hypothermia could all be construed as events. The characteristic response to such stresses is crying and activity. These responses are defensive and carry adaptive qualities, that is the eliciting of care. These do not constitute social events but their consequences, i.e. the success or failure to provide care, are crucial. Crying, which is greatest in the first few months of life, decreases in quality from thereon throughout childhood as the behavioural repertoire of the developing child emerges in the context of nurturing long-term experience.

Even in the presence of adequate nurturing mothers, events cannot be avoided. This is because mothers cannot identify on every occasion such intrinsic events as hunger or partially extrinsic ones as cold. They respond to the consequences, i.e. crying, shivering. There is a want–response paradigm, a system of mutual/reciprocal effects as a consequence of normative events between mother and child, and environmental circumstances influencing them both (Kagan, 1984).

Infants are easily distressed by alterations in their environment which may disturb their temperature, feeding and sleeping and comfort. Infant distress arises as a consequence of social and biological disequilibrium and no degree of maternal care can prevent all forms of distress response. Mothers who are described as overprotective may be so possibly because they misperceive the meaning of normative stressful events of infancy and early childhood.

THE PSYCHOLOGICAL PURPOSE OF PARENTING

The relationship between mother and infant is a dynamic one that involves the participation of both individuals. The emphasis on an active relationship as necessary for infant development and parental well-being and satisfaction provided the basis for Bowlby's theory of attachment for psychological development (Bowlby, 1969, 1973).

Bowlby has also proposed that intimate relations in early life exert a protective effect in the face of later adversity or stress (Bowlby, 1969, 1973, 1980,

1988). What is postulated is a continuity of some psychological process in the face of changing social experience and alterations in development including the form of expression of psychopathology. Attachment theory has been a catalyst for major endeavours in experimental and clinical investigations into the meaning and mechanisms of mother–infant relations (Murray-Parkes and Stevenson-Hinde, 1982; Reite and Field, 1985; Hinde and Stevenson-Hinde, 1988).

MATERNAL ADVERSITY AND MOTHER–INFANT RELATIONS

The significance of relationships for individuals

A focus for understanding the effects of parenting and the development of social relations for the child can be taken from understanding the purpose of relationships for well-being and normal development (Hinde, 1979, 1987). Interpersonal relations cannot be reduced to the characteristics of the participants (Hinde, 1979). There are therefore qualities about the relationship which constitute a legitimate unit of analysis. Studies using direct observational techniques have, for example, shown that relationship variables such as affection seeking, exploration, physical contact and gaze show different patterns for infant–mother pairs and same infant–different adult pairs (Main and Weston, 1981). In addition, there is evidence that the quality of relationship with caretaker in the first year of life predicts later relationship behaviour. For example, infants with secure attachments to their caretaker at 12 to 18 months are less likely to show high dependency on that caretaker in social interactions with other children and adults at 4 and 5 years of age (Sroufe, 1985; Sroufe and Fleeson, 1988). There seems to be a coherence and continuity in certain qualities of relationships even if they have changed in other ways as a consequence of development. Thus social–emotional processes at one age may predict similar processes at another despite changing social circumstances (e.g. playgroup relations rather than family relations). This suggests that early secure attachments provide a learning experience through which individuals internalise or represent relationships (Sroufe and Fleeson, 1988). This representation of relations seems to be carried forward to influence expectations and attitudes towards the self and others.

Thus early parenting experiences exert a significant influence on relations in later social interactions (for further discussion see Chapter 4 on the development of social relations).

The effects of competent early relations

The strength of early social experience can be seen in longitudinal studies which have used relationship variables to predict later social behaviour. For example, the quality of care-giver behaviour towards a 6-month-old predicts later attachment behaviour (Sroufe, 1985). This attachment behaviour itself predicts the mother's behaviour when the infant is 2 years old and behaviour between the child and another sibling some three years later (Matas et al., 1978; Sroufe and Fleeson, 1988).

The Minnesota Child Development Project has shown that children with insecure attachment were significantly more likely to take less positive attitudes into peer group relations and show increased rates of behavioural and social difficulties (Egeland and Sroufe, 1981; Sroufe and Fleeson, 1988).

These findings provide support for Bowlby's theories of the importance for early attachment, at least for the next immediate stage of social development. They also suggest that, again in line with Bowlby, a failure of attachment has psychopathological consequences for children. These findings do not address the question that early sources of insecurity such as maternal deprivation and separation predict psychiatric disorder in adolescence or adulthood.

We do not yet know of the mechanisms by which insecure attachments operate to increase psychopathological risk. Some of the factors are found in mothers and others in infants. A full discussion of attachment research is beyond the scope of this present text [see Murray-Parkes and Stevenson-Hinde (1982), and Hinde and Stevenson-Hinde (1988), for source texts in this area].

Maternal competence and quality of parenting

For some mothers the everyday stress of infant management proves extremely difficult. Indeed, for some mothers the very nature of infant care is difficult. Thus feeding, infant care and play may all become adverse experiences in the daily life of a mother or other care-giver.

Wolkind and Kruk (1985), in summarising a decade of research into factors contributing to psychiatric disorder in infants and young children, identify two conceptual areas that help to determine the degree of competence in mothers. Firstly, *structural factors* in the women's social backgrounds that put some women at a disadvantage when pregnant. In particular, adversity in their family of origin, coming from larger homes, being more likely to have fathers in unskilled or semi-skilled work and being more likely to be in this work themselves. Secondly, *functional factors* that result in undesirable psychological mechanisms facilitating a lack of competence. Mothers at risk show far less *current emotional support*. They see less of their parents and are more likely to feel unsupported by their family of origin, have poor relations with other women patients and have more disputes with other family members.

These findings illustrate an important role for *emotional support* in the lives of mothers and demonstrate that *a lack of availability* (many mothers were isolated or alone in care) and *poor adequacy* of relationships (as demonstrated by poor relationships and arguments) may determine *a lack of intimacy* in these mothers' lives which may be a major influence on their care-giving competence.

The role of *poor intimate confiding relationships* as a major factor in the social causation of depression in the lives of women (Brown and Harris, 1978), suggests that one substantial effect of long-term difficulties and poor intimate confiding relations may be to increase the risk of depression in women which may adversely influence maternal competence.

Associations between maternal structural and functional factors

These two conceptual areas of structural and functional deficits are clearly interrelated. The mechanisms of the relationship are not yet clear since it is apparent that not all women who experience structural difficulties in their lives have poor confiding relations, and communication difficulties with parents and friends do not inevitably lead to psychiatric disorder in young mothers. Therefore their influence on each other and on the development of sufficient maternal competence requires further investigation. For example, how do social difficulties with employment and housing influence confiding relations with parents or friends? Is there a third set of variables that mediate in some way in this relationship? How does the presence of poor emotional supports in the lives of mothers influence the relationship between mothers, their infants, and young children? Finally, why is it that for some mothers these adversities result in rejection or inattentiveness to their children whereas for others they give rise to overprotection and maternal preoccupation? These differences in individual responses to similar adversities are poorly understood.

Potential mechanisms of maternal deficits

We can see, however, that these factors may result in mothers who through adverse social experiences in their own lives may be unable to care for their own children. Clearly a range of adversities are possible candidates for influencing maternal competence. Poor maternal care in their own childhood may exert effects on current maternal care. But are these effects direct or do they operate through some other process? For example, perhaps current lack of confiding relations in mothers' lives is a consequence of early insecurities in relationships (Brown, 1988). It may then be that maternal competence is directly affected by *current life events and difficulties* in mothers, which are themselves determined by previous adversities including early insecurity in social relations. The patterning of maternal adversities and their model of effects for psychopathology in children are discussed further in Chapter 9.

For the clinician there is an important role in the assessment of maternal competence. Identifying pregnant women whose backgrounds contain risk factors would be an important first step in recognising an at-risk group of mothers to be. Mental health professionals, including psychiatrist, psychologist, social worker and health visitor, may provide a service in the obstetric department in collaboration with the obstetric team as well as to psychological surveillance and management in the primary care setting.

Implications for research

For the researcher these findings indicate that further understanding of maternal competence requires information, not just about the structural aspects of a woman's background (family size, social class, place of residence etc.), but also the process of relationships in early life. The recent work of George Brown and colleagues provides excellent examples of the sorts of life history enquiry methods used that will help determine which early experiences influence maternal competence (Brown, Harris and Bifulco, 1986; Harris, Brown and Bifulco, 1986).

In this research a semi-structured interview was developed to record not just recent life events and difficulties but the respondents' perception of their own quality of care as a child. This interview therefore seeks to obtain a narrative of both instrumental care and the quality of affectional care as recalled by the respondent. The reliability and validity of the method seems encouraging and similar to other research looking at adults' recall of childhood experiences. For example, Parker (1981) found that reports given by mothers as to how they had formerly treated their now adult children were correlated with reports of the mothers' care-giving given by the children themselves. In Brown and colleagues' work (Brown, 1988) similar results were obtained when sisters were asked to describe the childhood experiences of their sibling and results were compared with the other sibling's ratings. These findings provide important opportunities to obtain reliable and valid information about life experiences occurring at considerable distance in time from the present. Systematic collection of life history data concerning a range of social adversities, including loss of parent, indifferent care, confiding relations and recent life events and difficulties, has allowed Brown and colleagues to develop models of how social adversities exert their effects over time. In depressed adult women, for example, an important message seems to be that the past can influence the present through lowering self-esteem but only in so far as it is linked with troubles in the present (Brown, 1988). These findings suggest that systematic inquiry of early relations in the lives of children and detailed collection of other sources of social adversity in a child's life may improve our understanding of how early insecurity may influence psychopathology in childhood.

Some preliminary findings from interviews carried out with mothers and children attending a psychiatric clinic suggest that such studies would be worth while. Firstly, mothers were asked to describe their pregnancies and first 6 months of life with their babies. The interview formed part of a social inquiry into social adversities in the lives of anxious and depressed school-age children

(Goodyer, Wright and Altham, 1988, 1989a). The interview enquired about the progress of pregnancy, medical complications, the labour and delivery of the baby, the presence of any separations longer than 24 hours following birth, the degree of difficulty experienced by mother in infant care in the first 6 months of life, and the quality of support she perceived herself as receiving from her spouse in that period. Some 59/100 of the mothers of cases reported one or more of such early difficulties compared with 38/100 controls—a highly significant difference. Perhaps more surprisingly, more mothers of depressed children showed a trend to report one or more early difficulties over mothers of anxious children. These findings did not appear to be confounded by mother's present mental state or other factors such as ordinal position of the child, family size or presence of difficulties in mother's own life. Furthermore, a test–retest study on 20 mothers suggested satisfactory reliability of recall. These very preliminary findings suggest that life history methods are certainly worth pursuing in childhood and adolescence and may help to determine the effects of early maternal difficulties using interview methods with mothers. Such difficulties may exert their effects through mother–child relations.

Observational methods of investigating mother–child relations

Observing and evaluating interpersonal relationships between mothers with different backgrounds and present social supports and their infants and children is likely to improve our understanding of the processes which result in inadequate or inappropriate maternal behaviour at the times of normative stress, such as crying, screaming or event disinterest. Use of laboratory methods of controlled stress, such as the Ainsworth strange situation, for measuring relationship behaviour in normal and disturbed mothers allows detailed exploration of attachment behaviour and the dynamic association between characteristics in individuals and behaviours within relationships (Ainsworth *et al.* 1978; Dunn and Kendrick, 1982; Dunn, 1988b; Murray, 1988; Stevenson-Hinde, 1988). Normative stresses may, in the presence of vulnerable mothers, disrupt adequate caretaking and may adversely influence the path of normal development. In this sense it is not the life events or difficulties we wish to avoid or manipulate but the competence and coping abilities of mothers (or mother surrogates).

SOCIAL ADVERSITIES IN THE INFANT'S ENVIRONMENT

Children are active participants in building and maintaining interpersonal relationships with their care-giver (Murray-Parkes and Stevenson-Hinde, 1982; Hinde and Stevenson-Hinde, 1988). It is apparent that infants stimulate mothers or care-givers into social relations. Smiling, laughter, gaze and movement are expressions of internal affective states in the child that motivate personal and social behaviour (Emde, 1985). Throughout the first year of life there is an increasing adaptation between mothers and infants as a consequence of each one's qualitative behaviours towards the other (Sylvester-Bradley, 1981; Trevarthen, 1985).

Depriving infants of early social and emotional stimulation

Considerable research has established that neonates and infants engage in diversive exploratory behaviour under conditions of low stimulation such as might be experienced in the presence of a depressed or withdrawn mother (Lipsitt, 1983; Stern, 1985).

Observational studies have begun to demonstrate the mechanisms through which everyday stresses may exert some relatively immediate effects on a child. Recent research on mother–child interactions has shown that observations of depressed mothers and their 3-year-old children shows high negative transactions between mother and child such as physical smacking and negative verbal criticisms. In addition there was an absence of positive transactions such as smiling and embracing (Dowdney *et al.*, 1984, 1985; Mills *et al.*, 1985). Depressed mothers were often preoccupied, distracted and failing to initiate or respond to infant cues. Secondly, mothers seemed not to mesh the quality of their interchanges with their children. Mills and her colleagues point out that often these mothers do not make the transaction relevant to the toddler in terms of his own family and social context.

In Mills *et al.*'s study, reciprocal activities between mother and child and an episode of activity or talk was called a link. A verbal link contained two components:

(a) Content—which was the introduction or expression of material for discussion;
(b) Context—the context must be relevant to the child's ongoing behaviour.

An example of verbal linking given by Mills *et al.* is that if a child makes a statement 'that's a cow', mothers might respond 'do you remember the weekend when daddy took us on the picnic and the cow ate your hat?' (family situation) or 'it's like the cow who fell in the canal, you used to have that story when you were little' (child situation).

Depressed mothers make fewer links and verbal linking, making the context relevant to the child in his own world and family, was notably absent. In other words the transactions between mother and child were not congruent. Because of this the opportunity for reciprocal patterns of normative and adaptive behaviour between mother and child were significantly diminished.

Furthermore, these links appeared least likely in mothers who were depressed *and* reported *not having much fun* with their children. The direct role of maternal depression in link deficiencies between mother and child was less clear when other factors in mothers' lives were considered. Thus two groups of depressed mothers could be identified. The first group were a sub-group of women with personality difficulties and depression who were impaired in a number of areas of child handling and who:

(a) score high in controlling the child;
(b) were frequently staring into space;
(c) had a child often unoccupied;
(d) made few links, fewer responses to links, no verbal links;
(e) reported having little or no fun in their lives.

A second sub-group of women were identified who were depressed but were not identified as suffering from personality disorder who:

(a) were sensitive to children's verbal and non-verbal cues from interaction;
(b) score high (i.e. well) on all measures of links including having fun and spending time with the child.

Clearly it is not depression in mothers *per se* that predicts transactional problems. More profound difficulties in personality may be more important, and result in a failure of necessary reciprocal care-giving behaviour. This study suggests that the mechanisms of normal parent–child relations which involve mutual reciprocity are impaired over time. Normal signals to toddlers are flimsy or absent and there is a failure of normative transactions in the presence of poor maternal competence leading to inadequate coping with normative stresses. The evidence suggests, however, that brief deficits in maternal competence, such as may occur in maternal depression in the absence of other social adversities, do not impair the continuity of care in the young child. This may be because depression may be unrelated to maternal competence (unless severe) and cause only brief interruptions in maternal coping.

Infant Development

Whether or not the deficits in maternal behaviour are caused directly by depression or by more enduring characteristics in the mother it is important to establish if these deficits have effects on children's intrinsic development, such as their socio-emotional, cognitive and linguistic abilities. Investigations into the effects on children of impaired mother–infant relations have begun to indicate that some deficits can occur (Murray, 1988). Firstly, affective factors in the child as well as the mother are important in promoting social relations in such a way as to facilitate the child's development in all areas (Murray and Trevarthen, 1986). Smiling, laughter, gaze and movement are all expressions of the infant's affective state and appear to act as motivators of social behaviour as well as providing interpersonal reference points for subsequent interpersonal activity (Stern, 1977; Campos and Steinberg, 1981; Emde, 1985).

Throughout the first year of life there is an increasing adaptation between mothers and infants as a consequence of each other's qualitative alterations towards the other (Sylvester-Bradley, 1981; Trevarthen, 1985). These developmental processes are seen, for example, through alterations in maternal baby talk which becomes increasingly more complex and rich with time (Bruner, 1975). In addition, infant's facial expressions and motor behaviour are not unintegrated with responses to persons but goal directed and related to social cues such as maternal reciprocal activity (Stern, 1985).

It has recently been suggested that infants are markedly sensitive to perturbations in maternal communications such as speech, facial expression and motor activity (Murray, 1988). Ongoing qualitative deficits in these areas of maternal communication may result in emotional and cognitive deficits in children. On specific testing of tasks for object constancy, infants of depressed mothers appear to be less able to find hidden objects than infants of the same age of non-depressed mothers (Murray, 1988). Video analysis of the task and of mother–infant interactions show that the infants of depressed mothers were more easily distracted, showed less interest in the task and engaged in less affective expression with their mothers than infants of non-depressed mothers. The video also showed that depressed mothers were less infant centred and appeared to make greater numbers of critical comments about their infant and his or her performance under task conditions (Murray, 1988). These direct observational studies of young infants' interactions parallel the findings from the observations described above on 3-year-olds. They suggest, however, that effects of maternal difficulties on early infant development may be more significant in some cases than has been so far considered. To what extent these findings predict later developmental progress is unclear and as yet we do not know if deficits in social, emotional and cognitive development under the age of 2 years can be modulated by subsequent positive experiences in the child's life. Some recent evidence suggests that for some children at 2 years, deficits in cognitive function may persist. However, by 4 years no direct links are apparent between current behavioural difficulties and post-natal depression (Cogill et al., 1986; Caplan et al., 1989). We cannot tell if the findings at 2 years are a consequence of ongoing maternal or other adversities in the child's life or reflect a direct effect on intrinsic development. Neither do we know if these early infant deficits predict later intrinsic problems, social difficulties or learning problems at school.

Nevertheless the findings are clearly important for psychological theory and clinical practice. At present the evidence appears to favour multiple and diverse pathways from infancy, by which children may show emotional and cognitive deficits and that a range of social experiences are important for promoting adequate development or preventing effects of social adversity (Rutter, 1986b).

Fathers' parenting and adversities

Studies on paternal–child transactions have been few but indicate that fathers participate in important parenting processes and can influence social–emotional development (Lamb, 1977; Lamb et al., 1982; Lewis, 1986). The process by which fathers exert this influence and the similarities and differences there are with mothers is unclear. Present evidence suggests that fathers are at risk from depression following childbirth (Lewis, 1986). As infancy proceeds fathers increase the time spent with their off-spring and a year after delivery their relationship appears more substantial with a greater degree of interaction and expressed affection (Lewis, 1986). It is apparent that transactions with care-takers other than mothers is important and in need of further research. Important links may exist between the development of a lack of emotional support for mothers and paternal depression and for some families the origins of marital difficulties and childhood behaviour problems may stem from affective disorders in fathers during infancy.

The long-term outcome of ongoing difficulties in parent–infant relations

These studies should not be taken as indicating that an irretrievable deficit in social and emotional development has occurred. We do not know the longer-term effects of linkage deficits in mother–child relations. For example, there may be effects on how children relate to other children in the short term. There is, for example, evidence that siblings develop closer relations in the absence of adequate maternal care (Dunn and Kendrick, 1982) (see Chapter 3 for fuller discussion). Furthermore, longitudinal studies on children reared in the absence of biological parents tell us that outcome is far from gloomy in all cases, suggesting that important facilitative transactions can and do occur in later periods of life which may successfully influence subsequent adjustment (Quinton and Rutter, 1985b).

Past adversities in the lives of parents and present difficulties in parent–infant relations

It is a truism to say that present behaviour depends to some degree on past experience. The question is what past experience in the lives of individuals influences what kind of behaviour in the present? Do we accept that any form of severe adversity is likely to exert effects at a later date? Will mothers who were subject to adverse parenting be adverse parents for example? Recent studies have given some support to this hypothesis. Thus the association between maternal depression and behaviour problems in young children is strongest in those mothers with a history of adversity in their own lives (Cox et al., 1987). This study showed that women who were separated from their own parents for prolonged periods of time and/or experienced poor parenting themselves or reported the presence of a poor quality marriage were those most at risk. These findings suggest two somewhat different mechanisms. The first relates specifically to past experience of their own parenting and suggests that in some way this interferes in the quality of child care. The second is that being unsupported in their own lives in the present interferes with child care. In both cases the suggestion is that one mediating factor is maternal mental state. That is to say, it is depressed mothers with these factors who increase the risk for behaviour problems in the children. We know, however, that behaviour problems can and do occur in mothers who may be anxious and worried but not depressed and not all depressed mothers have problem children. The mechanisms are therefore suggestive of a link between past experience, present maternal adversity and depression in mothers and behaviour problems in children.

From the studies investigating the influence of maternal depression on mother–infant interaction we may conclude that the effects of early adversity in the lives of mothers are on personality factors related to parenting. We do not know if other areas of personality are also adversely influenced by such early experiences. Similarly it becomes apparent that maternal depression as a result of poor confiding relations with a spouse in the present is less of a risk factor to parenting and child behaviour problems in the absence of early adversity in the lives of mothers. Nevertheless these studies also suggest that maternal depression may exert effects not entirely dependent on previous adversities.

The appropriate studies to determine both the relative contribution of depression alone and in the presence of past adversities to infant development have yet to be undertaken.

FAMILY RELATIONS AND PSYCHOPATHOLOGY

Clinical implications of studies on parental competence

The major focus for the clinician is to consider the need for *encouraging* normative experiences between mother and children. Skuse and Cox (1985) summarise four findings that reflect differences in mothers who do or do not cope with everyday hassles.

1. The presence of parenting difficulties is associated with ongoing social and economic adversity.
2. Depressed mothers brought up in care seem at greater risk from failure to cope with everyday hassles.
3. One mechanism which may prevent the accomplishment of developmental tasks is a lack of maternal responsibility to the child.
4. The presence of intimate confiding relationships for women acts as a protective effect against maternal depression and may therefore facilitate

the responsibility in mothers to their children thereby allowing normative stresses to be dealt with.

The social and clinical implications of these findings relate to the need for
assessment of potential parenting failure because of personal inabilities to deal
with normative life experiences. Five clinical factors are suggested:

1. Identification of mothers at general risk because of past adverse environments in their own lives, in particular, having been in care or experienced
   continuous lack of intimate relationships with their own parents.
2. The assessment of supportive relationships to mothers in terms of their
   availability, adequacy and intimacy. Assessment of mothers' parenting
   and coping skills requires detailed interviewing about relationships as well
   as social conditions.
3. Observations of mother–child interactions should be part of any assessment procedure concerning the evaluation of normative stresses and reciprocity.
4. The importance of fathers must not be underemphasised as their involvement in assessments will allow the best clinical strategy to be adopted in
   terms of choice and compliance of intervention.
5. Child difficulties either as a failure of normative intrinsic or extrinsic
   events may interfere with the necessary relationships with caretaker and
   lead to behavioural disorganisation.

The clinical interventions required are based on a framework of developmental
transactions between persons and transitions over time which mutually influence
each other in certain respects. Skuse and Cox (1985) point out that 'there are
many different points at which a parent may enter a more vulnerable category'.
Sustaining good family life and managing the normative stresses of development
are major goals for a young family. Should stress-related difficulties arise, psychological interventions which may improve parenting qualities and the family
environment should be considered as an important treatment option for the
betterment of 'relations between relationships' as well as the improvement of
individual well-being and parenting skills.

Stress and the physical environment

The presence of adverse factors in the ecology of the environment may be a
contributory factor in family stress (Rutter, 1973; Richman, 1977; Quinton,
1980, 1988). For example, children need a safe place to play and a dangerous
play environment may increase the risks for life events (e.g. accidents, assaults)
to occur. The importance of parks, adventure playgrounds and play groups in
urban areas to replace the street or back garden cannot be underestimated, but

are all too often not available in areas that need them most or are inconvenient for parents to get to (Rose, 1973).

Flats, high-rise buildings and tower blocks predispose to increase rates of psychiatric disorder in pre-schoolers *and* in mothers who have been shown to have increased rate of depression (Richman, 1977; Brown and Harris, 1978).

Two factors in the environment have been discussed and investigated in some detail (Richman, 1985). Firstly, housing policy may influence rates of psychiatric disturbance by selectively grouping deprived and disadvantaged families together in housing estates. Secondly, increased social mobility may result in breaking ties and supports of adults and young families. The effects of these environmental factors on children appears to be through the loss of social and emotional supports and increasing low morale in adults.

These findings illustrate how physical structures can influence social structures in people's lives. These physical structures then result in changes in children's well-being through their effects on parental well-being. Therefore the impact of these stresses on children is indirect, operating by increasing adversity and its effects on their parents.

It seems unlikely that the physical environment exerts no direct effects on children however. For example, the lack of play space or equipment, or the absence of a secure exploratory social environment seems likely to exert direct effects perhaps on children's capacities to learn coherently about the world, as well as increasing the risk of psychiatric disorder. We know little, however, about children's perceptions of their physical environment and how this may directly effect their lives.

Family adversity and emotional disorder in school-age children

Few studies have been carried out investigating the effects of family adversity on the school-age child and the transactional patterns of behaviour between persons in this age group are far from clear. Epidemiological findings have established that *chronic family adversity* is associated with conduct disorder (Rutter, 1985b; Rutter *et al.*, 1979). These findings showed that at least six significant family stressors were associated with conduct disorders. Three of these reflect *structural factors*: (i) father having an unskilled or semi-skilled job; (ii) large family size; (iii) child having been in care; and a further three reflect *functional factors*: (iv) maternal psychiatric disorder; (v) criminal history in fathers; (vi) ongoing marital discord.

The presence of any one of these adversities does not increase the probability of conduct disorder in the child. The combination, however, of two or more of these stressful factors substantially increases the risk, suggesting that the adverse effects of chronic stresses do not simply summate but interact with each other (see Chapter 9 for further discussion of interactions between stressors).

These findings have been broadly confirmed in other studies (Shaw and Emery, 1988).

What these studies have identified are some of the social and family factors that are stressful in family life. The mechanisms by which they exert their effects and their interrelations with each other require further investigation. Their effects, however, often impact on more than one child in the family, suggesting that the focus of these family stresses is pervasive and markedly disruptive. Clinically, a diagnosis of conduct disorder can often be made in siblings of the referred case.

Associations between chronic and recent social adversities

Furthermore, it is not clear what the association between these *chronic stresses* and more *acute life events* may be. There is some evidence to support the notion that acute events are indeed associated with both conduct and emotional disorders (Goodyer, Kolvin and Gatzanis, 1985). The present slim evidence suggests that recent events which occurred in the 12 months prior to the onset of disorder, were moderately to severely undesirable and classified as family, marital, accident or illness events were potentially causal factors in emotional and conduct disorders. Interestingly, similar events which were judged as only mildly undesirable were significantly associated with conduct disorder only, suggesting a different effect for different qualities of recent life events on the form of expression of disorder. More recently it has become apparent that such recent adversities do continue to exert pathological effects on children and adolescents in the presence or absence of more chronic social adversities in the child's life (Goodyer, Wright and Altham, 1988). It appears, however, that it is the patterning of adversities, both recent and more long term, that is likely to predict the probability of emotional and behavioural disorders in most cases.

Two factors associated with anxiety and depression in school-age children are mothers who are emotionally unsupported and mothers who report emotional symptoms in themselves (Goodyer, Wright and Altham, 1988). Both these factors are relatively chronic stresses in the lives of children, and in their presence acute events continue to exert effects of importance on the probability of being emotionally disturbed. The presence of two or more stresses significantly increases the risk of emotional disorder in the child, suggesting that as with conduct disorder family stresses (in this case both acute and chronic) summate each other's effects. Interestingly there is no particular patterning of these adversities that discriminates between anxious and depressed cases. There are different psychological and statistical forms of interaction between social factors which are discussed in detail in Chapter 9. The main point here is that recent adversities are important in exerting psychopathological effects. The overall probability of being emotionally disturbed, however, is explained by the combination of effects of different forms of undesirable life experiences.

The findings on the association between different forms of social adversity and anxiety and depression in children are few, and the above results are no more than a beginning in our attempts to understand how family disturbance may result in psychopathology in the child. The patterning and interactions of both acute and chronic family factors require further study. The sensitivity of interview methods must be improved to examine the connections between different forms of adversities. The introduction of observational methods, so successful with younger children, could help answer some of the many outstanding questions.

FAMILY TRANSACTIONS AND SPECIFIC LIFE EVENTS

The classic studies on infant deprivation documenting the protest–despair–detachment sequence and the observations on withdrawn young children in institutions document, among other things, what can happen to children's normative responses to inadequate maternal care (Spitz, 1946; Bowlby, 1969, 1980; Robertson and Robertson, 1971). Although the meaning and mechanisms of these phenomena remain far from clear these early observations on the effects of disturbed relationships between parent and child have had a major impact on the theory and practice of child mental health over the past 30 years (Rutter, 1972, 1988a). They illustrate an important developmental concept: that of an alteration in the form of behaviour in the infant as a consequence of a socially undesirable stimulus that has disrupted the parent–infant relationship. These effects, however, have been shown to be reversible in the case of short-term separations of a few days (Rutter, 1972; Wolkind and Rutter, 1985a). In other words, the observations made on infant's responses to separations pertained more to those children where separations had been prolonged. The acute life event of separation from caretaker may result in transient symptoms of anxiety and social withdrawal in the child, and these can be undesirable and distressing for all family members. The evidence suggests clearly, however, that the re-establishment of child with parent results within a few days of a return to good relations and a loss of symptoms. In addition, there is no evidence that such brief separations have any long-term effects on the child who is not at risk from subsequent psychiatric disorder as a result of such an acute event.

The provision of a normative stressful and facilitative social environment will result in the optimum reciprocal and mutually rewarding association between care-giver and care-receiver. The relatively large contribution made by the care-giver is important but diminishes as the child matures physically and mentally. The transition from infant care-giver to toddler care-giver therefore requires a mutual re-defining of reciprocal ongoing life experiences and relationships between parent and child. In other words, we need to be concerned with what

Hinde and Stevenson-Hinde (1988) have recently described as the study of relations between relationships. In particular, how specific events and difficulties may influence such processes as well as individuals.

Disruption of maternal competence by recent life events

There may be effects on maternal competence as a result of acute life events such as bereavements or separations and longer-term difficulties such as chronic marital disharmony. Such adverse social experiences may impact on normal infant development as well as acting as potentially causal factors in psychiatric disorders in mothers and behaviour problems in pre-school children (Rutter, 1985a,b; Hinde and Stevenson-Hinde, 1988).

Separations between mother and child

Separations of children from their mothers can have undesirable effects under certain conditions, e.g. prolonged hospitalisation as a result of infant illness may have adverse effects if maternal support is not available. Hospitalisation practice has radically altered on this basis with regular visits to see children and many children's wards and hospitals operate a live-in policy for parents.

Duration of separation experiences

Separation of infant and child from care-giver can give rise to a variety of effects (Wolkind and Rutter, 1985a). Stress may result either from the *circumstances* surrounding the separation or from the *consequences*. As an event, separation disrupts normative experiences, for both mother and child. But if it is brief and innocuous it is not likely to result in adverse consequences for the relationship between child and mother.

The quality of care before separation

The presence of adverse ongoing social experiences in the life of the family may well alter the likely impact of separation. Thus, infants and children who experience poor relationships with their care-givers, may exhibit substantial distress at the time of separation (Rutter, 1985a,b). Therefore the impact of separation is increased because of the absence of an adequate relationship with a care-giver. This suggests that such a relationship confers important psychological effects of protection against the negative impact of separation.

If separations are going to occur then clinical evaluation of the quality of maternal care and maternal–infant relations may be important prior to separation experiences. For example, assessments of the effects of hospitalisation on the child may help not only to determine the need for psychological intervention for potential adverse separation difficulties for infant and mother but also to improve the efficiency of medical procedures that are required.

The assessment of maternal or parental capacity to nurture and facilitate development and protect and buffer the child against adversity in the environment can be achieved through direct observation of parent–child interaction at home, in the nursery or in an adequate play room in hospital, as well as through discussions with the mother which can be carried out prior to the separation.

Further clues to potential difficulties in this area of parenting may be obtained by evaluating the number of risk factors in the backgrounds of caretakers. Thus poorly supported and isolated mothers, socio-economic hardships, and the presence of poor parenting skills represent some of these possible risk factors (Wolkind and Rutter, 1985a). Mothers with previous difficulties in separation or with no experience of being separated from their children may require psychological support during such a period to alleviate any anxieties that brief separations may interfere with her role as a parent or reflect on her capacities to care for her children.

Separation—long-term effects on infant and child

For some children, however, separation is not a single acute event such as hospitalisation but represents a chronic difficulty in their lives. This may occur because of repeated separations occurring frequently throughout a period in their childhood, or because of a continuous separation such as being received into care on a permanent basis and spending a large amount of their formative years in an institution.

Longitudinal studies on children raised in care, and children with marked deprivation and social adversity in their early years, provide important evidence to show that it is the continuity of exposure to adversity that seriously impairs a child's chances of normal social–emotional and cognitive development (Miller, Kolvin and Fells, 1985; Quinton and Rutter, 1985b, 1988). If these social environments can be altered, there is clearly an opportunity to decrease the risks of adverse outcomes in later childhood and adolescence and adulthood. The risks appear to be not in the formation of a specific type of psychopathology (such as depression) but to the individual's emergent personality. Of course this reflects a substantial risk for subsequent episodes of depression because of problems that such children may have with later aspects of adjustment, such as personal achievement and interpersonal relationships. These risks for specific psychiatric disorder are a consequence of the effects of early ongoing adverse life experiences on personality development.

Quinton and Rutter's (1988) findings also demonstrate, however, that some women find later adaptive social pathways to ameliorate their early negative life experiences.

BIRTH OF A SIBLING

One method of investigating the effects of stress on mother and child relations is by observing their transactions before and after a life event. Such a model can be seen in the work of Judy Dunn and colleagues in their study of the effects of the arrival of a sibling on firstborn development and mother–child transactions (Dunn and Kendrick, 1982; Dunn, 1986, 1988a).

The birth of a sibling disrupted transactions between mother and firstborn and resulted in clear change of behaviour in the child in the first 2–3 weeks. However, there were considerable individual differences between firstborn children. Most, but not all, showed an increase in demands for attention and in negative behaviour directed at mother, and incidents of deliberate naughtiness were observed to increase markedly after birth. However, the expression of distress varied from social withdrawal from mother to others who were more clinging and aggressive. Several children developed somatic disturbances with sleep problems and in some who were toilet trained there was regression and setbacks in this area.

Firstborns who were rated as more displaced had an associated sharp decrease in sensitive maternal attention and a resultant escalation of conflict and punishment.

In addition, about half the children showed more positive changes, including an increased independence for feeding or dressing, going to the toilet alone and a preparedness to play independently.

These findings demonstrate important effects of a normative life event. Firstly, the event clearly results in alterations in transactions with firstborn children; mother's preoccupations with new infant may decrease links with the firstborn. Secondly, the event's consequence are not uniform; a variety of outcomes are possible. Thirdly, the quality of outcome is not predictable, neither is direction; some children become difficult and distressed, whereas others increase their individual coping skills.

Dunn and colleagues did not feel able to make inferences about the causal direction between maternal change and child behaviour. The question may in any case be misleading if we are considering the effects of an event on a relationship rather than on individuals' behaviour. A further interesting finding, from the point of view of family transaction, was that where the firstborn had a close supportive relationship with the father, the negative effects on the relationship between mother and firstborn were less marked.

The authors were only able to speculate on the mechanisms for this. For example, fathers may provide emotional support for their wives, emotional support for the firstborn or more direct instrumental infant care. Whatever the exact explanation it is likely that paternal competence may involve all three factors depending on the social circumstances. Thus it is likely that the maintenance of adequate links in mother–child relations is facilitated by father. Fathers, and perhaps other adult carers, are therefore able to buffer the impact of the normative event of sibling arrival in those children where such an event is likely to cause undesirable effects. The speculations concerning the role of fathers as modulators of normal and difficult social experiences also indicate that much greater understanding of the role of fatherhood is required.

This study illustrates that a common major life event of birth of a sibling exerts markedly different effects on children. These individual responses to a relatively uniform and ubiquitous life event indicate that there are multiple social and psychological components that determine its effects. But why should some firstborn children show their increased capacity for autonomy at such a stressful time? Does this reflect a more intrinsic mechanism, something related to the child itself—a sense of personal competence? If so where does this personal competence derive from—perhaps his or her own early maternal experiences? We are in no position as yet to answer these questions. However, some clues can be found in the results from recent research.

For example, the birth of a sibling for some children produces marked positive and adaptive behaviour not only for themselves but for family relations. It can be suggested therefore that such life events exert *steeling* effects. That is, although their *hedonic qualities* may predict undesirable and distress consequences, the result of their *effects* is to improve the child's personal competence. For other children, however, the event appears to result in unwanted and distressing symptoms. In other words, the effects of the event *sensitises* the child in an undesirable way and produces difficult behaviour which increases the everyday difficulties in family life.

These individual differences in response to similar life events require further investigation. There may be many other factors that determine how individuals respond to family adversity. Intrinsic features of the individual, such as temperament, and extrinsic social factors outside of the family, such as the physical environment and social supports, may exert effects on responses to family stresses.

Maternal experiences as indirect influences on siblings

The effects on children may not be as direct as implied in the above hypothesis however. Consider, for example, the focus of effects of the event of a newborn child. Such an event clearly has an impact on all family members to varying degree and direction, i.e. positive or negative. The direct impact on mothers, for example, may be influenced by a range of other social experiences, e.g.: structural factors in their environment; alterations in their present relationships; past experiences of child rearing; past experiences of their own childhood. All these factors may, if present, configure to alter the effects of childbirth on mother and therefore exert indirect effects on the impact of the event on the child. We must await the findings of future studies to determine how such indirect factors may influence children's reactions.

Some lessons from children's reactions to birth of a sibling

The ways in which some children utilise everyday hassles and prior undesirable experiences or survive major traumas apparently intact, suggest that clinical interventions could benefit through a better understanding of steeling effects of experiences (Patterson, 1983; Parmalee, 1984; Garmezy, 1985). Certainly an important area of personal development is that which relates to overcoming hardship, and coping successfully with unexpected and unwanted stresses. Furthermore, learning skills for problem-solving and perhaps improving recognition of potentially stressful events could be a clinical task for children as well as adults.

DIVORCE

Since the 1950s industrialised countries have experienced a steep rise in the divorce rate. To some extent this phenomenon has been paralleled by an increase in cohabitation, particularly within the last 20 years (Richards, 1988). Over the past 15 years there has been an accumulating body of research focusing on the impact of divorce on child development (Hetherington, Cox and Cox, 1982; Hetherington, 1988; Richards, 1988).

The demographic characteristics of divorce

Recent studies have shown that between 1 and 2 per cent of marriages end per annum (Richards, 1988). In one study in New Zealand, however, between 10 and 30 per cent of these divorces were reconciled within 12 months and at 4 years some 33 per cent are remarried and 34 per cent reconciled (Fergusson, Dimond and Horwood, 1986; Richards, 1988). Within 5 years 70 per cent of the reconciled parents had parted and 53 per cent of the remarried group had undergone further separation. It is apparent that divorce, from the child's point of view, can result in multiple alterations in family living circumstances in many instances and the consequences of divorce on an individual child will be determined in part by the quality of these social disruptions.

Demographic factors can also help in identifying children most at risk from the divorce process. Richards (1988) has provided a useful summary of this data and suggests that the probability of divorce is significantly increased with marriage at a younger age; briefer periods of going steady before marriage; prenuptial conception or conception soon after marriage; closely spaced conceptions after marriage; four or more children; marriage not taking place by religious ceremony.

These factors exert their effects on children through altered family relations. At first glance it is apparent that not all these factors will have negative effects on children even if they serve to bring about divorce. For example, as we have already discussed, a close relationship with a sibling of a similar age may protect against the negative effects of a poor relationship with parents.

Furthermore, some of the risk factors for divorce, such as the absence of religious ceremony or short length of pre-marriage relationship, are not psychologically important factors for children's adjustment to divorce.

The variety and complexity of the divorce process, the quality of pre-divorce relations and the nature of post-divorce relations have all been shown to exert effects on children's social and emotional adjustment (Hetherington, 1988; Richards, 1988). There are no easy generalisations about the effects of divorce. As well as the aforementioned social factors surrounding divorce, the child's age, developmental status and environment outside the home (school, peers and non-nuclear family relations to grandparents, aunts, etc.) can all contribute to the effects of a permanent alteration to the family status quo that occurs with the divorce process.

The divorce process

Divorce is an outcome event of ongoing difficulties between two adults. Conceptually one difference between divorce and other adverse social experiences is that it is arrived at intentionally in an effort to end unwanted and intolerable marital disharmony. We know that children chronically exposed to marital disharmony have a substantially increased risk of psychiatric disorder, particularly if the marriage has been violent (Wallerstein, 1983; Quinton and Rutter, 1985). It is therefore important to disentangle the antecedent effects of family relations from the impact of divorce itself. Thus the social origins of divorce do not necessarily provide clues to the impact of divorce on children. Thus targeting adults at risk for divorce is not the same as targeting children at risk from the *effects* of divorce.

There may be important antecedent factors other than parental relationships in determining a child's adjustment, and sibling relationships may be one of the most significant.

One further antecedent feature, however, has been identified by the researches of Block and colleagues (Block, Block and Morrison, 1981; Block, Block and Gjerde, 1986, 1988). In these studies prospective longitudinal investigation was undertaken of marriages before and after divorce proceedings. These important investigations showed that the marital environment was a predictor of child adjustment. Thus parents who showed greater agreement and consensus about child rearing values and practices showed significantly less marital disruption *and* less behavioural disturbance in their children. The duration of adverse family environment prior to divorce was as long as 11 years in some cases (Block, Block and Gjerde, 1988). Furthermore, boys in such adverse environments tended to be impulsive, undercontrolled and aggressive compared with boys whose families remain intact, suggesting that the increased difficulties in boys compared with girls post-divorce are influenced by antecedent family environments and may not be a consequence of divorce itself (Block, Block and Morrison, 1981). The greater post-divorce conflict between parents and sons rather than parents and daughters may be a consequence of their antecedent family environment. These findings do not discriminate between different types of attitudes and parent agreements.

In a recent study on the role of emotions in the family system, confirmation of Block's thesis that agreements and attitudes are important for marital adjustment was found for affective features of parent–parent and parent–child relations, but not for attitudes for discipline and control (Easterbrooks and Emde, 1988). These findings for young children only (6–24 months) suggest that different forms of agreement and consensus between family members may be important at different stages in the family life cycle. In Block, Block and Gjerde's (1988) discussion of their own findings, for example, they highlight again the modulating effect of the presence of fathers on mother–child/adolescent relations. In divorced families mother–son relationships are consistently described as more tense and conflict ridden in the absence of fathers. In their presence (i.e. when mother–son dyads are transformed into mother–father–son triads) the harmony of mother–son dyads improves markedly (Dombush, Carlsmith and Bushwall, 1985; Gjerde, 1986). The absence of positive paternal influence in single-parent mother–son families in particular raises the possibility of further deterioration over time.

The introduction into such dyads of a new step-father has markedly different effects than the maintenance of the biological parent. Step-fathers may amplify existing difficulties both in mother–son dyads and in child adjustment (Hetherington, 1988). This amplification effect of step-fathers seems greatest when they remain disengaged from the everyday affairs of the child. The findings suggest that the children, especially boys, see this lack of affective and instrumental contact with themselves as indicating a rival for affection of their mother.

These latter findings suggest significant interdependencies between emotional and instrumental factors in the adjustment of family relations in a reconstituted family.

Specific effects of divorce on child adjustment

As well as influences on relations and adults, divorce has effects on children's emotions and behaviours. Despite the caveats and clear influences of antecedent factors, divorce does appear to exert effects as a life event and post-divorce factors may influence these effects.

Pre-school children

Sex differences between boys' and girls' responses are apparent in the 3 months following divorce. Firstly, impairments in both sexes are apparent with aggression, acting out, anxieties and sleep disturbance and depressive features in some children. Greater attention seeking and proximity was apparent for all. Boys are particularly interested in adult males and show greater amounts of difficulties than girls. Social impairments are apparent with less interpersonal activity, solitariness and social withdrawal being common. Less positive responses to others, such as hugging, and smiling, and greater negative responses, such as scowling and crying, are reported (Hetherington, 1988). Boys show greater levels of aggression and both sexes show increased behaviours reminiscent of an earlier period of development.

As time passes the general trend is for all symptoms to improve but at 2 years post-divorce social, emotional and cognitive features of post-divorce children remain quantitatively different from children of non-divorced parents. Social difficulties, greater impulsivity and attention problems occur more frequently in everyday circumstances. The relative contribution of post-divorce adverse family relations to continuing deficits in the child are significant (Block, Block and Gjerde, 1988; Hetherington, 1988).

It should be noted, however, that some children do not develop significant difficulties whereas a small group may become clinically depressed (Wallerstein and Kelly, 1980). These uncommon polar reactions of resilience and psychopathology are not well understood but clearly cannot be accounted for by the effects of divorce *per se*.

School-age children

By middle childhood the child's responses are dominated by affective symptoms: tearfulness and fearfulness, especially of parental replacement, are characteristic. Social withdrawal and educational underachievement are reported. Boys again show greater quantitative responses and are more likely than girls to be affected. Anger may be reported by the children but fears of further parental loss may direct anger away from parents towards siblings, teachers or peers.

Although the children were better able to understand the changes occurring in their lives they showed little cognitive capacity for ameliorating their emotional difficulties and social deficits (Whitehead, 1979; Richards, 1988; Hetherington, 1989). Again however there is evidence to show that there is little social and emotional maladjustment for many children and adolescents following divorce (Amato and Edgar, 1987). Those children post-divorce who experience further multiple family changes are more likely to produce aggressive, antisocial behaviour, especially boys (Fergusson, Dimond and Horwood, 1986; Hetherington, 1989).

Interestingly, low self-esteem is reported for girls only. This finding would fit with life history investigations that loss of parent before the age of 11 is significantly more common in depressed young women and the effects of loss of parent may be transmitted through subsequent 'lack of care' and deficits in self-esteem (Brown, 1988). Whether the sex differences reflect insensitive measures of self-esteem in boys or real differences in the impact of divorce on the self-system is not yet clear.

Adolescents

The short-term impact on adolescents can be quite marked (Wallerstein and Kelly, 1980). Depression may be a more rapid and apparent response but overt anger also occurs, with blame placed on the parent who left for the divorce. Educational and social difficulties may arise as in middle childhood. Adolescents may find themselves being drawn into adult-confiding relations with their remaining parent. Sexuality becomes more obvious as parents often engage in a series of multiple relationships following divorce (Burgoyne and Clarke, 1982). In some, adolescents sexual relationships may be brought forward by divorce and a raised incidence of teenage pregnancies and illegitimate births is reported (Richards, 1988). These findings of increased sexuality have only been reported for girls, although the risk of poor social and emotional outcome 6 years post-divorce shows no significant sex differences (Hetherington, 1988, 1989).

The effects on children and adolescents of divorce show that the form of expression of difficulties varies with development; the importance of understanding children's appraisal of divorce at different ages is apparent. Different attributions and therefore different coping strategies are likely to occur at different ages. For example, Hetherington, Cox and Cox (1979, 1982, 1985) have shown that in pre-school and early middle childhood, divorce is likely to be attributed to personal feelings in the child, whereas the older child is likely to blame an adult.

The effects of social and cognitive factors on emotional and social difficulties, such as a sense of loss, personal blame, shame, guilt and anger, has yet to be evaluated.

The offspring of divorced parents

Large-scale demographic studies from a number of countries indicate that children of divorced parents are more likely to divorce themselves. A lower commitment to marriage has been suggested as a causal explanation for the intergenerational effects (Belsky and Pensky, 1988).

The Berkeley longitudinal study of human development provides the best evidence that children of divorce are at risk of diversity as adults because of styles of behaviour that are set up through their adverse social experiences, which may lead a person (i) to select environments and relationships in which behavioural patterns are readily enacted; (ii) to use ambiguous social situations which can be structured to permit the behavioural pattern to be expressed (Caspi and Elder, 1988).

Thus children of divorce are at more risk of subsequent adult social relationship difficulties. The mechanisms for this effect seem to be transmitted via the style of behavioural interaction and the mental representations of relating that children use subsequently. What is not clear, however, is the specific effect of the divorce process, since these children are more likely to have experienced a range of social family adversities prior to divorce and perhaps as a consequence of divorce. Clearly tracing out these patterns and associations requires further research.

BEREAVEMENT

There are surprisingly few studies on the effects of bereavement as a stressor in childhood (Garmezy, 1983). In the only prospective controlled report to date, Van Eerdewegh and colleagues (1982) compared a cohort of children, randomly selected and aged 2 to 11 years, 1 and 13 months after the death of one of their parents, with age- and sex-matched controls with no such loss. At 1 month there were signs of depressive mood in over three-quarters of the bereaved children compared with a third of the non-bereaved controls. By 13 months, however, the reactions in the bereaved group were considerably diminished, and depressive symptoms were rare, although disinterest in school persisted in some adolescents. The results suggest that, in comparison with earlier clinical descriptive studies (Furman, 1974), for many children the immediate consequences of bereavement may be severe but of a relatively short duration. We do not know if such events exert effects in later life. Nor do we know if these children now possess a vulnerability factor only operating at the time of future life events.

There is a suggestion that in adolescence the loss of the same sex parent is more likely to result in prolonged and more depressive type symptoms (Rutter, 1966; Raphael, 1982). At present, however, it has to be said that we know little of either the short- or medium-term effects of bereavement on children. The long-term effects of bereavement in childhood have received greater attention in the adult literature, as researchers have examined the relative contribution of bereavement to adult depression. The present evidence suggests that where bereavement exerts a long-term effect into adulthood, it may do so because of its consequences for the child's subsequent care rather than because of the impact of loss *per se* (Brown, Harris and Bifulco, 1986).

Retrospective studies of separation and loss effects at different times in childhood have indicated that it is children of middle childhood who may be the most vulnerable to later difficulties as adults, perhaps because it is children of this age group who respond with greatest difficulty to institutionalisation, either in a children's home or with foster parents (Tennant *et al.*, 1982). The research to date, however, has not considered in any systematic way the developmental effects that may influence the impact of bereavement. For example, the relationship between cognitive understanding of death, coping responses used by children and their subsequent adjustment merits systematic study.

Overall, the immediate impact of bereavement carries an understandable degree of stress. The duration of bereavement, however, may depend on the quality of relationships antedating the loss and the subsequent relationships in the child's life. The clinical implications of bereavement and the treatment of the bereaved child and their family has been the subject of systematic inquiry and is discussed in detail in Chapter 10.

LIFE EVENTS THAT IMPACT ON THE CHILD

So far discussion has focused on events and difficulties disrupting relations by interfering with maternal competence and coping. However, events may disrupt children and the direction of effects on relations may be from child to mother.

This is an important area for family transactions because it focuses on the role of the child in maintaining normal relationships with its care-giver. The question here is what are the conditions that are inherent in the child that may disrupt normative relations and increase the risk of psychiatric disorder in child or mother.

Physical handicap as a life event

Wasserman and Allen (1985) reported findings from an observational study of physically handicapped, premature and normal children, at play with their mothers at 9, 12, 18 and 24 months of age. They chose to measure episodes of 'maternal ignoring', which was defined as an episode 10 seconds or greater of no interaction, verbal or non-verbal, between mother and child.

Their results show that there is an increasing divergence of the mean number of episodes of ignoring between the three groups over time. By 2 years the mothers of physically handicapped children have significantly withdrawn from interaction, both compared with other mothers with a non-handicapped child and with themselves when their child was less than 18 months old. The authors point out that this is not an effect of the child's IQ, although ignored children overall perform less well on tests of intellectual and developmental abilities at 24 months by up to 20 points. Why should mothers of physically handicapped children become withdrawn from their offspring at this age and not before or at birth? The authors suggest that it is the maternal appraisal of the physically handicapped child's failure to develop as expected.

As time goes by and the markers of development are not achieved, there is increasing maternal detachment. In other words, the absence of expected normative events of physical development in the child act as adverse social life events to the mother. The absence of these normative events results in disruptions to mother–child relations through maternal detachment. Thus one form of deficit in maternal competence is the loss of proximity between mother and child.

The effects of maternal detachment

Maternal withdrawal has been described by others in relation to handicapped children (Ritchie, 1981). The appraisal of handicap by mothers may be an important indication of the quality of maternal–child relationship. Affective expressions between mothers and physically handicapped children, such as smiling and laughter, may be impaired (Wasserman, 1986). These impairments of maternal processes have been shown to be significantly more common in handicapped children with behaviour problems (Wasserman and Allen, 1985).

Of course physical handicap is not conceptually a *social* life event to the child but it is to the mother. Furthermore, it has the inherent capacity of altering permanently the status quo of family life and increasing the burden of developing normal social and emotional competence to the child as well as to the child's relationship with its parent.

The adverse impact of the event appears delayed because until the child is 2, mothers do not seem to alter their care-giving behaviour. This suggests that the personal meaning of handicap influences mothers responses to the event. As mothers' expectations for normal development are not met, so the undesirable impact of the event increases. Perhaps also here for the first time mother has to re-evaluate her personal competence for the future. In other words, the events of normative failure in her handicapped child may raise new doubts and ambivalences about the future, or allow a reconsideration of disappointment and frustration experienced at the time of diagnosis of her child's difficulties. Certainly it highlights the 'predictive future' that events may bring about in people's thinking. As indicated in Chapter 1, some life events promote anticipatory thoughts about future life events, which for mothers of handicapped children may include worries about future child development. What is also unclear, however, is which psychological component of the failure of normative development results in maternal preoccupation and withdrawal. Is it thoughts of disappointment subsequent to failed expectations about her child's abilities or the loss of a cherished idea arising earlier in her life or during pregnancy about how her child was going to be? Perhaps there are other emotional and cognitive factors associated with the life event of normative failure in a handicapped child. As yet there are no studies to delineate the different potential effects on the parents of specific failures of expected developmental milestones.

POSITIVE EFFECTS OF LIFE EVENTS ON
THE FAMILY ENVIRONMENT

So far we have focused on events and difficulties whose hedonic qualities and effects have been undesirable and stressful in most (but not all) cases. The notable exception is the potential steeling effects of events on children's adjustment, either following an event, such as the arrival of a new sibling, or in the future when a similar event may be coped with more effectively as a consequence of the previous adverse experience.

By comparison, surprisingly little is known about the effect of events and experiences whose hedonic qualities are considered beneficial for development. Richman (1985), for example, points to the effect of introducing stimulating environments in the form of play groups, nurseries and adventure playgrounds to underprivileged children, but this does not examine the differential effects of these apparently beneficial life experiences.

Similarly, we know little about the psychological qualities of personal success and achievements. For example, doing well in examinations or sports or successful completion of a task at home or school may contribute to the child's ability to withstand the effects of undesirable events in his or her life. There certainly seems a need to examine the value of events where hedonic qualities 'appear' positive in the family and social context and whose effects are assumed to be desirable and constructive in all circumstances. If we take the lessons learned from events considered to be 'undesirable' or 'adverse' it is clear that for some children they result in greater personal striving and competence. Similarly, therefore, we might expect that some positive events including personal or perhaps family achievements might have unexpected and unwanted effects on children. At present the issue remains speculative.

It would seem worth while for researchers to examine the influence of success in the lives of children and families, particularly as it is often a central goal of many clinical methods when dealing with demoralised and distressed parents and children.

ADOLESCENCE, EVENTS AND DIFFICULTIES

Parry-Jones (1985) highlights the emerging differentiation of the adolescent as an individual with an identity to develop, and discusses the role of parents, among others, in this process. As adolescence proceeds, certain options for life experience are closed by parents. These 'closures' may influence a wide variety of life experience, schools, friends, behaviour values and morals of the individual adolescent.

Very little is known about the event of closure in family life. In general the 'stress' of adolescence is popularly associated with disagreements and conflicts between the adolescent and parents. This conflict is generally regarded as related to the change from family or parental dependence to greater individual responsibility and decision making. Little is said, however, about the areas of accord and similarity between adolescents and parents. Even less is known about how foreclosures and family life cycle factors may influence the frequency of everyday hassles or specific life events. At present there is little to suggest, for example, that the rate of family life events is any different in children or adolescents (Goodyer, Kolvin and Gatzanis, 1986). It has to be said, however, that the data is sparse and further studies are much required. The social experiences of parents may be crucial in understanding the impact of family life and its effects on adolescence. As already discussed, epidemiological finds have shown that conflict between adolescents and parents is rarely substantial or longstanding (Fogelman, 1976; Rutter *et al.*, 1976).

Parental experiences of entry into middle life may coincide with entry into adolescence or late childhood of their offspring. We know little of the epidemiology of events and difficulties in relation to these life-cycle changes. Perhaps everyday hassles may alter in quantity, for example, less arguments with children who are also spending less time with their parents. There may be alterations in the quality of such arguments as the nature of life experiences alters and the form of conversation between parent and adolescent, for example, becomes more equitable.

It is likely that the prevalence of different types of life events change over time. Again, for example, accidents in the home are significantly less in teenage years than in earlier childhood. Other events may be more common as a consequence of life cycle changes, for example death of grandparent or parent. Similarly, the quality of events may change so that whilst accidents are less frequent in teenage years when they do occur they may have wider personal and social consequences, such as an involvement with road traffic accidents rather than home based accidents.

Leaving home

Perhaps a key adaptation life event in late adolescence is leaving home. Leaving home is a complex social and psychological process (Fisher, 1988). Firstly there are social disruptions, with a discontinuity of lifestyle. Secondly there are psychological consequences dependent on the nature of leaving home.

Thus adolescents who leave home may experience reduced control over their environment as they learn about new places and procedures (Fisher, 1986). The novelty of new social exploration can often off-set the immediate impact of a loss of familiar surroundings (Fisher, 1988). However, this novelty effect is generally over within weeks and preoccupations and thoughts of home may become uppermost in the adolescent's mind. The frequency and intensity with which such thoughts occur may be expressed in behaviour used to adapt to new surroundings. Increased work effort and social activity indicate successful adaptation, whereas a decrease in both work and social activities indicates a failure of adaptation (Karasek, 1979; Fisher, Frayer, and Murray, 1984; Hormuth, 1984).

Homesickness—a psychopathological effect of leaving home

The life event of leaving home may have undesirable consequences in some cases. A recent study investigated homesickness by asking boarding-school children to keep records of when they felt homesick (Fisher, Frayer and Murray, 1984). A descriptive study had identified the phenomenology of homesickness to consist of cognitive, emotional and behavioural symptoms of anxiety and depression but focused specifically on the home. In adolescents at boarding school episodes of homesickness symptoms were common in the majority of pupils and were strongly associated with periods of passive mental activity (Fisher, Murray and Frayer, 1985; Fisher, 1986). Interestingly, only one in four of the episodes were prompted by external reminders of home, such as familiar music or a letter from home. From the results of a study of newly entered university students who kept daily records of episodes of homesickness many episodes of homesickness were triggered by negative experiences in their new environment (Fisher, 1988). Thus a cycle of recrimination, inactivity and social withdrawal was set up in the 'fond memories' of home, perhaps as an internal method of coping with current difficulties.

The effects of homesickness

Substantial undesirable effects can occur in homesick students (Fisher, Murray and Frayer, 1985). Deviant behaviour is measured by poorer lecture attendance, and handing work in late was significantly more common. There was also increased reporting of minor psychiatric symptoms (dizziness, palpitations, somatic symptoms and anxiety) and physical symptoms (colds, 'flu-like symptoms and mild infections). Thus present findings suggest that homesickness may be responsible for a substantial proportion of minor morbidity in first-year undergraduates.

The mechanisms of homesickness

A number of factors appear important in promoting a state of homesickness. Firstly, homesick students had moved a greater geographical distance. Interestingly, however, although they desired more visits to home the number of visits did not differ from non-homesick students. The desire for visits may be related to greater cultural and environmental differences between home and university. The same number may be due to the lack of possibilities as a consequence of money, free time or social pressure to integrate.

Secondly, homesick students were significantly more likely to report psychological disturbances prior to leaving home. Furthermore, the pattern of reported signs of symptoms was similar to those reported in homesickness episodes, i.e. anxiety, and the symptoms and fears of phobias (Fisher and Hood, 1988). Clearly in some adolescents homesickness may occur as a response to the life event of leaving home. For some, however, homesickness represents a continuity of distress. In the latter cases, leaving home may enhance the frequency and intensity of distress but does not cause distress.

In conclusion, we know very little about the associations between everyday difficulties, life events and the family composition. What happens to the impact of events and difficulties on children where there are both pre-schoolers and teenagers or where there is marked disparity in the ages of parents? It seems probable that both the quantity and quality of events and difficulties are influenced by these other family factors but the mechanisms are far from clear.

Finally we need a much firmer understanding of the association between family composition and the presence or absence of events and difficulties at different points in the family life cycle. In other words, what are the continuities and discontinuities of behaviour over time in family life and how are these difficulties influenced by social adversities? (Rutter, 1983b; Hinde and Bateson, 1984).

Life history studies, both retrospective and prospective and involving systematic collection of social experiences in both cross-sectional and longitudinal samples, will continue to provide the data to confirm or refute theories such as Bowlby's (e.g. Belsky and Pensky, 1988; Caspi and Elder, 1988).

Studies of specific life events and difficulties alone are insufficient to explore the mechanisms of stress on developmental processes. Other investigative models, such as the use of observational techniques of family relations, can contribute important insights into the mechanisms operating between as well as within persons in the face of adversity (Hinde and Stevenson-Hinde, 1988).

The stressful effects of both everyday difficulties and life events require better understanding (i) to promote and facilitate normal child development; (ii) to develop a better understanding of the causes of psychiatric disorders in young persons; (iii) to formulate intervention policies, such as education about family life, and treatment strategies for disturbed and distressed children and their families.

SUMMARY

1. Relationships between parents and children are dynamic social and psychological processes. Life events and desirable or undesirable experiences are inevitable in this reciprocating system.
2. Competence is derived, in part, from the successful negotiation of everyday

adversities, events, and difficulties that occur as interaction between family members.

3. Early social–emotional deprivation has a significant adverse effect on child development. The mechanism appears to operate through an on-going deficit in the quality of parenting rather than through episodes of psychiatric disorder in mothers. The latter may, however, lead to the former showing how *events* of illness may contribute to an *on-going difficulty* in parenting.

4. Life events may alter the status quo of family relationships and social structures. The impact of family events depends on their social context and the child's developmental status.

5. The hedonic qualities of some family life-cycle events may be desirable but the effects can result in difficulties. *Entries* into and *exits* from family life are examples of major adaptation events.

Chapter 3

Peer Relations and Friendship Difficulties

FAMILY AND SOCIALISATION

As children develop, the balance of relations within family life alters. By teenage years there is less reliance on parents for attachment and security. As children's social experiences become more extensive the world begins to include strangers as well as family members. The process of social relationships becomes more complex, more exploratory and increases in interactions with others (Hartup, 1983; Hinde and Stevenson-Hinde, 1988).

These normative and necessary social and environmental alterations involve major life event changes and may cause difficulties for some children. The mechanisms and processes involved in socialisation, and their relationships to previous individual and family experience, can provide important insights into child development and the genesis of some forms of developmental psychopathology, involving interpersonal difficulties and disturbances of emotions and behaviour.

FAMILY BACKGROUND AND SOCIAL EXPERIENCE

The first feature of the child's social world is the mother and family, itself a complex multivariate system of varying compounds and characteristics. It is not surprising, therefore, to find that social relations with other persons are an outgrowth from early family experiences (Sroufe, 1979a,b; Hinde and Stevenson-Hinde, 1988). There is considerable evidence, however, to show that child–child contacts alter both qualitatively and quantitatively with age and vary according to the context within which the child lives (Berndt, 1983).

The importance of attachment to care-givers in early life and its influence on normal socialisation has been the subject of much research and many reviews. Although no clear theory or consensus on the relative importance of the links between attachment and friendship-making exists, there is reason to believe that the psychological similarities in close ties between persons share similar features at all ages (Rutter, 1981b). In other words, there is a considerable purpose to close and affectionate ties from infancy to old age. The maintenance of emotional well-being may be this purpose (Henderson, 1977).

PEER RELATIONS

The stresses and strains of friendships have received relatively little attention compared with those of mother–infant and family relations. At present we lack both adequate theory and research with which to explain the undoubted importance and complexities of friendship. An account of our present knowledge of the influence of normative stress on peer relations is worth while, however, to demonstrate the potential continuities and discontinuities in the psychology of relationships and the possible effects of events and difficulties between these relationships and with other components in a child's life, such as family or school.

Infancy and pre-school years

Although the most crucial relations in the first year of life are within family and between mother (or surrogate) and child, there is a suggestion that babies are aware of others from an early age. Social interest in others is evident but the skills necessary for social interaction are not (Rutter, 1987a).

The evidence suggests that responses to other infants occur more or less in invariate order, i.e. looking first, followed by touching and reaching and later co-ordinated activities (Eckerman, Whatley and Kutz, 1975; Hartup, 1983). In the early weeks and months of life these interactions are rarely sustained and there are marked individual differences (Bronson, 1981). In other words, there is no clear behaviour pattern towards peers, the processes are the same as for mother–infant relations and of considerably less frequency and duration.

Social context is clearly an important facilitation and inhibition of early peer relations. For example, by the end of the first year of life the presence of mother appears to stimulate interest in other females, and the presence of inanimate objects such as toys results in a greater frequency of infant–infant contact and more frequent social exchanges (Eckerman and Whatley, 1977; Vandell, 1980).

However, the reciprocity and intensity of interactions seen in mother–infant relations are absent even in intense circumstances, such as two babies in a playpen and adult–infant contact remains the most dominant interaction in laboratory, home and institutional settings such as day-care services (Eckerman, Whatley and Kutz, 1975; Finkelstein et al., 1978; Vandell, 1980). These patterns and processes appear relatively uninfluenced by familiarity with each other.

These very loose peer relations increase in complexity in the second year of life but remain rudimentary. The evidence to date suggests that frequency of contact between infants increases with a corresponding but smaller increase in complexity, including the early signs of reciprocity of behaviour. The reciprocal interactions, however, are infrequent, short-lived and essentially dyadic, the concept of group involvement seems undeveloped. Furthermore, the interactions appear emotionally neutral (Mueller and Bremner, 1977; Bronson, 1981). Towards the end of the second year, emotionality between child dyads is more apparent; although mainly 'positive' there are also early signs of negative emotions (Mueller and Rich, 1976; Rubenstein and Howes, 1976).

The introduction of emotionality may serve to sustain or support social interactions (Ross and Goldman, 1976) and suggests an important early role of intimacy in relationships. There is, however, no evidence that at this age children are extensively sought out by their peers. By and large, social relations remain a product of maternal/care-giver relations providing a secure base for social exploration which will be more frequent with familiar faces (Ainsworth, 1972; Hartup, 1983).

Social events and difficulties in infancy

What can we conclude from this brief overview about the influence of social adversity for social development in infancy. Firstly, it is likely that the frequency of life events and difficulties involving non-related children will be low. Secondly, when they occur there may be little effect because of the relative lack of importance, in emotional terms, of strangers. Indeed it is the overt introduction of emotionality into social interactions with strangers that may be the turning point for an increasing prevalence and impact of stressful events and difficulties in children's lives.

Again we know little about the relative frequencies of events and difficulties before and after the age of 2, so we are unable to confirm or refute the importance of emotional factors in the *prevalence* of stressful experience. It does seem likely that from the age of 2 the increased level of intimacy with others will be associated with a greater degree of personal salience or meaning. This would suggest that the impact of events and difficulties that may occur are more likely to result in emotional and cognitive changes in the child, indicative of an undesirable or desirable social event. In other words, disinterest in others is not the only predictable response to strangers, the presence of interest and the behavioural consequences of interest, such as exploration and activity, heralds the opportunity for everyday hassles and life events to occur within the context of non-parental and non-sibling social contexts.

Friendships in the pre-school years

From 2 years to 5 years there are substantial alterations in child–child relations. Inefficient and immature social exchanges which are brief, rarely more than dyadic and generally emotionally neutral, are abandoned for more complex social interactions that contain many of the components of even adult social exchanges (Mueller, 1972). Commonly, 4- and 5-year-olds engage more in talking and playing and less in crying, pointing and submissive-flight behaviours (Smith and Connolly, 1972). This does not mean, however, that the quality of these social exchanges reflects reciprocity, intimacy or emotional ties. Indeed the evidence suggests that, whilst social exchange is correlated with adult features (e.g. eye-contact, body posture/movement) of social behaviour, the success of verbal exchange in producing co-operative behaviours is the same at 3 and 5 years of age (Mueller, 1972).

The increase in socialisation is accompanied by social differentiation between persons. More time is spent with peers and less with adults. Earlier affection-seeking behaviour is replaced by 'attention-seeking' behaviours (Smith and Connolly, 1972).

In other words, selectivity of persons begins and overall socialisation is more efficient. Solitary activities remain in the child's repertoire. However, even the quality of these activities is altered, in part due to socialisation processes. There is a notable increase in the range of emotionality, thus quarrels are fewer but longer, competition and rivalry become more apparent but sharing and sympathy increase to a lesser degree. In 4-year-olds paired co-operation in task performance can improve results; in 3-year-olds social pairs perform less well in a task than singly whilst in 2-year-olds pairing has little effect (Hartup, 1983).

Middle childhood and adolescence

Social exchange becomes increasingly complex throughout middle childhood and adolescence. School attendance results in an increase in social contact and represents a significant normative life event (see below). The decline in egocentrism results in increasing recognition and (to a lesser extent) appraisal that individuals have ideas and points of view different from their own (Hartup, 1983).

Interestingly, far less attention has been paid to social development in middle childhood than any other period and little is known of the nature of peer group interaction or of its purpose at this age. There is, however, a substantial literature to show that communication skills increase in effectiveness. Reciprocity between children impairs their exchanges and increases their awareness of others. Group behaviour becomes more apparent and complex with co-ordinated utilisation of problem-solving based on multiple sources of feedback (Smith, 1973; Girgus and Wolf, 1975; Hartup, 1983).

Furthermore, emotion alters in quality. Aggression is less marked in both boys and girls and is person-focused rather than object-focused (toys etc.) as in younger children. Quarrels become less but abusive language is greater. Hartup (1974) has shown that it is in middle childhood and adolescence that threats to self-esteem arise through insults and derogation both in dyads and in groups. There are also sex differences in aggression, with hostile aggression in boys taking the form of physical beatings and in girls more accusation and teasing (Venkatamiah and Bosathi, 1977). By adolescence peer time exceeds time spent with family or others (Medrich *et al.*, 1982).

This brief overview of social development charts the nature of socio-emotional maturation and the alteration to individual responses to others. The management of everyday hassles and difficulties becomes more self-orientated with age. The increasing complexities of emotional development widen the opportunity of complex responses to stimuli as seen, for example, in the decrease in aggression when an undesirable interaction occurs. In middle childhood the aggressive 'coping response' of earlier years is less predictable because children learn to consider others and have a greater emotional responsiveness (see Chapters 6 and 7 for further discussion).

Sex differences and pre- and post-pubertal differences herald the importance of considering developmental factors in how distress responses to everyday difficulties can occur. Finally we note that the concept of the self as in self-esteem is identified in social groups. The occurrence of life events and difficulties may adversely impact on these personal qualities that derive from social experience.

THE EVERYDAY DIFFICULTIES OF NORMAL
SOCIAL DEVELOPMENT

Pre-school years

The process of socialisation is active and demanding. As with family relations some core components can be seen at all ages. It has to be said, however, that the normative stress and strain of peers does not seem to exert itself substantially until after the pre-school years. Until around the age of 5, children remain predominantly within the family, using other children as excursions into socialisation rather than as unique events in themselves. The major stresses are likely to be those that influence family life and the circumstances that surround it. Specific events, such as loss of peer relations are unlikely to exert the impact that might be expected in middle childhood and adolescence.

The pre-schooler does not appear to make substantive emotional investment in other children nor to have the cognitive maturity to appraise the likely benefits of peer relations. These intrinsic factors are developmentally controlled. It would appear that young children are *protected* from social stress both by their immaturity and their affiliative ties to care-givers.

Middle school years

This picture changes with increasing development and by middle childhood emotional and cognitive development appears sufficient to allow peer relations to occur. If social conditions prevail (i.e. there are others available to relate to) there is the capacity for normative stressful exchanges. These appear to occur as a consequence of the emergence of emotional investment in others, and cognitive factors, i.e. the ability to appreciate another point of view that may be of value but demand personal time and energy. By middle childhood there may be everyday difficulties in peer relations as a consequence of their own actions not only as a function of family life. The events of making and losing friends, joining or leaving groups are stresses in their own right. As development proceeds child–child (as opposed to parent–child) interactions occupy more and more time. This change in social orientation from family to peers represents a *developmental transformation* of structure and is an example of a discontinuity in development. The child brings individual qualities to these interactions (emotions and cognitions) which influence reciprocal behaviours between dyads. These qualities exert effects of a similar nature for both parent–child and child–child relations. For example, the use of feelings such as shyness, interest and excitement occur with both parents and friends, although the relative contributions of these emotions in the two forms of relationship may be different. The different use of the same emotion over time illustrates a continuity in development of a psychological process termed a *developmental transition*.

SIBLING INFLUENCES ON SOCIAL DEVELOPMENT

Important insights into the effects of non-parental relations have been found by Judy Dunn and her colleagues investigating the influence of sibling relations on child development (Dunn and Munn, 1986; Dunn, 1988a).

Aggression and conflict between siblings

Firstly, studies have shown a marked range of individual differences in sibling pairs on measures of friendliness, conflict, rivalry and dominance and that such admissions appear relatively independent of one another (Dunn, 1983; Furman and Buhrmeister, 1985).

Secondly, longitudinal investigations have indicated that aggressive relations between siblings play a shaping role in subsequent aggressive relations between peers (Patterson, 1984, 1986b). Epidemiological studies also suggest that poor sibling relations at 4 years predict clinical behavioural problems at 8 (Richman, Stevenson and Graham, 1982). There is also evidence that children with a recent history of truanting and delinquency in adolescence have a significant past history of poor sibling relations. Disentangling, however, the causal influence of these early sibling relations from concurrent family adversities has yet to be undertaken (Dunn, 1988b).

Empathy and friendliness

The degree of friendliness, co-operation and empathy shown by siblings to each other appears to be an independent dimension from the dimensions of conflict and rivalry at all ages (Furman and Buhrmeister, 1985; Dunn and Munn, 1986). There appears to be a significant correlation between friendly co-operative behaviour by older siblings in association with younger siblings and similar behaviour 6–12 months later (Dunn and Munn, 1986).

Whilst the influence of maternal behaviour is likely to exert a significant effect on empathic behaviour between siblings, there is some suggestion that certain aspects of prosocial behaviour develop independently of parents. For example, co-operative social fantasy play is more common in children whose older siblings have been very friendly towards them (Dunn and Munn, 1986). Mothers rarely participate in such pretend play and there seems to be little evidence that mothers influence the development of social co-operation in play with other children (Dunn and Dale, 1984; Dunn, 1988b).

DEVELOPMENTAL TRANSFORMATIONS AND TRANSITIONS

Developmental transformations of structure are clearly not sudden. For example, child–child relations occur over time concurrently with parent–child relations. In other words, interactions with parents do not cease just because a child finds a playmate. There are, however, gradual realignments as a consequence of greater social engagement. It is the relative change over time that unfolds as a part of normal development.

As this transformation unfolds it is apparent that the feelings and thinking involved in the different relationships are very similar across these two social structures. The gradual transfer of a process of socio-emotional interactions from one social structure to the next appears biologically and socially adaptive. Such a process may provide a 'net' against the risks of social failure. In other words, the normative negotiating task of peer relationship building involves emotions as drives and modulators of social behaviour. But if the effects are undesirable the individual can turn to other relationships. For example, if social interaction results in conflict, anger and avoidance of a child, family relationships may buffer the effects on self-esteem through emotional factors, and ameliorate the social difficulty through behaviour such as helping to patch up quarrels and misunderstandings. Young children who experience difficulties with peers (e.g. anxious, shy and socially withdrawn) may therefore be vulnerable to subsequent normative peer group stresses. It is not until these relationships become necessary, however, that difficulties arise. The coping and problem solving mechanisms in these circumstances may be maladaptive, such as aggression or social withdrawal and may lead to deficits in friendships (Pettit, Dodge and Brown, 1988).

Social difficulties and their effects

Aggression arises early as a response to conflict in child–child interactions and by the second year of life can be found throughout peer relations. The focus of aggression changes, however, with development. Thus in the pre-school years the adverse behaviour associated with aggression as a result of social difficulties is generally directed at objects and may result in breaking valued toys or household items. As development proceeds this focus is gradually replaced by aggression and related behaviour focused on persons. A pattern which predominates in adolescence. In other words, the same social difficulty and its concomitant emotion show continuity of psychological process but developmental transformation (discontinuity) of focus.

Positive emotions of empathy, understanding and concern for others increase in the emotional repertoire with age. These increasingly complex socio-emotional exchanges between children become important for the individual's development. For example, contingencies of both adult and peer reinforcement are known to affect children's assertiveness, aggression and associative behaviour. This is why the difficulties of everyday life *between* persons have led many workers to see events and difficulties as interactional concepts (Hinde, 1979; Patterson, 1983; Kagan, 1984; Hinde and Stevenson-Hinde, 1988).

Although much research has been conducted on relations within and between family members, surprisingly little is known about interactions between non-related children. We do know that acute upsetting events such as arguments and disputes between children do lead to rapid changes in friendship (Hartup, 1983). But we know little about the long-term effects of such changes. There is, however, some evidence that children who show a fairly consistent pattern of aggression and impassivity to their peers, perhaps as a consequence of everyday difficulties and stresses, are more likely to be socially isolated with less close peer relations and be at greater risk for maladjustment (Rutter, 1980; Hartup, 1983). This emphasises that a continuous long-term effect on social relations may arise from repeated adverse responses to short-term everyday social difficulties.

THE INFLUENCE OF ADULTS ON CHILD–CHILD RELATIONS

Adult attentiveness can change the character of children's play (Harris, Wolf and Bauer, 1967). Stresses that influence adults, either as events or as ongoing difficulties, will therefore remain potentially important influences on children's sociability. As yet, there is little evidence, however, to explain how and under what conditions adult stresses and their acute events or ongoing difficulties influence children's peer relations.

Finally, it is apparent that rather than a series of sensitive social periods where the child is vulnerable to stress and strains at a particular point in time, socialisation like family interaction is a dynamic ongoing process with intermittent but frequent opportunities for everyday hassles. Whilst episodic brief disruptions of socialisation may not result in long-term effects on social development, repeated social failures may well do so and increase the risk of psychiatric disorder (Hartup, 1983).

What connections lie between the developmental processes of sociability and the quality of different kinds of peer relations is far from clear. It seems likely that it is not until middle childhood that children will differentiate their relationships. In other words, friends and confidants will be discriminated from acquaintances and strangers. The social differentiation of persons may result in improving the quality of some peer relationships through greater social and emotional involvement. Such qualitative alterations may, however, carry a risk of experiencing the psychological consequences of social adversity such as loss and disappointment.

FRIENDSHIP AS A PROTECTION AGAINST STRESSFUL EVENTS

The concept of friendship

When children themselves are asked what are friends and why they spend time with them, their answers often reflect instrumental values, such as the sharing of games and toys, and the absence of family values, such as not having to complete household chores, pay attention to personal cleanliness or look after siblings, and to a lesser extent, the recognition of emotional preferences for one over another (Rubin, 1980).

Studies on the conception of a friend by children have noted that as with peer relations a general reciprocity has been evident throughout childhood and seems central in conceptualising a friend. Some theorists have emphasised that the concepts of friendship develop with increasing cognitive maturity whilst others have suggested that the features and behaviours of interactions have themselves been responsible for friendship development.

The cognitive interpersonal model is best illustrated by Selman (1980) who postulates that there are stages in the development of friendship conceptions that closely correspond to levels of social perspective-taking reality. Selman asserts that children move through stages of friendship development, moving from a singularly personalised view of friendship, with little understanding of another person's view of themselves, through to the ability to appreciate mutual reciprocity, seeing the value of others and sharing. Selman's construction of friendship parallels stage trends with younger children in the least cognitively mature stage and by adolescence reaching a cognitively mature one (Selman and Jaquette, 1977; Asher and Gottman, 1981).

The purpose of friendships

The constant changes of children's friendship conceptions reveal that sharing and reciprocity occur early in pre-school years but other attributes such as loyalty, sensitivity and intimacy occur later.

Selman's stages of the development of friendship conceptions may not consist of the emergence of new concepts as development proceeds but reflect developmental transformations as a consequence of reciprocal behaviours between children over time (Hartup, 1983). Certainly the evidence suggests that 'reciprocity action' is viewed differently at different ages and may determine the development of what a friend is for (Younnis, 1980). In other words, it may be reciprocal social behaviour *per se* that governs notions of friendship not structural cognitive development.

At present the relative continuities of social and cognitive processes to the development of friendship remain unclear. That both are critical is not in doubt, and present research builds on the views of earlier cognitive themes of Piaget (1970) and Bowlby (1969) as well as those of the psychoanalyst Sullivan (1953), who saw the pre-adolescent development of friendship as a critical interpersonal feature of healthy adult personality development.

Predicting how children would behave towards each other as friends has begun to attract the attention of researchers in child development. There are many methodological and conceptual problems in investigating interactions between persons, but in recent years progress in this area has been encouraging and new insights into the mechanisms that operate within and between relationships are beginning to be elucidated (Hinde, 1979; Berndt, 1981; Hinde and Stevenson-Hinde, 1988). The majority of this work has concentrated on family relations but some findings on child–child relations are of interest. In particular, the notions of helping, supporting and sharing with friends may be of particular value if we are to examine the function of friendships when children are subject to stressful events.

Further discussion of the emerging field of peer relations is beyond the scope of this book and the reader is referred to the recent work of Steven Duck and colleagues for an in-depth analysis of this area (Duck, 1988).

Friends as a source of support at times of stress

The studies to date suggest that emotional investment in friends and the development of intimacy is a relatively late occurrence in childhood. Presumably children remain emotionally dependent on family rather than friends, although we know little about intimacy as yet. The matter is of importance in view of the considerable literature on the value of social support at the times of stress in adults (e.g. Henderson, Byrne and Duncan-Jones, 1981; Brown *et al.*, 1986). Considerable discrepancies in research methodology, design and analysis of results exist in this field but the general consensus at present suggests that an intimate relationship with another person is an important protection or buffer against social adversity.

The dispute about the role of non-intimate close friends and what constitutes the meaning of support are important considerations in this literature and it is unclear at this stage to what extent acquaintances and other social restraints may mediate against stress or provide an individual with support (Vieil, 1985).

If the notion of stress-buffering effects of social supports is problematic in adults, adding a developmental dimension serves only to increase the difficulty. Our present knowledge can serve only to provide clues as to the potential for confiding relationships between children at times of stress.

There is considerable evidence to show that under adverse family circumstances where adults are unavailable to the child that children will use other children. Freud and Dann's (1951) reports of the support children gave each other as survivors of Second World War concentration camps is an extreme example. Investigations of the relationships between siblings provides evidence that in the presence of social difficulties greater proximity seeking occurs and reflects interpersonal support and perhaps protection against family and parent difficulties (Dunn and Kendrick, 1982; Dunn, 1988a).

It seems that in young pre-school children other children can become important in social and emotional terms if there are long-term stresses in parents. We can speculate, however, that the relative contribution of friends to psychological support will become greater with age. Overall it seems that in early childhood friendships are less likely to be required at times of stress as caretakers will act as protective agents. It is apparent, however, that if adversity is a consequence of parent or caretaker difficulties siblings may turn to each other for some form of protection. Whether this support is the same in emotional and cognitive terms as that of later childhood or adulthood is not clear.

Sex differences in friendships

Children's intentions and behaviours are different between the sexes and are dependent to a degree on interactions which may alter depending on the social context (Berndt, 1983; Barrat and Hinde, 1988), as friends may interpret each other's behaviour in more personal terms. Thus, girls seek closer more intimate relations than boys and distinguish more sharply between close friends and acquaintances (Berndt, 1981, 1983). These gender-related findings were constant across younger and older girls. By contrast, boys' friendships showed a change in the ratio of competitiveness to equality, the former predominant in friendships amongst younger boys and the latter amongst older boys.

The findings concerning sex differences are similar to previous research findings which have also shown that girls tend to make fewer close friends, make new friends less rapidly and prefer single friendships more than boys (Waldrop and Halverson, 1975; Elder and Hallinan, 1978; Savin-Williams, 1980; Berndt, 1983).

These research findings emphasise that the intention and behaviour of girls towards their friends is different to that of boys and, in particular, may be more emotional and more intimate than boys in middle childhood (Berndt, 1983; Douvan and Adelson, 1966).

What implications does this have for confiding relations and supports? The implication appears to be that girls may show greater distress at friendship failures because they are more likely to have close ties to peers at an earlier age. Are girls also more capable of using friends at a time of acute crisis? The data is insufficient to answer the question at this time.

Psychopathology and deficits in friendships in school-age children

Two broad themes are apparent from the friendship literature. First, good peer relationships are probably necessary for healthy mental development. Thus they may operate by promoting a child's self-esteem and developing instrumental skills and emotional ties with other children (Harter, 1983; Hartup, 1983).

Second, the absence of close relationships with others may increase the risk of psychiatric disorder (Rutter, 1985b). For example, Elder (1974) found supportive relationships between parents greatly reduced the likelihood of difficulties in their children after life stress. Considering family relations further Rutter (1979) has demonstrated that for children who come from discordant families a close relationship with one parent exerts a protective effect against conduct disorder. In other words, the psychological effects of sufficient close relationships with a member of a family provided the child with a sense of personal worth that ameliorated the potential adverse consequences of peer group difficulties. An example of the links between interpersonal relations of different social dimensions within the same time frame. Whilst there is evidence that children with conduct disorders and delinquency have difficulty in making and keeping friends, the issue is less clear in children with emotional difficulties (Rutter, 1985b). In particular, it is not clear if difficulties with friendships are a cause or a consequence of disorder or illness related behaviour.

As we have discussed, children discriminate between friends and peer relations on the basis of how well they know another child (Berndt, 1983). The meaning of 'friendship' for children requires a consideration of the availability and adequacy of a child's social relations as well as the emotional components of particular relationships (Hartup, 1983). Friends are only likely to arise if children have sufficient opportunity to meet other children (Berndt, 1983).

Therefore the formation of friendships from a peer group is likely to come about as a consequence of family, school and social factors as well as the child's developmental status. There is an interdependence between physical activity or instrumental play and the socio-emotional components of friendships. It is also clear, however, that the nature of the support required at a time of difficulty may well determine to whom the child turns.

Therefore parents may be used as important sources of emotional support into adolescence even when peer relations are well established (Hartup, 1983). This suggests that for some children both peer relations and family members may contribute to aspects of friendship at different ages, perhaps dependent on social circumstances.

The construction of a friendship interview

The multidimensional nature of children's social relations indicates that both instrumental and emotional components of friendship should be evaluated in any measurement of friendship. A recent study decided to investigate friendships in children and adolescents incorporating these principles and using a semi-structured interview method to collect information on the full nature and circumstances of children's friendship patterns in the last 12 months (Goodyer, Wright and Altham, 1989a). The study interviewed both mothers and children independently using a standardised interview.

Firstly we were concerned to measure the effects of recent friendship rather than attempt to make inferences about longer-term relations over years and different developmental stages. We therefore confined ourselves to enquiry about the last 12 months.

Secondly we were concerned to measure the everyday organisation of friendships and not a particular set of circumstances that might arise. Therefore we established that we were not identifying patterns of friendships occurring at a time of substantial crisis, such as a family death, or as a consequence of a unique experience resulting in unusual notoriety, such as gaining admirers through recent personal achievement.

We therefore took into account components of social network, frequency, duration and number of contacts with children, the social setting in which contacts occurred, the reciprocity of contacts and the preference and affiliation of contacts.

Children presenting with long-term continuous difficulties in socialisation were excluded because they would not meet entry criteria for recent onset emotional disorder described below. Some children, however, may well have had episodes of friendship difficulties in the past and these were not measured in the present interview.

A semi-structured interview schedule was developed which obtained substantive information about the ongoing nature of friendships over time.

The interview consists of 10 cue items with a Yes/No response. The cue items are:

1. Do you have friends near your home?
2. Do you have friends at school?
3. Do you play out with friends or see them in the evening?
4. Do friends come and see you at your house?
5. Do you go to friends' houses?
6. Do you have a special friend or person whom you can share a secret with?
7. Do you belong to a team, club or gang?
8. When something troubles or worries you do you talk to anyone about it?
9. Are your friends the same age as you?
10. How long do you usually keep your friends?

A series of secondary questions are asked whether or not the response is yes to a cue item. These secondary responses provide the contextual information concerning the exact nature, circumstances, frequency, duration and general outcome of each experience for either positive or negative terms. Secondary questions and contextual information are collected for each item whether responded to positively or negatively. We were particularly concerned to minimise the risk of including information likely to be a cause rather than a consequence of emotional disorder. Therefore, in psychiatric cases, respondents were continually prompted after each cue question, and again during the collection of contextual information, to describe only experiences that occurred before the onset of disorder.

A description of the child's friendship is then constructed on the basis of all available information derived from the interview, including background information collected concurrently from mother. A further check on potential independence was carried out at this stage by two of the researchers (I.G. and C.W.) using a consensual rating so that only information considered certainly or almost certainly independent of disorder was included in the vignettes. These vignettes form the basis of the friendship measurement.

The focus of the interview

The semi-structured interview was conducted with both child and mother (or main care-giver) independently at the same period of time. Contextual information is therefore derived from two sources. The description of the child's friendship behaviour used for rating consists of the confluence of child's and mother's contextual information. Clearly in some cases discrepancies may occur in reporting. We attempted to clarify and gain consensus between mother and child where possible. Some adolescents, however, were not willing or felt unable to reach consensus with their mothers, which is in line with previous findings that mothers may know less about older adolescents' social experiences (Monck and Dobbs, 1985). Unresolvable disagreement between mother–child pairs over contextual information occurred on only two occasions however, both psychiatric cases and both 15-year-old female adolescents.

Rating the quality of friendships

Friendship is rated on a 3-point scale: good, moderate or poor, based on the descriptions from all information. Thus the ratings reported by Goodyer, Wright and Altham (1989a) refer to an overall global measure of the degree of friendship incorporating the three conceptual features of the instrument, i.e. the availability, adequacy and intimacy of friendships.

We found that both mothers and children were reliable reporters of friendship details in the past 12 months. We also discovered that mothers and children showed good agreement with each other. This suggests that in the age group 8 to 16 years there is a substantial degree of shared information about much of the quality and quantity of friendship behaviour between parent and child.

Finally, we showed that the ratings of the quality of friendship showed good agreement between different pairs of raters, suggesting that the measurement is both reliable and valid, at least as measured by adults (Goodyer, Wright and Altham, 1989a).

Two examples of friendship vignettes serve as illustrations of the detail collected to form the basis for a measurement:

Example 1

Background information   John is a 9-year-old pre-pubertal child. He is the younger of two (having a brother aged 11). He is free of present medical illness and has no permanent disabilities. He attends ordinary school and ordinary class. He shares a bedroom with his brother in a house situated on a quiet street in a suburban area on the edge of a large city. He walks to school. Both parents live at home and there are no other persons in the household. There are no financial worries: father is an advertising manager; mother is a part-time secretary.

Social contextual information   John has a number of friends near his home, at least two in his street whom he sees frequently, almost every day, and will see in an organised manner at least once a week after school. He has friends at school who are mainly the same as in his residential location. Most are boys but there are two or three girls. The school is mixed. The children are all aged between 8 and 10. He and his mother consider he sees more than six different children to play with (weekends or weekdays) per week. He often plays out spontaneously with his friends and sees them at his house and at their houses.

He does have special friends with whom to share secrets and named two boys in his street (one at his school). He does not belong to an organised club or gang but plays in the school cricket team and goes to computer club.

When troubled or worried he talks to his mother or father or brother and would talk to his friends, he thinks, but has never had the need to do so. Mother confirmed this view. His friends are of the same age and 'playtime' out of school may be for hours and is rarely less than 30 minutes. He likes to keep his friends and has known most of his friends more than 2 years and his special friends for 7 and 5 years respectively.

Rating—Good

Example 2

Background information   Michael is a 12-year-old pubescent child. He is the middle child of three with a sister aged 7 and a brother aged 18. He is free of present medical illness and has no permanent disabilities. He attends ordinary school and ordinary class. He has his own bedroom in a house situated in a busy main street of a suburban area some 10 miles outside a large city. He takes a bus to school. Both parents live at home, as does maternal grandmother. There are financial difficulties, father is a self-employed builder and mother works in that business as an administrator.

Social context information   There are a number of boys and girls of his age in the immediate location. Michael says he has no friends. He initiates no contact and prefers to stay indoors. This information was confirmed by his mother. He says he has friends at school who are mostly boys and felt there were at least four in number. They were of the same age. He admitted rarely initiating social contact with them but felt more that he was swept along. He felt that he had not known them very long and that he has changed company on more than two occasions in the past 12 months. He does see his friends after school but they have to call for him and he admitted reluctance to play out. Play activities rarely last more than an hour in the week—at weekends they may last all morning. Friends will come to his house but he prefers not to have them in and dislikes them initiating games with his toys or with his things. He does not spontaneously go to friends' houses, despite encouragement from parents and from his friends. He does not have a special friend whom he can share a secret with and prefers to keep things to himself, even from his parents. He does not belong to a club or gang but he goes to computer club at school. He does not play sport. When something troubles or worries him he would not talk to anyone about it but would have to be asked by parents who need to observe signs of disturbance.

The children he sees are of the same age. He sees them for less than 4 hours during the week and more than 4 hours at weekends. Contacts are initiated by them. Reciprocity is minimal although at weekends he would initiate play with a boy who has a computer in the neighbourhood. He does not keep his friends, both he and mother agree that the longest he has kept a friend is 4 months. At the present time he has no special friend. His general activities and play are solitary and secretive. He chooses records, books and computing work and has a television in his room. He rarely seeks the company of family members during the evening and believes that his behaviour in this respect has been constant since early childhood, which was confirmed by his mother.

Rating—Poor

Vignettes were obtained prospectively from 100 children and adolescents and their parents attending a routine mental health clinic and 100 matched controls from the local community free of psychiatric disorder.

The results confirmed a significant and potentially causal association in school-age children between emotional disorder and the presence of moderate to poor friendships in the 12 months prior to onset of disorder.

The degree of these difficulties was important. The greatest differences between cases and controls were for the proportion of children rated as having *poor* friendships in the 12 months prior to onset. Indeed poor friendships were extremely uncommon in community controls (2 per cent only) compared with cases (14 per cent). The presence of moderate friendships, however, was also significantly associated with the onset of disorder occurring in 25 per cent of cases compared with 14 per cent of controls. These findings also tell us that having friendship difficulties is not sufficient to produce emotional symptoms in many children since 16 per cent of community controls reported moderate to poor friendships.

This suggests that investigation of social factors that exert buffering effects against the presence of poor friendships would be worth while. Perhaps there are qualities in family relations for these children that protect against adverse friendships. However, it is also apparent that friendship deficits are not necessary for emotional disorder as 52 per cent of cases did not report such deficits. An intriguing finding was the suggestion that the form of expression of emotional disorder varies as a consequence of moderate to poor friendships and puberty. Thus prepubertal children with poor or moderate friendship patterns were classified as predominantly anxious or depressed, whereas postpubertal children with poor or moderate friendships, by contrast, were predominantly anxious. This suggests that puberty constitutes a point of change in the impact of friendship deficits on the psychopathology of emotional disorders. This possibility seems equally likely for boys as for girls. We were unable to say what the mechanism for these differences may be from these findings. Two broad areas of investigation could be considered in future studies however. Firstly, intrinsic changes at puberty in the child may result in a different appraisal of the same social circumstances. For example, the same friendships may be viewed differently as a result of changes in perceptions of the self with development (Harter, 1983; Rutter, 1987a).

Secondly, there may be changes in extrinsic factors within the child's family group which require a reorganisation of both the purpose and function of social relations. Clearly there may be an interdependence between these intrinsic and extrinsic mechanisms. These results are encouraging for two reasons. First, it has proved possible to use an interview method to examine children's friendships. Secondly, the results suggest that the effects of friendship difficulties on psychopathology are different at different points in development.

There are some important caveats that prevent us from considering these findings as conclusive. Firstly, although we have focused on recent friendships we cannot be sure that some children have not experienced previous difficulties in their friendships thereby influencing subsequent peer relations and social behaviour.

Secondly, it may be argued that recent experience of moderate to poor friendships is a consequence of incipient or sub-clinical illness and the potentially causal impact of these difficulties merely an epiphenomenon. We were unable to determine this possibility on the present data but recognise that the imposition of a 12-month limit on the retrospective exploration of friendships is to some extent a useful but possibly artificial boundary in examining the effects of social factors in the onset of psychiatric disorders.

Thirdly, we do not know what other factors may be influencing the development of moderate to poor friendships; in particular it is possible that friendship difficulties may be a consequence of other adversities in the child's life occurring in the family or as a result of social and economic hardship. (The relationship to other recent social experiences, such as life events both undesirable and desirable, are discussed in detail in Chapter 8.)

Fourthly, we cannot determine from this data the relative contribution made by other more intrinsic factors, such as temperament, to both the quality of the emotional disorder or the development of friendship difficulties.

Finally, the friendship vignettes suggest that the sharing of secrets with friends may not include the sharing of recent worries, which appear to occur with family members, including age appropriate siblings. This may indicate that different types of confiding relations have different purposes (for example, there may be differences between who is turned to at a time of personal crisis rather than at times of everyday difficulties) or that family are turned to because worries are in fact about friends. In spite of these caveats, these findings emphasise the significant contribution made by friendships to mental well-being and the potential psychopathological risks that occur for school-age children with friendship difficulties. However, as 50 per cent of cases attending the clinic reported good friendships in their lives prior to the onset of their disorder, friendship difficulties are neither necessary, nor sufficient in their own right, to cause anxious or depressive disorders. The question, therefore, is what makes them a causal factor for psychopathology in some children and not others? The presence of other recent stresses, the chronicity and poverty of prior social development? Factors related to temperament? Further inquiry will help us to unravel the possible factors and their mechanisms.

Friendship competition—steeling and sensitising effects

Sullivan (1953) suggested that younger children are likely to compete with their friends and older adolescents are likely to try for equality. What little research there is broadly supports this view (Berndt, 1983). However, co-operative harmonious relationships between friends, as seen in younger children, do occur more frequently than between acquaintances of the same age (Hartup, Brady and Newcomb, 1985). Furthermore, there seem times where friendship competition can be intense and it may seem that friendship reciprocity can allow rivalrous competition with it. However, there is some evidence to show that conflicts follow competition, which may explain why competition is less common amongst friends than acquaintances (Tesser and Smith, 1980). Boys may have more problems in competition than do girls. This suggests that emotional investment buffers or mediates the potential stress of competition and rivalry in friendships but has little effect on rivalry in acquaintances.

The competitive and rivalrous nature of friendship appears to be abrogated in the presence of essential investment in friends. This suggests that friendships provide a relatively safe socio-emotional environment in which to experience conflicts that are likely to be stressful. Such friendship conflicts, if resolved, are both adaptive and positive experiences for the child. These successfully negotiated events may result in steeling effects. Such effects may re-emerge for later social conflicts when past successful coping strategies may be remembered and used again. Whether or not this is *specific* to later conflicts that are themselves related to friendship is unclear. In other words, we do not yet know if steeling effects of earlier social experiences may have a *specificity* and only be accessed with events appraised as the same or similar.

Similarly, the failure to negotiate conflicts may *sensitise* a child and subsequent potential friendships may be at risk because of earlier failures which when remembered result in undesirable social behaviour. As yet we have little knowledge as to whether or not life events involving peers and friendships at one period of development do indeed exert such sensitising or steeling effects for another.

Self-control and interpersonal conflict

Selman (1981) described the conflict between responsiveness to a friend and one's own independence as a control issue and suggested its occurrence was mainly in late adolescence and adulthood. However, this conflict is found in early and middle childhood as well (Corsario, 1981). Children may also use a friend's responsiveness to indicate the closeness of a relationship (Kelly, 1979). The degree to which the conflict affects children's friendships is difficult to judge but deserves further research. The balance of responsiveness/independence negotiation may affect the satisfaction and stability of social relations, as has been demonstrated with adults (Burgess and Huston, 1979). Herein may be the clues as to how intimate friendships may be and how they may contribute to altering the effects of social stresses. We may also be able to see how events and difficulties alter children's quality of friendship making. For example, friends may provide intimate confiding relationships in the presence of family difficulties and major life events such as bereavement.

FAMILY AND PEER RELATIONS—SIMILARITIES AND DIFFERENCES

Pre-school children

In the pre-school and early years of life, play activity is earliest in child–child systems and the socialisation between children is object-centred, whereas it is person-centred with mothers and even adult strangers, although toys may be used (Eckerman and Whatley, 1977).

The mother–child relationship is emotional and secure based with little sustained play. Everyday events and difficulties in the environment, such as loss of a doll, result in proximity-seeking behaviour to the care-giver even if a choice is given between familiar adult and familiar peer in fear-producing stimuli (Ainsworth and Wittig, 1969; Hartup, 1983).

Peer relations seem less able to buffer or protect against social adversity under the age of 6. The psychological development of interpersonal relations, particularly the capacity for the development of intimate feelings for other children, seem restricted and children at this age appear to have an all or none response within their affective relationships.

Middle childhood

In older children different emotions are used in child–child relations compared to child–adult relations. In the former, emotions of interest and pleasure are commonplace; in the latter, affection as experienced in physical contact is more common.

In middle childhood family relations appear to consist of a combination of dominance and nurturance; resistance and appeals are uncommon and avoidance rare. Child appeals result in adult nurturance, and child submission result in adult dominance (Hartup, 1983). This work suggests that it is dependency and control that predominate in adult–child reactions. By contrast, child–child relations are less harmonious, more differentiated in emotion and behaviour but suggest that appeals and submission, aggression and compliance predominate but avoidance again is infrequent (Hartup, 1983).

These findings suggest that in middle childhood different emotions predominate to different degrees between family and peer relations. Emotional security and proximity seeking under social adversity still occur towards care-givers but social withdrawal from peers under stress is uncommon. More likely is the response of dominance–submission through the use of aggression. Again with peers, normative everyday stresses promote reciprocity and suggest the seeking of a balance between equality and confrontation with peers. Social withdrawal would appear to be a particularly uncommon and abnormal psychological response to everyday social difficulties. Furthermore, by middle childhood the peer system is not a duplicate of the family system. Rather than buffer all social adversity, family relations may now provide alternative sources of emotional support at times of peer group stress.

A study investigating the impact of pubertal change on adolescence and schools recently reported its findings (Simmons and Blyth, 1987). The study focused on the transition from childhood into adolescence by investigating the impact of age, gender, timing and school transfer on self-image and adjustment of white youth in the mid-west of the United States. A sample of 621 youngsters was interviewed at the age of 9 and again yearly until the age of 16. The results showed a number of important features of development in relation to adolescence and schooling. First, for many children, the transition into adolescence did not involve widespread negative effects. Secondly, the outcome of transfer from one school to another was dependent on:

1. The particular characteristics of the transfer.
2. The characteristics of the individual.
3. The perceived outcome of the transfer.

The study found that many children were thrust out of childhood into adolescence before they were ready for the change. Negative effects on self-esteem and behaviour were associated with an early transfer—at 10 to 11 years of age—from primary to junior school. Children who remained within a supportive school a year longer before moving to a high school did not exhibit these effects. Early physical puberty, early independence from parents and early dating of the opposite sex all carried risks to self-esteem, especially when occurring in a cumulative fashion.

Social hierarchies were important and children gained in social importance when they were the oldest in their year. Similarly, they appeared more at risk when they were the youngest.

Children who were not developmentally ready for school and social changes seemed more at risk. If such children were faced with additional life changes, such as sudden high school entry, they seemed unable to cope with this. It appeared as though pubertal changes demand a focus of effort and cumulative areas of difficulty resulted in a loss of coping and onset of difficulties.

Girls seemed more at risk from these transitions of adolescence than boys. Perceived good looks and perceived peer regard prior to the transition helped a child to cope well with change of school.

Finally, different aspects of transition had different effects. Thus, school change and educational achievement affected an adolescent's global self-esteem but pubertal change had a more narrow set of effects particularly on body-image.

Overall, this important study points to the satisfactory negotiation of the social, psychological and biological components of adolescence for the majority of this sample. It is apparent, however, that this period of development is complex and multidimensional. A configuration of factors involving the onset and timing of social and school change and puberty rather than age may result in difficulties for some children. These findings, from a longitudinal study, provide support for our cross-sectional findings and indicate an important role for puberty in psychopathology where there are friendship deficits.

Adolescence

By adolescence there is a complex and interdependent model of family and peer relations complementing each other in a variety of ways. Interestingly, peer relations in adolescence are valued for their here and now effects on values and behaviour and choice of friends, whereas for 'events of the future' adolescents look to their parents for assistance and problem-solving (Kendel and Lesser, 1972). By adolescence, the emotional range of response to peers includes intimacy and privacy.

The role of friends as supports and confidants seems more likely in pre-adolescence and adolescence but not as a replacement for parents. There may be an exercising of choice at times of stress as to who may be supportive. This latter finding emphasises, as with the development of peer relations, the importance of the social situation in determining who will be identified as potentially helpful at times of stress—family or friends.

By adolescence the family may not be able to act as alternative forms of support at times of social adversity. The determinants of supportive relations at these times may now depend on the type (specificity) of event or difficulty and the choice of action the older child and adolescent perceives is open to him or her.

FAMILY ADVERSITY AND SOCIAL DEVELOPMENT

The value of affectionate family relationships

There is evidence to support the notion that early family experiences influence later social development (Rutter, 1980). There is also evidence that good family relationships may be associated with high self-esteem and good peer relations in adolescence (Tizard and Hodges, 1978; Rutter, 1988a).

Children who have adequately negotiated normative family stresses of development and have an adequate affectional base to explore the world have a greater sense of individual instrumental competence, are often more well-liked, show greater leadership qualities and are more likely to be rated as self-reliant and explorative (Elkins, 1958; Baumrind, 1967, 1971). Hartup (1980) has indicated that a number of methodological difficulties require the above findings to be viewed cautiously. The inference, however, is that emotional ties in family relations promote exploratory behaviours in child–child relations and may mediate in the normative stresses and strains of these explorations. Rutter (1980) has pointed out that children with anxious attachment intensify proximity/affection-seeking behaviour towards their caretaker and inhibit exploration of new, novel or strange situations. As discussed in Chapter 2, in pre-school children there have been a number of studies which indicate that young children who are securely attached to their mothers, as characterised by positive reciprocal behaviours (looking, talking, smiling, encouragement), as opposed to anxiously attached, as characterised by continuous proximity seeking and distress in mother's absence, are much more likely to initiate peer relations with same-age children (Easterbrooks and Lamb, 1979; Waters, Wippman and Sroufe, 1979; Sroufe and Fleeson, 1988). These findings certainly suggest that good relations in one social system promotes successful adaptation in another. Everyday events and difficulties of social development may therefore be buffered by the presence of good family relations.

This raises the question åre good family relations a necessary precedent for good social relations? Perhaps children with deficits in family relations are less able to respond to normative social stresses of peer relations. Furthermore, are there particular components of parent–child relations that allow children to cope with the stress of friendship making?

For example, are anxious children who have difficulty in leaving parents to play with other children failing in a normal social developmental transformation because of the direct adverse effects of the experience? Is this because the process of interaction with their parents is not sufficient or of the wrong type for an appropriate developmental transition? Again, as we have discussed, the style of parent–child attachment does have significant implications for the style of subsequent child–child relationships and indicates that children who are securely attached during infancy have qualitatively better relations with peers in the pre-school period (Rutter, 1988a; Sroufe and Fleeson, 1988). In addition, the type of attachment seems to predict the form of socio-emotional and behavioural response to other children. Thus quarrels, fighting and disagreements *between* young children seem more likely when *both* have experienced poor attachments. There is also the suggestion that a well-attached child attempts to mollify a poorly attached one within their own relationship. These important findings demonstrate how the *normative everyday difficulties* of peer relationships may be coped with well or poorly dependent to some significant extent on previous parent–child relations. What is important here is that it is not merely the quantity of social contact that is being influenced by previous family experiences but also the quality of the social interaction. Is there, therefore, a potential continuity of failure or success between the form and type of family relations and the subsequent form and type of social relations? It will not be good enough, for example, to show that social development occurs by simply measuring the frequency and duration of peer group interaction. We need to know the adequacy and intimacy of those social interactions and the specificities they have with the degree of adequacy and intimacy of the child's family relations. Furthermore, we do not yet know if the failure to negotiate normative developmental stresses at one stage may influence the negotiation of everyday stresses at another, but the above findings concerning attachment and later relations do suggest this possibility.

This raises a further important conceptual point. We need to be clear about the duration of the effects of social difficulties. Family deficits may precede social deficits but their effects may continue. We need to distinguish between children whose social development is impaired in the *presence* of ongoing family adversity as opposed to where there is *previous* but no *ongoing* family adversity.

SCHOOL EVENTS AND THEIR IMPACT ON SOCIAL DEVELOPMENT

School entry

School entry constitutes a significant life event for all children, and there is a substantial literature on school difficulties (e.g. Hersov, 1985a) and school influences on development (e.g. Ouston, Maughan and Mortimore, 1980). There is clearly a period of difficult adjustment which gives rise to a number of problems in sociability, learning and attendance. Although many children settle, some appear not to cope with this transition and can remain with significant and serious psychiatric difficulties (Hersov and Berg, 1980).

In a study of children at normal school entry, Elizur (1986) has shown that adjustment to school is a consequence of parental co-operation and support and personal competence in the school environment. These findings illustrate the interdependence of family and social systems. Interestingly, this research points to the potential importance of differential roles of parents in school stress. Mothers engaged in affective support to a child when difficulties arose but both mothers and fathers provided instrumental and structural support, which often resulted in the involvement of disengaged fathers in the problem behaviour with the child. The importance of disengaged fathers in the psychiatric disorder of school refusal has been noted by clinicians and emphasised by some in support of family therapy techniques for this condition (Skynner, 1974; Hersov, 1985a). The study by Elizur (1986) illustrates the value in young children of significant external support and suggests personal coping may be dependent on secure attachments. The method of coping with school transfer at different ages has been less well examined. From previous discussion on the development of peers, however, it may be expected that personal coping and peer groups become more important in the older child and perhaps in the transfer from primary to secondary school.

School organisation

Social organisations have effects on children's friendship patterns, performance and well-being (Hartup, 1983; Rutter, 1985c). School as an organisation can be important in this respect as Rutter and colleagues (1979) have shown in their study of the influence of school adjustment. They showed that how schools were organised had an independent effect from children's social relationships on a child's social adjustment and educational performance. Well-organised schools with clear policies and structure were much more likely to influence beneficially the child's academic attainment at the end of his schooling. Rutter (1985b,c), drawing on this and other studies investigating school effects, highlights the causal effect of school environment on adjustment. These findings again show an important feature of the impact of ongoing experiences in which there is continuous exposure, i.e. there is a current relationship between the environment and child. In view also of the importance of reciprocities in stressful circumstances the opportunity for the child to influence school and teachers is evident.

These findings highlight the importance of school environment as a potential facilitation or inhibitor of child attainment over time. Of course there are many facets of school life, including individual teacher and pupil characteristics, intake differences and the type and quality of teacher–child interactions. The influences on a child's performance and adjustment will depend on the patterning of these factors with each other as well as their effects on the child. Further study of the resulting mechanisms as well as the search for further factors is required.

School organisation is only one form of group structure to which children are subjected from their earliest social interaction. The influence of group norms and values seems particularly powerful (Hartup, 1983). Developmentally, dominance hierarchies occur as a consequence of different attributes at different ages. In younger children it is possessions and knowledge of how to use them that determines the greatest social power. In middle childhood children who are adroit in directing play and games emerge as leaders more often. Adolescents who mature early, often with athletic and social skills, are invested with social power, whereas in late adolescence children who are bright and well-liked hold higher-status social positions.

Social power is then a derivative of social norms. It can only be developmentally non-normative to be outside group norms and without the hierarchy. Of course, this emphasises that membership of deviant groups increases the risk of deviant behaviour and that it may be more important, although stressful, to 'join' than not to. A detailed analysis of the social psychology of peer relations is beyond the scope of this book. The interested reader is referred to recent comprehensive publications in this area by Stephen Duck and his colleagues (Duck, 1988).

SUMMARY

1. Normal friendship development contains considerable elements of adversity through competition, conflict, and co-operation.
2. Reciprocity between children remains a central theme of relationships. The emotional components of friendships arise in middle childhood and adolescence and are expressed by an increasing intimacy with peers; initially of the same sex.
3. There are links between early family relations and subsequent peer relations. The quality of family relations can predict the form of peer relations, at least until the age of seven, and may contribute towards good sociability in adolescence and young adulthood.
4. Conflicts within friendships constitute important normative stressful experiences. They may contain steeling and/or sensitising effects which are important in the shaping of later behaviours.
5. Friendships constitute an important source of social experience for emotional well-being. Friendship deficits are potentially a causal factor in the onset of anxiety and depressive disorders in childhood and adolescence. Puberty acts as a biological *point of change* in the impact of friendship deficits on emotional psychopathology.

Chapter 4

Community Environments, War and Disaster

Major life events and everyday difficulties can be considered in societal as well as in individual and family terms. Adversities that effect small groups of individuals, however, are also likely to be different in orientation from those that influence hundreds or thousands of people.

Social and community adversities can therefore be considered in two different ways. Firstly, *the environment* in which people settle and live can be examined for its impact on individual adjustment. For example, we might examine the effects of living in inner cities or rural environments, on general physical or mental health. We might also investigate if there are particular effects of the environment on different types of problems. Cultural factors, the effect of migration, quality of housing and employment are examples of factors that have been investigated (Quinton, 1980, 1988). These factors can be investigated for their influence on mental health specifically or in a wider context on child development. The quality of everyday life, development and change of social groups, even the evolutionary purpose of urbanisation, which has been a striking world-wide phenomenon in the twentieth century, can be investigated in this manner (Basham, 1978).

Secondly, particular major life events can occur which impact on many rather than few people. *Disasters* are such examples and may be (i) natural—such as earthquakes or large-scale fires (e.g. McFarlane, Policansy and Irwin, 1987) or (ii) man-made—such as war, murder or transport disasters (e.g. Yule and Williams, 1988).

In these examples of community adversity it is the effects of a single major event on large groups of people that concern us. What is the impact of a disaster on an individual surviving the capsising of a ferry or making a new start in life after years as a victim of a war? Surprisingly little investigation of this area has been carried out in young people, despite the thousands of children and adolescents who have experienced these severe forms of major life events.

This chapter considers these two forms of *community stress* in some detail. Clearly we cannot hope to cover all aspects of social adversity occurring to communities at large, and therefore the particular social difficulties and major events discussed should be taken as examples of the potential effects that may occur. In particular, the effects of famine and infection as 'adversities' are not discussed as they fall outside the main focus of this book.

AREA DIFFERENCES AND STRESSFUL CIRCUMSTANCES

There is substantial evidence that psychiatric disorders vary greatly according to geographical area, with rates highest in urban, inner city areas and lowest in small towns and rural communities (Rutter *et al.*, 1975a,b; Quinton, 1988). Furthermore, this evidence suggests that these differences relate to a wide variation of diverse family and social problems affecting both children and adults (Lavik, 1977; Rutter, 1979). In other words, the processes of adversity result in alterations to family and social relations, and it is through these alterations that urbanisation exerts its effects rather than through the distinct qualities of urbanisation *per se* (Quinton, 1988). At present then, the evidence supports the notion that living in urban rather than rural areas is more stressful. There is also a strong implication, however, that moving away from urban areas decreases the risk of certain types of problems, such as delinquency (West, 1982). The evidence suggests that living in urban areas increases the risk of multiple adversities and stresses which tend to have a potentiating adverse effect on the risk of psychiatric disorder in young people (Rutter, 1979). These urban–rural differences appear greatest for chronic rather than acute disorders of childhood. Again we see that it is exposure to ongoing difficulties within urban environments rather than acute events in the environment that appears to exert the greatest risk as far as difficult behaviour is concerned. Therefore we can conclude that it is unlikely that acute life events can account for the urban–rural differences in the rates of psychiatric disorder (Wolkind and Rutter, 1985b).

Nature of influences

The question of whether the ill-effects of city life operate directly or indirectly on children has received some attention. The findings suggest that influences on children are indirect, through the impact of urban difficulties on the family. When rates of disorders are compared across urban and rural areas controlling for the presence of family adversities, there are no significant differences in the rates of psychiatric disorder in the children.

Overall, the higher rates of problems in the inner city appears inextricably linked to the multiple family adversities characterised by family discord, parental mental disorder and poor living conditions (Quinton, 1988). Disentangling the relative contribution of these stresses to children's personal suffering and psychiatric disorder is no easy task. The contribution of the social urban environment *per se* may lie in three areas. Firstly, people may lose a feeling of control over the environment in large cities (Rutter, 1981a). Relocation, urban decay and housing policies which people have no control over may constitute direct ongoing stresses.

Secondly, the nature of housing and everyday living conditions may be stressful because of the poor quality of housing and overcrowding. However, as Rutter (1983b) has pointed out, marked improvement in housing conditions this century has been associated with rises in delinquency rates and possibly an increase in some forms of psychiatric disorder (this is not to suggest a causal relationship between better living conditions and increasing crime rates).

Thirdly, the design of housing estates may decrease the opportunity for individuals to identify personal territory that they can feel responsible for; can share with neighbours and discriminate strangers. This concept of 'defensible space' (Newman, 1973) receives some empirical support because crime and vandalism is greatest in housing estates which have large public thoroughfares and whose layouts discourage social cohesion and a sense of personal caring for the environment (Waller and Okihiro, 1978; Wilson, 1978). Wolkind and Rutter (1985b) indicate, however, that adverse effects may be a consequence of difficulties in surveillance of persons and/or reflect people's attitude to their environment and their neighbours. It has to be said that whilst there is a general adverse effect of poor quality housing on the family it has been difficult to prove a direct effect between housing conditions and mental disorder (Quinton, 1988).

Thus living in adverse housing has not been consistently related to psychiatric disorder in adults partially because individuals of different ages and families at different life cycles respond differentially to their physical environment (Freeman, 1984; Quinton, 1988). Some groups are known to be more at risk than others, such as one-parent families and large or immobile families. Investigating the independent effects of the environment on mental state in these groups in combination with other social adversities has yet to be carried out.

Overall, there is an important effect of the physical environment as a stressor. It is the long-term difficulties that arise through urban structures and their adverse effects on family life which result in distress and disruption. The relative contribution of the environmental factors to psychopathology remains unclear and the mechanisms involved remain to be elucidated.

The urban environment as a predisposition to events and difficulties

A second suggestion about inner city life is that it predisposes individuals to more personal stress and perhaps to greater rates of acute life events (Milgram, 1970). The decrease in personal territory, defensible space and living area increases opportunities for personal conflicts because of unplanned encounters with other people. Neither 'stimulus overload', due to an excess of information as a consequence of the environment, nor 'social overload' (McCarthy and

Saegart, 1976), due to an excess of contact with unrelated persons, has been shown to have a direct effect on mental health or be a direct consequence of the environment in which people live (Quinton, 1988).

Intrinsic qualities of the individual influence both stimulus control and social relations in all environments. Also there may be greater deficits in social relations and networks because of greater house moves and a looser sense of social identity.

One of the most striking studies on the effects of urbanisation has been carried out on children in rural Sudan who have been integrated into the urban environment of the capital Khartoum. A field survey of children living in villages located on the outskirts of Khartoum showed that, in comparison with children in developed countries, there were fewer behavioural problems, in spite of poorer nutritional status and somatic health (Cederblad, 1968).

Fifteen years later social conditions in the area had changed. The outgrowth of the capital had absorbed the villages and transformed them into an integral part of Khartoum North Town. Thus, rapid urbanisation had occurred in a population the health of which had been evaluated previously. The population was, therefore, reinvestigated using the same methods as before (Rahim and Cederblad, 1984). The findings showed that urbanisation had indeed influenced the health status of the children but the changes were neither uniform nor adverse in all respects.

Firstly, there had been general improvements in the children's physical health. This could be attributed to the increased standard of living, including better housing, food and sanitation.

Secondly, there were two patterns of psychological health. Children under seven, of both sexes, still exhibited the same low rate of symptoms as in 1968, indicating that the urbanisation process had had little adverse effect on them. School-age boys, however, showed a tripling in the rate of symptoms. This was not the case for girls, whose rates were the same as reported in 1968.

The authors explained these findings in socio-cultural terms. Thus, young children and girls of all ages were effectively shielded from environmental influences by a rigid family culture which restricted their exposure to urban influences. Boys, who were allowed greater independence as they grew older, became more deviant in proportion to their exposure to new urbanisation influences including alcohol, violence and sexual activity. In other words, it was school-age boys who were most at risk from acculturation during transition from a rural to an urban environment. In those circumstances where there is a clear dissonance between family values and personal experience, are males rather than females responsible for the transmission of cultural changes within families?

The authors pointed out that extrapolating their findings to other societies, with different social and family structures, should be made with caution. Nevertheless, it was striking that, even with a tripling of symptoms amongst boys, the rates of disorder were far lower than those reported in developed countries.

The findings do, however, suggest that family relations, durable marital commitments, communal interdependence and the exercising of social control over children act as protective factors against the social adversity of urbanisation. These protective factors, however, may take their own toll as not only do they seem to filter out unwanted experiences they also act as a general block to the positive qualities of urbanisation. Girls, in particular, may thus have restricted personal freedom and limited access to the education, skills development and career prospects available in a more modern society.

Clearly, urban living exerts effects through a widening of social experiences. These findings suggest that it is the relation between family factors and these newer social experiences that influences the rate of disorder in towns and cities rather than the direct effect of such experiences *per se*.

Environment and personal disadvantage

There is much more clear-cut evidence that long-term difficulties in the environment are associated with personal disadvantage and stress occurring in some families and individuals. Homelessness, loss of job and long-term unemployment, poverty and growing up in homes lacking basic amenities for hygiene are all too frequent despite a general improvement in living standards both in the U.K. and U.S.A. (Brown and Madge, 1982; Nelson and Skidmore, 1983).

There has also been a marked rise in the proportion of children growing up in one-parent families (Finer, 1974).

All of these features are more common in inner city areas and they all constitute stressors in a general, non-specific sense. It has proved more difficult, however, to delineate the psychological mechanisms that these non-specific but important social stresses exert. For example, it has been argued that as unemployment rises so does the risk of child abuse, but links over time between changing levels of unemployment and psychosocial problems do not result in clear-cut associations or conclusions (Rutter and Giller, 1983).

Mechanisms of stress as a consequence of physical environment

Urban environments predispose children to psychiatric disorder but the mechanisms by which this occurs are not clear-cut. There is no doubt that personal suffering is associated with many aspects of social disadvantage. The association between these disadvantages and childhood mental disorders has been reviewed by Wolkind and Rutter (1985b). Overall there appear to be, first, weak associations with poor living conditions and personal dissatisfaction with these, suggesting individual differences in adaptation and coping with circumstances (Madge, 1983). Secondly, the impact of unemployment and homelessness on psychiatric disorders in adults may be mediated through influences on loss of self-esteem, perhaps as a consequence of social stigma and discrimination. Thus a potential mechanism whereby children are influenced by stresses of the physical environment is through effects on parent's self-esteem adversely altering relations between child and parents. Thirdly, there is evidence that there are family as well as individual differences to hardships, with some families exhibiting considerable resolve and determination under chronically stressful circumstances whereas others are easily broken. This latter point reflects how some individuals appear more resilient in the face of acute events or difficulties. This individual resilience may have beneficial modelling effects on other family members in the face of adversities.

From the child's point of view the social disadvantages appear to exert an indirect effect through family and parental factors. However, there is no clear-cut association even here. For example, the finding that maternal depression is significantly more common in women living in tower blocks does not translate itself into any consistent association with those mothers having consistently higher rates of disturbed children (Richman, 1985). Of course overt psychiatric disorder *per se* may be a less sensitive measure of childhood disadvantage than, say, the failure to provide adequate emotional and physical care. Under these conditions social disadvantage is likely to be associated with deprivation rather than disorder.

It seems likely that different forms of acute events and ongoing difficulties in the environment are likely to exert different effects on development and psychopathology. Thus lack of care seems to be the most frequent consequence of urban disadvantages increasing the risk for failures in normal socio-emotional development. Abnormalities that may arise in family relations as a *consequence* of lack of care may be the basis on which psychopathology occurs.

SEVERE SOCIAL AND COMMUNITY STRESS

In contrast to chronic difficulties as a consequence of urban disadvantages a number of researchers have focused on the effects of serious disruptive stresses occurring as a consequence of major upheavals in society as a whole. War, community disaster, such as a nuclear accident, and natural disasters, such as floods and earthquakes, provide examples of such stressors and will be discussed in the rest of this chapter.

War

War reflects perhaps one of the most devastating social experiences for human beings. Permanent injury, separation, loss and physical and emotional deprivation are commonplace events. War itself may last years and for many children this period of stress can include any number of these events, as well as the stressful process of conflict as a consequence of bombs, air-raids and the inevitable war-time lifestyle graphically portrayed in the histories of the Second World War in Europe and conflicts in South-East Asia, the Middle East and Northern Ireland. The effects of these war events provide important information for the understanding of how severe stresses impact on children at different points of development.

Evacuation

The Second World War is estimated to have disrupted 30 million families and within a span of a few days in 1940 1.5 million mothers, children and handicapped persons were evacuated from London. It is not surprising that under these circumstances scientific investigation of the effects of war were less than adequate. Although it is difficult to delineate the mechanisms and effects of evacuation in detail, there are some important observations as a result of those investigations that were made together with some more recent studies from war conflicts in South-East Asia.

Firstly, evacuation from a dangerous area did not result in the children appraising themselves as 'safer', for many developed signs of emotional and behavioural disturbance and difficulties in school performance. Accurate prevalence rates are difficult to establish but symptoms such as anxiety, enuresis and antisocial behaviour are reported to occur in 10 to 50 per cent of these children (Isaacs, 1941; Despert, 1942; Gordon, 1942).

Secondly, rates of disturbance were lower in children who remained closer to their families and stayed within the same social contact, i.e. those children evacuated with their families had low rates of disturbance and were better adjusted (see Garmezy and Rutter, 1985).

Thirdly, reports suggest that one-half of displaced children returned to their homes within a month because of close family ties, parental dissatisfaction with foster home placement and the economic pressure of maintaining two homes (Despert, 1942).

These findings illustrate that children's perceptions of events may not be congruent either with their objectivity (i.e. the country is safer than the town) or with adults' appraisals. There is also the implication that family supports and family proximity are more important than personal safety. This may also be true for the parents, whose dissatisfaction with separation may stem from the anxiety of separation and hence the concern about foster parents not providing adequate care.

The impact of evacuation may depend on the antecedent nature of family and social experiences, thus the children who adjusted best to evacuation were judged to come from healthy families, and were considered socially well adjusted. A number of psychological mechanisms are likely to be involved in children's responses to these events.

Firstly, evacuation constituted a separation event. For some children, more likely those who came from disturbed or difficult family backgrounds, the opportunity to derive social support from other children with whom they were sharing this experience was insufficient to prevent disorder (although we do not know if effects were less as a consequence of this peer support). This suggests that children with difficult family relations may make less use of peer relations than those with good family relations.

Secondly, the hedonic positive qualities of the separation were insufficient to prevent their negative effects. Whilst many of the children were fully capable of comprehending that evacuation was in their best interest, this intellectual appreciation of the circumstances was insufficient to prevent distress and disorder in many cases. We do not know how previous experiences of separation or loss may have influenced this response. It may be, however, that in order to fully appreciate the positive qualities of undesirable events a previous personal experience, rather than an intellectual understanding of what is about to happen, is required.

Thirdly, in some cases evacuation may have improved the instrumental quality of life in terms of healthier living but there is little evidence to suggest that this was sufficient in the short term to moderate the effects of separation. There may, however, have been longer-term positive effects from this experience, such as better social adjustment or a maintenance of some aspect of the lifestyle considered to be healthy. There is no evidence, however, to confirm or refute these possibilities. The notion that undesirable events may carry desirable consequences is an important one. The example suggests that undesirable events may result in a reappraisal of current circumstances, i.e. a cognitive effect, which may be adaptive, or an alteration in behaviour for the better. There is little information on the adaptive outcomes of undesirable events or on the relative contribution of the hedonic qualities of events in relation to their effects on longer-term adjustment.

Children's personal experience of war

A second example is found in the investigations on children with personal experience of attacks such as bombing, assaults and kidnapping.

Surprisingly little investigation has occurred of children who have experienced personal attacks. This may reflect adults' reluctance to examine the potential effects of such attacks or reflect the difficulties again of systematic enquiry. Studies carried out in Israel on survivors of Arab attacks on border settlements and in Ireland on children involved in sectarian violence point to the wide individual differences and differential outcomes that may occur to subjects experiencing the same form and quality of event.

When children have been injured and witnessed the death of friends, commonly there are immediate acute stress reactions with marked symptoms of anxiety, fearfulness, insomnia, fatigue, nightmares and psychosomatic complaints.

Feelings of depression seem less common but episodes of re-experiencing the event in the following days or weeks can occur frequently (Garmezy and Rutter, 1985). There appears to be recovery in time, although a small percentage continue to show poor social adjustment and school difficulties.

When children have witnessed the death of parents (as opposed to strangers) the acute reactions appear similar, but what evidence there is suggests that the longer-term adjustment may be poor for many (Allodi, 1980; Minde, Minde and Musici, 1982). Overall, however, the evidence suggests that the severity of the children's reponses to such acute and stressful events is less than might be expected (e.g. Malmquist, 1986). Furthermore, when reactions do occur they appear mainly to be expressed as emotional and antisocial states with no evidence that such traumas may result in psychotic states. There is evidence, however, that following acute emotional reactions the responses of friends will influence outcome. Thus deviant behaviours, such as refusing to work and staying indoors to protect against further attacks, and psychiatric disturbances in parents serve to facilitate and maintain poor adjustment in children.

This point illustrates that the effects of a life event on children require a full understanding of the social consequences of the event on the child's social and family environments. The findings illustrate that factors in the environment serve to facilitate or maintain the immediate effects of events.

Finally, we may need to consider that short-term effects of such events are different from their long-term effects. These differences may depend on the appraisal of the event by the child and family and their responses to it.

Further difficulties are apparent when children are severely injured and require treatment. Case reports suggest that immediate hospitalisation may reinforce the impact of the attack through two different mechanisms. Either by the treatment necessary for injuries sustained or by the continued separation from family. These mechanisms are not mutually exclusive and may influence each other.

These clinical and investigative reports indicate that both the contexts in which personal injuries or traumas occur and the child's background influence the social outcome following injury. Thus, being with friends who suffered similarly or were, at minimum, witness to the trauma, will provide an opportunity to discuss the event. Children with good family supports are more likely to adjust again to ordinary life.

Furthermore, children with good family supports before the injury are more likely to be well adjusted in the long term. In addition, children's adjustment may be influenced by the effect of similar injuries on others as much as on themselves.

These series of clinical reports suggest a number of points in relation to stressful events. Firstly, the salience of the event to the child may depend on other people's emotional and behavioural responses as much as his or her own. This may be because the child is less likely to appreciate the implications of a personal injury whereas parents and/or other adults do. Secondly, the personal injury experiences shared with others who have had similar experiences suggest a role for non-familial group support in the longer-term processes of rehabilitation from a personal injury. The value of group support with individuals of similar injuries may need to be balanced against the importance of normal social development with non-injured children. Thirdly, we see the importance of good family relations at two different points in time. Family support in the immediate phase following on injury may buffer the effects of necessary treatment procedures which are themselves potentially stressful. The maintenance of family support in the long term facilitates psychological rehabilitation perhaps in part through the importance of children's perceptions of how important adults in their lives are responding to their injuries as suggested above. It seems that children with good family relations before injury do have a better outcome. This suggests that such families provide necessary support after the event. Whether or not some families' support for their child is altered for the better as a consequence of personal injury is not clear. We may be able to plan better services for children with injury who require rehabilitation by evaluating individual and family supports and through interviews comparing family relations before and after the event. Families, and therefore children, at risk from poor support, and therefore worse personal adjustment, are particularly at risk, and could be targeted for interventions to improve support to the child.

As with evacuations, it is apparent that antecedent supports, the quality of disaster and the timing of the trauma, the nature of personal injury and the families' and society's collective responses will influence children's outcomes. Coping with such events by children may also be determined in part by these factors. There are indications, however, that many children show considerable resilience in the face of such adversity, with low levels of antisocial behaviour or emotional disturbance (Garmezy, 1983; Garmezy and Rutter, 1985). For example, research in Northern Ireland has suggested that contrary to expectations children do not appear unduly preoccupied with the troubles and there have not been epidemics of delinquency (McWhirter and Trew, 1981).

This suggests that children show strong adaptive capacities to the social contexts in which they live. The chronic social and physical difficulties associated with war become accepted realities, perhaps as a necessary part of coping responses.

Severe permanent separations as a consequence of war

The previous chapter discussed separations from the family as a consequence of a variety of individual and family experiences but not as a consequence of war. Under war conditions separation may occur because of the impact of the conflict on children, with death of parents and other relatives either in battle or as civilian casualties. In addition, there may be specific policies of separation and extermination of identified groups of people, using internment and concentration camps.

Concentration camps

Internment during the Second World War has been described as the most anti-human event in human history (Lifton, 1980). Among the millions who perished were 1 million children under the age of 16 years. The liberation of Auschwitz released a mere 300 live children. The chronic continuous degradation for all prisoners was characterised by hunger, cold and hard labour. There were no schools and no play for the very young. The overwhelming fear of death resulted in self-preservation being the main value system for each individual child. Perhaps only in South-East Asia in the 1960s can one find similar descriptions of the complete absence of protective, mediating or buffering factors of family, friends, social surroundings and peacetime experiences that children may utilise at times of stress. It has been estimated that between one-third and one-quarter of Cambodia's 7 million population perished in 4 years as a consequence of Pol Pot policies which resulted in widespread execution, starvation and disease (Hawk, 1982).

Descriptions of concentration camp behaviour indicated low levels of overt neurotic disorder but high levels of antisocial activity such as lying and stealing. There appears to have been containment of serious anxiety and aggression (Langmeier and Matejeck, 1975; Kinzie et al., 1986).

Both the Second World War and South-East Asia conflicts suggested a relationship between the quality of stress and the type of behaviours expressed. Whatever else, the child's adaptive capacity to promote personal survival was paramount, perhaps this is why emotional symptoms designed as signals for help-seeking were non-constructive in the absence of caretakers or other social forms of support. The need to promote exploratory behaviours as a means to seek food and shelter made sense in these terms, indeed given the context of the children's lives the term antisocial appears unwarranted as the norms and values of their society were survival based. It is not surprising that aggressive behaviours, and severe anxieties were contained as they would have been divisive and non-adaptive in these conditions.

The outcome of child survivors

The longitudinal impact of internment on children has been examined in both Second World War and South-East Asia survivors.

Research on outcome into adult life from Second World War concentration camp survivors has been conducted mainly through clinical-descriptive and treatment accounts with survivors. The overriding impression of this literature is the markedly different outcomes that have been reported. The degree of trauma suffered by these children clearly does not predict continuing psychosocial difficulties with relationships, educational achievement or persistent emotional or behavioural symptoms.

There is, therefore, a suggestion that for some children subsequent substitute care, education and normative socialisation were sufficient to facilitate social adjustment to this degree of early trauma. For example, Freud and Dann (1951) reported the adaptation of six toddlers who spent the first 3 years of their life in concentration camps. Initial symptoms of serious anxieties, social withdrawal, and fear of adults gave way to increasing use of adults and wider explorations of their social world.

Moskovitz (1983) reported 24 child survivors, only one of whom was in a mental institution whilst the others, although still re-experiencing the memories of their traumas, were functioning well in all aspects of their adult lives, although some had manifested 'survivor guilt' thoughts indicating a preoccupation with loss of parents and family. These memories led to thoughts of 'why am I alive?' and 'who am I?'. Attempts to make links with the past and a desire for belonging gave rise to a haunting anxiety where past experiences seem to interfere with everyday life. Expressing fears about their sense of self ('am I strange?') and a sense of being an outsider were reported. The same group of survivors, however, also reported remarkable positive qualities, such as an absence of anger and bitterness towards their captors, a zest for life and a stubborn durability for everyday hassles.

Similar qualities have been described in Cambodian student survivors of Indo-Chinese war (Kinzie *et al.*, 1986).

Resilience and survival

These positive appraisals of adaptation have been supported by more recent studies on survivors of the Second World War systematically compared with matched controls (Leon *et al.*, 1981). Interestingly, this good outcome group from such severe traumas converge with evidence from other studies of early adversities showing that some children raised in an institution, following severe early family adversities may have good adult functioning (Quinton and Rutter, 1985b, 1988; Rutter, 1989).

Thus positive social outcomes may occur in spite of previously difficult social experiences. It seems that in some children traumatic memories do not interfere unduly with normal socio-emotional development.

Disturbed survivors

It is equally apparent, however, that for many children there are significant subsequent difficulties. For example, the placement of camp survivor children with families after the Second World War showed that both family atmosphere and the child's personal adjustment appeared better compared with returning evacuees. But both groups were marked by considerable individual variations. Camp survivors from a stable family background seemed to survive the traumas with a much better degree of personal adaptation. Overt emotional and behavioural symptoms seemed to occur more in camp survivors from unstable backgrounds (Langmeier and Matejeck, 1975; Garmezy, 1983).

Not surprisingly, many children from the camps were not resilient and showed poor adjustment in the post-war years. Yet the clues to some components of resilience are surely to be found in the suggestion that early family and possibly social experiences antedating internment exerted positive effects on outcome following release. The consequences of a traumatic event involving internment, permanent separation from family and subsequent placement in a new home and a new culture can be enhanced or diminished depending on previous relations with family and possibly friends.

Long-term adjustment of survivors

Clinical studies on severely traumatised children suggest that, for many, family placements proved extremely difficult, although great care was taken over them. In many cases a survivor syndrome was described: they perceived themselves as unaccepted by the family, sought out the company of others with the same camp experiences and maintained close contact with them. Many physical symptoms were reported by this group, often associated with feelings of depression and anxiety (Garmezy and Rutter, 1985).

A systematic study of 40 Cambodian adolescents who had been interned reported high rates of psychiatric disturbance 6 years afterwards, with 50 per cent of them meeting criteria for post-traumatic stress disorder. Major symptoms included nightmares and recurrent dreams of their traumatic experiences, feeling ashamed of being alive and vague aches and fatigue, again many of these people were described as having episodes of depression.

Comparisons of the Cambodian adolescents' social adjustment in American families were made with six non-interned adolescents from Cambodia, and overall adjustment of the camp survivors was much more impaired. The characteristics of their impairment was that of social withdrawal and avoidance of discussion about their previous experiences. Antisocial behaviours, such as truancy and aggression, were not reported, nor were alcohol or drug abuse. The inference drawn by the researchers was that for these adolescents their problems were private and internal and much of their behaviour and thought served to avoid or deny the significance of their past (Kinzie, Frederick and Ruth, 1984; Kinzie et al., 1986).

Of particular interest was the suggestion that neither the amount nor quality of trauma as reported by the students, by age or sex, was related to the current diagnosis or global functioning. However, 13 out of the 14 adolescents living in foster homes or alone had a psychiatric disorder. The most important predictor of poor outcome, either in terms of psychiatric disorder or social adjustment, was not living with a nuclear family member since resettlement. These findings provide a clear illustration of the palliative and neutralising effect of maintaining good family relations following internment (Kinzie *et al.*, 1986; Sack *et al.*, 1986). There were developmental and gender factors that may have influenced this finding. For example, amongst all ages it was adolescent boys in particular who showed the poorest adjustment to divorce. Perhaps there is a similar effect for camp survivors of wars.

Further findings showed that after the Second World War children in Israel assigned to kibbutzims did best, those placed in foster homes had the greatest difficulty. Adolescent boys often showed anger and destructiveness and girls heightened passivity demonstrating gender differences in behavioural responses to the same stress.

It would appear that for some children the psychological coping skills needed for adjusting to a new family life are lacking and their personal adjustment, whilst likely to be impaired, may be best served by remaining in a caring institution with peers.

In conclusion, the massive traumas of war provide some important findings demonstrating the importance of different social, family and personal factors that make a differential contribution to children who have experienced internment.

Firstly, there is the suggestion that children who reported good family relations prior to internment were more likely to show better long-term adaptation and social adjustment.

Secondly, there is the finding that the quality and quantity of the experience itself did not predict outcome in either psychiatric or social terms. This is a less satisfactory observation as we do not have an adequate understanding of the personal salience of these events for the individual. Furthermore, the individuals who are survivors may be so for reasons to do with specific aspects of their experiences or their personalities and they may represent an atypical group of children who were interned. Nevertheless, as a general point it highlights the fact that the impact of stresses of this nature and duration does not automatically confer a gloomy prognosis for the children's future well-being.

Thirdly, the finding of marked variations in the children's psychiatric and social adjustment may reflect in part individual differences in their temperament and personality.

Fourthly, it is very clear that subsequent family and social experiences play a major role in adjustment. Children who retain contacts with a biological family being particularly more likely to show good adjustment in personal, social and educational terms. However, children who were successfully placed in caring environments with no biological relatives also prospered, particularly if they had experienced adequate parenting before internment. This latter finding raises the suggestion that coping with a new family life may be specifically dependent on previous family experiences. Does this reflect cognitive emotional mechanisms whereby the child relives good experiences and memories which in some way are 'matched' between past and present family experience?

Fifthly, in some children a particular form of psychopathology may occur which is characterised by constricted and withdrawn behaviours that may suggest *no disturbance* because the child is quiet and compliant. These children may go unnoticed in the societies in which they now live. They may not, however, be as well adjusted mentally as their good behaviour may suggest.

CHILDREN AND DISASTERS

Disasters during peacetime are unexpected undesirable stressful events whose effects depend on their form, speed of onset, duration and expectancy, and the quality and extent of their impact on the community concerned (Kinston and Rosser, 1974; Garmezy and Rutter, 1985; McFarlane, 1988).

Natural disasters

Many disasters are nature's contributions to stressful life events such as floods, earthquakes, storms, tornadoes and cyclones. Two of the best studied are an American disaster, the Buffalo Creek flood, and an Australian disaster, the bush fires of New South Wales.

In the Buffalo Creek disaster a giant flood of water burst through a dam above the mining village of Buffalo Creek in the Appalachian Mountains. The flood killed 125 people, injured many hundreds more and left thousands homeless (Gleser, Green and Winget, 1981).

A systematic inquiry into the cause of the disaster was the stimulus for research into the effects on the survivors. The study examined the well-being of 230 children (116 boys and 114 girls) and 23 infants under one year of age (11 boys and 12 girls). The children were studied concurrently with their parents so that comparisons between parents' and children's adjustment were possible. The results indicated a number of important findings (in the 2 weeks after the disaster).

Firstly, the children showed less symptoms and impairment than adults. Half of the children had no disorder, 20 per cent were considered to have moderate to severe anxiety and some 30 per cent some degree of depression. Thus again there appears to be no specificity in the type of stress and form of response. The fact that half of the children were not disturbed indicates the resilient nature of children but does not tell us if this is a consequence of their own experiences or temperament, or a consequence of family and social protective factors. The results did show, however, that there was an overall increase in the rate of psychiatric disturbance and poor adjustment with age. Young adults had the highest rate of disorder and infants the lowest. Furthermore, specific fears were most frequent among the young. Thus, when developmental factors are taken into account, the specificities of the associations between events and the form of disorder are enhanced. These specificities may, in part, be a consequence of cognitive and emotional factors determining the form of response. Thus phobias may be seen as cognitively less complex than other forms of anxiety and were a more frequent response in younger children.

Another developmental difference was that children tended to respond to the physical stress with a high degree of anxiety whereas adults responded with a high degree of depression. The presence of anxiety immediately following the disaster was the strongest predictor of psychiatric disorder for adolescents in the following weeks and months. This prediction was not the case for younger children, especially those less than 7 years of age. These children showed the least outward signs of distress at changes in their social community structure and appeared the least affected by the deaths of peers and other children. For adults, the strongest predictor of psychopathology in subsequent weeks was the presence of depression immediately after the event.

These developmental differences were accompanied by the finding that subsequent to the disaster girls of all ages rated higher than boys on anxiety, depression, and overall severity but lower on belligerence. Again, however, the overall patterns of the children's disturbances in the days and weeks following the disaster was non-specific characterised by tension, cognitive impairment, somatic complaints, vulnerability to new stressful experiences, depression, guilt and isolation.

One of the most significant findings was that the children's well-being tended to parallel that of their parents across all age groups. Furthermore, there seemed to be sex identification; disturbed fathers being associated with increased rates of disturbance in sons and similarly for disturbed mothers and daughters.

Furthermore, the associations between parental and child psychopathology were independent of the child's age, sex or race. These latter findings also showed that the impact of disaster (as measured by rates of disturbance) was greatest in children from discordant and violent home backgrounds and least in those from supportive families. Additionally, children who had lost family members showed greater rates of disturbance than those who simply lost material possessions. The overriding impression from this study was that the impact of disaster on children was mediated through its impact on parents.

Similar conclusions have been reached from a very different form of disaster: the bush fires of New South Wales in Australia (McFarlane, 1987, 1988). The findings from this study also suggest that the impact of the disaster on children is mediated through the impact on parents. Subsequent life events in the months following the disaster did not appear to make a significant contribution to the children's adjustment a year later. The children's adjustment was found to be improved if they remained in contact with their remaining family and social structures. This latter finding is similar to that for Cambodian refugees who showed better rehabilitation in the presence of surviving friends and family.

Finally, there is some evidence from the recent studies on Cambodian refugees that friends and social networks, perhaps facilitated through existing social structures such as school, can also serve to rehabilitate the disaster/war victim (Kinzie et al., 1986). In the absence of a family structure it may be important to consider the form of community that a new refugee may require in order to produce some type of fit between the person's values and past experience and their future life as well as to make the best use of their coping behaviours shaped in a different culture.

Three Mile Island—A man-made disaster

In March 1979 a nuclear power station in Pennsylvania, U.S.A., had a threatened meltdown of its nuclear reactor core. The possibility of widespread radiation prompted the governor to issue a public declaration advising all pregnant women and pre-school-age children living within 5 miles of the reactor to leave the area.

This potential disaster event and its immediate consequences of evacuation were elongated because although no meltdown in fact occurred, considerable contamination was present some four years after the initial event. There have been numerous reports of the effects on adult well-being (e.g. Dohrenwend et al., 1981; Solomen and Bromet, 1982; Collins, Baum and Singer, 1983).

The effect on parents and children over the next few weeks and months after the declared disaster were substantial with high levels of distress. Not surprisingly the most concerned were pregnant women and mothers with young children, three-quarters of whom left the area.

The longer-term effects were recently reported by Handford and his colleagues (1986) from Pennsylvania State University following extensive assessments one year after the event of 35 parents and one of their children, whose ages ranged from 6 to 18 (mean 13.2 years).

The children's level of distress was significantly associated with the degree of mother–father discordance in mood and reaction to the event. Four of the children were given a psychiatric diagnosis (one conduct disorder and three with emotional disorders).

The authors describe numerous post-disaster responses that may reflect the children's efforts to cope with circumstances. For example, the desire to flee the area and the attempted use of a denial, 'this didn't happen to me'. Furthermore, the children consistently reported *more distress* than their parents did for them. This suggests that parents may underestimate their children's anxiety to social stress, a feature reported in other descriptions of disasters (Terr, 1981).

Another study of the Three Mile Island accident retrospectively reported adolescents' ratings of distress at the time of the accident (Dohrenwend *et al.*, 1981). The highest stress scores were recorded by those adolescents who also had high rates of somatic symptoms. Although distress scores in the adolescents declined over the next few months, the scores of adolescents with a pre-school-age sibling remained higher than those of their peers. These findings indicate that siblings as well as peers may influence adolescents' adjustment to severe events. The mechanism involved in maintaining these adolescents in distress is unclear. Interactions between siblings as well as with parents may need consideration (Dunn, 1988a). The findings do suggest that the level of stress remains higher in those families with a younger child. Interestingly, at the time of the event, the administration of the area publicly identified potential at-risk groups. These consisted of mothers of young children and pregnant mothers. This may have sensitised these groups to their at-risk status of which they had previously been ignorant. This re-evaluation of risk through new information may reflect a cognitive factor in the appraisal and response to community stresses.

The inference from Three Mile Island is that individuals in powerful positions of authority exert an influence which extends beyond their immediate intentions (in this case, to clear the area).

Overall, the Three Mile Island disaster provides further evidence that the impact of a disaster event on children is mediated through the effects it has on parents. There is not a simple relationship, however, because the consequences of the disaster meant long-term difficulties for the community, i.e. continuous radiation exposure. Despite this, the overall rate of distress in children decreased over the 18 months and the rate of psychiatric disorder was low at all times following the announcement of the potential disaster. As Garmezy (1986) has commented, there is a case for examining these community events to see which factors discriminated between good and poor outcomes.

Social context, event and response

The impact of disaster events may be influenced by their own social context and perceived consequences. Thus when describing the detailed interviews of children who had been kidnapped in Chowchilla, California, Terr (1981) showed that it was the direct impact on children facing constant threats of physical harm or death that accounted for the high rates of psychiatric disturbance and extensive symptoms. The likelihood of danger to the self had, not surprisingly, had marked adverse effects on the children.

When there is a direct impact on children, such as at Chowchilla, it is not clear that parental adjustment is so determinative. Anecdotally, this study suggested that parents may have difficulty in comprehending the meaning of a personal disaster to a child if they have not shared in the experience. This matter would be worth examining in more detail.

Low rates of psychiatric disorder following disasters appear to be a consequence of family or parental coping factors. McFarlane and colleagues (1987) investigated longitudinally and prospectively the outcome of 244 children who had been victims of bush fires in Australia. In this study the authors demonstrate a rising rate of psychiatric disorder following the disaster, which was severe enough to devastate homes, livestock and livelihood for many hundreds of families. At 2 months 8 per cent of children were disturbed, at 8 months 23 per cent were, and at 26 months 23 per cent still were (although not necessarily the same children). The rising rates may be a function of alterations in parental appraisal of the consequences of the fire and may reflect different coping mechanisms at different times. Acute coping after events may be different to longer-term adjustment. This study also suggested that further stressful life events may not add to the risk of poor adjustment directly but operate by maintaining poor levels of family adjustment.

PERSONALITY AND FAMILY VIOLENCE

The anecdotal report of Chowchilla demonstrates that, where personal violence is concerned, the impact is substantially greater than in community disasters. Clearly events do not always operate through parents and may exert a direct impact.

The Chowchilla incident exposed all the children to severe personal danger and assault but did not include death. The children from this incident were interviewed 5 months later about how they felt (Terr, 1979). Three major fears were recalled at the time of the event: separation from family, death and further trauma.

Their adjustment at 5 months showed that nearly 16 (60 per cent) out of 26 children were definitely impaired with school and social difficulties as well as having nervous anxiety symptoms, such as panic attacks, nightmares and re-experiences of the day of the event, which resulted in clinging behaviour in some cases. Interestingly, at this stage there were no differences in response by age or sex. There were no signs of pseudo-normalisation, denial, aimless behaviour, amnesia or marked passivity. All the children at all ages provided detailed stories of their experiences.

Terr (1983) followed up the children at 4 years and found that whilst school and social adjustment had improved, substantial fear-related symptoms remained. Furthermore, there was a suggestion that whereas at 3 months anxiety was focused to thoughts about the event, some children were now anxious in more everyday circumstances. The worst adjustment seemed to occur in children with antecedent behavioural and social problems.

Witnessing the death of a relative

It is difficult to imagine a more severe event in the life of a person than witnessing the death of a parent by violent means. Malmquist (1986), in a study of 16 children who witnessed a parent being murdered, and Garmezy and Rutter (1985), who reassessed the clinical descriptive accounts in the literature, conclude that there is a wide individual variation in children's response to this form of stressful event.

It is apparent that the context of the murder, antecedent factors, such as the child's relationship with the adult concerned, and consequent social structure all contribute to children's responses in this severe trauma.

Malmquist provides examples of how the children responded with substantial anxious symptoms, particularly nightmares, restlessness, sleep disorder, constant vigilance, alertness to danger and poor social adjustment and school performance 12 months after the event. Some children were depressed but others appeared to show considerable resilience and made good adjustments at follow-ups.

Malmquist, in common with other studies on disaster events, indicated that good antecedent relationships with parents protect against the impact of events, perhaps by instilling self-esteem. Furthermore, he suggested that previously successful exposure to minor traumas may contribute to the development of coping skills for subsequent life events. In other words, previous minor everyday events may have a steeling effect for later events. This suggests that some internal coping mechanisms develop through a mastery of tasks.

Although everyday events, such as going to the dentist or doctor, have been implicated as significant factors in the development of both sensitising and steeling effects for later events (e.g. Parmalee, 1984) it is not clear how such relatively common events provide steeling effects for such rare and highly undesirable events such as witnessing a death. Indeed it is not clear what effect a similar prior experience may have. It seems likely that extreme examples of stress such as this require considerable caution when attempting to extrapolate psychological mechanisms to the commonly occurring experiences in life. This should not be taken to mean that such adversity is unworthy of study. Many valuable insights may well be gained from the direct study of children's response to extreme stresses, as many of the studies highlighted in this chapter demonstrate.

For example, Pynoos and Eth (Pynoos and Eth, 1984; Eth and Pynoos, 1985) gathered descriptions of over 200 children who have witnessed violence to parents, including murder, suicide, assault, accidental death, rape and kidnapping. This important work has allowed the authors to make a substantive contribution in the area of clinical intervention (see Chapter 8). It is of interest to note that the descriptions of the children's responses are similar to other forms of severe trauma. There is wide individual variation of anxious, somatic and depressive symptoms with reiteration of the event in nightmares and daydreams and re-experiencing of the event under subsequent stresses.

In conclusion, the literature on severe examples of community and personal stress provides many examples of how children can show resilience in the face of such adversity. The remarkable capacities of young people in such circumstances deserve further attention. Investigations into resilience as well as into risks will provide a clearer picture of the coping mechanisms involved in psychopathology.

We are already able to see that, as far as extreme stresses are concerned, complex interactions between antecedent and postcedent social factors make an important contribution to young people's responses, both in the short as well as the long term. The significance of more intrinsic factors such as temperament, arousal and cognitive and emotional styles in the presence and absence of different patterns of social factors has yet to be determined. Such studies would be worth while.

SUMMARY

Urbanisation

1. Urbanisation increases the risk of psychopathology but not as a direct effect of living in towns and cities.
2. The mechanisms of urban adversity depend on the configuration of a number of factors including the structure and fabric of housing, overcrowding, and unemployment, as well as family relations, quality of parental care, and educational opportunity and attainment.
3. Social policy and psychiatric interventions should be determined by an accurate assessment of the types and patterning of adverse factors pertinent to a particular urban community.

War

1. Good family relations prior to internment improve the likelihood of subsequent adaptation and adjustment.
2. The quality and quantity of the experience offered by survivors does not specifically predict either social adjustment or psychiatric outcome. Both antecedent and consequential factors influence mental and social adjustment.
3. Resilient characteristics in temperament and subsequent contact with surviving relatives or with families with good parenting skills improve the likelihood of better long-term social and mental adjustment.

Disaster

1. The impact of disaster on children is influenced in most circumstances by the impact on their parents. Where children have been personally involved, however, parental influence is less important and may be absent.
2. Long-term effects can be diminished by adequate on-going relations with family. Friendships are particularly important when the family is lost as a consequence of a disaster.
3. The child's age influences the impact of disaster and differences between the sexes, whilst small, may be due to *same sex* effects between parents and children.
4. The effects of disaster appear similar whether they are man-made or natural.
5. Adults may underestimate the effects of disaster on children, particularly when the form of expression of the disorder is dominated by social withdrawal and isolation.
6. It is apparent that children of all ages have private thoughts, moods, and interpretations of severe social adversities which may not be available to adults, including their parents.

Part Two

Personal Disposition

Chapter 5

Monoamines, Immunity and Social Adversity

The impact of social events and circumstances occurs through effects on individuals' psychology and physiology. The latter systems have been far less well researched than either the psychology of stress (see Chapter 6) or the social origins and causes of stress.

Physiological studies of responses to stress have used quite different conceptual frameworks to those in social psychology and psychiatry. The main differences have been that physiologists and psychophysiologists have been concerned with determining physiological responses to physical rather than social stresses.

For example, noxious stimuli, such as pain and rapid change in temperature, have been used as physiological challenge tests to investigate bodily responses in terms of change of chemistry, blood pressure and heart-rate. It is apparent that the meaning of stress to a psychophysiologist bears little relationship to stress as conceptualised and studied by a social scientist.

In this chapter we are concerned with social adversities and their association with the physiology and chemistry of individuals. However, an important prologue concerns the description of those biological systems that are concerned with stress response mechanisms.

ENDOCRINES AND STRESS

The endocrine system has been a major focus for investigating bodily responses to undesirable or noxious stimuli (Herbert, 1987). These studies were stimulated by the discovery that there is a release of chemicals into the bloodstream as a consequence of stresses. This occurs with both intrinsic stresses, such as pain and hunger, and extrinsic stresses, such as dangerous events, e.g. parachuting. The earliest work of Cannon (1928) was concerned with investigating how such stresses could lead to disease. Cannon's work showed that the autonomic nervous system was fundamentally important in the maintenance of an organism's viability under stressful conditions. Cannon postulated that a chemical he called sympathin, now known as noradrenaline, was in fact essential for an animal's survival. He deduced this following experiments which showed that noradrenaline was released in copious quantities into the bloodsteam during stress.

Since then our knowledge about neurochemistry and neuroanatomy has expanded exponentially. Animal studies have resulted in postulates about neurochemical pathways with differential behavioural effects (Henry, 1980; Herbert, 1987; Keverne, 1988) and researchers continue to increase our knowledge of sympathetic nervous activity and its association with stress and disease.

We now recognise noradrenaline as one of a related group of substances which are known collectively as catecholamines. The members of this family are dopamine, noradrenaline and adrenaline. They occur throughout the body and can act both as hormones and as neurotransmitters. Physiological responses to stresses result in alterations of the levels of circulating catecholamines outside the brain. These consist mainly of adrenaline but there is also a small proportion of noradrenaline. Once released, catecholamines have direct effects on numerous bodily systems.

Additionally, catecholamines are found in the brain and are synthesised mainly in the central nervous system, since the peripherally circulating catecholamines do not easily cross the blood–brain barrier. The central nervous system catecholamines are principally dopamine and noradrenaline. Their function is that of neurotransmitters. Compared with peripherally circulating hormones, the centrally acting catecholamines in man have received very little attention in stress research. In fact, the largest proportion of catecholamines are synthesised and degraded in the brain.

Function of catecholamines

The presence of catecholamines in blood, cerebrospinal fluid and urine means that sympathetic nervous system activity can be measured by collection of amines under controlled conditions. There is now general agreement that catecholamines are one of the major pathways mediating psychological influences on peripheral physiological function.

For example, the release of adrenaline from the adrenal medulla has important hormonal actions on the cardiovascular system by regulating heart-rate and blood pressure. Catecholamines are also included in fat breakdown and carbohydrate metabolism, and interact with thyroid hormones to potentiate their action. Whilst there are a number of techniques for monitoring sympathetic activity, there is little agreement about their adequacy and about the appropriate methods of measurement to be employed under different stressful circumstances (Steptoe, 1987).

Secretion of catecholamines

There is a characteristic pattern of secretion of catecholamines over a 24-hour period. Both adrenaline and noradrenaline levels are low during night rest, increase gradually during the morning hours and reach a peak in the middle of the day. This diurnal pattern is more pronounced and more independent of sleep–wakefulness patterns for adrenaline than for noradrenaline.

Adrenaline secretion and excretion is stimulated by stressful events appraised as desirable or undesirable as well as physical events such as pain, sexual activity and sport (Frankenhauser, 1975; Henry, 1980; Barnes *et al.*, 1982). By contrast, noradenaline seems more sensitive to bodily posture and physical activity than to social stresses.

Among the more potent events likely to result in a release of catecholamines in children and adults are the anticipation of threat, mental effort and emotional challenges (Lundeberg, 1983a). Release of catecholamines, however, can occur in the presence of under- or overstimulation (Frankenhauser *et al.*, 1971). It seems to be, therefore, that it is the magnitude of change rather than its quality that governs the sympathetic response.

Personality as well as environmental circumstances seems an important determinant of catecholamine release (Lundeberg, 1983b). Individuals who are competitive, aggressive and striving (often referred to as Type A personalities) are prone to depression at times of failure, have longer vasomotor responses, excrete more noradrenaline and are more prone to coronary artery disease (see Chapter 6).

Interestingly, whilst successful they cope well with stress. However, if they begin to fail this protection is lost and stress responses may develop (Glass, 1977). This may be a consequence of differential secretion of catecholamines under different environments. In other words, different social stresses may provoke differential adrenaline or noradrenaline responses. In general, noradrenaline levels in plasma increases with achievement which is stressful but desirable and provides some satisfaction. This appears to occur for both humans and animals (Henry, 1980; Herbert, 1987). In contrast, adrenaline release may be more associated with anxiety and feelings of loss of control, i.e. stressful and undesirable (e.g. Frankenhauser *et al.*, 1971, 1975). These findings suggest links between the environment and different catecholamine pathways modulating and expressing physiologically the impact of life experiences.

The majority of this work has been carried out in adults and we must be careful about generalising these findings to children at all ages. Major changes in development, such as those associated with puberty, may influence the nature and mechanisms of neuroendocrine processes for childhood.

Age and sex differences

Some very consistent sex differences have been found in adrenaline reactivity (Frankenhauser, 1983). During rest and relaxation there are generally no differences between male and females provided body weight is controlled for. However, during periods of achievement, women are less likely than men to respond with increased catecholamine secretion. Furthermore, on a subjective level, males generally report more confidence in their performance than do females.

These differences have also been found in children (Lundeberg, 1983a,b). It appears that whereas boys almost invariably respond to environmental demands with increased adrenaline output, girls appear to be more selective in their responses. The data suggest that performance efficiency in males is more closely associated with adrenaline excretion than it is in females. Catecholamine levels may also be affected by the menstrual cycle (Collins, Ensroth and Londgren, 1985; Herbert, 1987).

Studies examining the covariation of catecholamines and behaviour at different times in the menstrual cycle and in the presence and absence of life events, difficulties or daily hassles would be of interest. In particular, a longitudinal study of girls pre and post menarche may elucidate how the physiochemical changes in puberty influence the associations between social adversity and psychopathology.

Age also shows an important relationship with plasma catecholamine excretion. Resting plasma noradrenaline, but not adrenaline, increases with age, and responses to distress may also be enhanced (Aslan *et al.*, 1982; Barnes *et al.*, 1982). It has also been suggested from investigations in the elderly that noradrenaline may be an index of biological age (Christensen, 1986).

These sex and age differences may influence the potential importance of catecholamine responses in children to stressful events. For example, does the lowered responsiveness of catecholamine release to stressful circumstances in females exert a protective effect? What are children's general physiological states under resting and stressful conditions? The sex differences described are of interest but how do these relate to psychiatric disorders? Boys and girls appear equally as likely to show emotional symptoms in the presence of *acute* stresses whereas boys appear more likely to show disturbance in the presence of *chronic* stresses (Rutter, 1983b; Goodyer, Kolvin and Gatzanis, 1986). Whether or not there are differential levels of circulating catecholamine response at resting (basal) conditions and at times of exposure to stresses between the sexes is not yet clear.

We know little about the catecholamine responses in psychiatric disorders in young people. Studies investigating associations between different types of events and difficulties, endocrine change and psychopathology would seem warranted.

Measuring catecholamines

Problems of measurement and methodology have been highlighted in the area of catecholamine research (Steptoe, 1987). Thus catecholamine secretion and excretion are sensitive to several factors besides stress, including the consumption of coffee and alcohol, various medications and cigarette smoking. In children it is to be hoped that these factors would have little influence; they highlight, however, the importance of knowing a child's personal habits when engaging in this area of stress research.

Complexities of measurement have resulted in only a few centres investigating in this area. The choice of method and laboratory reliability vary a great deal from study to study, making comparison of findings difficult (Steptoe, 1987).

A further area of conceptual difficulty is the purpose in the minds of investigators. By and large, neurochemists and physiologists have been concerned with studying the details of a particular biological system rather than its relation to stress. Stress has therefore been used as an external challenge for exploring physiological responses. Examining contingencies between stress and response, and understanding the mechanisms invoked has been relatively ignored.

Additionally, the majority of the research has paid little attention to the temporal relationship between stress and response.

By and large, most inferences that can be drawn relate to acute changes in arousal, often in anticipation of a presented stimulus (desirable or undesirable). The relationship between acute life events and onset of psychiatric disorders, for example, is of a quite different order of time. There is, however, some suggestion that urinary catecholamine may not only reflect acute changes in arousal but may, under certain circumstances, be used as indicators of the 'physiological costs' associated with a particular situation, environment or lifestyle. Thus the ability to slow down or deactivate after a demanding situation may be more important for long-term health than the acute response itself (Steptoe, 1987). Do children exposed to single, multiple acute life events or chronic stress show different deactivations in catecholamines? This hypothesis has yet to be examined.

In conclusion, the major catecholamines investigated in stress research have been noradrenaline and adrenaline. Little is known about dopamine found in the central rather than peripheral nervous system. Catecholamine release occurs as a non-specific response to a range of social and physical stimuli. There may, however, be a different magnitude of release for adrenaline and noradrenaline under different social conditions. Endocrine response can occur as a consequence of exposure to acute or chronic social adversities. Such endocrine changes can influence the child's behavioural state. The sustained effect of the immediate release of catecholamines in children is not clear.

ADRENOCORTICOIDS AND CATECHOLAMINES

There is a close and dynamic relationship between catecholamine and adrenal glucocorticoid enzymes. Steady state levels of catecholamine enzymes seem to be determined primarily by the levels of adrenal glucocorticoid hormones (Ciaranello, 1979) This relationship appears complex and is not well understood.

For example, neither exogenous administration of glucocorticoids nor excessive endogenous production *increases* the level of enzymes controlling production of catecholamines.

There is some evidence that circulating glucocorticoids may play a role in maintaining catecholamine enzyme activity in peripheral nerve cells. Thus glucocorticoids and nerve impulses may work co-operatively to maintain the level of catecholamine enzymes at times of increased demand (Ciaranello, 1980). Neuronal stimulation increases enzyme activity responsible for catecholamine production whilst glucocorticoids inhibit the breakdown of these enzymes.

Under stressful circumstances both neuronal stimulation and pituitary adrenocorticotrophin hormone (ACTH) secretion increase. Thus catecholamine enzyme synthesis is increased and their degradation slowed down. Production of catecholamine at maximum rates is ensured. When the stressful circumstances cease, the system operates in reverse fashion. Enzyme production is slowed whilst enzyme degradation is enhanced. The result is a fall in catecholamine production. Whether or not this co-operative dynamic system works in the brain is not yet known.

Corticosteroids and stress

Selye's (1956) original physiological studies were concerned with the catecholamine release from the pituitary adrenal system. Since then the adrenocortical system has received much attention because it too can be used as a measure of stress. Some writers have treated the two as being synonymous (Ganong, 1963).

Certainly there are similarities and interdependencies between the two systems. Both have neurotransmitter and hormonal actions in the brain and periphery respectively. The release of ACTH from the pituitary occurs as a nonspecific response to both physical and social stress. As with catecholamines, there is evidence that changes in the ACTH levels are non-specific and occur in response to desirable and undesirable psychological and physical stresses (Levine, 1983).

Recently it has been proposed that the hormonal responses being elicited by a great diversity of stimuli are being released largely by a single physiological stimulus configuration that has the psychological consequence of emotional arousal (Levine, 1983). This hypothesis, if confirmed, would provide evidence for theorists who argue for the existence of a physiological basis of emotion (see Chapter 6).

Components of the pituitary axis system

The release of ACTH is controlled by releasing factors in the hypothalamus (corticotrophin releasing factor—CRF). Circulatory ACTH has a peripheral effect on the adrenals releasing cortisol which has hormonal effects on many systems, altering cardiovascular and gastrointestinal motility as well as glucose metabolism. A feedback system controls circulating levels of cortisol, which decreases the release of ACTH and diminishes CRF. This HPA circuit is mature by 18 months of age (Migeon, 1980). The factors associated with the development of maturity are not yet clear. There is a diurnal variation in cortisol secretion. Cortisol is normally secreted episodically, with rates of secretion occurring in bursts and gradually increasing from morning through to evening, and then decreasing so that secretion is eventually non-existent at night and in the early morning. In the central nervous system glucocorticoids are found as the monoamine 5-hydroxytryptamine. As with the central catecholamines these amines function as neurotransmitters. Raised cortisol levels in serum and a loss of diurnal variation of cortisol secretion have been found in affective disorders in adults, adolescents and to some extent in children (Cowen and Anderson, 1986; Deakin and Crow, 1986; Puig-Antich, 1986; Foreman and Goodyer, 1988). The present findings have suggested, however, that sustained elevations of cortisol in some forms of depressive illness may not be a direct function of life events or difficulties.

Although there is some evidence of raised cortisols from between 24 hours and 8 days in rhesus monkeys separated from their mothers, it appears very difficult to maintain elevations of plasma cortisol following the cessation of separation (Levine, 1983). This suggests that cortisol levels do change as a function of undesirable events but their nature and purpose for so doing, together with the residual effects, remain unclear.

The involvement of the cortisol system in stress-mediated responses needs to be further investigated but must take into account the possibility of other perhaps intrinsic causes of cortisol hypersecretion. If this were the case, then it may be that different pathophysiological pathways exist with the same resultant psychopathological expression, such as depression.

A MODEL OF BIOCHEMICAL RESPONSE TO STRESS

Human studies broadly confirm differential alterations in hormone responses to a variety of life events, such as examinations and hospital admissions (Cox, 1978; Rose, 1980). Overall, there appears to be an increase in cortisol and catecholamine secretion as well as a rise in growth hormone and its production but a fall in testosterone.

Although both catecholamine and adrenocortical hormonal systems respond to stress, there is some data indicating that differential responses may occur to different stimuli. Investigations into the alterations of these hormonal levels in parachute trainees suggests different correlates between hormones and different emotional and behavioural states. Cortisol correlated negatively with performance and positively with fear, while noradrenaline was correlated with activity and achievement (Ursin, Baade and Levine, 1978).

In general, the cortisol response shows a rapid adaptation to repetition of stressful stimuli. On the other hand, catecholamine secretion occurs with each event encounter, suggesting considerably less habituation to the stimuli.

The general trend of these group findings, however, must be considered against the very large range of individual differences that occur in response to stressful events. For example, the nature and timing of hormone response alters with further experience of the stressor so that the main reaction occurs in the anticipation phase rather than the consequential phase of the event. Clearly appraisal of the event and its meaning are involved in some way with the type of hormone response.

These peripheral hormone responses to events do not, however, describe how central neuroendocrine systems actively mediate in these processes. Since both hormonal systems act through the HPA axis it is worth considering what role monoamine neurotransmitters (noradrenaline, dopamine and 5-hydroxytryptamine) may play in stress responses.

A neuroendocrine model of stress has been suggested (Henry, 1980). In this theoretical model a two-stage hormonal response is possible. The appraisal and meaning of an event is critical in determining the neuroendocrine response. Two responses may occur.

Firstly, if the event is seen as a *challenge to control*, the *fight–flight* mechanism is triggered. This is mediated through the amygdala, a portion of the brain rich in noradrenergic neurotransmitters. In this system, activation of the amygdala ultimately provokes a response in the sympathetic nervous system and adrenal medulla, resulting in increased secretion of adrenaline and noradrenaline. Testosterone rises consistently but cortisol remains unaffected.

Alternatively, the appraisal and meaning of an event results in a *loss of control* with consequent *helplessness* and, perhaps, *hopelessness*. This results in firing neuronal impulses postulated to arise in the hippocampus and septum. These areas are rich in hydroxytryptamine and dopamine neurotransmitters as well as catecholamines. Activation leads to stimulation of the hypothalamic–pituitary adrenal axis. ACTH production and release leads to secretion of corticosterone; testosterone is now reduced whilst catecholamines are unaffected. No direct test of this hypothesis has been carried out in infants or children. Evidence from measurements of circulating monoamines following exposure to novel stimuli suggests a rather nonspecific elevation in both adrenal and cortisol levels (Kagan, Reznick, and Snidman, 1987). Further refinements to the measurement of both the stimulus–event and the monoamines concerned are required.

Evidence for a neuroendocrine model

Animal studies provide some encouragement for the hypothesis that chemical changes in discrete brain regions can occur after acute stress. These changes, however, are not as discriminating as postulated. Dopaminergic, noradrenergic, adrenergic and serotenergic neurons participate, albeit at different firing rates with different results. Perhaps it is relative differences rather than absolute stimulating responses that help determine, at a distance, the hormone response.

A second piece of evidence may be inferred from a consideration of the meaning of the event. Psychologically speaking, fight–flight is a less stable response than helplessness/hopelessness. It may be that the former equates with anxiety as the affective component of arousal and the latter with depression as the affective component of loss of control.

If this were the case, the challenge tests to neurotransmitter pathways using pharmacologically active substances with specificity for different central nervous system receptor sites should provide a way forward in differentiating neurotransmitter responses to life experiences.

To date the only studies which show that such investigations are possible have been concerned with identifying the role of neurotransmitters in adult depression (e.g. Checkley *et al.*, 1986; Cowen and Anderson, 1986). At present this evidence shows that it is possible to delineate symptoms that are *not due* to stress. However, this approach to understanding the neuroendocrinology of stress and psychopathological disorders is encouraging. Experiments predicting the endocrine patterns as consequences of social stimuli would be worth while.

The association between endocrine response and psychopathology

Clearly much remains to be done before a coherent story of psychobiological mechanisms and response to stress can be elucidated.

Firstly, the majority of endocrine responses are to acute events and the immediacy of this effect may bear little relationship to the impact of events and difficulties occurring at different points in time. Although it is quite possible that change in sympathetic nervous system activity and its patterning with adrenocortical activity may help clarify matters in this regard, such work has yet to occur (Steptoe, 1987).

Secondly, pleasurable events can result in catecholamine responses of the same order and magnitude as unpleasurable events, generally postulated to be associated with psychiatric disorders (Rose, 1980).

Thirdly, there is a marked lack of specificity between different forms of psychiatric disorders and endocrine responses. By and large, this seems to be because psychological mechanisms associated with appraisal, decision-making and coping (e.g. the use of denial) significantly influence both psychopathological signs and symptoms as well as endocrine responses (Rutter, 1983b).

In other words, present findings suggest that single endocrine responses may not help in identifying specific patterns of developmental psychopathology. Indeed it may be that alterations in endocrine responses to stressful circumstances are adaptive and helpful, perhaps working as regulatory mechanisms in adapting the body to change under conditions of life difficulties.

Clearly there is a paucity of information concerning brain mechanisms and their potential associations with cognitive–emotional functioning. The development of any theory specifying the type of stressor, its psychological meaning and associated changes in neuroendocrinological response is not yet a viable proposition. There is, however, sufficient evidence to encourage further research in this area. The ubiquitous nature of hormone activity does, however, suggest important biological roles in an organism's response to stress. The role of neuroendocrine mechanisms may be related to adaptive protective and coping reactions to stressful experiences as well as to the formation of distress responses in psychiatric disorder.

Recent investigations, for example, confirm that in schoolchildren neuroendocrine profiles may be different between individuals at times of examination stress (Tennes et al., 1986). In particular, associations between low aggression, poor achievement, low restlessness, low intelligence and low catecholamines was found predominantly in 8-year-old girls. The clinical significance of this is not readily apparent. Nevertheless these behaviour profiles will be less conspicuous and therefore less likely to receive attention than aggressiveness in boys.

These findings support the argument that there is a complex association between patterns of endocrine activity and patterns of human behaviour that warrants further investigation.

Overall, recent studies on children confirm that there are differential responses amongst behavioural and endocrine measures (Tennes and Kreye, 1985; Tennes et al., 1986). There is also the suggestion that personality and temperamental factors may play a greater role in hormone release and perhaps mediate between social stresses and neuroendocrine or hormonal response. For example, endocrine release may reflect a biological coping response to stressful situations and be more closely associated with temperamental characteristics of the child than the form of particular psychopathologies. In a study investigating the endocrine response of normal 7–8-year-olds to routine classroom examinations, cortisol release was better accounted for by personality and behavioural variables than by the stresses caused by the examination task (Tennes and Kreye, 1985). Cortisol release appears to be positively correlated with social competence and negatively correlated with aggression or hostility (Mattson, Gross and Hall, 1971; Tennes and Kreye, 1985). Similarly, noradrenaline release is positively correlated with mentally challenging situations requiring alertness (Lundeberg and Frankenhauser, 1980). If fear and anxiety accompany mental effort a rise in cortisol as well as noradrenaline is seen. In healthy Swedish children, those who responded with higher noradrenaline levels performed better than those whose levels decreased in the same situations (Frankenhauser and Johansson, 1975). Swedish children also had positive correlations between noradrenaline release, social competence and low aggression.

These studies did not investigate persistent responses to repeated emotional stimulus and the child's method of response to the environmental demands. This is important since it has been shown that anxiety arousing situations involving novelty and arousal stimulate production of cortisol, but individuals with good coping abilities, such as problem-solving or comprehension of situations, may show no alteration or even suppression of cortisol (Levine, 1983).

The findings by Tennes et al. (1986) confirm that endocrine responses in normal children reflect more closely the child's responses to situations. Both amine systems correlate positively with social affiliative behaviour. Noradrenaline correlated negatively with inattentiveness but positively with aggression. Noradrenaline also correlated negatively with restlessness.

These correlations with behavioural styles indicate that before we can identify significant associations between neuroendocrine systems and psychopathologies we need to take into account individual differences in endocrine activity, psychological trait and coping factors, and to control for these associations in analyses on disturbed groups. If associations exist between endocrine responses and psychiatric symptoms after these associations have been taken into account, then we may have good reason to investigate potential causal links between endocrine systems and psychiatric symptoms. Certainly further research along these lines is urgently needed.

Finally, there is evidence from research in non-human primates and from some studies in adults that social dominance may be an important variable in sexual and aggressive behaviour (Herbert, 1987). The role of competition and achievement and concomitant stress of success and failure in children's lives may covary with hormone response, for example around puberty. Recent studies have confirmed that levels of sex hormones covary with alterations in mood states in adolescents. Low testosterone and rises in oestradiol are reported during negative mood states in non-clinical girls. The relationship is not a simple one and complex interactions exist with social adversities, including life events and difficulties, as well as with behavioural styles (Brooks-Gunn and Warren, 1989; Wilson and Cairns, 1988). These preliminary findings do not indicate the direction of effects but suggest that further research investigating the role of sex hormones, monoamines, and social adversities in adolescents would be worth while.

STRESS AND THE IMMUNE SYSTEM

The central nervous system and adrenomedullary and adrenocorticoid hormonal systems have begun to be linked in a causal chain of biochemical events activated by psychological responses to social stimuli. A second biological system has been investigated as a potential stress related responder to the immune system.

The central nervous system and the immune system are major integrative networks now known to be interrelated and to be influenced by ageing and development (Schleiffer *et al.*, 1986; Buzzetti, McLoughlin and Scaro *et al.*, 1989).

The immune system

The immune system is a complex organisation of blood cells (lymphocytes) responsible for the maintenance and integrity of the organism in relation to foreign substances such as bacteria and viruses. Two sets of white blood cells are responsible for the majority of immune responses. The T lymphocyte, primarily involved in cell mediated immunity, and the B lymphocyte, primarily involved in humoral immunity.

An immunologic response develops when a lymphocyte recognises a foreign substance in the body called an antigen. Lymphocytes attach to antigens at specific receptor sites on the cell surface, which thereby stimulates the cell and effectively neutralises the foreign substance. This binding of antigen also stimulates a process of cell division and proliferation, permanently increasing the number of circulating lymphocytes with this specific antigen binding capacity.

The genetic information in each lymphocyte commits itself to develop a specific reaction by rearranging its structure to encircle and 'fit' the arrangement of the antigen structure like two jigsaw pieces. The result is a highly diverse system of cells in humans and animals with B and T lymphocytes recognising many millions of different antigenic structures.

B-cell function

The B cell's role is primarily secretory; this is termed humoral immunity. Through a process of stimulation and cell proliferation and resultant differentiation into plasma cells, these cells produce antibodies which are antigen specific; they are known as immunoglobulins. Five major classes of immunoglobulins have so far been described. IgG forms about 75 per cent of the immunoglobulin population and contains most of the normal human plasma antibodies. IgA is involved in the protection of body surfaces and is found in mucous secretions of gut and respiratory tract as well as in milk and colostrum. IgA and, in smaller amounts, IgM and IgD are found in response to a wide variety of antigens. IgE is the reogenic antibody binding to another cell in the blood: the mast cell. Under this condition mast cells release chemicals which mediate in hypersensitivity (allergic) reactions. These mediators include histamine.

T-cell function

T cells do not secrete antibodies but participate in the immune process directly (cell-mediated immunity). T lymphocytes passing through tissues are sensitised to antigens. They enter the lymphatic system of vessels and pass to a lymph node. In the cortex follicles of a lymph node they proliferate and differentiate. They are then released and recognise, bind and remove (lysis) anti-gens. They also release chemicals involved in the destruction of antigens. These cytotoxic chemicals (such as interferon) are capable of destroying antigens. A macrophage inhibition factor (MIF) is also released, which promotes the aggre-gation of T-cells in the antigenic locus to maximise the cell-mediated immunity process.

The function of immunity

The primary protective function of B cells is against infection by bacteria. At times, however, the response can be unwanted and pathological; asthma and anaphylactic shock are examples. Occasionally the body's own cells become recognised as antigens. Under these circumstances pathological auto-immune disorders may occur, such as systemic lupus erythematosus. The mechanisms of many of the pathological responses of immunity remains largely unclear.

In contrast, T-cell-mediated immunity appears to be predominantly involved in protection against organisms which invade host cells, such as viruses, fungi and intracellular bacteria. T-cell immunity also responds to foreign grafts and is important in transplantation secretions (rejection). T cells are also involved in immune responses to neoplastic conditions.

There are a considerable number of interdependent regulatory processes be-tween these two immune systems. There are a number of cellular and chem-ical controlling and releasing factors included in the immune process of both cell types as well as T and B interactions. Thus T-helper and T-suppression cells have been identified in facilitating and inhibiting T- and B-cell effec-tor responses. Lymphocyte activating factors known as interleukins have been identified as chemical mediators. IL-1 induces T-helper cells which themselves produce a cell growth factor IL-2, stimulating cellular proliferation. T and B cells have their own specific differentiation lymphokines.

A third small group of cells have now been recognised as natural killer (NK) cells, since they mediate in cytotoxic reactions without the need for prior sen-sitisation.

Advances in laboratory techniques have allowed detailed investigation of the immune system (e.g. Diamond, Yelton and Schorff, 1981). The potential asso-ciations between the immune system and stress have been investigated in both animals and humans by examining changes in immune function under different stressful conditions.

Concepts of stress and immunity

Investigations into the influence of stress on the immune system arise from the belief that stressful experiences may enhance or interact with an individual's vulnerability to certain diseases. This enhancing role implies two important conditions: first, diseases which interfere with immunologic mechanisms will result in significantly greater sensitivity to adversity in the environment. Secondly, the impact of social stresses will adversely influence the immune system, thereby increasing the risk of disease.

Experimental models of stress, immunity and illness

Experimental investigations in a number of animal models, including rats, mice, guinea-pigs and to a lesser extent monkeys, demonstrate complex effects of stress on disease susceptibility (Justice, 1985). In particular, alterations in the animal's environment can be associated with increased susceptibility to a number of illnesses, including viral diseases and tumours. Adverse alterations in immune function were found in the majority of affected animals (Joaso and McKenzie, 1976; Rogers, Dubey and Reich, 1979).

The acute stresses involved, however, were often physical stimuli (noise, shock, movement) and it is apparent that immune responses are influenced by many different qualities of the events, including timing and duration. For example, studies in animals have shown that *acute exposure* to a physical stress can produce suppression of humoral immunity (via a decrease in antibody synthesis), *repeated exposure*, however, may enhance the same immunologic responses (Hill, Greer and Felsenfeld, 1967; Hirata-Hibi, 1967; Solomon and Amkraut, 1981). Similar findings have been reported for effects on cellular immunity (Keller *et al.*, 1983).

Experiments more analogous to human stresses have been carried out with monkeys, indicating that acute separation experiences of infant monkeys from their mothers produces suppression of cellular immunity from previous normal levels. Reunion with mother, however, results in a return to normal levels (Reite, Horbeck and Hoffman, 1981; Laudenslager, Capitanio and Reite, 1985). It is not clear if prolonged separation (i.e. weeks) would have resulted in some form of maladaptive response in immunologic function or a similar response to acute separations and a return to normal levels.

Quality of early life experiences in general, however, may be important in the development of biological mechanisms. Animal studies have led some workers to postulate, for example, that the absence of an adequate ongoing mother–infant relationship (at least in rats and guinea-pigs), not just separation, may result in a generalised defect in the maturation of hypothalamic function (Keller *et al.*, 1980, 1983; Ackerman, 1981).

Separations of this nature have also been shown to decrease levels of ornithine decarboxylase, an enzyme required for protein synthesis, and growth hormone, which is required for normal development of the immune system (Butler, Suskind and Schanberg, 1978; Kuhn, Buttier and Schorberg,1978).

These animal studies demonstrate associations between maturation of biological systems and social experiences in non-primates. There are, however, no equivalent studies in humans. Indeed many infants are born with a higher level of immune maturation compared to rats or mice and may be less sensitive to impairments due to separation or poor parent–infant relations. We know very little as yet of the interplay between life experiences and neonatal humoral and immune development.

Links between adversity, immunity and neuroendocrine function

As already discussed, the endocrine system is highly responsive to life experiences. Secretion of corticosteroids has long been considered the mechanism of stress-induced modulation of immunity and related disease processes (Selye, 1956; Riley, 1981). Recent findings, however, indicate that adrenergic mechanisms may be involved by suppressing lymphocyte numbers (Keller et al., 1983). Other studies have shown that circulatory levels of thyroid hormones, growth hormone and gonadotrophins are altered by social stresses and have been reported to modulate immune functions (Stein, Keller and Schleifer, 1981; Schleifer et al., 1985). There is also some evidence to show that the hypothalamus, which plays a critical role in neuroendocrine functions, also modulates humoral and cellular immunity (Keller et al., 1980; Cross et al., 1982; Stein, Schleifer and Keller, 1982). Additionally, an immunoregulatory role has been suggested for stress-related peptides such as B-endorphin (Gilman et al., 1982; Sharit et al., 1984).

A direct link between the central nervous system and immunological function has been suggested by the demonstration of nerve endings in the thymus, spleen and lymph nodes (Bullock and Moore, 1980; Giron, Crutcher and Davis, 1980). The possibility is raised that neuronal innervation of immunocompetent tissues may be important for immune responses, and the absence of such pathways through disease, trauma or congenital deficiencies may compromise some immune functions and stress responses. Finally, there has been speculation that some lymphocytes may release neuroregulators which exert inhibitory actions on central noradrenergic neurones and often have the facility to release an ACTH-like substance following a viral infection (Smith, Meyer and Blalock, 1982). These experimental studies suggest a neuroimmune regulatory feedback system associated with aminergic circuits in the CNS. They demonstrate the potential for life experiences to exert effects at a biochemical and physiological level.

Clinical studies of stress and immune function

Disease states

There has been a long-standing interest in the relationship between mental functioning, immunity and particular diseases, such as tuberculosis and cancer.

Overall, it has to be said that findings for a causal role of life stresses, acute or long-standing, in physical disease are not convincing (Greer, 1983). Invariably it proves difficult to distinguish stresses that may be consequences rather than causes of illnesses. This is particularly difficult in disorders with chronic fluctuating courses making onset of disorder difficult to determine.

What seems more plausible, and of more relevance to clinical practice, is the influence of life stress on the course of illness and disease.

Infections and stress have been the subject of a number of investigations. An important early study was that of Meyer and Haggerty (1962), who followed prospectively over 12 months 100 children from 16 families, undertaking throat cultures for streptococci every 2 weeks and having the family keep a diary of upsetting events occurring for family members and child.

Although only a quarter of streptococcal infections were preceded by such stressors, the risk of infection increased several times after a stressful event. This pioneering study is one of the few to successfully demonstrate a link between social stress and infection. It may well be that a mediating factor was an adverse influence on the immune system, but this was not investigated.

Recent studies in adults continue to propose links between social stress, immune deficiency and infections. The common investigatory method is to show an increase in undesirable life events and a decrease in hormonal and/or cellular immunity in a group of patients with identifiable infections. Of particular interest has been the prospective study of groups of young adults by collecting concurrent information on life events and measuring antibody titres and immune competence. Thus the 20 per cent of West Point cadets who were identified as stressed by examinations, and who achieved poor results, were significantly more likely to become seropositive for infectious mononucleosis, with a quarter of these being diagnosed as clinically ill (Kasl, Evans and Weiderman, 1979). Similarly, women experiencing stress and separation following divorce, and medical students with work stress and reporting loneliness, were all significantly more likely to have high antibody titres to herpes viruses (Kiecolt-Glaser et al., 1987; Glaser et al., 1988). The important suggestion here is that only women and students who reported both stress and psychological disturbance had altered immune status. Other studies have suggested that a number of psychological factors, including social stresses and personality, may precipitate relapse of herpes infections (Luborsky et al., 1976; Goldmeier and Johnston, 1982).

These studies demonstrate potential links between infections and stress in some cases and suggest that a mediating role may be played by a compromised immune system. Of course we cannot say for certain the direction of this effect, i.e. we do not know if immune defects and social stress were not themselves consequences of infections.

Such studies have not been carried out on children and would seem worth while. We can speculate that such a mechanism may have been relevant in Meyer and Haggerty's study.

Life events and lymphocyte function

Bereavement

There is evidence in adults (though not in children) that bereavement increases the risk for later ill health and early mortality (Helsing and Szklo, 1981; Parkes, 1985). This risk may be greater for men than women. A link between bereavement and altered immunity has been suggested following the findings that decreased lymphocyte function occurred in bereaved persons compared with matched controls (Bontrap, et al., 1977).

Bontrap's study was of interest because there were no significant differences between 33 pairs of controls and bereaved subjects in lymphocyte suppression at 2 weeks. Significant differences were apparent, however, at 8 weeks. Furthermore, lymphocyte suppression could not be accounted for by alterations in endocrine function. More recently, a prospective study of spouses of 15 women with advanced metastatic carcinoma of the breast were studied longitudinally for 6 months until the death of spouse and after the bereavement for a 12-month period (Schleiffer et al., 1983, 1985). Both T- and B-cell lymphocyte stimulation was depressed in the spouses 2 months after bereavement compared with their own pre-bereavement responses. The absolute number of T and B cells were unaffected, showing that it is the immune response that is impaired. Pre-bereavement stimulation was the same for spouses and age and sex matched controls. Follow-up showed that in the majority of, but not all, cases spouse's lymphocyte stimulation returned to normal by 12 months. A similar finding has been reported for other populations of bereaved adult males (Linn, Linn and Jersen, 1982).

The evidence suggests a link between the stress of bereavement and immune dysfunction and provides preliminary evidence for a psycho-immunologic mediation of increased illness susceptibility among the bereaved. The link, however, is unlikely to be direct, and processes linking naturally occurring stresses and lymphocyte activity require considerable further investigation.

Firstly, a wide variety of physical factors, including nutrition, activity, sleep and drug use, influence lymphocyte function (Schleiffer et al., 1985). Secondly, depressed mood, which may result in all of the aforementioned physical changes, occurs in bereaved persons (Murray-Parkes and Stevenson-Hinde, 1982). Since depression is associated with significant change in neuroendocrine function, it may be that bereavement exerts an effect on the immune system through psychiatric disorder and concurrent neuroendocrine dysfunction in certain individuals.

This would argue for a change in CNS activity mediating alterations in lymphocyte activity. Present evidence suggests that this mechanism is more plausible than a direct stress–immune response (Schleiffer et al., 1983, 1985, 1986).

As yet, there are no clear clues to help disentangle the interaction between stress, mood and neuroendocrine-immune changes. There is certainly substantial evidence for neurochemical disturbance in depressive illness, which in some cases may be aetiological (Deakin, 1986).

Prospective studies investigating the neuroendocrine and immune functions of children who have been bereaved as well as their social and family adjustment may help to elucidate the potential contribution of alterations in their physicochemical function to mood disturbance.

Other events and immunity

Few other natural events associated with loss, separation or disappointment have been studied. Indeed the overriding absence of applying psychological constructs to social events has diminished the opportunity to advance knowledge in this area so far.

A number of authors have used life-change stress measured from self-report inventories of recent life events. The most frequent investigations have been between academic pressure and immune functioning in medical graduates. Overall, the findings confirm an association between the stress of examination pressure, suppression of lymphocyte stimulation, impaired antibody formation and a rise in minor respiratory tract infections in some cases in the 6 weeks following the examination (Dorian et al., 1982, 1986; Jemmott et al., 1983). In the majority of subjects immune function returned to normal within 2 weeks of examination. Students with high distress scores before and after examination were most susceptible to infections.

These studies provide some independent support for the impact of acute stressors on immune function. The inference, however, from examinations and bereavement is that personality factors, longer-term adversity and mood disturbance may be important intervening variables between stressful event and immune dysfunction.

Chronic stress and immunity

Of greater importance for stress–immune paradigms in humans would be the finding that chronic difficulties produced alterations in immune responses that were sustained.

Loneliness as self-reported by students and low levels of social support in elderly women have both been reported as correlating highly with depressed lymphocyte (killer-cell type) activity and raised antibody titres to herpes (Kiecolt-Glaser et al., 1984; Glaser et al., 1988). The findings of raised urinary cortisol in the students again suggests that depressed mood may arise as an intervening variable, particularly in view of the evidence relating absence of social support and poor confiding relationships to depression (Brown and Harris, 1978). It has also been suggested that continuing stresses, rather than acute transient shifts in immune competence, result in progressive decline of lymphocyte function, especially for those cells associated with the recognition and removal of tumour and virus infected cells (Locke *et al.*, 1984).

Similar findings have been reported from a 12-month longitudinal prospective study of accountants rated as highly stressed. In this latter study the strongest correlates of lymphocyte dysfunction and stress occurred in those accountants who were identified as hard drinking, work conscientious and ambitious. The strength of the association was greatest in the group of accountants identified as chronically stressed and highly symptomatic, the latter findings tended to occur in those subjects who exhibited extremes of the Type A behaviour pattern and who reported work overload, job dissatisfaction and failed to reach their personal goals (Dorian and Garfinkel, 1987).

Chronic stress may therefore predispose some individuals to immune difficulties, perhaps increasing their susceptibility to infection. Mediating roles for temperament, mastery of tasks and coping abilities, as well as psychiatric disorder, are all apparent and as yet uninvestigated.

In conclusion, the animal studies and some work on adults suggests a link between external stress and biological mechanisms. It is equally apparent, however, that the nature of these associations is insufficiently characterised to draw any substantial conclusions. In short, we do not have a coherent neuroendocrine–immune model of stress.

At present too many basic questions remain to be answered. Firstly, there is the non-specificity of responses between biological functions and life experiences. Despite elegant animal models for monoamine pathways being activated for different forms of stressor, we do not have studies in adults or children to support this work. Some support, however, for pursuing these areas of investigation further is derived from the greater specificity of neurochemical disturbance to depression (Checkley *et al.*, 1986; Deakin and Crow, 1986; Puig-Antich, 1986; Foreman and Goodyer, 1988).

Secondly, the regulatory mechanisms within the biological systems themselves remain largely unknown.

Thirdly, little research to date has explored the specificity between types of life experience and biological response. Whether or not there are long-term effects on neuroendocrine systems following life events is poorly understood.

Fourthly, it is unclear what clinical significance can be attributed to the behavioural effects of these mechanisms. Present evidence seems to point to an important role for stressful events and difficulties in the maintenance and adjustment of some illnesses which may influence monoamine and immune systems. This is a quite different model, however, from postulating a causal relationship such as social stress ⟶ neuroendocrine–immune system ⟶ subsequent psychiatric disorder. The evidence for this is unconvincing at best, and at worst misleading.

At present the quantitative changes described in biological systems may have very little impact on the overall risk of developing an illness. Investigating the patterning of these neuroendocrine–immune responses and their associations with behaviour and mental disorder in the presence and absence of social adversities would seem worth while.

Longitudinal studies in which behaviour, hormones and immunity are monitored concurrently in relation to the onset of pathophysiologically distinct health events are required. An epidemiological approach would require large samples as the prevalence of disorder is likely to be low. Such studies are expensive, time-consuming and difficult to undertake. Population-based studies can and should be complemented by clinical studies focused on specific clinical groups, such as anxious or depressed children or children with infections, as in the Meyer and Haggerty study. Animal studies will continue to provide important information concerning the role of experimentally induced stresses on the neuroendocrine and immune processes. At present we are in no position to generate a theory of neuroendocrine–immune–stress relationships in human development.

It seems timely to initiate the appropriate studies to help decide the relevance of neuroendocrine and immune systems in mediating the effects of life experiences and to determine their relative contribution to developmental psychopathology.

SUMMARY

1. Catecholamine release occurs as a non-specific response to a range of socially desirable and undesirable, as well as physical, stimuli.
2. Glucocorticoid hormones are interrelated with catecholamines but this association is not well understood especially in man. Cortisol hypersecretion occurs in affective disorders in children but its role in stress mediated disorders is unclear.
3. Catecholamines and glucocorticoid release have psychological and behavioural concomitants but no specific associations have yet been elucidated.
4. Immune dysfunction in lymphocytes may occur as an indirect effect of life experiences perhaps through the effect of lowered mood. As yet no firm evidence exists for this in young people.
5. No coherent theory linking endocrine–immunity and behaviour can yet be generated. Links between glucocorticoids and lymphocytes have been established and there are suggestions that behavioural links are likely, but the mechanisms have yet to be elucidated.

Chapter 6

Arousal, Emotions and Temperament

INTRODUCTION

In the last decade a revival of interest and research has occurred in the field of emotion. Some of this work has focused on investigating the mechanisms determining emotional responses to stressful events and circumstances. For example, recent findings suggest that in pre-school children emotional responses to stresses may influence the way children think and subsequently behave (e.g. Cummings, Zahn-Waxler and Radke-Yarrow, 1984; Pettit, Dodge and Brown, 1988).

In other words, some components of emotion may be causes of cognitive and behavioural responses to social adversities, whilst other emotional factors may be consequences of such adversities and subsequently influence cognitions and behaviour. This chapter considers the relationships between emotion and life experiences under three broad headings:

1. The influence of life experiences on normal emotional development.
2. The expression of emotions as a consequence of life experiences.
3. The association between emotions as symptoms, temperament, and life experiences.

THEORIES OF EMOTIONAL DEVELOPMENT

Introduction

There has been a rich history of the investigation and description of emotion, which gained its momentum from psychoanalytic theory and practice. Perhaps some of the loss of interest in this area has been because psychoanalysis has not fulfilled the aims of its early protagonists, neither as an effective treatment for many psychiatric conditions nor as a theory of psychological development (Eagle, 1984). A recent revival of interest amongst developmental scientists in the significance of emotion for normal development, and the publication of research findings indicating that some forms of psychotherapy in children which involve alterations of emotional state are effective, are sufficient grounds, however, for investigating further the emotions at the level of theory and practice.

Classical psychoanalytic theory has had emotion in a central explanatory role for psychiatric disorder (Breuer and Freud, 1893). Freud's own dissatisfaction, however, with emotions as causes of symptoms is apparent with his 'instinct' or 'drive' theories in which *abnormal affect* arises as a result of changes in *instinctual emotional drives* (e.g. Freud, 1954). Emotion therefore occupied an ambivalent position in psychoanalytic theory. Distinguishing between the primary instinctual emotions of normal development and the abnormal emotions of psychopathology was never truly clarified. Hence the difficulties with the reliability and validity of psychoanalytic classification of psychopathologies in childhood and adolescence (Freud, 1970).

In contrast to the writings of clinical psychoanalysts, experimental psychologists came, over a number of years, to see emotions as forms of stimulus that can be identified behaviourally as gestures or expressions, and measured through psychophysiological techniques such as skin response and heart-rate. In other words, emotions were merely terms for categorising behavioural events or stimuli dependent on social learning (Skinner, 1953).

This view prevailed in various degrees from the 1930s to the early 1970s amongst many experimental psychologists. Investigation increasingly focused on behaviour and physiological events.

Developmental psychologists too had shown interest in emotions, but mainly as an index for some other psychological phenomenon, usually a cognitive process (Schachter and Singer, 1962). In other words, cognitions were considered to come first in the flow of information and only after evaluations were made was there a subjective experience of emotion. In other words, the ontogeny of normal emotional development and behaviour was seen as a consequence of cognitive development.

Emotions no longer had a causal role in psychological theory. They had become, at best, transitional links between other psychobiological processes; at worst they were epiphenomena and therefore of minimal interest.

Modern perspectives on emotions

In recent times, however, the idea that emotional experience is purely an outcome of cognitive experience has been challenged. Emotion in modern theory is viewed in terms of it having an innate biological origin which is not necessarily dependent on social learning (Izard, Kagan and Zajonc, 1984). For example, no social learning is necessary for the reception or production of facial and gestural signals in rhesus monkeys or human infants (Ekman and Friessen, 1972; Kenny *et al.*, 1979; Boucher and Carlsson, 1980; Mendelson, Haith and Goldman-Rakic, 1982).

Three features can be identified in the present theories on the origins of emotions.

Emotion as a neurophysiological event

Firstly, some theorists emphasise the biological characteristic of emotions by defining the existence of emotion in neurophysiological and neurochemical terms. By so doing, emotion is seen as a motivator of cognition and action (Izard, Kagan and Zajonc, 1984). Emotions at this level of experience cannot be assigned psychological terms as they do not register in cognitive processes. They have been referred to as feeling tones in the sense that they register physiologically and have effects on motor function such as muscle activity, heart-rate and eye blink (Kagan, 1984).

Emotions as controllers and facilitators of thought and action

Secondly, emotions may have regulatory effects on physiological, cognitive and behavioural aspects of an individual's response to the environment (Campos and Barrett, 1984). Under these conditions innate emotional components may influence the quality and form of children's thoughts and behaviours under different social conditions, including responses to events and ongoing experiences. Moreover, this affective system can be seen as playing an integrative role in psychological functioning. Thus emotion may be influenced and altered by cognitions and behaviours, but it is neither dependent on nor secondary to cognitions.

Emotions as consequences of social experiences

Thirdly, emotions can be aroused at any stage of the cognitive process. Thus whether children are appraising, registering, encoding, retrieving or inferring about a piece of information, feelings may be aroused (Zajonc and Markus, 1984). The lack of a consistent relationship between stages of thinking and forms of feeling suggest that pathways of emotional and cognitive processes in response to external social stimuli are not the same.

Zajonc and Markus (1984) represent perhaps the most 'cognitive free' of the emotion theorists. They argue that we can like or be afraid of something without knowing what it is. For these authors affect arises and is controlled by the limbic system of the brain, which phylogenetically precedes the neocortex and, therefore, the evaluation of language and those cognitive processes dependent on language. It is a system not subject to attentional control, very rapid in responding and relying primarily on verbal channels.

They propose that the motor system may be a point of contact between affect and cognitive systems. They suggest that 'affect is not always transformed into semantic content but often encoded in visceral and muscular signals. Under these circumstances we would expect information contained in feelings to be disguised, organised, categorised, represented and retrieved somewhat differently than information having direct verbal referents.'

These ideas remain speculative and require further investigation. Nevertheless, they provide an opportunity for exploring the nature of emotions and their relationships to cognitions. They also suggest that stressful experiences may be appraised and responded to emotionally without recourse to thinking. Such responses might, for example, include somatic and behavioural expressions of emotion.

Temperament and emotion

Temperament is not a new concept. It interested both the Greeks and the Chinese, who provide some of the earliest writings on this aspect of human biology. More recently modern scientific approaches have led to a considerable literature on this subject. Evidence from psychologists, physiologists and other neuroscientists is beginning to provide an integrative framework for the emotional, cognitive and social aspects of personality (Derryberry and Rothbart, 1984; Kohnstamm, 1986). Temperament is important because it may represent the development of emotional-cognitive processes and therefore reflect the intrinsic traits an individual has. These traits may in turn determine the emotional-cognitive responses children have to social experiences. Three theoretical positions will be briefly mentioned.

General arousal theory

Firstly, emotionality and temperament can be considered in terms of general arousal of the cortex. This physiological model of temperament has been elucidated in Eysenck's theories of personality (Eysenck, 1981). The cortical arousal model argues that individuals differ in their basic physiology and consequently in their optimal level of stimulation. A relationship between optimal arousal and stimulation is sought by the individual and expressed in behavioural style. Individuals will be motivated to avoid stimulation that results in either under- or over-arousal and to approach stimulation that results in optimal arousal. These premises owe their origins to some extent to earlier optimal level concepts of the relationship between drive and central nervous system function (Hebb, 1955).

Other arousal theorists have suggested that cognitive processes mediate between arousal and stimulus, and that varied emotional states are a consequence. In other words, arousal signals cognitive processes which determine the priority to which an individual will appraise external stimulation and therefore influence behavioural response (Mandler 1975).

Shortcomings of arousal theory.   Recent research has shown that the physiology of arousal is considerably more complicated than at first thought. The nervous system needs to be considered as multi-dimensional with considerable differentiation in anatomical and neurochemical structure and function. Components of the system may serve different psychological functions (Ciaranello, 1983; Derryberry and Rothbart, 1984).

The pathways are not simply those of arousal but also involve inhibitory and modulatory neural networks both within the brain and the peripheral nervous system. External stimuli may act on one or more of these networks. It is apparent that physiological, biochemical, endocrine and psychological pathways are not only more complex than previously considered but also influence each other in highly complicated regulatory ways which remain unclear (Derryberry and Rothbart, 1984; Kohnstamm, 1986). The assumption that arousal *per se* elicits emotional response is questioned by at least two separate sets of research. Firstly, experiments have demonstrated that emotions in response to social stimuli elicit physiological changes in the autonomic nervous system. Alterations in facial and vocal behaviours, as well as heart-rate, respiration, cardiovascular and skin changes, are all examples of physiological responses (Gallistel, 1980; Izard, 1982). Secondly, ethological studies demonstrate that motivation plays an important role in how information from the outside world is detected, processed and subsequently responded to (Hinde, 1979, 1987). Accordingly physiological arousal may be secondary to emotional changes—themselves a consequence of social processes.

General emotion–arousal theory and behaviour

In general emotion–arousal theory, emotional systems are viewed as motivators of central nervous system activity. Different emotions can result in arousal and may involve complex neurochemical and physiological pathways which determine or regulate behavioural expression (Kohnstamm, 1986).

The simplest position has been described as one of a relative balance between two emotional systems in the limbic area of the brain. Both systems influence the cortical arousal of an individual. One, the behavioural inhibition system, is activated as a consequence of the appraisal of signals of punishment, non-reward and novelty. This system suppresses ongoing behavioural patterns, activates the cortex and directs attention to the external stimulus.

Another system using the same principles is activated as a consequence of signals of reward and non-punishment by facilitating approach behaviour (Gray, 1982).

In general emotion–arousal theory, interactions are proposed between reward-approach and punishment-avoidance mechanisms and different behavioural patterns are postulated to be associated with different neurochemical systems in the brain (Zuckerman, 1979). Further suggestions have been made concerning how these emotion–arousal systems result in different psychopathological syndromes, such as depression and anxiety (Gray, 1982). The theorising of the associations between emotions and physiology has begun to indicate the possible existence of multiple physiological systems with the potential for discrete circuits for certain types of emotion (Zuckerman, 1979; Kohnstamm, 1986). In childhood, the work of Kagan and his colleagues is an example of emotion-behaviour theory. This group have identified two groups of children who are differentiated by their emotion-behaviour style in the second and third years of life. One group are described as behaviourally inhibited and are characterised by a cautious and shy approach to novel stimuli. The other are described as behaviourally uninhibited and are characterised by a fearless and outgoing approach to novel stimuli (Garcia-Coll, Kagan and Reznick, 1984). These characteristics may reflect different expressions of different physiological responses to novel stimuli, and the activating mechanisms which control responses may be set at different physiological thresholds for different social experience.

The biological component of individual differences may therefore occur as a consequence of independent emotion-arousing systems with different priorities of behavioural expression in different individuals. These as yet tentative hypotheses also suggest the possibilities for genetic control mechanisms on individual circuits in the brain.

These patterns may have multiple autonomic central nervous system and somatic regulatory systems. It would be expected that in such a complex system expression of emotion and behaviour would consist of many mechanisms rather than a single one. This makes some intuitive sense in that both adults and children tend to report a range or cluster of emotions, feelings and behaviours, and most concepts of personality and temperament reflect not a single unit but a clustering of variables said to identify a discrete pattern of personality type or temperamental style (Thomas and Chess, 1977).

Specific emotion–arousal theory

There have been recent attempts to extend and consolidate general emotion–arousal theory.

At the end of the nineteenth century, observations on faces led Charles Darwin to establish a theory of human emotion which suggested that facial expression represented the external component of internal feeling states (Darwin, 1872). Modern research procedures examining emotions through facial expression have identified ten emotions as basic or fundamental (Izard, 1977, 1982). These basic emotions (interest, joy, surprise, distress, anger, fear, shame, disgust, contempt and guilt) are seen as arising from underlying neural systems with defined neuromuscular patterns and associated with distinct subjective experiences. As development proceeds there is increasing co-ordination of emotions and facial expression, so that from basic emotions are derived complex emotions such as anxiety, depression, love and hostility. In addition, as cognitive processes develop there is a continuing integration of emotion–cognition complexes resulting in relatively stable affective–cognitive styles (often referred to as structures). It has been suggested that there are hierarchical relationships between physiological, chemical, emotional, cognitive and behavioural expressions of these processes (Gallistel, 1980). It remains to be seen if such a hierarchy is present or not. Perhaps the most important difference between general and specific emotion–arousal theories is that physiological arousal is de-emphasised in the genesis of emotion. Some form of relationship between these processes clearly exists, however, for example, emotional processes influence the selectivity of perception and thinking (Izard, 1977).

Overall, the present position suggests that the concept of temperament is difficult to define and we do not have a firm view about its nature or effects. At present we can say that temperament has its basis in a multiple system of emotions and behaviours which have innate physicochemical origins. The precise nature of the relationship between these factors and the mechanisms governing their widely different emotional and behavioural expressions in individuals are far from clear. It is not, however, a 'closed biological system'. Social interpersonal factors may substantially influence the development and form of temperamental traits during childhood.

Emotions and the developing infant

Present thinking and research into the area of emotions and development indicates that the innate biology of the affective system may be complete at birth (Izard, 1984). Whilst this may be so, it is far from clear what factors influence the development of behaviours associated with this emotional 'hard-wiring'. For example, can alterations of the environment *in utero* determine the behavioural expression of this emotion physiology?

Some authors consider behaviours in the infant, such as crying, facial gestures and sucking, as expressions of feeling states, such as sadness, pleasure, fear and rage. Others interpret these early behaviours at a physiological rather than a psychological level of emotion (e.g. Emde, 1981). In other words, for many behavioural scientists, the development of psychological, differentiated and more complex forms of emotion is a developmental process. This process is likely to be related in some way to cognitive functioning, although how is far from clear (Sroufe, 1979a,b).

Thus the transformation of discharging moods in the infant (which communicate distress) into complex emotions such as pleasure and disappointment emerge with the infant's development of recall memory and increasingly sophisticated cognitive apparatus (Sroufe, 1979a,b). If, however, there is a true emotional system then independent effects of this system will persist. For example, certain forms of emotional-behaviour responses may be unrelated to the cognitive components of the appraisal of stressful events. Fear, alertness and rage may be examples. Additionally, such 'independent' emotions to stressful events and difficulties may carry behavioural consequences, such as withdrawal or flight, or physiological consequences, such as visceral effects, blood flow or alterations in hormonal or neuroendocrine functions. The appearance of different components of this emotional system may then be determined by their relative contribution to physiological function and the dynamic relationships between emotions, cognitions and behaviours. This suggests a complex pattern of relationships between different psychological and physiological systems in the body. As yet we know little about these complex interrelationships of function. Therefore our ability to predict their patterns of response to stressful life events and ongoing difficulties is unclear. Some clues, however, are available.

The physiology and psychology of behavioural inhibition

Activity in the hypothalamic–pituitary axis is usually increased following exposure to a novel event that cannot be appraised (see Chapters 4 and 5). Elevated monoamines, particularly cortisol but also noradrenaline, alterations in muscle tension with increased contraction and alterations in vocal sound occur. Recently these alterations in monoamines in the peripheral circulation have been correlated with behavioural inhibition in 6-year-old children to unfamiliar events or situations that pose a psychological challenge and cannot be handled without effort. Two cohorts of children were used who form part of a longitudinal study selected in the second year of life because of their cautious, shy, inhibited behaviour or their fearless, outgoing uninhibited behaviour to unfamiliar events (Kagan, Reznick, Snidman, 1987).

The study found these behavioural characteristics to be stable at the age of 6. In addition, more of the inhibited children showed signs of activation in monoamine systems and physiological circuits that are associated with a biological response to novelty. Whilst the findings did not demonstrate any specificity between physicochemical and behavioural systems they do suggest that the thresholds for responsivity in limbic and hypothalamic structures to unfamiliarity and challenge is lower for inhibited than uninhibited children. These findings provide some empirical basis for links between brain, emotion and behaviour, since it is emotion-behaviour characteristics that are the mutually exclusive criteria for the two groups of children in the study. Determining greater specificity between the physiological and behavioural systems seems an important task for the future. The results also indicate how many of the neuroendocrinological factors and mechanisms we discussed in Chapter 5 may be relevant in determining the style of emotion-behaviour response to social stimuli in children.

Emotion-behaviour styles and subsequent social adversities

The significance of early emotion-behaviour styles for later appraisal of social experience is not yet clear. From our overview of temperament, however, we need to examine the potential links between the persistence of emotion-behaviours that may become temperamental characteristics and those that do not, as well as the influence of such characteristics in the presence and absence of life events and difficulties at different ages and stages of development. Finally, we may need to examine patterns of emotional response at different ages.

It seems likely from the existing evidence that as development unfolds there is a complex patterning of differential responses of emotions and behaviours to stressful events and circumstances, which accounts for at least some of the different forms of expression of psychiatric disturbance at different ages to the same or similar life events and difficulties, such as those already discussed in previous chapters. The stability and constancy of certain emotion-behaviour patterns and the influence of cognitive devlopment on these psychological constructs is an important area for further research.

This brief overview and synopsis of the potential relationships between emotions, cognitions and behaviours does not do justice to the research and theory in this area of developmental psychology and further reading is recommended (see Izard, Kagan and Zajonc, 1984).

Type A Personality

Research in adults has identified a cluster of behavioural styles in some people which appear to mediate their response to environmental stimuli. These individuals are termed type A personalities and have excessive drive, an extreme sense of time urgency, competitiveness, aggression and hostility. Some children and adolescents exhibit these temperamental characteristics but it is not yet clear how such characteristics influence responses to environmental stimuli in younger people. However, some clues have been found in recent research.

Thus, type A individuals tend to respond to challenges with a greater increase in heart-rate and catecholamine secretion than other people (Lundeberg, 1986). In other words this cluster of behaviour styles has a correlate in the neuroendocrine system. It has been shown that everyday problems and environmental events contribute to the development of type A behaviour and its endocrine correlates. Present findings indicate that although type A adults, and perhaps children, are more reactive in response to environmental demands they do not differ from others in either their physiological baseline levels of circulating catecholamines or their type of behavioural response to stress.

For example, Glass and Constadd (1983) have shown that, during tasks which included competition, type A individuals only increased their catecholamine output to a higher level than control individuals when the competition was combined with harassment. In the absence of harassment raised catecholamine levels were present for all individuals. Similar experiments have confirmed this finding (Lundeberg, 1986).

Type A patterns of behaviour have been described in children from the age of 5 upwards and appear more commonly in boys (Lundeberg, 1986). Recent findings suggest that type A behaviour in adulthood may have its origins in childhood (Bergman and Magnusson, 1979).

It is not clear what the significance of type A characteristics in childhood are for psychopathology. Perhaps temperaments with differing clusters act as an intermediate variable between social adversities and psychopathology. Could, for example, type A characteristics interact with undesirable life events to increase the risk of conduct disorder? Alternatively, could the absence of type A characteristics increase the likelihood of emotional symptoms in the presence of undesirable events?

As well as the implications for psychopathology, type A characteristics in early childhood indicate an increased likelihood of repeatedly raised catecholamine levels exposing these children to elevated systolic blood pressure levels from an early age. Such temperamental characteristics may indirectly increase the risk of coronary heart disease and hypertension through neuroendocrine mechanisms later in life. The present evidence indicates that this is more likely in the presence of environmental adversity and shows the potentially important relationship between life experience, temperament and neuroendocrine factors in childhood as well as in adulthood.

SOCIAL INFLUENCES ON EMOTIONAL DEVELOPMENT

Everyday hassles and emotional development

The importance of understanding how the normal stresses and strains of life influence emotional development has been of interest to a number of researchers. In Chapter 2, for example, the problems of depression on a mother's ability to participate in the normative and stressful exchanges with her young child were described.

Naturalistic studies have been undertaken which have developed reliable and valid methods of measuring children's emotional reactions to emotional stimuli in their own homes and with their own caretakers (Zahn-Waxler and Radke-Yarrow, 1982). The results of these studies demonstrated that in infancy there appeared to be an increasing repertoire of emotional responses by the child when perceiving emotional events in their caretakers (Radke-Yarrow and Sherman, 1985). There appears to be a developmental progression of this increase. Thus at 10 months of age all children showed awareness of events by attending to them. Generalised distress to an undesirable life event appeared at 12 months, together with seeking and touching their care-giver. Somewhat later children imitated expressions of a distressed person, followed later still by attempts to intervene, indicating that they had processed the event and arrived at a decision to intervene. These behavioural interventions appeared to be aimed at diminishing the expression of distress in their caretaker.

The absence of an adequate comprehension of the social circumstances and meaning of distress may result in the child making incorrect interpretations about adults' responses and behaviours and therefore coming to a wrong behaviour decision.

In other words, distress in adults may represent a *reasonable* as well as an *unreasonable* form of response to a social event. In infancy the absence of cognitive development in relation to the capacity for relative emotional response to an event results in a likely 'all or nothing' response by the child. As cognitive factors appear with development, the child can enquire and receive an explanation for the adult's distress. This may modify the *behavioural expression* of his or her emotional response to distress but not necessarily the *emotional response* itself.

Therefore, as development proceeds the child engages in hypothesis testing about the reasons and purposes for distress. Cognitive processes, however, may not prevent emotional responses. They may modulate such responses as well as increase the options for an expansion of the behavioural expressions of these emotional responses.

For example, hypothesis testing is apparent in 2-year-olds where if one attempt does not seem to help the other person they will try one or more different strategies, indicating the role of thinking as well as feeling (e.g. empathy) (Radke-Yarrow and Zahn-Waxler, 1984). These increasingly complex responses to social experiences indicate how cognitions and emotions become intrinsically related to each other with development. A classification of cognitive–emotion abilities would seem an important research task to determine the common categories of appraisal that occur in normal children faced with everyday social hassles and major life events and difficulties.

These studies show an unfolding of young children's emotional development along a developmental timetable and indicate a sequence of reactions to potentially stressful stimuli as a function of development. However, these studies also indicate the substantial interplay between emotions, cognitions and behaviours in processing external stimuli. By 2 years of age there is considerable cognitive activity which is utilised in determining the child's response to distress.

Two questions arise as a consequence of the potential associations between external emotional stimuli and the child's internal emotional responses. First, to what degree are children's responses dependent on the social contexts of stresses? And secondly, what influences would social conditions have on the development of emotional responses over time?

Adult depression and child development

Events and difficulties in people's lives result in alterations in emotions, cognitions and behaviours. How people communicate their distress to others as a consequence is an important feature of the interplay between the effects of stress and an individual's response to that stress. Charles Darwin (1872) suggested at the turn of the century that facial expression was a crucial feature in this act of communicating the sense of stress. If parents, for example, engage in a dispute and show their anger with each other to their child, we need to consider that the perception of the emotion of anger by the child may exert an effect as well as the perception of parental behaviour between his parents. A similar argument may hold for affection and its consequential behaviour of physical contact.

In other words, a life event carries an emotional stimulus that may contribute to the child's intrinsic feeling state, cognitive appraisal and behavioural expression to that stimulus. Studies have found that changing the social context of an emotional stimulus changes the emotional responses in infants and young children. Together with a developmental unfolding of responses it is apparent that children are interacting substantially with their environments.

This implies that the quality and degree of emotional stimulus will influence the quality of children's emotional responses. Studies of children's emotional responses in the presence of depressed and non-depressed mothers indicates this is the case. Not only do depressed mothers fail to engage their children in adequate and meaningful interaction, but present evidence suggests that children's emotional development may be impaired as a consequence of exposure to maternal depression (Gaensbauer *et al*., 1984; Zahn-Waxler *et al*., 1984a,b, 1986). From the point of view of the child we can consider depression in his or her caretaker a major life event or, more likely, a severe ongoing difficulty. The social adversity associated with adult psychiatric disorder may therefore operate in part through emotional mechanisms modifying the child's own emotional development and not just through an alteration in social experiences such as poor maternal care.

In the series of studies by Zahn-Waxler and colleagues (1984a,b; 1986) the interesting finding is that although the children had the cognitive competence for age-appropriate play, the majority of their play was consistent with that of a younger age. That is to say, the children appeared emotionally less mature, more inhibited or less adventurous, timid and sensitive.

These findings indicated a failure of parents with affective disorders to promote normal interaction and play, with adverse developmental and therefore clinical implications. Developmentally this may put children of affectively disturbed parents at risk for subsequent abnormalities in emotional and cognitive development, and clinically it may put them at risk for psychiatric disorders in childhood, adolescence and adulthood (Weissman *et al*., 1987).

In other words, a depressed parent acts as an undesirable 'event-emotion', through her expression and behaviour interaction. It is not clear if children respond to emotion, behaviour or their interaction. We have already described how some evidence suggests that it is not depression *per se* but personality factors in the mothers that influence the risk of psychiatric disorders. This group of studies, however, suggests that emotion in the adult may act as an undesirable event for emotional development. Perhaps we should examine the forms of mood, their frequency and duration in the personalities of caretakers to evaluate the role of the emotional stimuli on children in these circumstances. Disinterest on the part of caretakers may prove to be important as a lack of normal emotional stimuli for such children. These findings support those discussed in Chapter 2, relating maternal depression to impairments in cognitive development.

The implication from studies on infant–mother relations is that both emotional and cognitive development can be impaired by adverse emotions. Maternal depression as an ongoing difficulty may operate by impairing emotional development in early development. So far the studies are few but suggest that the value of parenting programmes in primary care settings would be enhanced by assessment methods that systematically consider the emotional as well as the social and instrumental context of parenting. Many of the concepts are already in use. For example, clinicians are concerned to determine the presence of rejection, lack of interest or doubts a mother may have about parenting. What is needed is a method to determine the value of such observations for diagnosis, intervention and outcome for children whose development is impaired in these areas.

Children's responses to adverse emotions

Response patterns of children to the emotional stress of others could be of clinical importance. Patterns of children's responses may constitute an important link in the process of how social stressful events result in disturbed interactions as well as individual symptoms.

The exposure to emotions such as anger illustrates this point. Studies examining children exposed to anger have demonstrated that children's responses to this 'event-emotion' may be to develop emotional or behavioural symptoms or attempt to mediate or avoid disputes (Cummings, Zahn-Waxler and Radke-Yarrow, 1984). These responses occur at the time of the stimulus. There is also evidence, however, that exposure to anger may result in emotional disturbance at *future points in time*, distant from the original stimulus (Friedrich and Stein, 1973; Cummings, Zahn-Waxler and Radke-Yarrow, 1984).

If children can exhibit a repeated pattern of response distant from the original stimulus then two further questions are raised. Firstly, are children capable of rapid learning of undesirable emotional patterns to a single undesirable emotional episode such as anger or do they need multiple exposures (as seems more plausible). Secondly, does this indicate some degree of innate predisposition to respond to emotions of others in a particular way or is all the experience learned. For example, patterns of response to maternal separation show considerable continuity over time (Waters, 1978; Vaughn et al., 1979). Thirdly, are the same emotional responses more likely in the presence of further similar emotional stresses? Although the evidence is from studies on rhesus monkeys, such patterning can be expected in children. We do not know, however, if this form of emotional specificity is in fact the case (Suomi *et al.*, 1981).

A related but somewhat different question is whether or not emotional stimuli result in different forms of emotional response. For example, children between 18 months and $2\frac{1}{2}$ years of age often respond with anger and distress to anger in others but do not appear readily to translate their responses into purposeful behavioural interventions (Cummings, Zahn-Waxler and Radke-Yarrow, 1981). Affectionate stimuli in children of the same age, however, appear to elicit similar emotional reactions and result in purposeful behavioural interventions, chiefly attempts to join in other affection reactions or displays of pleasure.

These findings suggest that very young children possess the competence to interact and may do so in the presence of positive affection-laden emotions. Negative emotion-laden events, by contrast, seem likely to inhibit behavioural performance. By contrast, both positive and negative emotional events from others release performance in the child which has some *specificity* with the emotional event—i.e. anger elicits anger and affection elicits affection.

Clinical consequences of negative emotions

Angry emotional responses in children have been shown to increase with increasing exposure to anger occurring as a result of interparent conflict. Perhaps this is why violent aggressive marital disharmony is associated with psychiatric disorder in young people more than passive non-violent disharmony (Quinton and Rutter, 1985a). Indeed, perhaps the likelihood of producing conduct rather than emotional disorder in such adverse family circumstances is because negative emotions between adults lead to activating behavioural responses in the child which do not inhibit the stimulus until the child's response exceeds that of the adults'. Thus the greater the frequency of event-emotion the greater the chance of the same emotion expressing itself in the child. The findings suggest that children's emotions and their behavioural expressions are to some extent shaped by the form, frequency and duration of the patterning of emotional stimuli they perceive in their lives. Therefore events with similar social characteristics may result in differential emotional and behavioural responses in part because of the form of emotion expressed, its frequency, its duration and perhaps its focus.

Finally, it is apparent that the focus of the emotional stimulus need not be directly on the child to elicit an emotional response. In the above example it is anger *between* parents that elicits anger *within* the child. Future studies may be able to determine what effect the type and focus of the emotional stimulus may have on the child's response. That is to say, there may be different responses from a child when the focus is indirect (i.e. between adults) or direct (i.e. adult to child), and whether the type of emotion is anger or affection. Other emotions such as fear or interest may also evoke different forms of response, but have not been the subject of systematic research.

Longitudinal effects of exposure to negative emotions

What happens to emotional responses to event-emotions as children get older? So far we know that with age children (i) are less likely to express emotional responses overtly and (ii) develop an increasing behavioural repertoire, such as becoming more socially skilful (Zahn-Waxler and Radke-Yarrow, 1982; Buss and Plomin, 1984). Cummings, Zahn-Waxler and Radke-Yarrow (1984) followed up their toddler cohort at $6\frac{1}{2}$–$7\frac{1}{2}$ years of age and examined the associations between emotional stresses and children's responses. Firstly, they demonstrated that the frequency of naturally occurring episodes of anger and affection per month in the children as toddlers and as young schoolchildren were the same. Therefore we cannot assume that older children will be exposed to any more or less emotional stresses. There were, however, changes in the patterns of responses over time. Thus by the time children were of school age, emotional responses to angry stimuli resulted in greater behavioural responses. By school age, children's responses to anger events between parents included attempts to arbitrate and ameliorate in the conflict. They appeared more able to be selective in their responses to anger between parents and speak without substantial anger in themselves or necessarily scolding the parents.

In the same study the authors demonstrated that the social context and frequency of the anger stimulus from parents influenced the children's responses. The greater the rate of anger focused on the child, the greater the risk of overt distress in these children. It is apparent that as the child develops he or she contributes to a greater extent to emotional exchanges in stressful situations.

Secondly, negative emotions had become *motivators* for behavioural responses that may be adaptive by seeking to stop unwanted stimuli and not merely be imitative 'like-emotional' responses. In other words, the same stimulus has different effects at different ages.

Age brings both cognitive and personal awareness. The ability to act in a competent manner to solve disputes becomes increasingly greater when anger is focused on the self.

This latter point emphasises an important feature of the focus of emotionality. The direct impact of an angry emotional stimulus appears to have the alerting capacity to promote problem-solving cognitions and behaviours. This stimulus also carries the risk of overt distress, which may inhibit adaptive responses by the child. Thus the degree or intensity of the anger may determine the appraisal and response by the child.

This is in contrast to the infant and toddler where anger, whether to self or others, invariably inhibits problem-solving behaviour. Thus in the younger child the degree and intensity of anger may not influence the direction or form of the child's response. This shows that emotional responses in the child may alter with age to the same stimulus. As yet we do not know what developmental features result in a transformation of responses to the same stimuli. In this respect the effect of increasing social and cognitive experience on emotional responses and behavioural actions would seem to be centrally important and an area for further study.

For example, perhaps emotional response is related to an increasing association between a sense of self and the outside world. Children may learn to control the quality of their behavioural action as a consequence of emotional response because it is in their interest to do so, even if their own feeling states would predict behavioural disorganisation. In the presence of social adversity it may be important to 'keep one's feelings to oneself'. This well-known phrase implies a cognitive mechanism involved in modulating the behavioural expression of internal feeling states that arise in response to life experiences (see Chapter 7). Again, however, we see that the feeling state itself may not be a consequence of this form of cognitive modulation but becomes *subordinate* to it. We know surprisingly little about these important psychological mechanisms and their function in young people in the presence of different forms of life events and social difficulties.

Individual differences and emotional response

A further important observation is the marked individual differences in children's responses to similar stressful event-emotions such as anger. Relatively little attention has been paid to individual differences in children's responses to most stressful circumstances (Garmezy, 1983, 1985; Garmezy, Masten and Tellegen, 1984). Individual differences may be the result of factors in the child as well as the nature and social context of the emotional stimulus. Individual responses are particularly important to elicit in clinical work and often receive a high priority in the clinician's assessments. They are equally important to the researcher who seeks to understand how they arise, what influence they exert on development and how they can be incorporated into coherent psychological theory. The association of individual differences (idiographic features) *between* children and shared characteristics (nomothetic principles) *within a population* of children must be carefully considered in both clinical and research settings. The relative contribution of these two concepts to emotional responses and behavioural actions in the face of social adversities has only recently begun to be investigated. If some emotional features were continuous across different social circumstances then the case for believing they reflect the contribution of a biological predisposition to stress would be considerably strengthened. For example, Cummings's findings suggest that the form of children's emotional responses to adults' affection was consistent across social settings, age and time.

In events that contain anger, however, there were marked changes over time. Additionally, school-age children's responses to affectionate events were not associated with their responses to anger events.

These findings provide support (albeit modest at this time) for believing that some forms of emotional response to stress have a contribution from innate processes, which may vary from one individual child to another but may show constancy within a child over time and situation. They also suggest that different emotions may have different ontogenies and pathways. Some emotions may be *traits* in development others may be *states* that arise in response to emotional stimuli from outside. Temperament as a trait, may influence the state of emotional responses to social stresses. For example, trait (perhaps physiological feeling tones as well as basic psychological feeling states) emotions may act as regulators of state (complex psychological feeling states) emotions.

It has been suggested that some feeling states, such as reactivity or excitability, are innate expressions of physiological mechanisms in reaction to annoying or threatening events and constitute intrinsic (or temperamental) disposition (Buss and Plomin, 1984). The case is far from proven, however, and conceptual and methodological hurdles need to be overcome before a coherent picture of temperament will emerge (Kohnstamm, 1986; Graham and Stevenson, 1987; Rutter, 1987c). The significance of different styles of behavioural expression may be that children's responses to similar life events will be influenced by their temperamental trait-organised emotionality.

Individual differences may have some explanatory value in accounting for differences in response by children raised in the same environmental difficulties, such as ongoing marital disharmony. Individual different responses to similar stressful events may in part be accounted for by the associations and interactions between innate emotionality and environmental adversity. Thus acute life events of similar psychological characteristics which appear to be associated with different forms of psychopathology may do so not only because of the relative contribution of other social factors but perhaps because of the differential contributions of innate physiological and psychological responses.

Emotional and behavioural response to social adversities

Behavioural performance following a stressful life event may be a consequence of the form of emotional response that a child experiences as a result of the event. Behaviour and emotion may not correlate with each other and it may be incorrect to assume that the absence of a behavioural change to adversity implies the absence of an emotional response.

There is an implication here that some association exists between social adversities and emotions that is relatively independent of cognitive processes. Some social conditions may trigger an arousing emotive response which is not so much appraised as reacted to. Different emotion pathways may be activated by different external emotional stimuli. For example, anger-laden events generate arousal and anger in the child and, as discussed earlier, different forms of behavioural response, dependent to some extent on the child's age. By contrast, affection-laden events provoke affectionate responses and different forms of behaviour. The hypothesis that different physiological and chemical pathways will be responsible for different emotion-behaviour responses requires further investigation. As discussed in Chapter 5, many measurement issues need clarifying before we determine the validity of physicochemical–emotion-behaviour pathways. We may be measuring the wrong chemical factors, as well as psychological, at the wrong times; we need to consider the associations between behavioural styles and endocrine responses independent of social factors; we need also to consider that physicochemical responses may prime the individual for psychological responses. In other words, interactive effects between physiological and psychological states need investigating as well as independent effects.

Children are clearly exposed to substantial depths of anger and anger events throughout childhood relatively frequently. Indeed, Cummings and colleagues found that in the average American family anger incidents were 2–3 times as common as affection incidents! Children not only appear to be unaffected in many cases by anger events but may need to experience other people's anger for optimum emotional development. This may be a further demonstration, this time in emotional terms, that undesirable life experiences have necessary steeling effects for normal development. It may be the balance and range of emotional stimuli that provides infants and young children with the range of social contexts in which cognitive appraisal unfolds, and feeling states and their behavioural expressions develop.

Does experiencing angry event-emotions in the context of a secure environment exert a steeling effect whereas experiencing the same event-emotions in the context of an insecure environment exert a sensitising effect?

There is a remarkable lack of research in the area of negative emotions necessary for normal development at all ages (see Garmezy, 1985). The case for such research has perhaps been most eloquently summarised by Garmezy and colleagues at the University of Minnesota in their project on personal competence and Rutter's descriptions of the search for protective factors against stress (Rutter, 1983b; Garmezy, 1985; Garmezy and Rutter, 1985). The major observation which underpins these investigations is that many children *do not* become distressed in the presence of stressful life events and difficulties and do not go on to develop psychiatric disturbance.

Emotions as consequences of social experience

The investigation of social factors as potential causal agents for conduct and emotional problems has been a focus of research for a considerable period of time. For example, both marital disharmony and family discord have been established as significant and independent risk factors for conduct and emotional disorders (Wolkind and Rutter, 1985a; Rutter, 1985a). The meaning and mechanisms of these social events and their role as stressors is beginning to be studied in some detail. Whilst much has been discovered, we remain relatively ignorant of the mechanisms through which psychopathology may arise as a consequence of these life experiences (Rutter, 1983b, 1985c; Garmezy, 1985).

Identifying the mechanisms involved will require a consideration of emotional factors from at least two directions. First, emotions generated by the social event. For example, marital disharmony may generate anger, despair, silence or withdrawal, or a combination of these, in the adults and children. Secondly, children's responses to others' emotions may help to identify patterns of emotions and behaviours within the child and between the child and other persons. Patterns of responding to other persons' emotional reactions may provide an important link in the analysis of psychological processes through which stresses impact upon children (e.g. Dunn, 1986). This suggests that an area for future study is how the psychological components of relationships between two people may effect relations with another. Understanding the mechanisms of relationships between relations may provide us with an understanding of the emotions that are causes or consequences of relating (Hinde and Stevenson-Hinde, 1988).

EMOTIONS, TEMPERAMENT AND SOCIAL
ADVERSITY–CLINICAL IMPLICATIONS

Temperament as behaviour

Recent studies of temperament can be said to have begun in the 1950s, with the work of Thomas, Chess and Birch who began to collect data on the behavioural style of a sample of New York babies (Thomas and Chess, 1977). As clinicians, they were impressed by the fact that despite being exposed to social adversities, both acute and chronic, many children appeared unscathed by these adverse life experiences. They postulated that a set of largely inherited characteristics made children more vulnerable or invulnerable to social adversities. Later they modified their views to lay much greater emphasis on interactions between inherited characteristics and life experience, on the 'goodness of fit', between the child's temperament and the environment, to explain the psychiatric outcome. They remained firm, however, in emphasising the importance of temperament. These pioneering authors described nine categories or dimensions of temperament based on detailed interviews with mothers about their babies. They labelled the categories, established by content analysis, activity level; rhythmicity or regularity; approach/withdrawal; adaptability; threshold of responsiveness; intensity of reaction; quality of mood; distractability; attention span and persistence. They suggested that on each of these dimensions of temperament, children would show consistency across situations. In other words, whether at home with parents or at school with teachers, performing a task or reading a book, there would be a stability of behavioural style. They suggested that children could be grouped into three main broad categories. 'Easy' children, who are adaptable and regular in their habits, 'difficult' children, who show withdrawal in new situations, are irregular in their biological functions and show intense and negative emotional reactions, and finally 'slow to warm up' children, who are quiet and who initially withdraw from new situations but who, if handled appropriately, are gradually able to cope with new circumstances.

From these classifications it was suggested that easy children were relatively invulnerable to stress, difficult children were predisposed to develop aggressive or antisocial behaviour and the slow to warm up children to develop emotional disorders characterised by pathological withdrawal. Subsequent investigations confirmed some of these hypotheses (Graham, Rutter and George, 1973; Thomas and Chess, 1977). Child psychiatrists and other mental health workers began to change their practice as a result of these studies and to consider the child's own contribution to psychopathology and not lay all the emphasis on parental behaviour. Treatment was tailored to take into account the child's own behavioural style, and progress was determined by considering the child's own pre-morbid patterns of behaviour rather than an expected (and generally unknown) norm.

More recently, refinements to these classifications of child temperament have been made, through further research aimed at improving on some of the limitations inherent in the earlier work, in particular the emphasis on maternal reports of behaviour. Observational studies of children in different settings have been developed to improve the validity of investigations into behavioural style (Buss and Plomin, 1984). The studies of Buss and Plomin have led to a redefinement of the dimensions of temperament. Their findings suggest three dimensions of temperament. The first is emotionality, equated with distress and the tendency to become upset easily and intensely. This dimension underlies tendencies to demonstrate both fear and anger. They relate low emotionality to the New York category of the easy child and high emotionality to the difficult child. The second category is 'sociability'—the tendency to prefer the presence of others to being alone. This dimension underlies the presence or absence of the tendency to share, co-operate, be responsive to others and initiate social activities. The third dimension is activity. This involves a tendency, or lack of a tendency, to be energetic and restless, and is largely defined in terms of motor activity.

Buss and Plomin define two essential characteristics of temperament. The behaviour concerned must appear first in infancy and it must be at least partly genetically determined. It remains to be seen whether these two criteria are valid for all forms of stable behavioural style (Kohnstamm, 1986; Graham and Stevenson, 1987).

It does seem useful, however, to discriminate between emotions, cognitions and behaviours that are situation dependent and those that exhibit stability across social contexts and continuities over time. It is apparent, however, that behavioural styles do vary with social contexts (Stevenson-Hinde, 1988). Nevertheless there may be important patterns or core characteristics that are prominent if not dominant, across place and time.

Temperament and psychopathology

Graham and Stevenson (1987) discuss their studies of temperament, including longitudinal and twin studies, in terms of the relationships between premorbid characteristics of behavioural style and behavioural content. They suggest from their findings that the common emotional and behavioural disorders of childhood may represent predictable outcomes if the child's temperament were known. For example, traits such as restlessness were found in the majority of 3-year-old children who later developed conduct difficulties at age 8 (Richman, Stevenson and Graham, 1982). This suggests some degree of continuity between temperamental traits and behaviour disorders but does not tell us the mechanisms by which the latter is derived from the former. What intervening variables are needed for temperament to exert a risk for conduct disorder? Could life events and other social adversities be sufficient? These authors, when discussing their twin data (Graham and Stevenson, 1985), also indicate that whilst there is evidence that traits are inherited, the specificity between particular temperamental traits and psychiatric symptoms is not high. Thus monozygotic twins were very likely to share temperamental traits but neurotic symptoms may occur in one child and behavioural symptoms in the other. What modifying factors were operating in these twins to produce different symptom patterns? Again, should we be looking at the type of social adversities that these children have experienced to explain different forms of psychopathology? There has been little research investigating the interaction of temperamental characteristics and social adversities on the risk of psychiatric disorder in childhood and adolescence. Thus it is not known how different behavioural styles operate when social adversities are taken into account. It seems reasonable to investigate the likelihood that children considered difficult or rated high on emotionality would have a greater risk of disorder in the presence of life events than would easy or low emotionality styles. We also need to determine if the risk of anxiety or depression when exposed to social adversity is altered by different temperamental styles. In other words, is there any specificity between temperamental styles and psychopathologies that occurs in the presence of social adversities? In other words, do we need to discriminate between state dependent emotional responses to stressful social events and ongoing difficulties, and trait emotions that may themselves influence the form of emotional response to adverse life experiences?

Investigations into the contribution of trait and state emotions may help us to understand the form in which 'symptoms', both emotional and behavioural, emerge as a consequence of temperamental attributes as well as through the effects of social adversities.

At present there is considerable evidence that children show wide differences in behavioural styles, expression of emotional distress and disturbed behaviour. There is some support for the view that these differences may reflect temperamental factors, although how such factors arise is far from clear (Keogh, 1982; Rutter, 1985c; Kohnstamm, 1986).

If temperament consists of differential emotional patterns it becomes important to consider how stressful experiences may impact on multiple emotions. It has to be said that studies on the origins of temperament have only recently begun and there is much to be done (Plomin and Dunn, 1986). Present evidence suggests that the same stressful life events may result in different effects on children as a consequence of individual differences in temperament. For example, children's responses to the pain of vaccinations have a wide variation according to the time it takes to sooth. Slow soothers show proportionately more anger expression than fast soothers (Izard et al., 1982). This study provides an interesting example of the role of temperament in response to an undesirable stimulus (in this case pain). The findings suggest that pain results in arousal and anger as an emotion plus crying is a behavioural response and this response does not discriminate between children. What tells us the children are different is their refractory component of anger to soothing. This suggests that irritable temperaments are more refractory to subsequent external social attempts at soothing or coping.

This demonstrates that post-event inhibitory mechanisms in infants are different and perhaps illustrate a functional difference in intrinsic emotional or temperamental factors. At the present time there is very limited direct evidence on the influence of temperament in children's reactions to stressful events. There are grounds, however, for considering that temperament is likely to influence both the appraisal of and response to stressful events and difficulties in the environment.

Firstly, there is evidence linking temperamental factors with psychiatric disorders in children (Rutter, 1985c; Earls and Jung, 1987; Graham and Stevenson, 1987). Thus children with greater impulsivity, aggression and activity show increased rates of emotional and behavioural disturbance. These findings indicate that these clinical dimensions of temperament have some validity. Thus there are certain traits of behaviour that may remain relatively persistent.

Secondly, there is evidence to show that a normative family event, birth of a sibling, has a stressful impact on children and may adversely influence their behaviour for at least weeks (Dunn and Kendrick, 1980a,b). In this latter study it was found that a child's temperament significantly predicted changes in the child's behaviour after their sibling's birth (Dunn and Kendrick, 1982). They also showed, however, that there were significant interactions with the mother's mental state and with patterns of mother–child interaction. This indicates that temperamental characteristics of children may have a direct impact on the response to a stressful event (in this case an entrance event), but also may operate through the social interaction with a parent. How parents respond to their first-born's temperamental response may modify for better or worse the child's responses to parental behaviours between mother and newborn.

Thirdly, it may be that temperament may promote and alter the social conditions in which the child is operating at any one time. For example, children with adverse temperamental characteristics, such as impulsivity and aggression, are twice as likely as other children to be the target of parental criticism (Quinton and Rutter, 1985a). Both Dunn's and Rutter's findings highlight the complex interrelationships between parenting behaviour and child temperament.

The available evidence seems to suggest that temperament exerts its main effects through influencing parent–child interactions (Rutter, 1987b,c).

To date the majority of work on temperament in children has been related to pre-school and infancy. There is also some evidence that in pre-school children temperament exerts a greater influence on behaviour in boys than girls (Earls and Jung, 1987). The influence of temperament in older children and the effects it may have on stress events is not at all clear at this time. For example, how do individual differences in the form of different emotional expressions arise? Is there a continuity of emotional temperamental style over time? Undoubtedly there are discontinuities as a result of modification of emotions through development and experience (Campos and Barrett, 1984). What are the social conditions under which temperament may be viewed as an adverse stimulus to others? How does development and social experience influence emotion-behaviour responses in the child? Finally, what factors in others alter individuals' perceptions of acceptable temperament in children?

Temperament, past social experience and present social adversity

There is considerable evidence to show that the frequency and duration of previous social experience influences reactions to stresses (Rutter, 1985b,c). For example, in Cummings's study, differences in children's distress reactions to anger were associated with the frequency of exposure to interparental conflict (Cummings et al., 1984).

In attachment research, negative reactions to a reunion following separation in a strange situation have been linked to a history of negative interactions with mother (Ainsworth et al., 1978). In research on adult depression, early loss of a parent in childhood is significantly more frequent in young women who develop depression as a consequence of recent stressful life events or difficulties (Brown, 1988; Harris, Brown and Bifulco, 1986). In young children, social experiences do seem inextricably linked up with development of temperament. Thus there is an important environmental influence on temperament and some trait emotion-behaviours may indeed arise from environmental effects (Stevenson-Hinde, 1988).

Overall, however, there is sufficient present evidence to consider a biological component for temperament, the significance of which probably depends on interaction with the environment (Kohnstamm, 1986; Bates, 1987). We should again be clear about what we measure in this regard. For example, if we wish to know the origins of temperament then the contribution of intrinsic and environmental factors will be our focus of study. If we wish to know the effects of temperament we need to measure the emotions and behaviours that result from such factors.

Present evidence, however, supports maintaining the concept of temperament as it may be associated with positive as well as negative qualities (Rutter, 1987b,c). For example, high activity and being difficult can be helpful under adverse social circumstances such as poor caretaking or famine (Schaffer, 1966; de Vries, 1984). The latter example emphasises the possible protective effects of some dimensions of temperament against ongoing stressful circumstances and also highlights the importance of taking into account the impact of temperament according to the social conditions in which the child is operating.

Finally, a better understanding is required of the dynamic relationship between environmental variables and biological factors that determine temperament during childhood. For example, different dimensions of temperament may have different forms of development. Thus expressions of anger appear related to increased rates of autonomic reactivity as well as previous exposure to conflict (Cummings et al., 1984). Affection, by contrast, shows a continuity that seems relatively uninfluenced by adverse social experiences of a similar nature and not associated with an increase in autonomic reactivity.

These findings and arguments indicate that stressful and undesirable life events and difficulties will have differential effects on children in part because of their relationship to temperamental factors. The precise nature of this association has yet to be delineated and further research clearly seems worthwhile.

SUMMARY

1. Basic emotions have innate physiological origins which may not have direct psychological reference. Complex emotions have physiological and psychological components the evolution of which is influenced by life experiences.
2. Temperament is presently considered as a configuration of behavioural styles which has its origins in infancy and is partially determined by genetic factors. The form of temperamental characteristics are influenced and shaped by early life experiences.
3. Emotions as responses to social experience may influence emotional development and the subsequent risk of psychopathology.

4. Emotional responses to social adversity become increasingly modulated by cognitions with a resultant alteration in the behavioural expression of emotional response with age. The emotional response itself may remain little changed with development.
5. Temperamental styles show marked individual differences. The interrelationships between social adversities, temperament and emotional symptoms is unclear. Difficult temperamental styles may predispose to both increasing the risk of social adversities and emotional symptoms. Alternatively, desirable temperamental styles may decrease the risk of social adversities and emotional symptoms.

Chapter 7

Cognition, Coping and Behaviour

Perhaps the greatest interest in stress research other than the evaluation of external stressors has been the investigation of how individuals perceive, appraise and, in general, think about stresses. This chapter will consider how our present knowledge of cognition has been used to understand stressful events and circumstances. It is relevant to consider firstly some of the main arguments that have occurred in developmental studies concerning the place of cognitive development in childhood.

COGNITIVE THEORIES OF DEVELOPMENT

There are three broad areas of cognitive theory: (i) Piagetian; (ii) Information processing; (iii) Social cognition.

Piagetian theory

Piaget's enormous contributions to child development spanned over half a century. In his theories children are motivated by the *affect* of interest which engages the child in the world with objects and people. These conditions result in the construction of meaningful perceptual experience and imply the child's active involvement in the construction of reality.

At birth the infant is equipped with a restricted set of biological mechanisms with a small range of behavioural expressions, such as sucking and looking. Piagetian theory proposes that the infant's motivation to make sense of the environment is intrinsic and biological. Making sense and adapting to the environment occurs via the processes of assimilation and accommodation. From this position the infant proceeds to build schemata of the world through stages of development. The transition from stage to stage is characterised by the child's qualitative internalisation of his or her external experiences.

Piaget's work has generated considerable interest and research. Many of his concepts concerning the timing of developmental stages and the building of schemata have undergone modification (Bryant, 1974, 1977; Hobson, 1985). Nevertheless, Piaget's theories have made a major contribution to child development.

Information processing

The information processing view of cognitive development is not a single theory. Unlike Piaget, information theorists make an analogy between the ways in which human cognitions work and computer processing. This emphasises the understanding of cognitive processes rather than single mechanisms in isolation (Simon, 1979).

In development what changes is firstly the 'set' of cognitive processes, such as rehearsal and retrieval strategies, that the child has available to him in order to make inferences and solve problems. Secondly, the rate at which various processes can be performed alters with development. Thirdly, the amount, quality and organisation, and therefore usability, of knowledge increases with development.

These developmental changes in turn influence the quality, speed and likelihood of future cognitive activity. In contrast to the Piagetian position, information processing is knowledge acquisition which is gradual and innate. What appear to be qualitative shifts are, in fact, the result of a variety of quantitative changes that in combination produce observed behaviour.

In general, cognitive theory has not been overly concerned with studying the interface between cognitions and emotions, perhaps because the question of what motivates a person to perform cognitive activity has not been a priority in research to date (Radke-Yarrow and Sherman, 1985). For some cognitive theorists changes in affective functioning are derivatives of changes in the cognitive system (Sroufe, 1979).

The assumption here is that recall memory becomes a necessary cognitive capacity for affective processes, both the emotional representation of an object and its affective expression such as fear. Recall memory may be necessary but it is not sufficient to predict the form of affective expression. For example, there are marked individual differences in infants' emotional reactions to recall of objects (Radke-Yarrow and Sherman, 1985).

Social cognitions

The role of socialisation in the development of cognitions represents a third theory of cognitive development. In social cognitive theory there are proposed central links between social factors and cognitive processes. The earliest writers in this area propose that internal representations arise from social interactions, both verbal and non-verbal (Meade, 1934; Vygotsky, 1934). The development of an intrapersonal mental state effectively stems from social elements and processes (Flavell and Markham, 1983; Harre, 1984).

Subsequent interactions between social relations and thought determine important thinking and feeling processes which make up the self. The development of the self-system has indeed been a major area of research in the last few years (Harter, 1983, 1986).

The inclusion of a social dimension to the development of both cognition and affect draws support from ethological studies, which have shown that the way in which individuals form their relationships during ontogeny is similar in both primates and non-primates. Ethologists propose that individuals have been adapted to select relationships which promote both social and cognitive development and these relationships promote further socio-cognitive skills which contribute to their biological fitness (Hinde, 1987). Studies in monkeys have, in particular, provided hypotheses concerning the dynamics of human relations (Hinde, 1979, 1983; Hinde and Stevenson-Hinde, 1988).

The importance of social factors in cognitive development is twofold: firstly, *the absence* of social experiences may result in cognitive deficits and secondly, *the presence* of social adversities may result in cognitive dysfunctions.

The present views of cognition and development are unlikely to be mutually exclusive. Certain interdependencies seem apparent. For example, it is apparent that children have intrinsic abilities that they bring into the world and that Piagetian motivation has as its purpose the acquisition of further information. It may be that motivation occurs because of the *affect* of interest, enquiry and inquisitiveness; clearly information processing of the world proceeds and the mechanisms of processing play an important part in how cognitive development takes shape, again, however, affect may modulate information processing. As we discussed in the previous chapter, certain cognitive variables, such as attention, are themselves influenced by the *affect* that accompanies them. Finally, it seems inevitable that the environment provides the content for information processes and promotes the biological basis of enquiry. It seems then that theorists have different points of emphasis when speculating on the developmental origins of cognition. Perhaps the argument is too firmly based on the desire to decide a hierarchy of importance; constitutional, functional and environmental factors are all necessary for normative cognitive development.

INTERNAL WORKING MODELS

The concept of an internal working model of relationships has been proposed to explain the nature of social experiences in development (Bretherton and Walters, 1985). On the basis of the attachment theories of Bowlby it is suggested that children derive a set of expectations about their own relationship capacities and how others respond to their social behaviour. Two possibilities arise as a consequence of stress. First, the presence of continuous exposure to adversity in the home will result in unwanted 'internal working models' with potential effects on subsequent personality development. Secondly, there may be different internal mental representations as a consequence of different life experiences.

For example, although the security of a good relationship with one parent does not predict the relationship with the other parent it does predict peer relationships several years later (Bretherton and Walters, 1985). These results provide some support for the notion that mental representations develop as a consequence of good social relations between mother and child. Furthermore, once developed these mental representations may be enduring over time and situations.

If this is the case does this mean that inadequate social relations predict inadequate peer relations and a greater negative responsivity to subsequent stressful events? Bowlby's writings certainly postulate that insecure attachments increase vulnerability to later disorder in adult life in the presence of stresses (Bowlby, 1980; Wolkind and Rutter, 1985a). As we have already noted, social cognitive factors may be the mediating experiences in this process linking past and recent social experiences.

It has been argued, for example, that social experiences only have long-term effects as a consequence of cognition (Kagan, 1984). Furthermore, research in adults has suggested that, in line with Bowlby's argument, loss of parent in childhood creates a negative cognitive set which itself creates a vulnerability to later stresses (Brown and Harris, 1978; Brown, Bifulco and Harris, 1987). The suggestion is that the effect of early loss is to irrevocably influence cognitions through lowering self-esteem. Indeed, negative cognitions have been emphasised as causal and maintaining factors in some forms of depression (Beck, 1976; Bebbington, 1985). Finally, it may be that early loss determines a social pathway which individuals select because of their social cognitive deficits. In other words, the probability of subsequent losses is increased because individuals bias themselves towards relationships that have a high risk of failure as a result of their social cognitive set determined through their early adverse experience. Early loss may therefore have lasting effects on cognition through maintaining adverse social pathways. It is apparent, however, that the effects of early social adversity depend on when they occur in a child's development. For example, lasting psychological sequelae from adverse social effects in infancy may be uncommon because of the infant's limited ability to process experiences (Kagan, 1980, 1984). The effects of disrupted attachment may only exert effects when the child has the cognitive apparatus to develop undesirable internal schema.

The interesting point here is that exposure to social adversities continuously or for a substantial period of time constitutes a potential hazard for the development of undesirable cognitive patterns or internal working models, which may have a direct impact on subsequent social and emotional development.

The self-system

As children develop they learn that they are coherent persons with physical boundaries that separate them from others. In addition, they come to recognise themselves psychologically. The notion of self is complex and a full discussion is beyond the scope of this volume. What constitutes self, how can it be recognised and when does it emerge, as well as its importance in the world are some of the questions that have been examined in order to produce a coherent view of the psychology of the self-concept (Kagan, 1980; Harter, 1983, 1986; Harre, 1984).

There are perhaps two central notions in many of the writings and researches conducted on the self. The first is the role of self-image, in which we see ourselves as existing in the world and attribute to ourselves various qualities which may describe our self-concept. For example, to consider oneself humorous or dull or competent or incompetent. In this respect our self-image contains those components that determine our degree of self-esteem.

The second concept is self-awareness, in which we respond to others on the basis of their attributes rather than our own. In this respect we respond to our precepts and not just their immediate behaviours. Our precepts will be influenced by what information we are given and what we are able to see. For example, it has been found that we respond negatively to people regarded as aggressive even when at that moment they behave in a prosocial or compliant manner (Dodge, 1980; Dodge, Murphy and Buchsbaum, 1984). Similarly, we are liable to respond to individuals on the basis of the label 'male' or 'female' and not just their tendency to behave in male or female ways (Condry and Ross, 1985).

What is apparent for both these notions of self is how social factors initially influence our self-esteem (Rutter, 1987a). The view that self and mind are developed through social experience without which both are deficient has been argued philosophically and demonstrated in a number of research enquiries (Harre, 1984; Rutter, 1987a). Social adversities, therefore, may well influence different components of the self-system. For example, responses to task-failure have been shown to discriminate between secure and insecure infants (Lutkenhaus, Grossman and Grossman, 1985), and adolescent boys and girls (see Dweck and Elliott, 1983).

The self-system is not merely a function of childhood development but may change for better or worse throughout life. Secondly, the self-system may influence how individuals respond to life situations as well as be shaped by them. Thirdly, individuals seem to vary markedly in their levels of self-esteem (Harter, 1986).

The existence of a self-system has substantial implications for a number of important psychological concepts (Rutter, 1987a). Perhaps the most salient for social stress is the fact that personality is not just a collection of intrinsic traits or temperamental attributes which are constitutionally determined but is influenced by and responds to life experiences.

Furthermore, the quality of life experiences in childhood and adolescence has implications for personality development (which is therefore not explicable solely on the basis of intrinsic properties or generalised tendencies to be emotionally stable or unstable). The social components of personality may be the factors which explain why there are large variations in individuals' personality characteristics and why individuals' behaviour can be so different when exposed to similar adverse social situations. These individual variations may be determined by thought processes that are derived from social experience.

Psychoanalytic theories have suggested that personality development involves intrapsychic cognitive processes as modulators and controllers between emotional states and social experiences. In particular, psychoanalytic theories have focused our attention on the meaning individuals attach to social experiences, the importance of early family relations and the subsequent relationship between social experience and meaning. Of course we know that many life events, such as early loss, do not constitute universal and irrevocable disadvantage to personality development. Such undue emphasis in psychoanalytic writings has not been helpful in understanding how social adversities influence the construction of internal working models or socio-emotional development (Eagle, 1984). Many changes and modifications will be required to present thinking in this area before a psychological theory concerned with the effects of stress on personality development will be credible.

SOCIAL EXPERIENCES AND COGNITIVE DEVELOPMENT

Attachment deficits and cognitive development

In the chapters dealing with family and social events and experiences a number of studies were described which investigated the impact of maternal depression on children. The studies, whilst few in number, have been impressive in demonstrating that there is an increased risk of disrupting the mother–child relationship in the presence of maternal depression. These studies suggested, however, that it is exposure to *continuous* maternal difficulties that may impair the development of a child's cognitive abilities as indicated by intelligence and developmental quotient tests (Cox *et al.*, 1987; Mills *et al.*, 1985).

The matter is of importance in view of the findings that cognitive abilities may regulate susceptibility to life events and experiences. The suggestion here is that everyday social experience in early life with an adequate caretaker is instrumental in the development of a child's mental representation of the world. Thoughts and feelings become a consequence of these mental representations and may in turn influence responses to stressful events and difficulties.

Brief episodes of everyday social difficulties are unlikely to exert long-term adverse influences on mental development as a sufficient quantity of desirable social experiences prevail in everyday social interactions.

Prolonged exposure to months of poverty of early social experience may have a significant effect on subsequent cognitive development. In other words, attachment is important for the development of adequate mental representations of social relations and therefore for cognitive development.

For example, children older than 5 who have experienced adequate attachment to their caretaker in infancy are less vulnerable to the effects of separation because they have acquired the psychological capacity to maintain relationships in the absence of a parent (Wolkind and Rutter, 1985a).

This example demonstrates the value of mental representation in dealing with the potentially adverse events of separation. These findings suggest that children with deficits in attachments as a result of difficulties with a caretaker in early infancy may have a particular cognitive deficit in the form of inadequate representation of a secure relationship. These deficits may result in children not possessing cognitive characteristics required for coping with life events such as separation. Are they now, therefore, at risk of disorder in the presence of a stressful experience such as separation? Psychoanalytic writers have commented on the central role of a 'good-enough mother' as an example of the infant introjecting good objects as a prerequisite for the capacity to be alone (Winnicott, 1968). This cognitive mechanism is a product of early social experiences and may operate by allowing the child to think about the existing relationship, thereby retaining a safe feeling tone which does not motivate the need for proximity seeking behaviour.

Bowlby has hypothesised that insecure attachment acts as a risk factor for later psychiatric disorders in the presence of subsequent adverse life events and difficulties (Bowlby 1980, 1988). This theoretical position indicates the active function of thinking in psychopathology and emphasises the importance of social cognitions and memory when an individual is exposed to social adversities which require a behavioural response.

Deficits in internal working models—risk for psychopathology

If social experiences determine the form of internal working models then social adversities may exert substantial and undesirable effects on the mental representation of social experience. In other words, a direct contribution to the cognitive aspects of psychopathology can be made from life events and difficulties.

For example, conduct disorders in childhood and adolescence occur significantly more often in children from disadvantaged backgrounds with a number of factors such as criminality and chronic discord in the family. Is it perhaps in these children that adverse internal working or cognitive models are derived as a consequence of undesirable social factors and subsequently have a direct causal effect on their behaviour? There is no doubt that such long-term social stresses influence cognitive development (Rutter, 1985c). There is, however, no marked critical period for such influences, although effects appear more striking from pre-school years onwards and show less impact in infancy where maturational (biological) effects appear more important (McCall, 1981). Furthermore, the more severe and gross the stress is, the worse the cognitive deficits. Thus children reared in substantial social isolation and subject to severe physical confinement can show no speech or language and exhibit signs of marked intellectual retardation (Skuse, 1984).

Overall, it is apparent that children who are exposed to long-term stressful experiences, ranging from severe privation to exposure to chronic family discord and disturbed behaviour in their parents, may be at considerable risk from cognitive deficits, which themselves may determine later behaviour and psychiatric disorder. There is, however, surprisingly little known about the long-term effects of such privation on psychopathology or subsequent interpersonal behaviour. Thus we do not know if the presence of cognitive deficits as a consequence of early social adversities are only important in the presence of subsequent life events and difficulties or whether they exert important effects independent of later adversities.

Altering the adverse environment in early childhood

There is a suggestion from the above that severe adversity in infancy and early childhood has markedly irrevocable and undesirable effects for the child. The same may be inferred from the role of chronic adversity and the risk of conduct disorder. The outcome is not, however, always poor and other social factors may compensate in varying degrees for such stresses. There is, for example, evidence to show that changing the environment of children can lead to marked cognitive recovery in severe privation (Skuse, 1984). In the few cases reported in the clinical literature, normal levels of intelligence and language occurred within months of rescue in a number of cases. Unfortunately there is no systematic data on other aspects of children's functioning, such as self-esteem and interpersonal relations, to help us decide if such effects may result in specific deficits relating to social cognitive function rather than intelligence *per se*.

The above examples although rare demonstrate the dramatic positive effects of altering a child's total environment. There are also opportunities to ameliorate negative effects in children's ongoing social environment and enhance normal social cognitive development.

In the case of chronic adversities and conduct disorder, for example, it has been shown that many children may be protected from chronic family difficulties by a good relationship with one parent (Rutter, 1985b).

This suggests that desirable social experience involving intimate relations may be sufficient to enhance social cognitive functions in the presence of ongoing adverse social experience. The evidence, however, suggests that the effects on cognitions may be indirect. For example, it seems that chronic family discord is more likely to have a negative effect on scholastic performance by influencing socio-emotional and behavioural functioning than by producing cognitive deficits (Rutter, 1985c). These findings suggest that ongoing social adversities exert effects on social cognitions through socio-emotional dysfunction. These findings, together with the small data on severe deprivation, suggest that intelligence and learning are more robust cognitive skills than social cognitions, and can recover from severe social adversities more substantially and rapidly than the qualities (e.g. self-esteem) associated with interpersonal and emotional development.

Acute events and social cognition

Can recent life events adversely influence social cognitions? Certainly the evidence suggests they can, and indeed social cognitions may be rather sensitive to environmental changes.

There may, however, be counterbalances from other social factors to prevent or limit the negative effects of social adversities on cognitions. For example, protective effects against the impact of bereavement can accrue as a consequence of maintaining confiding and supportive relations with a surviving parent. This protection seems to stem from the continuing presence of a confiding relationship with a parent or care-giver. It is not clear, however, what the mechanism of this protective effect is. Are the emotions of loss and sadness directly buffered by a confiding relationship, such that they occur with less negative intensity?

This seems unlikely since, as we have already discussed in previous chapters on disaster events (Chapter 5) and emotional arousal (Chapter 6), children can feel intense loss even in the presence of close family relations. It seems more plausible that a confiding relationship provides a continuing secure base from which the child's cognitive emotional response to loss can be discussed, explored and eventually ameliorated such that cognitive memory can be explained without intense emotional memory.

It has been hypothesised that early loss increases the risk of depression in adulthood through alterations in the quality of care as a consequence of loss (Brown and Harris, 1978; Brown, Bifulco and Harris, 1987). Such losses as we have described are hypothesised to exert their negative effects through cognitive mechanisms by increasing the risk of experiencing a sense of hopelessness in the face of recent life events and difficulties.

Little systematic information is available to determine if recent loss events exert this type of effect in children or if cognitive mechanisms are important in this respect. It seems reasonable to conclude on the basis of what we do know that social adversities in early life can exert significant effects, and the development of a coherent social cognitive system is likely to be contiguous with an adequate social system.

One further cognitive mechanism that may influence appraisal of recent social adversity is the perception about one's own self-worth. The suggestion is that it is easier to cope with a stressful event, and perhaps an ongoing difficulty, if you feel good about yourself as a person (Rutter, 1987c). However, concepts of the self are not as straightforward as they initially appear (Harter, 1983,

1986). The central notion lies in a system of beliefs in oneself in a number of ways. Firstly, *self-determination* in one's life to meet and deal with life's challenges (e.g. Bandura, 1977). Secondly, *self-confidence* that survival will occur in the face of adversity. Thirdly, *self-control* to ensure that taking action is within one's capabilities (e.g. Pellegrini, 1985). It is as yet not clear when or how these three differing forms of the self become utilised at times of stress. Clearly, however, they all may contribute and indeed may have a connectedness to each other.

Problem-solving skills may depend on one's confidence and belief that such processes are both possible in general and can be achieved by oneself or with important others, such as a spouse or a parent.

Of course the implications for responding to stresses and their subsequent re-evaluation are multifaceted. It seems that in some circumstances stresses can be turning points in people's lives and result in a positive reappraisal of both past experiences and future expectations. Such events may not be pleasant. Often undesirable events for adults, such as divorce, can have adaptive qualities that may benefit the self-system through a positive re-evaluation of life. Such events have been termed 'fresh start events', and have been shown to exert a beneficial effect on the resolution of adult depression (Brown, Bifulco and Harris, 1987). The success of problem-solving adversities may be extremely powerful for dealing with future stresses and difficulties.

The evidence for events exerting such effects in childhood are not so clear. Social achievements, educational success and sporting powers all promote the self-system and may be regarded in some senses as desirable. We do not know if such experiences will be of benefit to the self-system in the long term.

Indeed, recent preliminary evidence suggests that social achievements occur with equal proportions in disturbed and non-disturbed children (Goodyer, Wright and Altham, 1989b). The *failure* to obtain social achievements, however, indirectly increases the likelihood of psychiatric disorder in the *presence* of recent friendship difficulties, but *not in the presence* of recent undesirable life events. This specificity of social adversity is of considerable interest since both friendship difficulties and recent stressful life events are known to exert significant and direct risks on the likelihood of school-age children becoming anxious or depressed (see Chapter 3 for discussion of friendship difficulties) (Goodyer, Wright and Altham, 1989c). The relationship between these adverse factors is discussed in more detail in Chapters 8 and 9 when we consider models of the social origins of psychopathology.

For present purposes, however, the findings propose that different social pathways exist for recent adversities and may exert their effects through different components of the self-system. For example, social failure and friendship difficulties may exert effects on cognitions related to future success and personal capabilities and engender doubt about self-efficacy. By contrast, recent stressful life events whose social contexts are predominantly family based and include accidents or illnesses may exert effects on cognitions related to past experiences and raise doubts about the validity of the past, thereby adversely influencing self-confidence.

These social cognitive pathways remain speculative. If effects like this are proven to exist we will need to investigate patterns of alteration in the self-system in relationship to the patterns of social adversities in the social system.

Long-term difficulties and social competence

Perhaps the most intriguing of psychological premises is that of the long-term effects of early social experiences. As already discussed in this chapter and in those on family and social influences, early adversities seem likely to exert negative long-term effects through the consequences of their experience, even if there are immediate or short-term inputs as a direct effect of, say, painful separation. But are the long-term consequences operating by cognitive or non-cognitive mechanisms? And, why is it that similar experiences can result in such different outcomes? (Rutter, 1987c). It is apparent that the effects of long-term stressful experiences are unlikely to be accounted for by any single process, cognitive or non-cognitive.

At present, the evidence required to disentangle the relative contributions of social effects on cognitions is modest. Two findings suggest, however, that two different forms of desirable social experience are associated with later social competence and problem-solving. Thus security to one parent in early childhood predicts peer relations several years later (Bretherton and Walters, 1985) and early positive peer group experiences were predictive of later social competence in the classroom (Pettit, Dodge and Brown, 1988). Could the characteristics that facilitate later friendships be cognitive? And if so what? Perhaps a sense of self-esteem or self-image or the ability to attribute to others good qualities? As yet we do not know.

It is clear, however, that some social adaptation *per se* does occur in children even in the absence of early secure relations. For example, children raised in institutions, and therefore experiencing an absence of close ties in infancy and early childhood (when selective attachments normally arise), can develop close intimate ties with their adoptive parents in late childhood, and do not necessarily show a greater risk for psychiatric disorder in later life and are capable of marriage and rearing children without substantial difficulties (Tizard and Hodges, 1978; Quinton and Rutter, 1985b). Peer relations, however, and intimate confiding relations were impaired in institutionally reared but adopted children, suggesting that although social circumstances had altered for the better and the children had shown the general capacity for making social relationships, impairments in the qualities of those relationships may still persist (Tizard and Hodges, 1978). It is the styles and qualities of interpersonal relationships that seem to be impaired following severe continuous early life experiences. But are the impairments operating through thinking processes? Similarly, one might ask the same question for those individuals who appear to have their lives remedied by later positive social experiences, such as a good marriage.

Of course such studies do not directly provide evidence for alterations in cognitive processes. They do, however, strongly suggest that both persistence and change occur in association with social and cognitive features. The hypothesis that early secure experiences may operate through the self-system on later peer-group behaviour is one conclusion.

The internal working model concept (Bretherton and Walters, 1985) suggests that children would derive a set of expectations about their relationship capacities and other people's responses. This expectation may be shaped by early experiences but it is apparent that internal working models *are not* fixed cognitive concepts but alter and change with life experiences. In this respect, and returning to the severe social privation cases mentioned earlier, it is presumably apparent that children may also have *an absence* of desirable internal working models which may be altered and shaped by the input of wanted social experiences during the course of development.

SOCIAL EXPERIENCE, MEMORY AND MENTAL DEFENCE

If cognitive schemata can, as it were, be manifold and remembered over time, then might different schemata at different points in time influence each other? For example, it has been suggested that later social experiences and even later thoughts about earlier experiences may alter the meaning of earlier experiences and thereby alter their impact.

Of course, this presupposes that the relevant past experiences are available, i.e. remembered. In psychoanalytic theory the notion of repressing unwanted experiences can be construed as an attempt to cope with unwanted stresses (Freud, 1946). Repression as a psychological process is a central notion in psychoanalytic writings together with denial. Both these mechanisms are assumed to have a developmental sequence and there is a further suggestion that children move from overt non-cognitive behavioural defences or avoidance to ideational avoidance by cognitive defences, such as denial, rationalisation and later projection (Sjoback, 1973).

The mechanisms which underlie the use of these cognitive processes and the purposes they serve are less than clear. In psychoanalytic theories these mental 'defence mechanisms' make the assumption that the child utilises cognitive processes to control undesirable levels of anxiety arising from social experiences which may threaten well-being (Freud, 1946; Winnicott, 1968).

Curiously, many of these ideas have subsequently received little attention, resulting in very little improvement in our understanding of how memory and mental mechanisms operate at times of life events and difficulties. Unfortunately, many traditional psychoanalytic views have not stood up to the empirical test (Rutter, 1987a). In addition, a wide range of concepts have been abandoned, or completely integrated into our understanding of mental mechanisms [see Dare (1985) for an overview]. In all, this has resulted in little interest in researching these concepts. This is unfortunate and further research in this area in children is required.

It is interesting to note, for example, that the notion that 'what happens to the organism is a result of experiences good or bad' has received very little attention from social scientists or developmentalists (Rutter, 1987a).

Mental mechanisms

Thoughts may be used as a method for coping with some forms of social experiences, such as acute life events. Already we know that experiences do not operate solely through the acquisition of habits, styles or emotions. Investigations into children's thinking may help us to understand how a cognitive mechanism may arise, the conditions under which it is used and its degree of effect.

We have discussed how internal working models develop through social experiences, the consequences of which lead children to derive expectations about existing relationships. The notion of internal working models is a dynamic one, suggesting active mental processes appraising, filtering and coping with external social information. These mental mechanisms have been suggested as the ways in which external experiences may be reorganised to assist in shaping social schemata of the world. For example, it has been suggested that later social experiences or thoughts may alter an individual's comprehension of earlier experiences and by so doing alter their impact. It may be adaptive for an individual to reconceptualise maternal rejection as a consequence of mother's depression or social circumstances rather than dislike of him or her as a person (Ricks, 1985). If one generalises this view a little, it argues for a dynamic mental apparatus involving cognitive and affective schema that result in a coherence of social experiences, and an internal working model of the world that is both salient and offers the least degree of personal undesirability. In these terms cognitions are the components of mental processes that regulate the emotional effects of social experience. In such circumstances a primary task of cognitions would be to minimise the connotation of personal failing and to enhance, maintain or re-establish self-esteem. For example, recent life events may result in a reappraisal of previous social experiences or a new orientation to new social experiences which may operate through cognitions. Such events may be either undesirable or desirable, depending on the child's ability to think about past or future social behaviour. The impact of cognitive development on the propensity to appraise acute life events remains unclear.

We discussed in the previous chapter how emotions influence cognitive abilities and may promote or inhibit appraisal processes of social experiences. It may be that the capacity to think and appraise events in order to produce an understanding that minimises undesirable effects is influenced by the degree and duration of emotional intensity that an event produces. In other words, the emotional response inherent in appraisal influences the cognitive interpretation of the event.

In most cases, however, the onset of disturbance is days or weeks from a life event, suggesting that cognitions are playing an important role in the intrinsic mechanisms regulating the effects of social adversity—perhaps as modulators of the emotional response to the event.

The clinical value of mental mechanisms is not in question and many important concepts concerning their use have been integrated into everyday clinical practice, particularly, but not exclusively, involving psychodynamic psychotherapy (e.g. Malan, 1979).

Attempts at a systematic classification linking mental mechanisms with the form and expression of psychopathology in childhood have been made, but as yet lack adequate reliability and validity (Freud, 1970). The clinical ideas have therefore provided a basis for the necessary scientific research to investigate the nature and purpose of these mental processes in a systematic manner. At present they remain largely untested but provide important pointers towards our need to develop adequate measures of the cognitive appraisal of life experiences. Considerable advances have been made in the field of cognitive psychology including how thoughts, as a means of coping and adapting to undesirable social experiences, may operate (Fisher and Reason, 1988). Work has recently begun in children and adolescents but as yet we know little of the mental processes involved in recall, appraisal, etc., at different ages. The point here is that cognitive processes have a potentially important role in modulating the emotions that arise from social experiences. A mental mechanism in these terms is one which allows the organism to continue to function efficiently knowing that adverse life experiences may be interrupting behavioural efficiency.

Cognitive mechanisms, therefore, may be called into play under different social circumstances. In these terms, cognitions act as facilitators of coping behaviour. As with the clinical classification of mental mechanisms and the form of psychopathology, we have no reliable or valid classifications for these 'cognitive-behavioural' processes. Some may represent 'defenses' against unwanted anxieties, others facilitators of vigilance or arousal, yet others as promoters of information storage and retrieval.

Denial repression and development

Two methods of investigating thinking and development have occurred in recent times. Firstly, a few studies have examined developmental changes of denial during childhood. Secondly, rather more attempts have been made to document changes in children's understanding of the usage of different defences. The latter area of research has also documented changes in children's understanding of emotions over time.

Firstly, some findings have suggested that children's understanding of what denial is increases with age. This increase occurs from approximately 5 to 14 years, in what appears to be a gradual increment rather than sudden alterations and consequent new levels of comprehension (Dollinger and McGuire, 1981). Others, however, have suggested that there may be associations between degrees of development and understanding of defence mechanisms in a more Piagetian sense. Children classified into pre-operational, concrete and formal operational abilities showed an increasing understanding by category (Chandler, 1985). This appeared to be substantially non-linear for the concepts of denial and repression, suggesting that some new aspect in cognitive function had occurred.

In the above study 10 per cent of the pre-operational group appeared to understand what denial and repression were compared with 75 per cent and 80 per cent of the concrete and formal operations groups respectively. These results suggest that by the age of 9, three-quarters of children may have a substantial understanding of what defence mechanisms are and how they may be used.

Thirdly, use of defence mechanisms in general, and denial and repression in particular, appear closely related with general levels of intelligence both in adults and children. It has been suggested that more intelligent individuals are less ready to employ such mechanisms (Rump and Court, 1971; Smith and Rossman, 1986).

Forms and patterns of denial

Furthermore, recent findings suggest that there may be more than one form of denial. *Denial of affect as a trait* appears unrelated to *denial of arousal under conditions of stress or personal failure* (Smith and Rossman, 1986). This suggests that different mechanisms may operate for the use of denial under different social conditions. Studies in adults confirm denial as a complex multifaceted concept, often situation dependent (Lazarus and Folkman, 1984). The use of denial may have social consequences unrelated to its purpose for 'blocking' undesirable social stimuli. For example, it seems that being defensive is regarded as undesirable in childhood and may lead a child to being viewed as undesirable by friends (Dollinger and McGuire, 1981). This suggests that using denial for *intrinsic adaptation* to minimise thoughts of failure may in some circumstances be *extrinsically maladaptive* and illustrates the costs and benefits of denial as a coping process.

As yet, many of these ideas concerning defensiveness and stress remain largely untested. We need to understand more about external social factors that influence the production and maintenance of a defensive response as well as the internal factors of appraising, making associations and recall of social experiences.

Appraisal of adversity

Research in adults suggests that how a person perceives a life event strongly influences his or her behavioural response (Lazarus and Folkman, 1984). For example, even after substantial and severe difficulties, such as fleeing your country of origin, events such as relocation can be considered beneficial (Hinkle, 1974). There appear to be two cognitive factors in appraising life events. *Primary appraisal*, consisting of recognising that an event has occurred, and *secondary appraisal*, consisting of determining implications and how to react (Lazarus and Folkman, 1984). Sex and developmental differences have been found in how children appraise events. For example, boys respond with greater efforts than girls when receiving feedback from adults that they are failing, girls appear more likely to give up and attribute their failing to their own lack of ability (Dweck and Bush, 1976; Dweck *et al.*, 1978). One of the reasons girls give up may be in the sex-differentiated patterns of feedback from adults. This appears more likely to increase a girl's tendency to feel she cannot succeed no matter what, compared with boys, who appear to receive the message that they could do better if they chose to do so.

These studies confirm how external circumstances influence perceptions of oneself. They also introduce the notion that children's self-image and attributions can be considerably influenced by powerful adults, such as parents and teachers, for example. The appraisal of events such as exam failure may be influenced by the responses of parents and teachers. Children's views of themselves as a consequence of stressful events becomes dependent in part on the views of others. This may even result in children developing negative self-images or low self-esteem. We do not know, however, if this appraisal mechanism is influenced to any degree by earlier experiences. For example, are children with early adversities more likely to appraise events such as exams as potentially more stressful? In other words, are they more 'vulnerable' at times of life events.

The cognitive processes involved in appraising stress seem to be worth further investigation in young people. Cognitive treatments have been developed whose efficacy for some forms of depression and stress-related anxiety disorder have been established. Such theories and treatments have not been put to the empirical test in children, although the case seems favourable (Pellegrini and Urbain, 1985).

THINKING AS COPING

Coping can be defined as those processes that are brought into action to deal with change. In social terms, coping reflects an individual's responses to life experiences. As already indicated, coping has at least two functions: problem-solving and relief of emotional distress. Whilst it is apparent that cognitive processes are involved, it is equally the case that behavioural factors play an important function in coping mechanisms for stress.

To date, however, reliable and valid concepts and measures of coping have proved elusive. As yet there is little evidence to help us disentangle the relative contributions of intrapsychic and environmental factors.

Types of coping response

Environmental alteration (problem-solving) and *emotion regulation* probably represent the two main categories of coping (Lazarus and Folkman, 1984). Coping modes may be categorised further into information seeking, direct action on the self, direct action on the environment, inhibition of action, or the use of internal mental mechanisms, in particular denial (Lazarus and Folkman, 1984).

For example, coping may firstly be anticipatory and initiated before the expected stressful encounter. Secondly, coping may be initiated after a consequence of the event (and presumably during the event in some circumstances). Thirdly, coping may *not* be adaptive in all cases and in some circumstances may increase the risk of maladaptation and psychiatric disorder.

It is apparent that coping is not easily subject to simple unitary variable analysis. Furthermore, it makes no evolutionary sense for human beings to have only one form of coping. The phylogenetic development of the neocortex equips us biologically with a range of new options for appraising and coping in the world compared with other animals, including other primates. The single coping response can be seen at once as less desirable, regardless of efficacy, than a range of responses that may be brought to bear on life strains and stresses (Pearlin and Schooler, 1978).

Developmental influences on the form of coping

Developmental studies demonstrate that different forms of coping occur at different ages or stages of development. In pre-school and early school years the concept of coping may depend less on cognitive factors, and reside more in the patterns of behavioural response seen in child, parents and others. In this respect children may be protected in varying degrees from stresses by the actions of others. However, the cognitive aspects of coping may well develop as a consequence of earlier experiences, including the notion of how protective social and family environments may have been. Numerous studies have demonstrated marked variations in children's responses to stressful events and difficulties both in the short and long term (Rutter, 1981a, 1987b,c). The cognitive components associated with coping in childhood and later life may, however, be influenced by these early social experiences. Past experiences may alter the meaning of new ones or may influence the way events are appraised. Thus the findings that previous hospitalisations in the pre-school years increases the likelihood that some children will develop a psychiatric disorder following a later admission suggests that something may have altered children's mental sets towards similar experiences (Douglas, 1975; Quinton and Rutter, 1976). This suggests that thoughts of past experiences about hospital and/or about separation from parents increases their vulnerability to similar experiences later. It is also the case that for many, previous hospitalisations do not influence the risk of later psychiatric disorder. This suggests that other factors may protect children from this early adversity.

Furthermore, this raises a more general notion, namely that it is a common occurrence for people's responses to stress and adversity to be modified by prior experiences that either increase their vulnerability or protect them from the undesirable effects of life experiences and do so via some effect on cognition. Is it that cognitive styles are in some way formed through social experiences that are negative and undesirable, or is it that an absence of desirable experiences results in a bias of memory or recall towards negative experiences?

The importance of desirable social experiences in protecting people from stress has been well documented. Thus adequate available and intimate relationships with others, successful task accomplishment and effective mastery of previous stresses are all capable of exerting protective effects (Rutter, 1979, 1985c; Garmezy, 1985; Masten and Garmezy, 1985).

Thus social experiences may have an effect on the development of cognitive sets, including the self-concept. The mechanisms by which young people appraise and respond to life experiences and how individual cognitive sets influence their coping reaction to events is unclear.

Cognitive control of event-related emotions

As we have discussed, when a person is subject to a stressful event or difficulty, both emotional and cognitive consequences are likely to occur.

This may be because emotional arousal in the face of a stimulus is likely to have cognitive consequences (Gilligan and Bower, 1984). Furthermore, the emotions and cognitions generated as a consequence of an event may occur automatically without intention and without interfering with another mental event (Posner and Snyder, 1975).

In contrast to such automatic processes there are also control processes which require awareness, command attentional resources and need time and effort to implement. Under these conditions interference with other ongoing mental processes is likely (Posner and Snyder, 1975; Clark and Isen, 1982; Gilligan and Bower, 1984).

In automatic responses to a life event or difficulty, arousal may be controlled by cognitions. Events that are salient and evoke feeling states are associated with thoughts arising in consciousness through, for example, self-talk procedures. These cognitive consequences of event-emotion arousal are recycled together with the event. The production of thoughts to arousal act as a means of ameliorating emotional responses to stressful events and have been termed control cognitions. Control cognitions may be held in short-term memory, their functions may be to distract and counter immediate thoughts associated and activated by the emotional arousal of an event. Their value has been in self-control treatments of a range of anxious states as well as depression (Meichenbaum and Novaco, 1978; Meichenbaum and Cameron, 1983). If there is a deficit or lack of controlling thoughts, no self-talk or rehearsals of thoughts can occur and activated negative thoughts may accrue in response to social adversity. Under these conditions short-term memory becomes filled with undesirable thoughts in relation to emotionally arousing events. Although the event-related emotion may die out the negative cognition may remain in memory (Gilligan and Bower, 1984). In other words, new undesirable thinking has been brought about by the absence of control thinking.

Reappraisal of events from memory

If negative cognitions develop and remain embedded in memory, could this be the basis for negative appraisal of other life events and difficulties in the future?

It has been proposed that an event causing an emotional reaction would be stored in memory as a triad. Thus: (i) The social experience episode, (ii) The emotions aroused, and (iii) The emotion-cognition consequences (Bower and Cohen, 1982). An emotional interpretation connects event appraisal and emotion response. An example given by Gilligan and Bower (1984) is IF someone harms you (appraisal) then feel anger at that person (response).

The social context and the emotional state of an individual at the time of an event may determine what forms of emotion and cognition will be produced. This suggests that the response to an undesirable event will differ according to the individual's mood at that time. To be happy at the time of an accident may result in a different emotion-cognitive response than if one were already angry or sad. What is *not* clear is whether or not such immediate appraisals have an impact on later emotions and thoughts concerning subsequent events perceived as similar by an individual.

However, storing the emotion-cognition interpretation may provide an explanation as to why an individual had the emotional reaction he did. Secondly, it may be that the memory of the event-emotion reaction may be used in reinterpreting or changing one's thoughts of an earlier event. In other words, a different emotional reaction may be assigned to a subsequent event because the meaning of the earlier event has been reconsidered in the light of present experience and its intrinsic impact altered.

But how might such a reappraisal occur? There are at least four possibilities. Firstly, there may be new information concerning the event, altering its meaning and explanation. For example, concern for a child's fall becomes relief when no fractures are found. Secondly, a change in values or attitudes may occur. For example, pride associated with antisocial behaviour may later become shame as concern for people and property replace earlier disregard. Thirdly, the impact of an event may be neutralised by subsequent social experiences. For example, rejection for a higher education placement with its feelings of sadness may soon be dissipated by subsequent acceptance and feelings of joy. Another example of neutralisation may arise by recognising the 'shared experience' of the event. For example, the recognition of a particular handicap in oneself and its associated feelings of despair can be lessened by recognising similar handicaps in others and appraising their subsequent mood and behaviour. Fourthly, the nature of one's mood may determine the appraisal of an event. Tired and exhausted parents may experience irritation at a young child's behaviour but when rested the next day may feel gaiety about their handling of the situation.

Of course the adaptive importance of cognitive control processes in the presence of social adversities is self-evident. To be able to reconceptualise events and difficulties in such a way as to shift the connotation away from personal negative impact may decrease a sense of distress.

Secondly, it may be necessary to accept the reality of past negative events and experiences and to integrate them into a coherent understandable framework whose rules and reasons make sense (Main, Kaplan and Cassidy, 1985). It may be that to appraise and apply meaning to stressful events and difficulties resulting in an unpleasant, even undesirable, concept of the world is preferable to experiencing stresses that remain chaotic, distressing and inherently non-understandable. These 'cognitive control' models, whilst attractive and intuitively plausible, remain largely untested.

Nevertheless, the development of cognitive therapies for a variety of emotional difficulties in both adults and children owe some of their techniques to these theoretical postulates (Beck, 1976).

DEVELOPMENTAL INFLUENCES ON EMOTION COMPREHENSION

Children have different cognitive abilities at different ages. The ability to appraise adversity and comprehend the emotional effects of adversity are likely to influence the form of response that the child exhibits.

In Chapter 6 we outlined the developmental principles in emotion theory. In this chapter we have described how some form of mental mechanism, denial for example, alters both with age and with social contexts. There is, however, evidence to suggest marked changes with age in the knowledge that children have about situational, personal and strategic factors which are responsible for variations in memory performance (Flavell and Wellman, 1977; Brown, 1978).

Reappraisal of stressful events from memory therefore seems likely to be different at different ages. Furthermore, emotions, as we have seen, have motivational components and influence social behaviours and task performances. Happiness encourages altruistic behaviours and facilitates performances on cognitive tasks whereas sadness depresses both (Moore, Underwood and Rosenhan, 1984).

At present, the evidence suggests that children change their concept of emotion as development unfolds. This has implications for the way in which children think about identifying and controlling the effects of emotion (Harris, Olthof and Terwogt, 1981; Carroll and Steward, 1984; Harris, 1989). It seems that 5–6-year-old children do not make reference to the inner mental events that are a consequence of stress but direct their efforts to external features, such as the emotions of others and the situation itself. In other words, identifying one's own emotion in pre-schoolers and children under 7 occurs by noting reactions in others and the social setting.

Control processes over stressful events do seem in this age-group to be essentially *non-cognitive* and will operate either by *displaying reactions (behaviours)* that are different from those normally elicited by a situation (such as laughing at being told off) or *altering the situation itself* and therefore allowing different emotions to dominate as a consequence (for example, altering a game or content of play after a quarrel with another child). In other words, coping with undesirable life experiences requires changing the environment rather than a redirection of inner mental processes.

As children get older, inner mental states do become recognised and utilised in emotion-event episodes. As well as attempting control through the environment, redirecting one's mental state using thoughts will also occur. Older children are also more likely to offer mentalistic explanations of the effects of emotion as a consequence of social experience.

These differences in children's understanding of emotions and use of cognitive coping processes reflect on the child's general developing awareness of his own mental and motor activities. Thus it may be that in memory cognitive associations may serve as retrieval aids even for a young child without him being aware he does, or could, use them (Gordon and Flavell, 1977). Overall the qualities of memory seem to be different in pre-schoolers with little use of past performance when involved in a task that involves remembering or forgetting (Miscione *et al.*, 1978; Wellman and Johnson, 1979a).

Moral judgement seems to exhibit a similar progression, suggesting that young children evaluate acts in terms of their overt consequences and it is only later that intention of the person's actions is taken into account (Kohlberg, 1969; Rest, Davison and Robbins, 1978). We may conclude that stress events in pre-schoolers, and perhaps children up to the age of 7, will not be appraised and understood with the same mechanisms as in the older child. The mental apparatus may be different and less reliance on cognitive control processes seems likely. Clearly emotions can operate as motivators for behavioural change and this seems the likeliest coping strategy following stress and difficulties. Furthermore, the presence of cognitive control processes does not imply that such coping methods will be used in all cases and emotion motivated behavioural mechanisms may still be used, perhaps when there is clear proximity between stress impact and behavioural response.

These developmental mechanisms require further investigation to determine how early social experiences may influence the development of internal working models of cognitive coping (Rutter, 1987a). Greater clarity of the age-related nature of these processes could help in promoting interventions which include the level of development of a child as well as the presenting complaint. For example, cognitive based treatments may not be successful in 6-year-olds without attention to the social environment, or an understanding of their emotion-behavioural style of response to changes in their environment.

SUMMARY

1. Current theories of cognitive development are unlikely to be mutually exclusive. There is an important role for life experiences from infancy onwards in the formation of social cognitions.
2. Internal working models and self-system are cognitive processes which probably develop from the life experiences a child is exposed to and interacts with.
3. Early adverse life experience may result in deficits to internal working models and the self-system. Such deficits can be ameliorated by subsequent positive life experiences. It is not clear, however, if there are persistent deficits in some components of the self-system as a direct consequence of chronic social deprivation in infancy and early childhood.
4. Mental mechanisms are important cognitive processes that are involved in the appraisal of life experiences. The type of mental mechanism employed depends on the age and stage of development and involves the use of memory.
5. Coping processes are brought into action to deal with change. Regulating emotions and developing problem solving skills represent the two main categories of coping. Styles of coping are influenced by intelligence, social environment and past experience.
6. Cognitive controls and emotion regulation of responses to social adversities vary with development. In young children psychological processes used at times of events and difficulties are often non-cognitive. As children get older, inner mental states become increasingly used in emotion–event episodes.

Part Three

Psychopathology

Chapter 8

Life Experience and Psychiatric Disorders

RECORDING LIFE EVENTS

Following in the footsteps of the life history approach proposed by Meyer came the first life research events inventory developed in the 1960s by Holmes and Rahe (1967) and called the 'social readjustment rating schedule'. This scale assigned stress scores to each life event on the basis that all events which resulted in a change in social circumstances were stressful and some will be more stressful than others. Individuals simply ticked those events that had occurred in the previous weeks and months and the stress scores, or life change units as they were known, were summated to provide a total score. Comparisons between different groups of individuals with medical and psychiatric disorders could then be made. Over the next 2 decades considerable interest and modification of the scale occurred, and child and adolescent versions were developed (Masuda and Holmes, 1967; Coddington, 1972a,b; Tennant and Andrews, 1977; Dohrenwend *et al.*, 1978; Monaghan, Robinson and Dodge, 1979; Yamamoto *et al.*, 1987). There remained, however, considerable methodological difficulties with both the reliability of individuals reporting events and the validity of the life change units. In other words, it became clear that self-report checklists were unsatisfactory as a method for understanding either the prevalence or the meaning of stressful events in people's lives. The original intention of these scales had been to find a method of predicting illness rates (especially physical illness) from stress. By the 1970s George Brown and colleagues were arguing that a different approach was needed to examine this question and, more importantly, to test the hypothesis that social factors *caused illness*, particularly psychiatric disorders (Brown, Harris and Peto, 1973; Brown, 1974).

Brown and his colleagues argued that only the use of a comprehensive, wide ranging and detailed semi-structured interview carried out by trained interviewers would be able to produce information of sufficient quality to measure the degree of stress in people's lives (Brown and Harris, 1978). This interview procedure records the details of each event and the social context within which they have occurred. The information obtained from a good informant is thus considered to be both a comprehensive and a highly specific account of that individual's recent life events. The number, scope and specificity of the data is limited only by the interviewer's persistence or the subject's reluctance to disclose either embarrassing events or those considered too trivial. This data gathering technique was a considerable advance in life events research methodology.

THE ARGUMENT FOR A LIFE EVENTS AND DIFFICULTIES INTERVIEW

The precepts upon which measurement of causes are based are different from those of prediction to the extent that self-report methods are both insufficient and, more importantly, invalid methods for causal inquiry. Brown (1974) indicated that the measurement of a selected variable can easily be contaminated by the very causal process an investigator wishes to study. He described two sources of invalidity that must be taken into account at the level of measurement.

Direct contamination

First, the measurement of the selected variable can be directly *contaminated* by the very causal processes an investigator wishes to study. In this example a person is asked to recall life events at the time he or she is ill, and recall of events may be directly contaminated by the process of recall. In such circumstances events may be over-reported as occurrences and may seem more significant than they were; events may be forgotten or details distorted as a consequence of mental state difficulties. The effort to explain present difficulties as a consequence of past social experiences (effort after meaning) underlies this source of direct invalidity (Bartlett, 1932).

Indirect contamination

Secondly, other variables not measured in the research may be important in determining the rates of psychiatric disorder. For example, careful interviewing may have delineated that a life event had occurred before the onset of symptoms but a third factor, such as chronic social adversities in a child's life or a difficult temperament, had important causal effects on the onset of psychiatric disorder. In these circumstances *indirect contamination* of life events measurement may occur because the causal effect of events would be removed once the third factor was taken into account. Thirdly, a spurious relationship between events and subsequent symptoms may be inferred because of a third factor that has causal associations with both events and disorder, i.e. both life events and symptoms are dependent on other social factors or intrinsic factors in the child.

These crucial conceptual arguments concerning the validity of life events reports led Brown and his co-workers to argue that the only valid methodological procedure was to separate as carefully as possible events from disorder in time and to investigate the relative contribution of events in the presence of other social adversities. They developed an extensive semi-structured interview method to record face to face the full details surrounding any social experience in the recent past. The interview proved to be reliable and to show an acceptable degree of validity. Adults were capable of recalling life events more consistently in the interview situation and were able to date accurately the time of onset of disorder and the event, so that events that may be a *cause* rather than a *consequence* of disorder could be separated. As well as determining the event's independence it was argued that the personal meaning of an event needed to be taken into account in order to understand its full nature and circumstances for the individual. It was this second measurement concept that led to the development of life event vignettes that contained the social context of events. Rating vignettes by mental health professionals for their degree of threat to the individual provided a method of evaluating the causal impact of events which took account of social differences between individuals and prevented the index patient from receiving a rating which may have been distorted for reasons described above under 'effort after meaning'.

The independence of life events from disorder

The interview method allows for events that are *consequences* of disorder to be discriminated from those that are potentially *causes* of disorder. Such events can be truly said to be independent of disorder, although as we have discussed they may be dependent on other factors in the environment or in the child. Life events which are independent of illness and whose context is known can be classified according to a variety of features. The most successful methods have involved those which take into account the psychological meaning that events are likely to have for an individual (Brown and Harris, 1978, 1986; Paykel, 1983; Paykel et al., 1969, 1980).

ADULT PSYCHIATRIC DISORDER AND LIFE EVENTS

The studies of Brown and Paykel showed that, when asking causal questions, it was events that carried a moderate to severe degree of threat or undesirable negative impact that were most likely to be causally associated with psychiatric disorder, particularly, although not exclusively, with depression (Brown and Harris, 1978; Paykel et al., 1969).

These studies demonstrated that the qualities of events that caused disorder appeared rather non-specific and pertained more to some general notion of stress than to some specific tie between events and types of disorder.

Because of this, a number of refinements to event measurement occurred. Classifying events according to some form of permanent and personal loss has received most study (Paykel *et al.*, 1980). Such exit events (i.e. events that result in the permanent removal of an individual from a person's social field) have been reported as significantly more common in depressives than in controls (Paykel *et al.*, 1969). A number of other studies in adults confirm that separations are significantly more common in depressives than controls (Paykel *et al.*, 1980). The converse entrance events (the permanent entry into a person's social field) are not associated with depression (Paykel *et al.*, 1969). There is also a suggestion that exits, undesirable and uncontrollable interpersonal disruptions, are reported more by depressed than anxious adults (Barrett, 1979).

Overall, adult studies suggest that major interpersonal losses become increasingly important as age increases, occurring mostly in later phases of the life cycle.

It is apparent, however, that the relationship between depression and loss events classified in this way is not specific. For example, separations have been shown to precede other disorders (Paykel and Rowan, 1979). Events have been associated with a variety of psychiatric disorders, including a variety of anxiety states, suicide attempts and as triggering factors in schizophrenia and mania (Brown and Birley, 1968; Paykel, 1974; Tennant and Andrews, 1978; Kennedy *et al.*, 1983).

However, events considered as dangerous to self and as losses have been shown to be significantly more common in anxiety and depression respectively (Finlay-Jones and Brown, 1981). The latter findings suggest that some specificity and magnitude of the association can be identified between adversities and psychiatric disorder. For example, neurotic depressives are more likely to report multiple interconnected events with a variety of meanings whilst the severity of their symptoms may be associated with the intensity of the events (Uhlenhuth and Paykel, 1973; Benjamissen, 1981).

Dimensions of life events

Recent findings have shown that refining the event measure can improve the specificity of events to psychiatric disorder. For example, Miller and Ingham (1983) categorised events on six dimensions (loss, threat, social action, hopeless situation, uncertain outcome, choice of action) and found that the number and pattern of these characteristics within a single event provided a better estimate for predicting adult depression than any one single dimension alone. These improvements in event measurement can be important in improving the magnitude of the association between events and depression.

Despite the crucial refinements in the measurement of life events and ongoing difficulties, the relationship between events, recent difficulties and depression is far from all embracing. In many clinical studies a substantial proportion of adults do not report events preceding disorder and in many controls events occur without subsequent depression.

The magnitude of association between events and psychiatric disorder

The precedence of events before disorder establishes the basis for the argument that events cause disorder. We have already discussed the qualitative pitfalls that need to be considered if such an argument is to become credible. A second concept to be considered is the relative magnitude of the causal effects that events preceding onset of disorder may bring to bear. For example, we may determine that events are not the result of a third variable and do indeed exert potentially causal effects, but the size of that effect needs to be known in comparison with, say, other putative causal factors occurring in the child's life. Knowing the increase in risk for psychopathology as a consequence of a life event may help to decide whether or not exposure to such an event should be avoided at all costs or whether such risk is considered acceptable.

Measuring the quantity of causal impact for recent life events has been the subject of a number of research reports in recent years (e.g. Paykel, 1978; Cooke and Hole, 1983). Two of these have been used relatively frequently and will be briefly described. They are both developed from epidemiological principles for measuring the association between exposure to a particular factor and risk of a certain outcome, and are termed relative risk and attributable risk (MacMahon and Pugh, 1970).

Relative risk

Relative risk is the ratio of a disease (usually the incidence) amongst those exposed to the rate compared with those not exposed. Paykel (1978) has shown that the use of relative risk statistic is appropriate for calculating the magnitude of association between life events and psychiatric disorder from case–control studies where cases have been identified from hospitals or selected outpatients. Such reports are unlikely to be representative of all cases in the general population.

Relative risk can be calculated from a fourfold table as shown in Table 8.1.

Table 8.1

Suspected cause	Cases	Controls	Total
Present	a	b	$a + b$
Absent	c	d	$c + d$

Relative risk $= \frac{ad}{bc}$

Using this relative risk formula an estimate of the risk of psychiatric disorder when exposed to life events can be calculated. Examination of a range of studies shows that events increase the risk between 2 and 7 times in the 6 months after an event has occurred (Paykel, 1978). Many individuals are exposed to an event but do not become ill, indicating the importance of interactions between events and other factors to produce disorder.

Attributable risk per cent

Attributable risk per cent (Lilienfield and Lilienfield, 1980) is the rate of disease in exposed individuals that can be attributed to the exposure. A relatively precise enumeration of the incidence of disease in the exposed and non-exposed population is required, making this statistic unsuitable for case–control studies but suitable for epidemiological cohort studies. It is derived by subtracting the rate for disease among non-exposed individuals from those exposed.

Attributable risk per cent can be calculated as shown in Table 8.2.

Table 8.2

Suspected cause	Cases	Controls	Total
Present	a	b	$a + b$
Absent	c	d	$c + d$

Attributable risk $= \frac{ad - bc}{(a+c)(c+d)} \times 100\%$.

Cooke and Hole (1983) applied this risk estimate to cohort studies where the rates of psychiatric disorder had been identified in the community and argued that some 32 per cent of all psychiatric cases of anxiety and depression in adults could be attributed to stressful life events. Within female samples approximately 41 per cent of cases of anxiety and depression could be attributed to life events and rates may be higher when specific life events were associated with specific psychiatric disorders.

Recent findings suggest that if ongoing difficulties are included with life events then some three-quarters of depressive episodes are proceeded by a provoking agent, either a stressful event or difficulty. However, only about one in five women who experience events go on to develop depression (Brown and Harris, 1978; Brown, Bifulco and Harris, 1987).

This explains why the correlations between events and disorder rarely account for more than 10 per cent of the variance (Andrews et al., 1978). Clearly many other factors besides recent events and difficulties are causally important in psychiatric disorder in adults.

The statistical issues surrounding the correct use of these estimations are beyond the scope of this book and the reader is referred to other texts (Everitt, 1977; Lilienfield and Lilienfield, 1980).

Recently the magnitude of association between events and depression in women was improved when a range of life events measures were examined for their match with other contextual areas in a woman's life and their ability to predict the onset of depression. This notion deals with the potential congruence between the configuration of different meanings inherently possible in a single life event and other adverse social experiences (Brown, Bifulco and Harris, 1987). The study reports some further refinements in the methods of rating life events and difficulties, including improvements arising from collecting further life history information in the same systematic way as for recent events and difficulties.

Firstly, long-term threat was dichotomised into upper and lower, indicating whether a threat was imminent or had already occurred. Secondly, six types of loss were considered: (i) death, (ii) separation, (iii) unemployment, (iv) physical illness, (v) disappointment, (vi) loss of a cherished idea. The first four of these classes of loss are identifiable in terms of social experience, i.e. they have an identifiable frame of reference. The last two classes do not and therefore concern a conceptually different area of stress based on an internal frame of reference. Descriptive information provides the basis for these ratings.

The last two concepts are not easy to discriminate and careful definitions were used to assist in maintaining independence of the ratings. Thus disappointment is considered to have occurred when an event results in an undesirable revision of a previous life experience. Loss of a cherished idea is defined as a disruption of an expectation of trust, faithfulness or commitment, which may lead the individual to question these qualities in herself (these measures have so far only been reported in women). A rating of loss of a cherished idea therefore excludes a rating of previous experiences and is made on the basis of undesirable changes to ideas. This rating is therefore an attempt to measure the symbolic appraisal of loss. The concept of danger to the self is further divided into present danger and anticipated danger, which might occur in the future as a consequence of an event in the present. The results confirm that multidimensional ratings of events and their match with previous social experience substantially improves both the prediction of depression and our understanding of the mechanisms that cause such disorders.

These findings continue to emphasise the importance of systematic interview methods using life history techniques to collect reliable information about an individual's past experiences. They also continue to illustrate the importance of using this information to develop scales of measurement based on the potential meaning of social experiences in people's lives.

Timing and onset of disorder

Ideally, the causal link between life events and psychiatric disorder would be investigated by studying events as they occur in the community, following up the population and noting the rate of illness in the days, weeks and months after event occurrence. The incidence of such disorder occurring within days and weeks of an event would give the best estimate of the causal fit of events to disorder as it reflects the proportion of new-onset cases.

Prospective studies on adult psychiatric illness

The need for such prospective designs to examine the nature of the causal link between events and illness has been emphasised by a number of researchers (Lloyd, 1980a,b; Tennant, Bebbington and Hurry, 1981). However, Paykel (1978) has pointed out the practical implications of such studies and indicated that whereas they are both feasible and desirable for those conditions which occur relatively frequently in the community (such as neurotic disorders) they would be difficult and expensive for disorders that are uncommon in the community. Andrews (1981) reported a community based prospective study of events occurring in 407 adults initially free from symptoms and found that the incidence of neurotic symptoms was significantly associated with life events that had occurred in the 4 months prior to symptom onset. The size of the association was similar to that of other retrospective studies. Andrews examined the path analysis of events to symptoms and found that 8 months later the association between events and symptoms was negligible and that previous symptoms were a better prediction of present symptoms than previous life events. A possible interaction between persistent symptoms and life events was noted. The findings are consistent with other studies which have examined the time-course relationship between events and symptoms and suggested complex interactions between these factors and possible other mediating variables (Clayton, 1974; Eaton, 1978; Warheit, 1979). A case–control prospective study by Grant et al. (1981) arrived at the conclusion that the relationship between life events and symptoms depended on specific qualities of both variables and that undesirable and uncontrollable events had a direct association with both dysphoric and somatic symptoms.

A further strategy used with community samples consisted of examining the relationship between life events and the remission of neurotic disorders in adults (Tennant, Bebbington and Hurry, 1981). In this study the authors concluded that 30 per cent of all remissions in 108 subjects defined as cases according to Wing's criteria (Wing et al., 1978) were due to a 'neutralising' life event, defined as an event which specifically neutralised the impact of an earlier threatening life event. Further recent advances in the association between anxious and depressive disorders in women in the community have been found by investigating the quality and timing of events in relation to onset of disorder (Miller et al., 1987).

These findings suggested that the duration of symptoms and the course and nature of women's disorders were related to the form and timing of the life event. Events rated as likely to be of uncertain outcome were associated with illnesses of relatively longer duration, whereas events involving impaired interpersonal relations were associated with continuing illnesses. Events containing neither of these factors were associated with transient disorders of a few weeks' duration only. These longitudinal studies have tended to emphasise qualities in events that are either positive with respect to previous experiences or possessing varying degrees of undesirable effect on the subject. A recent report suggested that some events may exert a positive influence on the outcome of disorder because they intrinsically alter the person's appraisal of their life circumstances. Such events have been referred to as 'fresh start' events. These events may be desirable *or* undesirable in themselves, such as a serious personal accident, sudden unemployment or divorce. The notion is that social change exerts cognitive effects causing an alteration mental state (Brown, Bifulco and Harris, 1987). These findings demonstrate links with social cognitions discussed in the previous chapter. The findings suggest that there is an effect on the reappraisal of past life circumstances for the better, even if cognitive-emotional responses to the present life event is unpleasant. A clinical use of this premise may be to investigate the positive effects an acute experience may have after acknowledging and treating the distressing effects. In a sense this suggests cognitive restructuring of past experiences may be beneficial if this helps the individual to appraise that there are opportunities for the future as a result. Perhaps divorce is an example here; it is distressing and emphasises interpersonal failure but it can be used to examine an individual's cognitions about the purpose of relationships. Perhaps if a more constructive thinking approach to relationships can arise then the divorce process may have served a purpose for the future (see Chapter 2 for details on the effects of divorce). Such an approach may help to minimise second failures in marriage that appear all too common. This suggests that for many individuals re-evaluating past experiences and learning for the future has not occurred.

LIFE EVENT CHECKLISTS IN CHILDHOOD AND ADOLESCENCE

Life event checklists have been in use for over a decade. Both paediatricians and psychiatrists have employed them for methods that are similar to those of previous adult studies (Coddington, 1972a,b; Heisel *et al.*, 1973; Kashani *et al.*, 1981). The majority of studies have indicated that life events are reported significantly more often by the parents of children with both physical and psychiatric illnesses. When other factors, such as chronic family discord or parental psychiatric illness, have been measured in the study the results suggest that life events are less important (Steinhausen and Radtke, 1986). Unfortunately all of these studies suffer from the same sources of invalidity as for checklists used in adults. Life events may not be reported because lists are too short, events may be consequences of disorder and occur *after* onset of illness, parents may not be able to distinguish events from ongoing difficulties without careful discrimination and life change units may not estimate qualitative differences between single or classes of events.

Life events as provoking help-seeking

Life event checklist studies have indicated that event occurrence is significantly related to help-seeking from primary care physicians. A study investigating psychiatric morbidity in children taken to their primary care physician showed that almost one in three of the children with somatic complaints had emotional disturbance and that the presentation was significantly associated with stress in the lives of child and parents (Garralda and Bailey, 1986). Mothers reported life events as occurring significantly more often than controls not attending their physician. Whilst events may have been illness related, a reasonable interpretation of the findings is that in some cases life events were causing families to seek help. The mothers of the cases also reported greater levels of psychiatric morbidity in their own lives as well as significantly more social stresses, such as relationship difficulties and housing problems. It may be that a recent undesirable life event occurring in the presence of other difficulties is a sufficient reason for these families to seek help from their physician. If this were true we might predict that it is families with existing ongoing social adversity in whom life events act as a help-seeking variable. As yet we do not know what mechanisms may be included. Intuitively, however, it seems possible that a new acute event is perceived as an additional burden that is out of the parents' control. Exactly why this should promote behaviour activity in some persons, however, is not clear. Investigating life events as mediators in the process of health care delivery as well as causal models of psychiatric disorder seems well worth while.

Measuring events—some issues for childhood

In adult studies the patient is invariably the person interviewed about recent stressful life events. But can we expect children reliably and validly to report recent adversities in their lives? We do not know if adults' concepts and perceptions of threat, undesirability and other dimensions of events are necessarily the same as those of young people themselves (Yamamoto *et al.*, 1987). This issue needs addressing and investigating, perhaps using well children at different ages to rate how threatening events might be perceived. Furthermore, what of subjective ratings of the child patients themselves? Whilst patients with acute disorder may overrate the undesirable qualities of events, this may not be true for more quiescent phases of illness (e.g. recovering).

Some early findings suggest that events rated by adults and adolescents show high concordance when severely undesirable but low concordance when only mildly undesirable. In particular, adolescents with psychiatric disorders are significantly more likely to rate mild events as severe compared with well adolescents or adults (Gannon, Goodyer and Rivlin, 1989). This suggests that adolescents with recent disturbance may overestimate the impact of events and this may be a function of disorder. Young people's ratings of events may therefore be prone to the same sorts of invalidity as ratings for adults with similar errors due to overestimating the degree of undesirability and therefore confounding the association between events and disorder.

Methodologically there will be developmental limitations in obtaining children's ratings of events and it is unlikely that children under 7 or 8 years old would be able to evaluate the impact of life events over time.

A further measurement issue concerns the conditions in which an event occurs. Children and adolescents may not be in a position to (a) take independent action or (b) guard against being adversely influenced by events happening to other family members. In some events, the impact may be filtered by parents or others dealing with the practical issues required, e.g. nursing a sick family member at home, or providing direct support to the child by explanation and reassurance of their sibling's condition. In other circumstances the effects of events may be amplified, e.g. the failure to nurse a sick sibling adequately may indirectly increase the effects of this event on a child.

A CHILD AND FAMILY LIFE EVENTS INTERVIEW

Collecting life events

Because of the well-known shortcomings of checklists Goodyer and colleagues (1985) decided to develop an interview for children and families to overcome the methodological problems described by George Brown and discussed earlier in this chapter (Brown, 1974; Brown and Harris, 1978).

Mindful of the fact that life events for children and adolescents may not be the same as those occurring in the lives of adults, a life events inventory was drawn up and each event was used as a basis for gathering information through interviews about the nature, context and circumstances surrounding each prescribed event. The original child and family life events interview consisted of 66 potential events with guidelines for their collection. Thus interviews had to (i) establish that events occurred prior to the onset of symptoms or illness-related behaviours, (ii) determine the time, duration and social context of each event, (iii) establish that event occurrence included all event circumstances.

For example, marital disharmony may have resulted in a physical assault to a spouse, and a permanent separation of parents. Should this be rated as three events (disharmony, assault, separation) or should this be seen as a single event separation with the other factors considered as social context and used to decide the nature of the life event.

It was decided that the life event should be the end-stage or resultant experience of the social circumstances, providing the duration of the social context was less than 4 weeks and circumstances were clearly linked. If they occurred in a linked way over days *rather than months* they would not be rated as independent events. In this way the rules for deciding what constituted an event were developed. The work of Brown and Harris (1978), Paykel *et al.* (1980) and Paykel (1983) investigating life events in adults was used in helping to develop rules for how a life event should be defined and recorded.

The interview was developed for school-age children and therefore the events represented what might occur across a large age range (6–18 years). The present schedule contains 70 key items, including events that reflect social, educational and personal achievement, that may carry desirable as well as undesirable connotations.

The schedule was designed to collect life events from mothers as it was considered likely that mothers would be equally as good as children in rating events that had occurred in family and personal terms, and likely to be better in describing the details. This *a priori* assumption has proven to be reasonable except for late adolescence (i.e. over 16 years of age), where personal and sexual events of teenagers may not be known to parents (Monck and Dobbs, 1985). Equally, however, parental events likely to have an impact on children (such as parental disharmony) may be known by children but the details only available from parents.

Events are collected by interviewers who use a semi-structured interview schedule to elicit (i) the date of onset of disorder, (ii) event occurrence, (iii) event description.

Interviews were able to delineate reliably the onset of psychiatric disorder in recent onset cases whose symptoms had occurred in the previous 12 months (Goodyer, Kolvin and Gatzanis, 1985; Goodyer, Wright and Altham, 1988). Dating onsets in a retrospective manner from parents of disturbed children is clearly a difficult task. Whilst parents may be reliable we cannot always be sure that they are being valid. They may, for example, have failed to notice symptoms until a certain threshold of social difficulty or overt distress was present in their child.

Rating life events

The descriptions of life events were transcribed into vignettes (see below). As in adult studies, it was decided to make judgements of the effects that events were likely to bring to bear on a child. The vignettes were free of mother's or child's subjective reports or interpretations of the events' effects. In this sense an objective account of events had been obtained.

Two ratings of events were made in the published research but, as indicated in Chapter 1, the classification of life events suggests that a range of evaluations on life events are possible and may add to our understanding of the likely mechanisms of their effects.

The first rating is the degree of undesirability. Based on the work of Paykel (1983) and derived from Brown and Harris (1978) this rating was defined as the degree of negative impact an event would be expected to have on a child when its full nature and circumstances are taken into account. The convention has been for two raters to discuss the vignette and assign a rating on a 5-point scale, varying from no negative impact to severe negative impact. It has been shown that there is good agreement between pairs of raters whether or not the vignette is known to come from a case or control (Goodyer, Wright and Altham, 1988). This was a useful finding as it could have been that knowledge of a child's status (case or control) biased the raters into a favourable or unfavourable view of the event. The findings suggested that this is in fact unlikely to be the case. In practice the 5-point scale has generally been dichotomised into events with no or mild impact and events with moderate, marked or severe impact.

The inter-rater reliability of objective negative impact has been shown to be satisfactory for both childhood and adult events (Paykel, 1983; Goodyer, Kolvin and Gatzanis, 1985).

Rating negative impact provides a qualitative measure of an event with an undesirable effect. If we are concerned with investigating the potential causal effects of events it is important that the negative effects are not overestimated. One area of concern in this regard, other than undesirability, is to be confident that only events independent of disorder are included. An independent event is one which was not a consequence or potential consequence of illness or illness determined behaviour. The interviewers will have filtered out most of these events at interview. But, as we have noted, some events may be included by the interviewers because mothers believed them to have occurred prior to the onset of disorder. In order, however, to retain a 'conservative model of effects' it is useful to have a second filter. Thus raters are asked to judge an event's likely independence on a 5-point scale, from independent of illness to certainly not independent of illness. Events that are considered possibly or certainly not independent of illness, even if included by the interviewer, are then removed from any analysis that is investigating the potential causal links between life events and onset of disorder.

Should significant associations then be found between life events and disorder from retrospective accounts of life events by respondents, it can be argued that a potentially causal link has been established in part because of the conservative selection procedures used to include events. Note that in a retrospective interview, even in a prospective sample of children, a true causal link cannot be assumed, hence the phrase 'potentially causal link or effect' must be retained. A prospective study of community children free of disorder followed until events and subsequent illness occur remains the best model for determining cause. We have, however, already discussed the significant methodological and resource implications for such a study. The replication of cross-sectional findings and conducting short-term longitudinal studies on at-risk populations, such as recently bereaved children or children of recently divorced parents, remains the most realistically promising way of advancing causal psychological theory in this area.

Classifying events

In Chapter 1 we discussed in detail the range of classifications possible in theory for life events and difficulties. To date, however, in the two studies in which events have been collected and measured classification has occurred in four dimensions: (i) by the degree of undesirability, (ii) by the degree of independence, (iii) by their social characteristics, (iv) as exit or entrance events (i.e. permanent separations or gains to the child's social field). Examples of life event ratings are given below: the classifications by social characteristics are followed by the ratings of independence and undesirability assigned to each event.

Examples of measuring objective negative impact of life events

(1) Marriage and family events

    Background information   An $8\frac{1}{2}$-year-old prepubertal boy with no permanent medical disabilities. He lives with his biological parents, father aged 28 and mother aged 26, and is the elder of two children with a younger sister aged 5. They live in rented council-house accommodation in an urban dockland area of the city. Father is a maintenance foreman in the docks and has been employed in his job for more than 5 years.

    Life event   An episode of marital friction occurred 10 months prior to onset of illness and lasted approximately 4 weeks, following a change in father's work roster with a resultant decrease in take-home pay as part of the general recession in his employment. Parents disagreed as to how to handle the financial changes, in particular whether or not to receive help from maternal grandparents who had offered financial assistance, particularly with the children. The matter was resolved amicably.

    Event rating—No undesirable impact

(2) Marriage and family events

    Background information   A prepubertal 10-year-old girl with no permanent medical disabilities, who lives with her biological parents. Her father is 42 and her mother is 40. She is an only child. Father is a coalminer and mother is a part-time domestic worker in a block of offices. He has been in his job for over 5 years. They live in rented accommodation in rural Northumberland.

    Life event   On three occasions over the past 12 months mother had asked the father to leave the family. The most recent had been 5 months before the onset of illness in the child. On this occasion there had been a considerable argument in the house in front of the girl. Father had not left. The argument was over money and the father's suspicions that mother was having an affair. Although his wife declared his fears were groundless, their relationship remained difficult.

Event rating—Marked undesirable impact

(1) Accident and illness events

Background information   A 12-year-old girl in early puberty with no permanent medical disabilities. She lives with her biological parents, mother aged 41, father 42, and is the middle of three children, an elder brother aged 14 and a younger brother aged 10. The father is employed as a heating engineer for a private company and has been in this employment for more than 5 years. The mother is a housewife. They are owner/occupiers and live in an outer suburban area of the city.

Life event   Seven months prior to the onset of her illness, her elder brother sustained a fractured leg during a football match. He required surgery under general anaesthetic and was in hospital for 4 weeks. Deborah was considerably upset by this episode and made many visits to the hospital, and following his discharge spent 3 weeks following him around both in the house and on his occasional social visits. The boy was off school for 3 months but made a full recovery from his fracture and returned to school with no difficulty. Deborah no longer paid him the attention she had during his illness.

Event rating—Mild undesirable impact

(2) Accident and illness events

Background information   A postpubertal $12\frac{1}{2}$-year-old girl with no permanent medical disabilities. She lives with her biological parents, both of whom are 49 years old. She is the elder of two children with a brother who is 10. Father is a carpenter in the local ship-building yard. He has been employed in this capacity for over 5 years but in the last 18 months he has been on shortened hours. They live in rented accommodation in an urban area of the city.

Life event   The identified subject experienced abdominal pain which resulted in an emergency operation and the removal of an abnormal appendix. She has post-operative complications with the development of an abscess and a chronic sinus. She was in hospital for 6 weeks and was absent from school for 3 months. Her operation was 6 months prior to the onset of her psychiatric disorder. By the time she returned to school it was a new term and her medical condition was said to have markedly improved but not completely resolved.

Event rating—Severe undesirable impact

(1) Exit events

Background information A 10-year-old prepubertal girl with no permanent medical disability. She lives with her biological parents, father aged 37, mother aged 35, and is the elder of two children, her brother being 8. Father is a computer engineer. He has been in his present employment for some 18 months. Mother is a part-time office worker. They are recent owner/occupiers in an outer suburb of the city.

Life event Six months before onset of illness paternal grandfather died suddenly of a heart attack. He was 70 years old and although known to Angela was seen only once or twice a year. He had been ill with heart trouble in the previous 12 months, although this had been kept from the grandchildren. His death was not a shock to the family and although Angela was distressed at the news, some 3 weeks after the funeral, which she did not attend, she appeared to show no pre-occupations or concerns about the loss. She had visited her grandmother in the meantime and paid her respects without any difficulty.

Event rating—Mild undesirable impact

(2) Exit events

Background information A 12-year-old pubertal boy with no permanent medical disability. He lives with his biological mother who is 35 and step-father who is 36. He is the eldest of three children, all boys, the others being 10 and 7 years old. The step-father has been unemployed for more then two years and has been in the family for over 5 years. Mother works as an office cleaner and is away from the house by 5.30 a.m. She also works in the evenings. They live in rented accommodation in the city and are poorly off financially.

Life event The boy had a close relationship with his maternal grandmother who was in her late 50s. He regularly visited her for tea following the end of school. On one occasion whilst with her at the kitchen table she had sudden chest pain. She fell to the floor and died within a few minutes in front of the boy. Only two of them were in the house at the time. She appeared to have been well with no suggestion of illness.

Event rating—Severe undesirable impact

The use of interview techniques and ratings of contextual information has been applied in few studies to date (Goodyer, Kolvin and Gatzanis, 1985; Goodyer, Wright and Altham, 1988). There have, however, been a number of useful clues to the role of recent stresses from studies that have examined a single stressor such as divorce or bereavement in childhood. Further clues have also been obtained from studies that have used life event checklists designed for rating the effects of stress in children's lives (Steinhausen and Radtke, 1986; Bailey and Garralda, 1986, 1987; Garrison, *et al.*, 1987).

As can be inferred from adult studies, by and large, acute events are best understood when their potential psychological meaning to the subject is taken into account. To date it is only the broad notion of undesirability that has been used in studies with children, together with classifying events according to their general characteristics, such as family, accident or financial events and according to whether or not they are exit or entrance events.

The prevalence of life events

The Newcastle life events study compared the prevalence of life events that occurred in a prospective sample of children and adolescents attending a child psychiatry clinic with a sample of community control children of the same age and sex who were free of psychiatric disorder at the time of interview. The study focused on school-age children 5–16 years old. The clinic cases were classified into four groups according to their presenting clinical features. Firstly, a conduct disordered group who met ICD-9 criteria for this diagnosis (anti-social behaviour, lying, stealing, destructiveness, cruelty or bullying of more than 2 weeks' duration and two or more symptoms). Secondly, emotionally disordered groups, divided into three clinical classes mutually exclusive on the basis of their predominant clinical features: (i) somatic presentation, (ii) mild anxiety disorders, and (iii) severe anxiety and depression disorders.

The Newcastle study—not taking into account the quality or independence of events—showed that mothers of cases reported a mean number of five events per child during the 12 months prior to onset of symptoms, compared with four events per child in the controls during the 12 months prior to the day of interview. When raters examined the vignettes of both groups it was judged that some 19 per cent of all events, for all subjects, were *not independent* of illness or illness determined behaviour.

If interviewers' reports had been taken without reference to further checks on independence there may have been an overestimation of the effect of inde-pendent events. Clearly despite careful interviewing a large proportion of events collected may be a consequence rather than a cause of psychiatric disorder. All four clinical groups had events removed by the raters but the trend of results indicated more dependent events were found in conduct disorders, 26 per cent of events, than emotional disorders in general, 18 per cent of events, and severe emotional disorders in particular, where only 13 per cent of events were rated as not independent.

In a second study conducted in the city of Salford, interviewers were more conservative in researching independent and dependent events separately and the rate of not independent events for emotional disorders was less than 10 per cent, suggesting that judgements of independence can be incorporated into the interview schedule and depend on careful collection of the timing of events in relation to the onset of disorder (Goodyer, Wright and Altham, 1988). Inevitably some events, perhaps 10 per cent, will require judgements about their suitability for inclusion, even with careful interview technique. Overall, the findings from the two studies suggest that a child will experience approximately three independent life events per annum.

The quality of life events

The Newcastle study dichotomised independent events into those with no or mild undesirability (or negative impact) and those with moderate, marked or severe undesirability. Of the remaining independent events some 75 per cent were classified as no or mild undesirability and only 23 per cent as likely to contain moderate, marked or severe undesirability.

These findings indicate that life events may be common in children's lives but events that are qualitatively severe enough to be potential causes of psychiatric disorder appear to be infrequent. There was approximately one moderate to severe independent event per case in the 12 months prior to the onset of disorder. Reporting the mean number of events is, however, misleading as some children had one or more severe events in the 12 months prior to psychiatric disorder and therefore some had none. These findings for events were replicated in the second study (Goodyer, Wright and Altham, 1988).

Thus the preliminary findings from these early studies using interview techniques indicate that substantial improvements in the quality of information are obtained by utilising the measurement and methodology pioneered by George Brown in studies on adult depression. The next question is whether or not events exert potentially causal effects of any significance in the onset of psychiatric disorder.

Do events exert a potential causal effect?

The two studies carried out on clinical populations confirmed a potentially causal effect of recent stressful life events in childhood and adolescence for conduct and emotional disorders (Goodyer, Kolvin and Gatzanis, 1985; Goodyer, Wright and Altham, 1988). In both studies moderately to severely undesirable events occurring in the 12 months prior to psychiatric disorder were found in 60 per cent and 70 per cent of new cases respectively. These findings confirm that recent stresses may provoke new episodes of disorder in some two thirds of new onset cases. Interestingly, however, both studies indicate that some 30 per cent of cases and 20 per cent of controls experience one or more recent events without developing psychiatric disorder. These findings suggest that children can be protected in some way, perhaps by other social experiences in their family or social environments, or as a consequence of different intrinsic factors such as temperament, cognitive methods of appraisal, or physiological responses.

These studies also showed that rating events for their degree of undesirability or negative impact results in important differences between clinical groups. Thus events that are rated as only carrying no or mild undesirable or negative impact are significantly associated with conduct but not emotional disorders. These findings suggest that for conduct disorders the quality of event is relatively less important.

Classifying events

Events may be classified in other ways besides their degree of undesirability. For example, events may be classified according to their general characteristics (such as marital, family, illness or accident) and as to whether or not they constitute permanent separations (termed exit events) or additions (entrance events) to the child's social field.

Although exit events appear less commonly, they may be more important for severe anxious and depressive emotional disorders and somatic presentations (Goodyer, Kolvin and Gatzanis, 1985). These tentative findings are made on the basis of rather small sample size but are of interest as they are analogous to the associations between this class of life events and the onset of depression in adults.

The associations between psychiatric disorder and events may be improved by considering certain other psychological qualities which events may carry. For example, a single event may be undesirable, out of the child's control, impact directly on the child or indirectly via a parent, and have consequences that inevitably alter the child's environment (e.g. divorce) or return it to the previous state (e.g. serious but successfully treated illness). Unlike adult studies, such multidimensional measures of life events have not been examined in children, although the evidence from adult studies suggests exploration would be worth while (Finlay-Jones and Brown, 1981; Miller and Ingham, 1983).

The number and timing of events

Timing

The argument that there is a causal relationship between events and disorder may also be strengthened if there is an association between event occurrence and the time of onset of signs and symptoms. Thus in depressed women Brown and Harris (1978) showed that events with severe long-term threat led quickly to depression, most often within 9 weeks and generally within 6 months. It was also apparent that some events may have even longer-term effects in some cases. These findings strengthen the argument that there is a causal relationship between severe events and onset of depression in women. The Newcastle data were examined for the timing of events in the 12 months prior to onset of psychiatric disorders in clinic attenders. Investigating the timing of events requires the respondent to recall events retrospectively. It can be argued that the further back in time mothers have to remember, the greater the risk of underreporting important events. If there is a large fall-off in reporting events then the collection of life events may be unreliable and invalid. The fall-off in reporting of all life events was low, the disparity in the number of life events reported per month over a year was less than 1 per cent. Thus it is unlikely that there has been serious underreporting of life events.

For example, in school-age children, whilst events occurred throughout the 12 months prior to the onset of disorder, they tended to cluster in the 16 weeks closest to onset of symptoms, supporting the inference that events cause disorder (Goodyer, Kolvin and Gatzanis, 1987). Some 70 per cent of school-age children experienced an event in the 6 months before symptoms. Furthermore, children who have experienced two or more events in the preceding 12 months are more likely to report an event in the 16 weeks before onset.

The patterning of relationships and form of interaction between events, such as the suggestion that the effects of events may add to each other, is an important area for further investigation. Models of developmental psychopathology are likely to be determined by the patterning and interactions of social factors of differing types and effects. We return to this area in more detail later in this chapter and the next.

Number

Clustering of events improves the hypothesis that a severe life event causes the onset of symptoms. We know, however, that in this sample of children some had experienced more than one life event in the preceding 12 months. What effects are brought to bear on the risk of onset of symptoms if children and adolescents have been exposed to two or more events in the time before their illness?

To some extent this question will surely involve understanding the psychological relationship *between* life events as well as the statistical associations with psychiatric disorder. The strength of interview methods is seen again here since we can say with a degree of confidence that each life event is effectively independent from each other. We can say this because in the collection phase social context information is included in the ratings of events. Therefore we have not counted information twice. Connections between events therefore cannot be explained by social links, such as a severe argument leading to divorce or a road traffic accident leading to an operation. In both these examples the event constitutes both the context and the end-stage experience. If events are linked it must be through their appraisal by the individual.

A reanalysis of events was carried out which separated all the cases into two groups:

1. Those with only one event in the previous 12 months, which consisted of 56 per cent of (54/96) of the children.
2. Those with two or more events in the previous 12 months, which consisted of 44 per cent (42/96) of the children.

The first observation was that roughly equal proportions of children were classified into the single and multiple event groups. When cases were classified by clinical diagnosis the proportions for each group were not significantly different.

Both single and multiple events were significantly more common in cases than in controls. Whilst there was no significant specificity between number of events and diagnosis there was a suggestion that such a difference may be found in larger samples. We discussed findings in adult depressives suggesting that neurotic depressives are more likely to report multiple interconnected events and it would be of value to investigate if such reporting occurred in different diagnostic groups in younger persons.

Given the lack of diagnostic differences in single : multiple event classification, the distribution over 12 months of these two groups of cases was analysed separately. The results suggested that multiple event cases were significantly more likely to be exposed to a severe life event in the 16 weeks closest to onset than were single event cases. It may be that the probability by chance alone of this occurring is operating, since these children have, by definition, more events. This seems unlikely as the majority have only experienced two events (less than 10 per cent had three or more) and we have prevented the inclusion of connected experiences as separate events. An alternative explanation may be that the occurrence of some types of events increases the risk of further events occurring. The findings suggested that there may be an additivity of effect in multiple event cases. The data is insufficient to confirm or refute this hypothesis but warrants further investigation.

A second finding from the distribution of single:multiple cases was that where onset occurred within 4 weeks of disorder there was no significant likelihood of the case being classified as a single or multiple event case. In other words, there seem to be rapid effects of an event that may cause emotional or behaviour symptoms which were unrelated to the number of events that may have occurred in the previous 11 months. Such a rapid effect cannot be due to additivity. This latter finding also provides further support for the argument that single : multiple event differences are due to chance alone. If the multiple effects were chance there would continue to be significant differences between the two groups even at 4 weeks.

A third observation showed that single event cases appear significantly more likely to report an event in the 36–52 weeks prior to onset, but no more likely than multiple event cases to report an event in the 16–32 week period before onset. Since there are no diagnostic differences from this effect it suggests that either the qualities of these events occurring further back in time from onset are different in some respect other than just undesirability *or* different appraisal mechanisms are operating for different types of event.

Mechanisms as a consequence of the number and timing of events

The type of mechanism involved in an additivity effect of stressors may be different for different types of disorder. For conduct disorders there appears to be a non-specific quantitative addition, dependent perhaps on the number of events. Under these circumstances, therefore, symptoms may occur independent of any meaning inherent in the events, implying a quantitative threshold of stress above which psychiatric disorder is likely.

The association for emotional disorders is less clear, and more qualitative factors may also influence additivity as well as impact. These may be the presence of particular links or connections between the events or perhaps through the personal significance unrelated to the events but reflecting intrinsic psychological associations made by the child. Under these circumstances the meaning of events may be more important and symptoms are more likely to occur as a consequence of the salience of events. These potential differences in the additive associations within events as well as between events and psychiatric disorder may be considered in at least four ways as suggested by Brown and Harris (1978).

1. Mechanical additivity—Which may occur independent of meaning of events, implying a threshold of stress above which psychiatric disorder is likely.
2. General additivity—Where although events appear unrelated the subject feels unable to cope with any further stressors.
3. Specific additivity—Where events have particular meaning and implications for the subject which indicates that one event may be psychologically related to another through the overt social experiences of the events themselves.
4. Symbolic additivity—Where the first event influences the second through individual personal significance probably unrelated to contextual information, but reflecting intrinsic psychological associations made by the sub-

ject, which others could not make from a knowledge of the life events themselves.

Present knowledge suggests that for conduct disorders events may exert a degree of mechanical additivity, as they appear to exert effects independent of the nature of social context (Goodyer, Kolvin and Gatzanis, 1985). For emotional disorders, however, some degree of qualitative appraisal seems likely. Whether this is general, specific or symbolic for one or all of the groups cannot be clearly stated from the present knowledge. The relatedness of events and other social experiences is an important issue and further work in this area appears essential.

It may be that there are differential effects of both the timing and number of events at different ages. The study described above was carried out in school-age children, and similar systematic research has not been carried out for children of other ages. There are suggestions in the literature, however, that age effects are important in determining the effects of events. For example, studies on hospitalisation in childhood suggests that it is multiple not single admissions that are likely to result in long-term distress (Douglas, 1975; Quinton and Rutter, 1976).

It is also apparent that the appraisal of events occurring in the 12 months prior to onset of psychiatric disorder may be different in different time periods. For rapid effects it seems possible that there is little cognitive processing and an emotional or arousal response may determine effect. Perhaps overdoses reflect this form of response. Certainly in many such cases events such as arguments with boyfriends or relatives can trigger parasuicide attempts in adolescents within days (Paykel, 1974; Hawton, 1986).

What, however, might be the mechanisms that determine the effects of events that occur in the weeks and months more distant from the onset of disorder. Indeed, is it possible to consider that a life event occurring some 36–52 weeks previously can have a significant direct effect on the onset of psychiatric symptoms? Certainly it is a common clinical finding to elicit that children have been affected by events occurring at a distance in time and some possible mechanisms have already been briefly described. We need to consider further aspects of how events occurring 36–52 weeks before onset of disorder appear to have a delay in their effect. Some reasons are perhaps more apparent than others, for example:

1. Buffering factors may dilute or slow down the influence of events. Such buffering factors may occur in the child's social supports or family relationships (Rutter, 1985b).
2. The nature of the event may be such that protective factors are activated subsequent to the event, e.g. serious illness, family loss or death may mobilise support for the child.

3. The salience of the event may determine its impact. Thus an event may not be fully understood at the time of occurrence and its personal meaning and impact may not become explicit until later.

These potential mechanisms have yet to be examined in any detail in childhood and adolescence. They suggest the need to investigate carefully the interrelationships between factors in the environment that exert both positive and negative effects on psychopathology. Such models of effects are discussed in the next chapter.

The influence of sex differences on recent life events

The influence of sex differences on the impact of stressful social experiences is an important factor in developmental research. There is evidence that there are sex differences in the appraisal of stressful events but not necessarily in the occurrence of such events. Thus Burke and Weir (1978) have suggested that girls perceive more stress in their lives than boys, and Dweck and colleagues (Dweck and Bush, 1976; Dweck *et al.*, 1978) have reported observational data in a classroom setting indicating that boys respond with greater efforts following criticism of performance from adults, whereas girls tend to give up and blame their own lack of ability. Perhaps girls are more likely to attribute external stressors to their own personal shortcomings, insurmountable through personal effort alone. Adverse social experiences that adults bring to bear on children may be important in this regard, for example, the popular view that girls are emotionally more labile or more suggestible than boys is not supported by research findings (Maccoby and Jacklin, 1978).

These appraisal differences are important, but it is not clear if they are a result of the events *per se* or the consequence of adults' responses to events, as seems the case with classroom experience. The evidence, at least for school-age children, is that there is surprisingly little difference in the number and type of stressful life events occurring in the lives of boys and girls (Goodyer, Kolvin and Gatzanis, 1986; Goodyer, Wright and Altham, 1988). The present evidence suggests that girls may be more likely to experience severe mood disturbances than boys, but overall it is the lack of sex differences that is striking. However, the consequences of adults' responses to events impacting on children may well be influenced by a child's gender. Sex differences appear to occur in the response to social adversity. Boys and girls are equally as likely to be exposed to some social adversities but demonstrate different forms of response.

SUMMARY

1. The most reliable and valid method of recording recent life events and difficulties is with a semi-structured interview.

2. Events and difficulties may be important causal factors in the onset of psychiatric disorders in children, particularly anxiety and depression. They are, however, neither necessary nor sufficient in all cases of emotional or conduct disorders.
3. Measuring the qualities of an event may help determine the specificity of the association with a particular type of psychiatric disorder.
4. The magnitude of effect can provide a quantitative estimate of the risk for psychopathology carried by an event or difficulty when a child is exposed to it.
5. The psychological mechanisms of events may vary according to their number and timing in relation to the onset of the disorder.

Chapter 9

Models of Social Adversities
and Psychopathology

In Chapter 8 we discussed in detail the conceptual, methodological and measurement issues involved in life events research. It is apparent that severe life events and difficulties independent of illness or illness determined behaviour, may be causally associated with emotional and conduct disorders of childhood and adolescence. As we have seen, however, such events, occurring singly or multiply, are neither necessary nor sufficient to cause these disorders. The *effects* of acute life events will only be clearly understood when investigated concurrently with other factors that exist in a child's life. For example, for some children acute stresses, such as bereavements, occur against a background of a happy and secure family life. For others such events occur in the presence of adversity, such as marital disharmony, financial difficulties or chronic illness. It is apparent that these other factors may influence the impact of events. Positive experiences may diminish undesirable effects. Negative ones may enhance such effects.

Over the past two decades research has identified factors considered to put individuals 'at risk' for psychiatric disorders. It has become apparent that a range of social factors are involved in both the production of psychopathology and the individual's protection from it (Rutter, 1987b). A number of conceptual frameworks have been proposed to explain how acute events might exert effects in the presence of other undesirable social factors (Golden and Dohrenwend, 1981; Rutter, 1987b). We will review the models proposed for risk and protection in this chapter.

PATTERNS OF SOCIAL ADVERSITY IN EMOTIONAL DISORDERS

Family adversities

Acute events most commonly occur in the presence of other chronic adversities, such as ongoing marital or family disharmony or chronic psychiatric illness in a patient. In such circumstances the impact of an acute life event may be difficult to estimate. Three broad questions arise: first, what contribution to psychopathology can a recent life event expect to have in the presence of ongoing difficulties? For example, the onset of behavioural disturbance following an argument with a parent may be due to the presence of a continuous poor relationship and not directly as a consequence of the argument. Clearly in this example the relative contribution of the event to disorder is in question and its aetiological significance unclear.

Secondly, the relationship between adversities may be important in determining the effects of stresses. In the above example it could be argued that the event was important because it provoked symptoms that might otherwise not have occurred because a good relationship between parent and child existed.

A third and related question concerns the aetiology of the events themselves. Using our example again, it could be hypothesised that the argument itself would not have occurred if it had not been for the presence of a chronic poor relationship between parent and child. This hypothesis now suggests that acute undesirable events are a product of chronic stress. If this is the case we might expect some events to be significantly more common in children who experience chronic adversity. These three questions formed the basis of a second study investigating the relative contribution of life events to anxious and depressive disorders in school-age children (Goodyer et al., 1988). In this project a number of recent social adversities and achievements were measured in the lives of mothers and their children.

For example, there is considerable evidence indicating an important role for confiding relationships in protecting children from conduct disorders (Rutter, 1985b). Furthermore we know that depression in the lives of mothers is significantly associated with psychiatric disorders in children (Quinton and Rutter, 1985a; Rutter, 1985b). What, therefore, might be the relative contribution to anxiety or depression in children from mothers who are distressed and lack confiding relationships in their own lives? Could these forms of adverse life experience for mothers exert a direct effect on emotional symptoms in their children or would they only be important for psychopathology in the presence of acute stressful life events? To investigate this question these three factors were measured concurrently in a prospective sample (n = 100) of emotionally disturbed children and community controls (n = 100). The quality of maternal confiding relationships was determined by interview, collecting information about mothers' intimate relationships. The interview was derived from that of Brown and Harris (1978) and asked each mother about the availability, adequacy and intimacy of her personal relationships with her partner, or her closest confidant. A contextual picture of mothers' long-term confiding relationships prior to the onset of the children's symptoms was obtained and rated as good, moderate or poor by a pair of researchers. In addition, mothers completed a questionnaire known to be a reliable and valid indicator of maternal distress (Rutter, Tizard and Whitmore, 1970; McGee, Williams and Silva, 1985).

In the cases, 24 per cent of mothers had poor confiding relationships, 30 per cent reported maternal distress and 71 per cent of the children experienced one or more severe undesirable life events. A logistic analysis showed, however, that all three factors exerted significant independent effects on the onset of symptoms. We can conclude that acute recent undesirable life events exert effects of importance in the presence *or* absence of other more ongoing adversities in the family. The findings demonstrated, however, that the probability of developing anxiety *or* depression was greatest in the presence of all three adversities. In other words, there was a cumulative effect on the risk of disorder. The psychological mechanisms through which these three factors exert their effects depends, however, on the configuration or relationship they have with each other. All three act as provoking agents, i.e. exert a direct effect on the risk of disorder. In the absence of a life event, maternal adversities are not related, i.e. they have different *origins* from each other. For example, a mother may have a poor confiding relationship with her husband but be distressed or depressed because of employment difficulties for herself. When a life event occurs, however, the likelihood is that the three factors are related and share some common origin. For example, death of a relative may impact on maternal and child mental state and may adversely influence the mother's ability to confide. This suggests that maternal adversities may either increase the probability of exposure to life events or alter the intensity of impact of events. In other words, some children may become 'life event prone' as a consequence of their mothers' difficulties. For example: (i) mothers may 'fail to buffer' the effects of events under the circumstances of their own difficulties and these children experience the impact of life events more intensely but not more frequently; or (ii) mothers may 'fail to protect', in which case the intensity of events may be the same but more are experienced.

Clearly this is only one mechanism through which events may arise or exert their effects. For example, we described in Chapter 8 how some events exert rapid effects, probably in the absence of other events or perhaps other social adversities.

Friendships and life events

We have noted in Chapter 5 that the development of adequate peer relations and friendships constitutes a major social experience for social adjustment. There are also findings to suggest that friendship difficulties occurring in the 12 months prior to onset of emotional symptoms is a potentially causal factor in the onset of anxiety and depression in school-age children (see Chapter 5).

If, therefore, friendship difficulties and life events occur in the same time-frame, do they have the same psychological and statistical associations as maternal adversities and life events have to each other and to psychopathology?

When undesirable events and friendships are investigated together the results suggest a different mechanism to that found for events and maternal adversities. Thus 71 per cent of anxious and depressed cases experienced one or more major life events, and 48 per cent moderate to poor friendships; 30 per cent of the cases experienced a combination of the two factors. When the two factors were investigated for their effects on the likelihood of provoking an onset of emotional disorder it was found that they had independent effects, as had events in the presence of ongoing maternal adversities. The findings therefore indicate that again two different forms of recent severe adversities, life events and friendship difficulties, exert independent effects. Again, the likelihood of being a case of anxiety or depression is best explained by the cumulative effect of these two different types of recent social adversity. Overall, the findings begin to suggest at least two relatively independent environmental pathways through which children may become anxious or depressed. A 'family pathway' involving maternal adversities and family life events, and a 'social pathway' involving interpersonal non-family relationships. The second question concerns the *relationships between* these two recent social adversities. First, the patterning of these events and friendships, i.e. occurring singly or together, does not discriminate between predominantly anxious or depressed children. Secondly, unlike the three-way relationship between maternal adversities and life events, there appears to be no association between friendship difficulties and life events. Therefore we must consider that these factors are independent from each other in both their effects *and* their origins.

Thus recent friendship difficulties *do not* operate as an event-prone mechanism, as may be the case for maternal adversities. Similarly we cannot suggest that events may themselves provoke recent friendship difficulties. These findings suggest that recent friendship difficulties exert their effects through different mechanisms to that of recent life events. In addition, friendship difficulties seem to provoke onsets through a social dimension in which family pathology may not be required, since they exert effects independent of maternal adversities, as well as of recent life events (Goodyer, Wright and Altham, 1989b).

In conclusion we can consider that first, there are a number of family and social factors which have direct provoking effects on the onset of emotional disorders in childhood and adolescence. Secondly, it is the patterning of these recent adversities that leads to a significant increase in risk of causing onsets of emotional disorder. Thirdly, a family pathway exists involving mechanisms which may operate within maternal adversities and events impacting on the child's life. And fourthly, a social mechanism independent of family mechanisms exists suggesting at least two different pathways through which social adversities may cause emotional psychopathology.

COMBINED AND POTENTIATING EFFECTS OF ADVERSITIES

The magnitude of risk

The independent effects of recent events, friendship difficulties and maternal adversities can be evaluated for the magnitude of risk each carries. The relative risk of onset of emotional disorder is increased by approximately 5 times when a child is exposed to a life event, a distressed mother or a friendship difficulty and about 3.5 times when exposed to poor maternal confiding relationships (Goodyer, Wright and Altham, 1988, 1989a). Individually these do not represent large risks. As we have seen, however, most cases experienced more than one recent adversity and under these circumstances the risk or odds of being a case increase by the combined risk of each variable, which in quantitative terms is obtained by multiplying their known risks. In the case of maternal adversities and life events this risk is equivalent to $5.5 \times 5 \times 3.5 = 96.25$ times increase in the likelihood of anxious or depressive symptoms. This represents a substantive risk for the development of emotional symptoms.

Overall, the studies on both acute and chronic social adversities demonstrate that the combined effects of adversity exert significantly greater quantitative risks than single adversities. Psychologically this indicates a potentiating of the effects of social factors when they occur together.

Cumulative effect of chronic social adversities

The model of cumulative risks can be found in other forms of social adversities. For example, Rutter and colleagues (Rutter, Tizard and Whitmore, 1970; Rutter 1979) identified that a number of social and family factors increase the risk of psychiatric, particularly conduct disorders, in children. Unemployment, parental psychiatric disorder, being taken into care of the local authority, paternal criminality and large family size have all been shown to increase the risk of psychiatric disorder and reflect ongoing adversities in the life of the child. Evidence of a cumulative effect was inferred because the risk of being a case increased with the number of these adversities. However, the increase in risk did not seem a straightforward summation as the probability of being a case was substantially greater in the presence of two or more stresses than would be expected by summation. In other words, one or more chronic adversities of different types and qualities seem to potentiate the risk of disorder. These findings have been broadly replicated in other similar research on the impact of chronic stresses for child adjustment (Shaw and Emery, 1988).

A similar finding has been reported for chronic stresses influencing the child's response to acute stresses. Evidence from a specific event (hospital admission) suggests this may be the case (Quinton and Rutter, 1976). In this study the effect of repeated hospital admissions in provoking emotional disturbance was greater in conjunction with high psychosocial adversity than it was in more focused family circumstances. Again these effects were not merely cumulative but potentiated each other so that the combined effects of the two together was greater than the sum of the two considered separately.

MEASUREMENT AND STATISTICAL MODELS OF STRESS

Cumulation and potentiation imply different forms of interaction which may be investigated statistically. There have been a number of different statistical models used to test for conceptual models of stress, such as vulnerability–provoking agents (Everitt and Smith, 1979; Bebbington *et al.*, 1984; Brown, Bifulco and Harris, 1987). It is apparent, however, that our present understanding of stress does not allow for a definitive answer in this area. Firstly, we have yet to agree on how social adversities may be conceptualised. For example, should life events be viewed merely as undesirable or should their psychological properties be further clarified to improve the associations with psychopathology (Brown, Bifulco and Harris, 1987; Miller *et al.*, 1987). Secondly, we do not have adequate ratio scales of measurement for stress, unlike height for example. These conceptual and methodological shortcomings prevent dogmatic views being held concerning the best statistical model for determining the effects of stresses on the probability of being a psychiatric case. For example, it has been shown that in women an interaction between intimacy in relationships and life events can be demonstrated as present or absent on the same set of data depending on the assumptions of the measurement (i.e. whether or not the data is treated as categorical or continuous) (Parry and Shapiro, 1986). This study demonstrates the importance of recognising limitations inherent in our present knowledge. It is important to recognise that many assumptions are made at different levels of argument concerning stressful experiences. Defining concepts, developing reliable and valid measures and deciding on the best methods of analysis all represent differing and important forms of assumptions. It is apparent that results and therefore interpretations of psychological mechanisms will be influenced by the assumptions made in the course of the investigation.

Interactions between social factors

The term 'interactive processes' can be misleading as psychological and statistical interaction are not synonymous (Rutter, 1983a, 1987b). An example from the work of Rutter and colleagues demonstrates the distinct issues.

In their studies on institutionally reared women, institutional rearing was associated with a worse outcome compared with a general population control group. Marital support in early adult life, however, almost obliterated the adverse effect of an institutional upbringing. This appears to suggest two independent main effects with no statistical interaction. However, Rutter points out this may be misleading because an institutional rearing made it much less likely that the women would make a harmonious marriage that would lead to the provision of emotional support. This is a powerful psychological interactive process.

Finding statistical models to explore these important psychological interactions is important for research of the future. Determining whether or not a variable has an effect in both the presence and the absence of other variables is an important test of the usefulness of such models. It is not correct, for example, to assume that a significant main effect in a standard regression analysis means that a variable has an effect on its own. What it means is that a significant main effect is present after other variables have been taken into account. Significant main effects of individual variables and their interactions should be looked for simultaneously. If an interaction is present then the variables concerned cannot be interpreted as having a single main effect. This is different to determining an effect in the absence of all other variables. The latter is seldom thought of because it is uncommon for social adversities to occur in isolation.

It is the patterning and multiplicity of these factors that gives rise to the mechanisms associated with different psychiatric disorders. Single adversities are unlikely to result in a high proportion of cases within a general population. This is possibly why even chronic family discord, if occurring as a single factor, is only a weak predictor of psychiatric disorder (Rutter, 1979, 1985c; Emery and O'Leary, 1984).

This emphasises that methodologically sophisticated studies are needed to examine the relationships between variables as well as the impact of these variables on individuals.

As we have discussed, maternal distress, poor confiding relationships in mothers and life events focused on the children are all potential causal factors of emotional disorders in children (Goodyer *et al.*, 1988). The findings demonstrated that all three variables exert independent effects. Acute stresses therefore exert significant effects in the presence of more chronic adversities. The likelihood of developing anxiety or depression was best predicted, however, by considering all three factors together.

Vulnerability and provoking factors

In the section above, the relationship between social factors concerns variables, all of which have a direct effect on the likelihood of psychiatric disorder.

The mechanisms of their effects and the origins of these factors have been considered within this 'direct effects' model. There are social factors, however, that do not exert direct effects but nevertheless may be important for increasing the risk of psychiatric disorder. Such variables exert modifier effects on risk. If risk is intensified then the variable carries a *vulnerability effect*, if the risk is diminished the variable carries a *protective effect*. In either case the social factor involved exerts its effects *indirectly* in the presence of other social factors which exert a direct effect. This is, therefore, a form of interaction. Furthermore, a variable of this type can be considered as catalytic, as it changes the mechanism and the effects of another variable (Rutter, 1986b).

Under these conditions, vulnerability and protection may represent the negative and positive ends of the same concept rather than different concepts. We may consider, for example, that the *presence* of a given social factor may be protective and its *absence* may result in vulnerability. Alternatively we may consider one social factor as inherently a vulnerability factor and another as inherently a protective factor.

The theory of effects does not depend on the hedonic classification of the social factors investigated. Acute events, friendship difficulties and ongoing recent difficulties exert similar direct effects. Similarly, factors with vulnerability or protective 'effects' may not be intuitively obvious on the basis of their characteristics. As Rutter (1987b) has pointed out, medicines that work are often of the type that taste bad! And many protective mechanisms are promoted by exposure to the noxious agent, as with vaccination.

Vulnerability factors and provoking agents in adult depression

In adult depression, for example, it has been proposed that recent life events and difficulties in the lives of young women are provoking agents for depression and considerably more likely to cause depression in the women made vulnerable by other social factors in their lives (Brown and Harris, 1978, 1986). Although these social factors may be of various types, particular attention has been focused on the importance of close personal relationships. There is evidence to indicate that women who lack intimacy in their own lives are significantly more likely to be depressed after experiencing a provoking agent than women who are not vulnerable (Brown and Harris, 1986). The most extreme form of vulnerability would be a stress that exerted no effect on the risk of psychiatric disorder except (and only) in the presence of a provoking agent (recent life events and difficulties). In practice most stresses are likely to exert some effects, it is their relative contributions under different social conditions that require investigation.

For example, in the work of Brown and Harris (1978), for women without a provoking agent the presence of children does not predispose to depression. With a provoking agent the presence of young children increased the risk of depression some $2\frac{1}{2}$ times. A number of studies have replicated these findings for the role of the presence or absence of intimacy (Brown and Harris, 1986).

Vulnerability and provoking agents in anxious and depressed children

An example of an indirect effect on anxiety and depression in children and adolscents was found in the Salford Life Events and Social Difficulties study, which had concurrently enquired about the social achievements that children had made in the same time period as they may have experienced life events or friendship difficulties. Both mothers and children were asked to record the successes that had occurred in the child's life in the previous 12 months. A social achievement was considered as any event that had social and personal connotations of desirability and would be seen by others as expressing a degree of personal competence. Achievements in education, physical skills, art/craft, technology and community service were recorded.

The results showed that anxious and depressed children were *equally* as likely as their controls to report one, two or more social achievements in the previous 12 months. The hypothesis that social achievements would *directly protect* against emotional disorders seems unlikely on the basis of these results. A *direct protective effect* would predict a significantly greater proportion of control subjects reporting social achievements. It would seem that this is not the case, at least in this sample of children and adolescents. If recent social achievements occur with equal likelihood in both cases and controls, how might they exert an *indirect effect*? It may be, for example, that having or making achievements decreases the risk for experiencing recent social adversities such as life events or friendship difficulties. This hypothesis can be tested by comparing the proportion of cases and controls with recent achievements and those with none, in the presence and absence of recent social adversities. When this analysis is undertaken a marked interaction between friendship difficulties and an *absence* of recent achievements is found, but no interaction between life events and an absence of recent achievements. These findings are the same for anxiety and depression.

Thus some two-thirds of cases with moderate to poor friendships also reported no social achievements, whereas some two-thirds of controls with moderate to poor friendships reported at least one achievement (Goodyer, Wright and Altham, 1989c). These results now allow either of the indirect mechanisms discussed above to operate for social achievements. We may say that if a child has moderate to poor friendships but socially achieves, this protects him or her from the known direct provoking effects of friendship difficulties. Alternatively, we may argue that no achievements acts as a vulnerability factor, i.e. the adverse effects carried only operate in the presence of friendship difficulties.

A further consideration about the potential mechanisms of effect is that both factors relate to deficits in the child's social competence. Thus whether we argue for the loss of protection effects or the presence of vulnerability effects for a lack of social achievements, we can assume that these factors and mechanisms are occurring in the dimension of social competence independently from family life.

A practical implication is that the lack of social achievements carries unseen risks. In children and adolescents who lack achievement there may be no overt emotional or social difficulties. Assisting children to succeed, according to their own personal yardsticks, may decrease the inherent covert risks associated with the absence of social achievement.

If a child has poor quality friendships the development of a socially achieving programme may be a way of protecting him against the effects of poor friendships. It may be crucial in these circumstances to ensure that the child succeeds in an area which has social connotations.

The final common pathway is strongly suggestive of social influences on the development of self-efficacy, where being valued by others of the same age and status is a central notion. Perhaps if others do not value you sufficiently or you come to believe you are not valued, it may be crucial to find ways of valuing yourself. Perhaps non-social achievements that require only oneself become important in this respect. It seems likely that both personal and social achievements contribute to a sense of well-being and self-worth. As yet, however, we have little notion of the effects of private achievements in children's lives or of their relationship to social experiences either good or bad.

Latent vulnerability factors

Finally, vulnerability factors do not have to exist in the immediate circumstances of an individual. For example, a lack of adequate parental care in early childhood may be a vulnerability factor for later depression in some young women (Bifulco, Brown and Harris, 1987).

This raises an important point concerning how early vulnerability factors may exert their effects. We have previously described how women raised in care (and therefore experiencing a lack of adequate parental care) are not doomed to failure as adults and a significant proportion of them may become parents, employed and develop socially without serious psychiatric disorder. This suggests vulnerability effects may operate at an intrinsic affective-cognitive level and are not socially apparent until later stresses arise. If cognitions are implicated in the vulnerability process it is not clear if such 'cognitive schemas' arise at the time of the early adversity, become formed as development progresses or occur only as a consequence of subsequent stressful events and difficulties.

This potential cognitive effect of vulnerability factors has been the subject of some investigation in adults suffering from depression but has yet to be investigated in children (Teasdale, 1983; Bebbington, 1985). Mental representations of past experiences may be retrieved from memory as a consequence of recent acute events and difficulties. The affective connotations of these memories may also be retrieved and exert an effect in the present. In other words, affects that occur at the time of an acute event may be connected to the events of the past that are re-experienced as a result of the present provoking agent. If control cognitions are deficient, might the expression of the event be a complex affective-behavioural response to both past and present experiences? A speculative formulation such as this seems testable perhaps through more experimental rather than epidemiological methods. For example, computer-aided prompts could be provided in the form of vignettes on a screen which children had to analyse in terms of appraisals they might make if it were their event in affective, cognitive and behavioural terms. Epidemiological research will provide predictions such as children who have experienced an exit event in the past would have a different appraisal pattern to an exit event they were being asked to evaluate from a child who had experienced no such exit event.

TURNING POINTS IN CHILDREN'S LIVES

For many people life may change as a consequence of a key event or set of events at a moment in time (Rutter, 1986b, 1989); life may change for the better or worse as a consequence. In other words, the pathway that a person is on may be altered. This may mean an alteration from a way of life which constantly renders them vulnerable to psychiatric disorder to a way of life which protects them from psychiatric disorder. A change in developmental trajectory may occur and alter the process of living.

There are numerous examples where developmental trajectories have been changed (Rutter, 1986b, 1989). Staying on at school and obtaining higher qualifications improves the trajectory and increases the protective mechanisms associated with academic success (Maughan and Rutter, 1986).

By contrast, teenage pregnancy may alter downwards the trajectory of a previously well-functioning teenager by decreasing options associated with protection and increasing those associated with vulnerability, such as the risk of a one-parent family. Altering to a vulnerability trajectory may be very difficult to change. For example, once set in motion disruptive-aggressive patterns of response behaviour to social stress can be quite resistant to change (Patterson, 1986a).

The avoidance of a vulnerability process in a life path may be a more attainable goal than the treatment or amelioration of vulnerability processes in motion. Clearly many such vulnerability processes are unforeseeable or unavoidable, for example, the birth of a handicapped child or the death of parents. Others may be amenable to social policy decisions. For example, social skills training and counselling young adults brought up in residential care may decrease the selection of unsuitable partners likely to increase the risk of disharmonious marriages.

NON-SOCIAL VULNERABILITY FACTORS

Perhaps vulnerability factors require a wider consideration. It seems reasonable that other factors in the individual, such as genetic predisposition, temperament or personality, intelligence or gender may exert effects either in combination with social factors, perhaps as vulnerability–protective factors, or directly as provoking agents in their own right (Paykel, 1978). Such considerations may prove specially useful in childhood and adolescence.

Effects of sex

There is considerable data to show that boys are more likely than girls to develop emotional or behavioural disturbances when exposed to marked family discord (Rutter, 1982). The evidence suggests, however, that girls take longer to respond to discord and that sex differences in disorder diminish with time (Rutter, 1986a).

Boys may be more vulnerable because of a biologically determined greater susceptibility to social hazards. For example, family discord may have a qualitatively more adverse impact on boys. Thus boys are more likely to go into care than girls at the time of family break-up (Packman, 1986) and boys are exposed to more parental quarrels than girls (Hetherington, Cox and Cox, 1982).

Boys are more likely to respond to adversity with difficult oppositional behaviour, girls are more likely to disengage and withdraw (Rutter, 1982; Masten et al., 1988) and this male reaction is more likely to elicit a negative response from parents and may become a coercive cycle of disruptive-aggressive response patterns (Patterson, 1986a,b). These intrinsic response patterns may reflect the biological component of sex differentiated responses.

Finally, adults may place a different meaning on aggressive responses in boys. They may be more positive to sons than daughters. Similarly, peers and strangers may respond with negative reactions to aggression by more aggression or retreat, whereas responses to girls' disengagement may be more enquiring (Maccoby and Jacklin, 1978; Dunn and Kendrick, 1982; Masten et al., 1988).

These mechanisms indicate that 'female' protection may depend on biological factors in males and the socio-cultural aspects of gender difference rather than specific differences in the psychology of males and females.

Different mechanisms for boys and girls in relation to stress may operate under different conditions and are not mutually exclusive. Biological vulnerabilities may need to be considered in the context of family discord. The chain of effects that follows may bias further the risk to boys as a consequence of socio-cultural mechanisms.

The diminution of sex differences for psychopathology can be seen in children attending the clinic. Thus the rate of new onset depressive illness is approximately equal in boys and girls (Goodyer et al., 1988). Furthermore, boys and girls are equally likely to be exposed to severe recent life events, suggesting that gender does not protect or promote exposure to these types of recent social adversities (Goodyer, Wright and Altham, 1988, 1989a).

This suggests that protective effects of femininity, biological and socio-cultural, have thresholds for their effects. Cases attending clinics represent the severe end of disorder where gender effects have been overcome, at least as far as the development of significant psychopathology is concerned.

What is not clear is what are the mechanisms which operate to overcome the effects of gender. For example, biological factors may unfold both genetic and acquired factors such as prenatal damage. Females from families with high genetic loading for affective disorder may have a greater biological propensity towards psychopathology than females with no such genetic loading. Secondly, there may be differences in sex-rate stereotypes between females that differen-tially influence response to stress by girls and by adults.

Thus attributes such as the determination to succeed, competitiveness and self-aggrandisement are seen as components of 'maleness', whereas character-istics such as empathy, nurturance and warmth as 'femaleness' (Spence and Helmreich, 1978). Concepts defined as masculine may be stronger correlates with positive mental health (Taylor and Hall, 1982).

Recent findings indicate that depressive symptoms in females is correlated with a low level of masculine attributes (Wilson and Cairns, 1988). Thus low masculinity was related to depression in both sexes in this study. The results do not support a direct effect of sex-role attributes on depressive symptoms as the level of masculinity was constant across all ages, but the prevalence of depressive symptoms showed a significant increase with age. The findings suggest that the origins of sex-role attributes will be found in pre-school and pre-adolescent years but their effects as indirect vulnerability factors only become apparent during the teenage years.

Puberty

Puberty may be more important in this respect than age. For example, as we have seen, there is a significant interaction between puberty and friendship dif-ficulties and the form of psychopathology but no sex effects in this three-way interaction. The point here is that puberty acts as a 'point of change' in the effects of friendship on the likelihood of being anxious or depressed. Being ex-posed to friendship deficits in prepuberty results in an equal likelihood of being anxious or depressed. In postpuberty this results in an increased likelihood of being anxious rather than depressed (Goodyer, Wright and Altham, 1989a). The mechanisms through which puberty exerts its effects are not clear but sug-gest that the physiology of pubertal change deserves much closer investigation as a mediating factor which influences the effects of social experience.

Temperament

As discussed in Chapter 5, temperamental qualities of children have been shown to be relatively stable global descriptions of traits of emotions and related behaviours.

These intrinsic qualities may play a role in the interactions of the individual with social adversities. For example, children with adverse temperaments, as characterised by low regularity, low malleability, negative mood and low fastidiousness, are more likely than other children to be the target of parental hostility, criticism and irritability (Quinton and Rutter, 1985a). When parents are depressed interpersonal conflicts occur more often with children who have difficult temperaments. Similarly, toddlers with difficult temperaments are not only more resistant to maternal control but their negative behaviour is more likely to be met with coercive responses by mothers (Lee and Bates, 1985).

Some children with irritable and impulsive characteristics are more prone to psychiatric disorders. What is less clear is how such characteristics exert their effects. For example, does the presence of irritability increase the risk of other stresses in the child's life? There is an association between disturbed family relations and irritability in the child, but the direction of that association is not always clear (Rutter, 1985a,b). In some cases there may be effects from the irritable child to the parents (suggesting a temperamental effect) rather than irritability being a consequence of disturbed family relations. Disentangling the direction of such effects requires a longitudinal design, ideally using children with and without temperamental difficulties and in the presence and absence of family disharmony. Cross-sectional studies can give clues, however, to the relative contributions that irritability and family disharmony may make to the probability of being a psychiatric case without disentangling the causal processes between these two factors. In other words, it may be important to know the relative risk of intrinsic factors (such as temperament) in the presence and absence of social factors when determining the risk of different forms of psychiatric disorder. We may be able to examine vulnerability and provoking agent models in childhood and adolescence using a range of factors, both intrinsic and extrinsic. For example, the associations between epilepsy and psychiatric disorder in childhood and adolescence clearly involve a complex series of factors related to neurological, psychological and social and family factors (Rutter, Graham and Yule, 1970; Goodyer, 1985; Hoare, 1987). The mechanisms, however, remain uncertain and the relative contributions of such factors in the presence and absence of each other deserve further examination. It may be, for example, that the factors involved in producing the significant increase in risk for psychiatric disorder associated with epilepsy in childhood do not all exert direct effects but operate through different types of mechanisms, depending on their relationship to each other as well as to epilepsy and psychiatric symptoms. The vulnerability and provoking agent model may provide one conceptual framework for examining such relationships.

Personal competence

A recent study investigated the relationship between personal competence, social adversity and individual attributes of children (Masten *et al.*, 1988).

Personal competence was assessed through measures of peer relationships and classroom behaviour (Garmezy, Masten and Tellegen, 1984). Two dimensions emerged: engaged versus disengaged children and classroom disruptiveness.

These measures of personal competence were used in 6–9-year-old children and interview methods recorded from mothers for the quality of parenting, parent–child relationships, family adversities and recent life events. Children's intellectual abilities and school achievements were also recorded on psychometric tests (the WISC-R). A number of 'stress-models' were tested on the data with support best found for a 'vulnerability–protection' model when the competence criterion was classroom disruptiveness, life events were the provoking agents and intelligence, social class and parenting qualities were the vulnerability–protective moderating variables.

When the competence criterion was altered to educational achievement the effects of life events and all modifying factors except I.Q. were lost. In other words, the level of the intelligence quotient had a direct effect on educational achievement.

An interesting speculation from the study was that personal attributes may function by altering the form of behavioural response to events. Thus, possessing a high I.Q. and being middle-class do not protect against undesirable responses to stresses but do cause more disengagement than disruptiveness. This finding appeared less likely in girls, suggesting a covariation of social factors, intrinsic dispositions and gender status on the form of expression of competence failure.

The impact of temperament in such studies has yet to be evaluated.

PROTECTIVE FACTORS AGAINST PSYCHIATRIC DISORDER

Protective factors can be defined as having the ability to reduce the effects of stresses on an individual (Rutter, 1979, 1987b,c). Questions that are concerned with identifying protective factors against stresses are equally important as those concerned with identifying factors that exert potentially causal effects on psychiatric disorder.

The general findings from epidemiological studies searching for protective factors highlight good relationships with parents, a positive caring family atmosphere and an external supportive system that envisages and reinforces a child's coping efforts and encourages a positive view of the self (Rutter, 1979; Garmezy, 1985).

A second set of positive/protective factors which are more intrinsic are found from a longitudinal study over 30 years on the Island of Kauai, examining the growth and emotional development and social and physical outcome of the islanders (Werner and Smith, 1982).

In these studies the authors identify a group of resilient children who shared many of the positive social and family characteristics with children from the Isle of Wight study by Rutter and colleagues (Rutter, Tizard and Whitmore, 1970). In addition, however, resilient children had better health histories, fewer accidents and appeared to recuperate from illness more quickly. These children were more likely to be rated as active, socially responsive, autonomous and given to a positive social orientation.

These latter features point to intrinsic qualities of the child as protective factors in terms of innate (genetic?) predisposition, quality of early upbringing and temperamental characteristics.

In terms of protective qualities, the triad of positive disposition, family work and cohesiveness, and social achievement and supports appear as repetitive themes throughout the literature (Garmezy, 1985; Rutter, 1987b,c). It should not be assumed, however, that protective factors are always positive social experiences, interpersonally or socially rewarding. In other words, beneficial experiences are not synonymous with protection (Hultsch and Plemons, 1979).

Examples from animal studies show that acute physical stress in early life can lead to neuroendocrine changes that increase an animal's resistance to later stress experiences (Levine, 1983). Exposure for young children to separation experiences from parents through to the use of babysitters or grandparents may decrease the risk of disturbance as a result of hospitalisation (Rutter, 1985b). These are examples of environmental stresses whose qualities appear *undesirable* but whose *effects* may be beneficial. If protection is considered in terms of effects, undesirable events may have protective qualities. These are examples of steeling effects from social experiences mentioned. The potential steeling effects of events have received little attention but are important for study if the mechanism of protection as a consequence of social factors is to be elucidated.

Other qualities may also protect individuals. There is a considerable literature suggesting that individuals who seem most immune to stress have an almost sociopathic quality to their personality, in that they make shallow attachments to others and appear to easily shift relationships (Hinkle, 1974; Rutter, 1981b; Brown, Bifulco and Harris, 1987).

This data applies to adults and it is not known if such intrinsic qualities operate the same way in children. The findings demonstrate, however, that certain individual qualities which may not make that person desirable to others may provide a protective effect against stresses.

Such personal qualities are not socially adaptive and the life path of such a person may be much more isolated than for others who expose themselves to greater risk through increasing social exposure to relationships and achievements.

There may be a trade-off between personal qualities and sociability aimed at minimising the risk for psychiatric disorder in some persons. The avoidance of social experience will result in a lowering of social adversities experienced. Do gregarious sociable individuals with high social exposure have greater rates of social adversities? Much more work is required to understand the relationship between personal disposition and selection of environments.

SUMMARY

1. Being exposed to a recent undesirable life event exerts a significant risk for the onset of anxiety or depression in school-age children in the presence or absence of other social adversities.
2. The likelihood of anxiety or depression occurring in a school-age child or adolescent is best explained by the patterning of social adversities rather than any single social factor.
3. Two independent pathways of effects are present. A 'family pathway' and a 'social pathway'. There is as yet however, no specificity between the patterning of social factors and the form of disorder, i.e. anxiety or depression appear equally as likely for family and social adversities.
4. The role of non-social factors is poorly understood. Sex differences may depend on sex-role behaviour rather than gender *per se*. Puberty acts as a point of change in the form of expression of psychopathology in the presence of friendship deficits. Temperament and personal competence may influence individual psychopathological responses to social adversities.
5. Social factors can protect against adverse experiences. Protective effects may arise from earlier positive experiences in family life but not all protection stems from desirable events. Steeling effects can be protective for social adversity and arise from unpleasant experiences.

Chapter 10

Clinical Issues and Intervention

We have discussed the various ways in which the nature and consequences of social adversities may contribute to psychiatric disorder in some children and adolescents. In this chapter we will consider a range of interventions that have been used to treat the adverse effects of stressful life events and difficulties.

DISTRESS AS A SYNDROME

The inclusion of distress as a possible 'syndrome' in DSM-III-R has usefully focused attention on the consequences of severe life events. The diagnosis of post-traumatic stress disorder can be made if the following criteria are met:

1. The existence of recognisable stresses that would evoke significant symptoms of distress in almost everyone.
2. Re-experiencing the trauma as evidenced by at least one of the following:
   (a) Recurrent and intrusive recollections of the event;
   (b) Recurrent dreams of the event;
   (c) Sudden acting or feeling as if the traumatic event were re-occurring, because of an association with an environmental or ideational stimulus.
3. Numbing of responsiveness to a reduced involvement with the external world, beginning some time after the trauma, as shown by at least one of the following:
   (a) Markedly diminished interest in one or more significant activities;
   (b) Feelings of detachment or estrangement from others;
   (c) Constricted affect.
4. At least two of the following symptoms that were not present before the trauma:
   (a) Hyperalertness or exaggerated startle response;
   (b) Sleep disturbance;
   (c) Guilt about surviving when others have not, or about behaviour required after survival.
5. Memory impairment or trouble concentrating.
6. Avoidance of activities that arouse recollection of the traumatic event.

7. Intensification of symptoms by exposure to events that symbolise or resemble the traumatic event.

Three forms of syndrome are suggested. Firstly, an acute syndrome, which has an onset within 6 months of the event and a duration of symptoms less than 6 months. Secondly, a chronic syndrome, which has a duration of symptoms 6 months or more. Thirdly, a delayed syndrome, which has an onset of symptoms at least 6 months after the trauma.

The development of this diagnostic category has resulted in a substantial degree of clinical and research activity in an effort to establish the reliability and validity of diagnosis in both adults and children. The publication of a recent book entitled *Post-Traumatic Stress Disorder in Children* testifies to the significant endeavours in this field of child mental health (Eth and Pynoos, 1985).

At present, however, the reliability and validity of 'post-traumatic distress syndromes' remains unclear. The present classification, for example, allows us to group together virtually any life experience and misfortune that may have aetiological significance, including bereavement, natural disasters, warfare, life-threatening illnesses, rape, suicide and witnessing acts of personal violence. At first sight the list seems overinclusive as in some respects a number of these events are conceptually quite distinct. For example, effects of events that have resulted in personal assault seem of a different order to those of witnessing such acts to others. Events that occur once appear different to the chronic fluctuating difficulties of a child with cancer or physical handicap. The qualities of the event may be important to the effects. Thus physical or sexual abuse can take a variety of forms, from a single event, ranging from voyeurism to rape, to chronic fluctuating and repeated assaults over weeks, months or even years.

The clinical criteria highlight emotional, cognitive and behavioural features, many of which appear in the criteria for differing forms of anxious and depressive disorders. This suggests a range of emotional response that does not clearly identify a specific clinical syndrome.

The emotional responses described in the post-traumatic syndrome seem to suggest a rather non-specific clinical picture of disinterest, detachment and preoccupation. It is not clear how these feeling states can be discriminated from those of depression. The most distinct clinical feature is the presence of an intrusive thought focused on the event that disrupts mood and behaviour.

Other cognitive features include guilt, specifically about surviving. Interestingly, no suggestion about the shame of surviving despite the suggested useful separation of guilt and shame in the phenomenology of affective disorder (Block Lewis, 1986).

Behavioural actions such as social withdrawal or the re-enactment of behaviour 'as if' still experiencing the event appear only possible as secondary effects of cognitive features through one of two mechanisms. Firstly, through intrinsic 'automatic thinking' resulting in associations in the present with events from the past. Secondly, exposure to further social stimuli such as other similar events or perhaps symbolic features of apparently dissimilar events likely to trigger memories of the original undesirable experience.

Perhaps the least specific clinical features are the biological responses of sleep disturbance and exaggerated startle response.

The criteria for diagnosis do not indicate a cognitive–behavioural hierarchy as implied above and present evidence suggests that it is premature to accept the face validity of a specific syndrome of post-traumatic stress disorder. We may, however, be usefully reclassifying a range of emotional reactions to social adversities in a more systematic manner (rather than delineating a new diagnosis).

Continuing to delineate the qualities of social adversity will help determine the social origins of distress reactions and psychiatric disorders that may ensue. Additionally, the clinical characteristics may become clearer as research proceeds in this area. We have already noted individual differences in children's reactions to events, the importance of personal meaning, the effects of intrinsic characteristics, such as temperament, and possibly physicochemical factors. Clearly we are unlikely to develop a coherent view of the causal associations between social adversities and psychopathologies without taking into account a range of non-social factors.

Overall, it is encouraging and important that a clinical literature has begun to appear on the psychopathology of stress. Like all beginnings many questions as well as answers are being produced at present. For example, differences between adults and children are beginning to emerge. Thus, with respect to severe traumatic events children appear to show less amnesia for an event,

However, they tend to be sensitised to react adversely to subsequent milder stresses and have more frequent re-enactments with nightmares and fears. In addition, developmental factors are likely to influence the form of response to stressful events as we have described previously.

Recent findings suggest that interviewing children directly as well as talking to their parents is an important clinical procedure in identifying psychiatric disorders (Earls et al., 1988). The present evidence not only indicates a lack of uniformity in children's clinical pictures in the weeks and months following a disaster but suggests that the symptoms present are greatest in those with a pre-existing psychiatric disorder and those whose parents reported a high number of symptoms in themselves (McFarlane, 1987, 1988; Earls et al., 1988).

With this diffuse clinical presentation occurring in many cases of post-traumatic disorders it is perhaps not surprising to find a lack of clear procedures for the management of severe stress reactions in childhood and adolescence. It is also apparent that the application of the general principles of good clinical practice will apply to these children as much as to any other presentation. In other words, careful, systematic and comprehensive assessments of the child, family and the environment should be undertaken and an adequate formulation of the case be made before treatment is undertaken.

The rest of this chapter is concerned with describing the common forms of intervention that have been used to alleviate distress and disorder in children and their families. The emphasis is on interventions for children and their families who have experienced some form of recent stressful life event. In addition, some mention is made of the management of separations in general, the role of physical illness as a life event and the management of dying children.

PSYCHOLOGICAL TREATMENT

Psychodynamic psychotherapy

Individual psychodynamic psychotherapy, including traditional forms of relationship building between child and therapist in the here and now to promote emotional well-being and improve the personal meaning of previous acute adversity, has not usually been employed in the management of stress, reactions or disorders. This may be because the substantial cognitive component in stress reactions indicates that patients are not uninsightful nor are they using defence mechanisms to avoid the emotional consequences of previous or early unresolved conflicts. It may also be because the re-enactment of traumatic memories does not appear to result in satisfactory alleviation of distress in many of these children. It is not that re-experiencing the memories should be avoided (on the contrary, such avoidance has poor prognostic consequences, see below) more that interpreting the relationship with the therapist 'as if' it had sufficient treatment value for those memories appears not to be the case. In other words, the development of an adequate relationship with the child such that painful memories can be elucidated and discussed seems to be a necessary prerequisite for successful treatment but does not constitute an end in itself.

The use of re-experience

It is apparent that the continuing re-experience of adverse stress is a central feature of psychopathology. As a result, some clinicians have focused on manipulating these thoughts as a method for alleviating distress. This introduces cognitive (and indirectly behavioural) techniques into the treatment of individuals.

The therapeutic core appears to be in helping children develop a more adaptive appraisal of what happened during their traumatic experiences. There are a number of components to this process as follows:

1. To clarify what the child's perception of the event is.
2. To evaluate this 'biography of an event' with what is known from other sources.

3. To determine what the child views his or her role in the event to have been, including:
   (a) personal blame for the event or its consequences;
   (b) actions that may have been taken at the time but were not;
   (c) subsequent reflections on how the event has influenced his or her life.

The purpose of these procedures is to develop a coherent and meaningful understanding of a traumatic experience that does not inhibit the child's social and emotional development. Thus the regaining of self-esteem and developing effective coping mechanisms for life difficulties are goals of treatment. There is some evidence that failure to provide such opportunities, at least in severe traumatic events such as personal assault and kidnapping, may lead to chronic anxiety states (Terr, 1983). There may also be difficulties in relating experiences in everyday terms to friends and family members, sometimes referred to as forced silence (Lister, 1982).

The clinical techniques for treatment success, however, will depend on factors other than the type and nature of the event itself. The child's age, stage of development, family and social support networks, including school and friendships, all require evaluation. Adequate assessment and evaluation of these factors should precede any treatment decisions.

Play and the physical reconstruction of events

Group methods

A number of authors have published reports of the use of non-verbal methods to facilitate reconstruction of stressful events. These may be primary or central methods of treatment in young children perhaps less than 8 years old, whose vocabulary as well as their socio-emotional development and life experience may not be sufficiently adequate for a talking treatment approach only (although it should not be assumed they are unable to do so). In older children non-verbal methods may ameliorate the emotional difficulties of discussing aspects of the trauma and can be helpful in facilitating a reappraisal of the experience. For example, having children make drawings of a traumatic event has been used as a method to relive the experience in the here and now (Blom, 1986; Pynoos and Eth, 1984). Such techniques can be enhanced by fantasy and story-telling methods which promote the discussion and reconstruction of events but deflect the personal implication.

For example, children who had been victims of earthquakes in central Italy drew pictures while listening to a story about a child who was fearful and too timid to ask for help. This was followed by group discussions of the children's drawings and their feelings about them and the story which they were encouraged to discuss with each other (Galante and Foa, 1986). In subsequent discussions in groups, the thematic focus of the drawings became the earth-quake experience itself. The move to a more realistic drawing of the experience together with expansion of drawings to include personal possessions (toys etc.) was complemented by the children acting out in a mini-play the realities of the earthquake. Following this application of psychodrama principles in controlled group circumstances, subsequent sessions focused on survival activities and the resumption of everyday life. Through these sessions the children's productions grew less fearful, and losses the children had sustained were discussed more openly. The symbolic re-enactment of the earthquake, and subsequent sugges-tions of being able to control their environment and plan for the future, appears to have helped to relegate the traumatic loss to the past.

Furthermore, this interpretation appears to have decreased rates of subse-quent psychiatric disorder in children who received this integration compared with those who did not (Galante and Foa, 1986). The children involved in the project were mainly school age and from a relatively isolated rural community. Perhaps benefits were gained by using groups of children who knew each other or shared a similar social value system. Certainly children as young as 3 or 4 can turn to each other for support at times of great trauma, such as surviving concentration camps or the stress of parental disharmony (Freud and Dann, 1951; Dunn and Kendrick, 1982).

It is not clear, however, if some or all of the methods used exerted a therapeu-tic effect. The logical progression of story-telling, play and the use of fantasy through to re-enacting events and discussing coping suggests a basis of stress management therapy of considerable merit whose principles are translatable to children who may have experienced more common and less substantially traumatic events, such as divorce, bereavement or illness.

Group behaviour seemed to play an important part in the intervention stra-tegy. This made sense because the event had been a collective experience for all the children. It seems worth while to consider that when traumatic events are common enough and contain similar characteristics impacting on children that group therapy may be the treatment of choice. It would, however, be insufficient merely to consider a group treatment on the basis of exposure to event. Evaluation should probably contain an assessment of the qualities of the event and the degree of impact on the child.

We do not know if group techniques would be more effective if children shared a general similar degree of impact. Neither do we know the degree to which therapeutic factors associated with group therapies in general are contributing to the children's outcome (Bloch and Crouch, 1985). In particular, factors such as self-disclosure, learning from interpersonal action, acceptance, guidance and the installation of hope all seem apparent and known to be associated with positive outcomes in group treatments.

Additionally, the role of the therapist in the treatment is unclear. There seems no doubt that they are actively participating and providing structure and guidance in the re-experiencing of the event. We know little, however, of how the therapists are perceived by the children. It is not clear if this latter factor is important in the management of stress-related symptoms. There is evidence, however, to suggest that active therapists may be more effective in group treatments with children (Kolvin *et al.*, 1981). Findings from adult studies emphasise that therapists occupy an important role in group treatments and cannot be viewed as exerting no effect on the outcome of treatment (Bloch and Crouch, 1985).

In Chapter 4, however, we discussed the therapeutic techniques used for the children of the North Sea ferry disaster. Interestingly, the reports indicate that the children perceived the therapist as somewhat intrusive on their shared experiences. The anecdotal findings from this group of disaster victims suggests that the children worked better with no therapist at all! Clearly a more systematic analysis of therapeutic factors in these groups would be worth while.

Finally, it is apparent that in the treatment of severe events, emotional, cognitive and behavioural methods are being used. Far from being mutually exclusive there seems to be necessary linking between different psychological models to develop effective treatment strategies.

Individual treatment strategies

Relieving distress from events in young children either pre-school or between 5 and 7 may require more individual rather than group approaches. Contextual play techniques involving some structured play combined with non-personalised story-telling have been developed for interviewing 5–6-year-old children and may help to evaluate the role of such interventions in the resolution of distress following life events (Lentz, 1985). Such techniques can be helpful in common and unavoidable separations, such as school entry (Barnett, 1984). In one such project, 3-year-old children were observed in nursery school settings following separation from their mothers. Children's level of anxiety was determined physiologically using a palmar sweat index, and behaviourally by direct observation evaluating (i) the degree of clinging to parent at time of separation, (ii) verbal responses such as pleading, whining, begging, etc., asking parents not to leave, and associated tears, screaming, sobbing or tantrums. Children were then divided into two groups, 'high' or 'low' anxiety, on the basis of the two scores, which were highly correlated.

Children in each of the high and low anxiety groups were further divided by order of appearance into two conditions, either play or no play. The play condition consisted of a 15-minute period in a room containing a variety of toys. The children were told they could do whatever they wanted and a teacher was present in the room, seated in the corner, but NOT participating. Half of the play group children found other children in the playroom and engaged in social play whereas the other half were alone and therefore in solitary play.

The 'no-play' condition consisted of a group who were instructed to sit at a small table and listen to a story about various types of trees and shrubs that could be found in a forest. Children were retested at the end of the two conditions. The results indicated that for children with low anxiety there were no differences in pre and post sweat measures in either play or story settings nor were there any significant differences in sweat measures between the two settings. Low anxiety children had not described separation as stressful and therefore were made no better or worse by play or a story.

For high anxiety children, however, there were highly significant reductions in the sweat scores pre and post play. There were no significant reductions in the sweat scores for the high anxiety group in the story conditions.

It seems reasonable to conclude that in children where the life event of separation was stressful, the resolution of that distress was significantly more likely through play than story-telling. Further analysis of these results showed that highly anxious children were not helped by the presence of peers (regardless of their level of anxiety) in the play setting. This finding is contrary to previous suggestions that the resolution of distress depends on the presence of peers (Rubin, Maioris and Homung, 1976; Rubin, Watson and Jambor, 1978; Rubin and Krasnor, 1980). A fine-grain analysis of the children's play suggested that high anxiety children choose to play alone or in parallel with peers rather than interacting with them. Highly anxious children were found to engage in more dramatic/fantasy play forms and less functional and manipulative play styles. The amount of dramatic/fantasy play markedly decreased in the presence of peers.

This study demonstrated a number of factors in relation to the treatment of young children and the event of separation.

First, it was individual rather than group treatments that appeared efficacious. There seemed to be an important place for social dramatic play but no evidence that there was a re-experiencing or reconstructing of the events. This suggests that any cognitive factors of treatment are either intimately related with action and in a sense hidden by the behavioural expression to the event. Alternatively, there is no substantive cognitive factor and play is motivated through the emotional effects brought about by the event of separation.

There does seem to be greater emphasis on emotion–behaviour links through fantasy to improve mood and lower anxiety. For young children there seems to be less need for a participating therapist, although there is a suggestion that a familiar adult and perhaps environment is necessary.

The suggestion that a highly anxious pre-school child may be inhibited by peers following separation from mother suggests that in such circumstances nurseries, playgroups etc. should consider having a period of solitary and supervised play as part of their programme. This could be made available to those children identified as markedly anxious at the time of entry. Firm efforts to have the child join in group activities to take his or her mind off the separation event may not be the best strategy in the first instance.

These results demonstrated that a substantially different approach to the management of a life event involving separation is required to that of a disaster event. In particular, it is clear that these children need secure private space for the purposes of treatment and anxiety reduction. Although life events of separation and disaster may have similarities, we see that the effects of the two events involve substantial personal meaning that is different. Some of these differences may be a consequence of their developmental status. Clearly, however, the markedly different context within which separation occurs is a major factor. Studies of anxiety reduction to school entry at other stages of development would be helpful in this respect.

The role of anxiety reduction in a transitional event such as going to school or school change may have an important role in assisting children's adjustment. Certainly school change can be perceived as stressful, particularly when there are new stimuli and a reorientation of the child to his or her environment is required (Field, 1984b; Elizur, 1986).

The treatments discussed so far demonstrate that developmental differences must be taken into account when planning a treatment strategy for stress induced fears and worries.

Thus the value of cognitive approaches must be considered in the light of the child's cognitive development. Group approaches may benefit from the children getting to know each other in the group setting before task focused work related to the stressful event is introduced. Solitariness following a stressful experience may be a sign of adaptation rather than a sign of disorder and may indicate the need for individual rather than group oriented work, at least in the first instance. It has to said, however, that prolonged solitariness is unlikely to be adaptive in the long term.

Do these findings provide sufficient information to consider if these techniques can be applied to psychiatric disorder as a result of other life events involving separations, such as parental separation, divorce or migration?

Whilst the present findings are of interest and provide important clues as to how children cope with distress, there are substantial limitations in their generalisation to other stressful life events. The measures and methods require further improvements, design of controlled trials of treatments is needed and replication of present findings required. Nevertheless, important aspects of managing stress are highlighted in these studies and provide a framework for individual and group treatment for distress and psychiatric disorder arising from life events.

Family therapy and bereavement

The discussion has so far concentrated on treatment of children in individual or group settings. We know, however, that many events will have an impact on the settings in which children live. In other words, institutions such as family systems, schools and communities are affected by life events and may need to be the focus of intervention rather than individual children.

Surprisingly little has been written about treatment for bereaved children in comparison with the literature on adults. Thus a range of treatment techniques have been used in adults who are bereaved, including intervention in normal grief following perinatal death (Forrest, Standish and Baum, 1982; Woodward *et al.*, 1985) and guided mourning in adults in whom the grief process has gone wrong (Mawson *et al.*, 1981).

The child's ability to cope with bereavement was recently investigated by the application of a family therapy technique aimed at increasing the child's understanding of his loss and thereby aiding subsequent adjustment (Black and Urbanowitz, 1987).

An unselected group of children at the time of death of a parent were identified over a 3-year period and randomly allocated to family treatment or control groups.

Treatment consisted of six family sessions spaced at 2–3 weekly intervals, taking place at home about 2–3 months after the bereavement. The therapists were all experienced psychiatric social workers in child mental health settings and trained in bereavement counselling techniques.

The aims of the treatment were to promote normal mourning in both the children and remaining parent and to improve communication with them, especially about death.

Photographs and mementos were used during treatment, as were active techniques, such as play and observing, to encourage verbal communication. Control families received no intervention or planned visits.

Approximately 1 year and again 2 years after bereavement both treatment and control families were contacted by another interviewer. The interview was structured and covered the children's health and behaviour and the death event surrounding it.

At the first year follow-up the children from the treatment group were significantly less likely to be restless, bite their nails or have depressed parents. In addition, mothers from treatment groups were less likely to have sought help from professional agencies. There were no significant differences in the number of subsequent life events following bereavement in the two groups. By the second year the major difference between the two groups lay in the parents. The control group had significantly more health-related problems in the surviving parent.

A further interesting trend in the data was the suggestion that a favourable outcome (i.e. less emotional and behavioural difficulties in the child) was associated with the child having cried and talked about the dead parent in the month following bereavement, especially in those children over 5. Furthermore, by 2 years there seemed to be an association with the avoidance of talking about the dead parent if a substitute existed. At the first year avoidance of talking about the dead parent showed a trend towards an unforeseeable outcome. Avoidance of talking was also shown by children whose parents scored highly on a composite score of grief, worry, depression and suicidal thoughts. In other words, the therapeutic potential for the child of an emotional display together with discussing the loss can be inhibited by disturbed parents. This suggests an important role of evaluating adult well-being and satisfaction following bereavement and the need to intervene with the surviving parent if psychiatric disorder is identified, for the well-being of the family.

The results of this study are encouraging and some of the clearer findings deserve further discussion.

Firstly, it is apparent that the well-being of the surviving parent is of considerable significance, suggesting the life event impact on the parent must be evaluated if the impact on the child is to be assessed adequately. This demonstrates the mediating influence of parental health on a child's well-being following bereavement and other life events carrying a potentially severe impact (McFarlane, 1987, 1988). These findings demonstrated that some forms of severe events, which involve loss of persons, carry significant personal meaning and irretrievably alter the family's status quo. The impact of the main effects on the child were exerted through their substantive effects on parental well-being. These effects may have maintained child difficulties. What is less clear is how this mechanism related to the onset of disorder and whether or not it required children to possess other factors, such as a past history of disturbance or poor family relations. In other words, does this mechanism operate in the presence of vulnerability factors or is it sufficient in itself? Perhaps the answer lies in the qualities of the event as well as past experiences. Certainly the nature of events, their severity, duration and effect on the individual's overall status quo (i.e. their general living circumstances, social and family composition) have been shown to influence the course of emotional disorders in young adults (Miller et al., 1987). It is apparent that for the clinician the analysis of the type of event, its social impact, personal meaning, focus (i.e. whether impact is directed at child, parent, family others etc.) and amplification (i.e. if the effects of the event spread beyond the immediate persons and if so how) may be important in determining the range of intervention and help in predicting the psychopathological effects of stress.

Secondly, there was a suggestion that talking and crying were important in promoting good adjustment in the child and these emotional features may be attenuated if a reconstituting of the family occurs. This suggests that when surviving parents remarry, there may be a place for further assessment of communication about the bereavement as in some cases the children may be in a 'forced silence' position rather than being well adjusted.

Thirdly, the interventions appeared to have been appreciated by the families and may have shortened the period of distress following bereavement. This finding suggests that the adverse consequences of life events may be diminished in duration if psychiatric assistance is offered.

These families were not in crisis nor had they identified any member as a case. They may not have received bereavement counselling although they are likely to have been offered general support from primary care services. This raises an important question about the service provision for bereaved families: should mental health services wait for abnormal grief and family difficulties before offering interventions or should all bereavements (whether unexpected or not) be screened for difficulties? The present slim evidence suggests that the active participation of bereavement counselling as a primary prevention measure should be offered, even in the absence of any overt difficulties. Such help could come from primary care teams (health visitors, nurses) who could be offered training in bereavement counselling and support by specialist child mental health professionals.

The development of a health-related policy as a consequence of research into bereavement is a good example of research into practice. Health policy development can be usefully influenced by reliable and valid information. Primary prevention policy could be advised to health authorities and service providers in the community. An argument can be put forward for the provision of resources at a primary care level on the grounds of preventing morbidity in children and their families.

Stress inoculation

Teaching children coping skills and problem-solving techniques to treat symptoms has become an increasingly well-used approach in child mental health.

The cognitive and behavioural aspects of these techniques are often prominent issues (Kendall and Bronswell, 1984; Nicol, 1987). Stress inoculation is a cognitive behavioural method which attempts to teach children coping skills that might serve as an 'immunisation' against stress (Meichenbaum and Cameron, 1983). The important treatment components are said to be (Meichenbaum and Novaco, 1978):

1. Guided self-discovery to make apparent the role of a person's own cognitions in adding to subjective distress.
2. Self-monitoring of maladaptive behaviour.
3. Learning problem-solving skills.
4. Encouraging effective coping methods.

5. Graduated exercises that emulate in their performance.
6. Behaviour therapy procedures, including relaxation training, coping in imagination and behavioural rehearsal, where the likelihood of disorder is a potentially repeatable occurrence (e.g. floods, earthquakes, etc.)

This array of concepts is used to facilitate (i) discussion of the sequence of stressful events and the types of likely response and changes that may occur in the environment, (ii) reassurance techniques to indicate how the impact of such changes can be controlled, (iii) methods of protection, such as the role of parents and teachers in the alleviation of distress in children and in the reinforcement of confidence that such procedures can be helpful in alleviating individual and collective distress. The use of 'paced mastery' is an example of a stress inoculation technique in which small units of stress are induced to train children in coping skills.

Whilst the concept of stress inoculation is to be commended, there is as yet little evidence of its efficacy in preventing distress reactions to life events or assisting in the avoidance of events by producing more efficient problem-solving in children. The use of such techniques has been advocated in some circumstances, such as coping with arsonist attacks in Israel (Ayalon, 1983). One novel introduction in this programme was the teaching of children to recognise and evaluate cues that indicated a potentially stressful event was about to occur (i.e. an attack).

In the present state of knowledge it is not clear if stress inoculation procedures will achieve their desired aims. No doubt some systematic studies will be forthcoming. There is, however, a certain technical, almost surgical, quality conveyed by some therapists and practitioners of such programmes. It may be that in certain circumstances, where practicable, with life events that are severe, perhaps catastrophic, a stress education programme of this nature will be substantially valued as a protection against mortal danger.

In many other contexts of life events, however, it remains to be seen if the components of cognitive behavioural methods do not in fact contain affective and communicative qualities at least as efficacious as the details of the programmes themselves. For example, paced mastery has much in common with the psychotherapeutic technique of recovering mentally painful thoughts and their associated affects in the here and now. The difference appears to lie in how the therapists then use this 'cognitive-affective scheme'. It remains to be seen whether or not it is the recovery on induction of cognitive-affective schemes *per se* or therapists' techniques with this information that exerts therapeutic effects. A third, and so far uninvestigated, variable concerns the child's perceptions of their treatment; inducing or recovering painful memories and feelings needs to be considered concurrently with what the child believes is expected of both himself or herself and the therapist.

MANAGING REACTIONS TO SEPARATION FROM HOME

The majority of children will find themselves subject to a separation from their homes during their childhood. Many of these will be brief, although the reaction to them will vary according to the quality of family relations, the age of the child and the nature and purpose of the separation (Wolkind and Rutter, 1985). It should be remembered that brief separations can be distressing and should be handled with sensitivity and compassion by caretakers. Adults may consider that certain separations are free of unpleasant circumstances. Staying with relatives or friends, however, can be a distressing experience. If the adults concerned are well known to the child and brief separations are carefully planned, distress may be considerably lessened, although not totally removed (Robertson and Robertson, 1971).

This principle of planning separations can be applied to a number of 'events' that are likely to arise. For example, approximately one-third of children in the U.K. will be admitted at least once to hospital and one in twenty will have multiple admissions (Douglas, 1975; Quinton and Rutter, 1976). It is well accepted that distress can be substantially alleviated by parental residence or regular visits to hospital. It should be remembered that alleviating distress can be helpful to the general medical care of the child who may receive a better quality of care if less irritable and fractious (Wolkind, Vyas and Haris, 1982).

Assessing the child's relationship to its parents is perhaps a crucial issue. It is very likely that an insecure child will react negatively to brief separations. In such circumstances where separations are inevitable it can be helpful in planning management to know what may happen. Provision of support can then be planned and substitute caretakers will not be surprised or made anxious themselves by a separation reaction. It should be remembered that separations may be beneficial if brief and happy and may provide a positive steeling experience for subsequent more-protracted separations.

Finally, as well as these general items on the management of separation we need to consider developmental issues.

For example, following separation, infants under 6 months are more likely to withdraw and become quieter whereas older pre-school children may become difficult and irritable, with the characteristic picture of protest, despair and detachment sequence. After the age of 4 this classical picture is seen less frequently.

The alteration in the form of expression of distress reflects developmental changes in the child. Before 6 months selective attachments to parents have not been developed sufficiently to result in a distress response. Between 6 months and 4 years attachments become selective and other distress reactions may occur. After this time children's reactions diminish because they have learned to maintain their relationship with their parents over a period of absence. This may be because of a better understanding of the transient nature of separation, and a developed sense of time as well as an established internal working model of their relationship. Planning management of separations may therefore be more efficient by taking into account these developmental factors. Observing children's behaviour in the presence of their parents may provide important information in this respect.

ILLNESS AS LIFE EVENT

The development and onset of physical illness constitutes a common stressful life event. Indeed, illnesses and accidents are the second most important group of recent undesirable life events likely to precede emotional or conduct disorders in school-age children (Goodyer, Kolvin and Gatzanis, 1985).

The impact of illness on a child's general adjustment has been studied from various points of view, including the presence of overt symptoms, general development, effects on the family and social development (e.g. Breslau, 1985; Taylor, 1985; Hoare, 1987; Marteau, Bloch and Baum, 1987). By and large, illnesses which leave no long-term effect on a child's physical health do not appear to have significant long-term psychological consequences even if hospitalisation has been involved (Quinton and Rutter, 1976). There are circumstances where illnesses may have profound effects, however. In particular, chronic physical illnesses such as diabetes or epilepsy that require continuous medical surveillance and monitoring of drugs and general lifestyle, such as diet. In spite of the obvious risks to general adjustment in such disorders there has been little systematic study of their associations with social stressful events.

Findings to date refer mainly to adults. The research suggests that in some circumstances acute events can be important factors in some physical symptoms, such as abdominal pain (Creed, 1981). The role of acute life events as causes of chronic illness such as diabetes however has not been substantiated (Graham, 1985).

Illnesses may, however, alter the probability of subsequent events occurring to children. Thus repeated hospitalisations, alterations in friendships, being described as different or less able, and being more vulnerable as a consequence of a chronic illness have been reported, for example, in children with epilepsy (Long and Moore, 1979; Hoare, 1984). Adequate control of seizures, glycaemic control of diabetes and respiratory control of asthmatic disorders may be influenced by life stresses and social adversities, but as yet we do not know of the specifics of these relationships and whether or not acute life events as opposed, for example, to ongoing chronic difficulties are important in the course of chronic physical disorders and whether or not they exert influence on the sequelae of the disease.

Despite the lack of substantive findings there is a place for practical health promotion measures (described in the next chapter) or in some cases the use of treatment techniques to assist children and parents gain a better understanding of how social adversities may influence medical well-being. Developing better coping strategies for such children seems an important area for mental health professionals and in some cases may form part of liaison health care practice in paediatric and medical settings for adults as well as children (Creed and Pfeffer, 1982; Graham, 1985).

For example, there is some evidence that asthma attacks in children can be alleviated by family therapy methods, although it is not clear if this process involved attention to acute stressful life events and their potential consequences for control (Lask and Matthew, 1979). What seems more apparent is that medical crises, such as acute respiratory difficulties, status epilepticus and diabetic ketoacidosis, are themselves highly stressful events which may adversely effect parents' and child's attitudes towards the chronic illness and result in undesirable alterations in both the management of the disease and general social adjustment. Further research in this area would seem useful and help to identify any stressful factors that may make a contribution to the disease process itself and stressful factors that may influence the child's and family's adjustment to the disease.

In some circumstances physical symptoms may act as social adversities for others who share some environmental characteristic with the individual. A rather unusual, but well-recognised, social phenomenon, termed epidemic hysteria, can arise from the presence of functional symptoms in a few individuals. Epidemic or community hysteria has been described in various age groups, but most typically in adolescence, and in many different cultures and social economic settings (Kagwa, 1964; Moss and McEvedy, 1966; Levine *et al.*, 1974).

The clinical picture is that of symptoms of fainting, headache, pins and needles, and hypertension often arising at a time of general life stress in school or institutional settings, such as during exams. The symptoms therefore arise in a few individuals because of impending life events although not always so. There is a spread of symptoms to include those people in close proximity to the original persons and soon a large number of individuals complain of identical symptoms. These episodes of contagion are often interspersed with days when no new cases are referred (Moss and McEvedy, 1966; Levine *et al.*, 1974). Children with a dominant or influential position in the school or institution appear to be important in the spread of symptoms. Transmission occurs readily within closely knit groups and the direction is usually from older to younger children.

Management requires attention to the social and anthropological concepts that underlie this response by children to the symptoms of others with whom they are in close proximity. Persons of high prestige, such as teachers and doctors, are capable of effectively allaying the process and prevent the 'spread' by prompt response that there is no serious illness in the school. Dispersion of the groups by sending older children home or closing the school or institution for 24–72 hours can be helpful. Interestingly, it has been suggested that press publicity of the event may be harmful, although the reasons for this are not clear but may be related to the implication of serious physical illness. Indeed, publication of the views that the disease is psychological may be helpful (Adomakoh, 1973).

Epidemic hysteria provides an example of some important social and anthropological concepts in considering how symptoms in others may act as stressful life events in close-knit groups. Two mechanisms have been suggested. Firstly, symptoms exert their effects through a shared social experience for a significant number of individuals who consider themselves to have close, possibly intimate, relations. Secondly, that individuals with predisposing vulnerability factors are more afflicted in the presence of a single person with symptoms. A past psychiatric history and chronic ongoing family difficulties have both been described in the children who first show symptoms but are markedly absent from those children to whom the symptoms spread. Contagion to others is dependent on proximity, the closer the physical proximity of children the greater the number of affected individuals (Moss and McEvedy, 1966). Identification with, or imitation of, other children appears to increase in these circumstances (Goodyer, 1986a).

Dying children

Perhaps fatal illness in a child captures the fullest meaning of a stressful life event focused on a family. Sudden death from accidents results in acute bereavements and the treatment clearly focuses on the consequences of loss to parents, siblings, extended relatives and perhaps friends. Many of these principles have been described in this chapter, including individual and family treatments. What of the uncertainty related to children with malignant disease, however, where the cause and outcome of disorder are unpredictable but certain to be stressful? The uncertainties of malignant disease never truly pass from the minds of the child or the family, often because of frequent hospital check-ups and attention to the routines of everyday life to identify as early as possible signs of deterioration. Even after children have been in remission for years there can remain a constant background feeling that events are, or might easily become, out of control, a state that has been termed the Damocles Syndrome (Koocher and O'Malley, 1981).

Cancer in children is rare, about 1400 cases are diagnosed each year in the United Kingdom. Prognosis has improved substantially and some 60 per cent of children can expect to reach long-term remission (Morris-Jones, 1987). However, some 40 per cent of patients still die and cancer remains the commonest illness causing death in children between 1 and 14.

The outlook for cancer is significantly better when children are treated in a recognised paediatric oncology centre with multidisciplinary teams, experience and facilities for physical and psychological care (Lansdown and Goldman, 1988).

The implication of present evidence is that alleviating child or family distress has a potentially good prognostic effect on the physiological outcome on the malignant disorder. The suggestion is not that stress reduction directly influences white cell counts (in the case of leukaemia) but that indirectly stress reduction improves the attention to detail of overall management, thereby enhancing the therapeutic methods employed. No studies have yet evaluated the possibility that anxiety management of the child may indeed have direct influence on the disease. The principles and practice of psychological techniques used in malignancy have recently been described (Lansdown and Goldman, 1988). Involving staff as well as families in group discussions about the ongoing progress of cases; providing individual play sessions for children as a forum for preparing children for the side effects of treatments, such as hair loss, and a secure place to act or play out their concerns and thoughts; the provision of home visits and the co-ordination of support services all have a role to play, depending on the individual nature and circumstances of the family concerned.

A major focus in this area concerns direct communication with children. A common problem for therapists is to gain access to the child for this purpose. Firstly, parents and children may engage in a defence where family members pretend nobody is worried about the future (Bluebond-Langner, 1978). Alternatively, as has been observed in families with a physically handicapped or chronically ill child, parents may assert that they have all the coping skills necessary (Goodyer, 1986b). In both cases these mechanisms prevent access to the child and in many cases to the child's siblings.

The value of communicating with children directly when they have malignant disease (and indeed for any disorder with effects lasting more than a few days) has been summarised by Lansdown in his work with dying children (Lansdown and Benjamin, 1985; Lansdown, 1987).

The thesis for communicating with children directly is that anxiety is commonly reduced when children can anticipate events. The provision of adequate information about their illness is a major focus of communication in dying children. Information about treatment, the nature and cause of illness, anticipated side effects reflect the instrumental communication. Indicating respect for the child and developing a language to describe the emotions related to illness and to dying reflect the affective communication.

Interestingly, there are no studies investigating how children come to understand their impending death from a fatal illness. Neither is it clear what the best procedure for communication might be for a child facing death. Lansdown and colleagues emphasise that getting close to the truth of the future event is a central concept when children seek answers to the question 'Am I going to die and will you visit me in heaven?'

In conclusion, there are encouraging signs that recent interest in the effects of stressful events in the lives of children and their families has resulted in modest advances in treatment in some circumstances. As our knowledge improves concerning the clinical features, natural course and outcome of stress-related disorders we will be able to improve our methods of evaluation and thereby our treatment choice and effectiveness. Present findings indicate that we should be careful in generalising possible interventions from one event-related disorder to another. For example, it is apparent that whilst death and divorce are both, in one sense, loss events to a child their differences in terms of social and psychological characteristics are quite marked (Richards, 1988).

The evaluation of a stressful event in terms of its characteristics, social context, personal appraisal by the child and other family members and effects on social and family structure remain the focus of a clinical assessment and should contribute significantly to decisions concerning management. Future studies should consider the clinical and research implications of investigating relatively common events, such as divorce, and necessary separations, such as school and college entry, where children and adolescents are known to be at risk from psychiatric disorder and distress.

SUMMARY

1. Post-traumatic stress disorders refer to psychopathology occurring as direct consequence of a life event. The clinical features are similar to affective disorders although survivor guilt may be a specific cognitive symptom.
2. The absence of overt symptoms in a child may reflect forced silence rather than good adjustment.
3. Clinical evaluation of the salience of the life event to the child and family is important and may help to determine the form of treatment.
4. Cognitive restructuring of past experience in association with the release of affect appears to be a common theme in many treatments.
5. Direct involvement of children using group, individual or family treatment appears important for subsequent adjustment.
6. Physically ill, handicapped or dying children may benefit from attention to the psychological consequences of their disorder. These illnesses act as life events and difficulties for family members.

Chapter 11

Social Adversities and Public Policy

LIFE EVENTS RESEARCH AND PUBLIC POLICY

One of the aims of mental health research must be to provide new insights or information to mental health practitioners, policy makers and the general public. Has life events research on children and families achieved this and if so to what extent and through what processes? It has to be said at the outset that many problems beset this important area of public policy, not just those of life events (e.g. Segal, 1975; Lynn, 1978). Firstly, it is important to impress upon policy makers that an understanding of psychological processes in the promotion and maintenance of well-being in childhood and adolescence is crucial for society. There is an impressive body of evidence that children's general development is influenced by chronic and acute life adversities. Both adverse social and psychological consequences for children can therefore be argued as arising from factors in the public domain and legitimately the concern of the public at large, mental health practitioners and policy makers (Segal, 1975, 1983; Graham, 1985).

THE PURPOSE OF PUBLIC POLICIES FOR CHILDREN AND FAMILIES

Interest in how the family and society value child care are far from new. At present it might be argued that we are in a rapidly changing perspective towards children. The role of the child, the moral, ethical and legal issues of children and parental rights are at the forefront of public debate.

This important debate has evolved through many reconsiderations of what childhood is for and how children may become socially responsible adults. An analysis of the medical, social and political factors included in this reappraisal is beyond the scope of this book. The role of public bodies and government agencies involved in child and family welfare has been growing steadily throughout this century in most areas of the world and has been the subject of legislation at the United Nations and World Health Authorities.

In the U.K. the instigation of agencies in the voluntary and public sector, such as the N.S.P.C.C. and social services, are evidence of both public concern for children and the view that children are not in the best position to determine what is in their best interest at all times.

The development of large-scale projects to determine the course of child development, such as the National Child Development Survey, reflect on the important need for accurate information about the general principles of childhood that are necessary for the development and implementation of policies towards children.

Four concepts can be elucidated about public policy. Firstly, attitudes in society seem important in determining to what extent priorities for public policy will be set. At this point in history we appear to be in a 'stage of concern' about children, with resultant questioning about previous assumptions concerning the value of children, their moral standing in society, their ethical and legal rights and the consequent implications for parents, families and the organisation of social structures.

This alteration in the perception of childhood seems an evolving process and it is difficult to determine the origins of the present position without a consideration of social, medical and political practices over many decades.

Therefore, a focusing on public education efforts towards child development provides an opportunity to alter public attitudes about the purposes and the needs of children. It must be recognised that in so doing no assumption is made about the relative importance of other radical alterations in social and political philosophy and policy over the recent historical period [for a consideration of such factors see Halsey (1986) and Loney (1987)].

Secondly, public education policy requires information on which to base its recommendations. The relevance of research is readily apparent, for it is only through systematic investigation that the identification of valid information can be obtained.

Thirdly, how is such information to be used by the public at large? In particular, what promotes the use of information and what impediments are there to the success of policies and programmes designed to educate the public about stress and well-being? (Segal, 1983).

Fourthly, there needs to be a reliable and valid method of evaluating the success of any public programme designed to alleviate the effects of stress in the community.

Evaluation research is notoriously difficult (Segal, 1983). A major hurdle to evaluation of a stress programme often lies with the planners and principals of evaluation programmes, who do not have either interest or expertise in research.

Evaluation programmes are also methodologically complex. Although there have been evaluation studies with adequate designs, including measures of subjects before and after the programme, often the measures are narrow and targeted to a specific question, making the results difficult to generalise to other forms of stress or population (Segal, 1983).

These four concepts can be examined in a little more detail with particular reference to how they influence public health education and specific life events.

The information base

Is it possible to provide adequate information on a life event for a public education programme. There is no doubt that there are many 'informed views' as to what one should do or say, for example, to children at times of crisis or difficulty such as divorce or bereavement. Indeed, parents can choose from a bewildering variety of 'coping and caring' concepts in books, magazine articles and now videos. However, the majority of these publications reflect a point of view and the practical experience of a particular author rather than research evidence.

In theory it is possible to obtain an adequate information base concerning areas of acute stress as well as chronic stress and ongoing difficulties. Some examples of education programmes can be used to illustrate these underlying principles.

Hospitalisation

The stress of hospitalisation has been the focus of a number of research programmes which have identified that hospitalisation may be stressful but long-lasting effects are apparent for those children with two or more hospitalisations (Rutter, 1981b). The younger the child the greater the likelihood of separation anxiety. This type of research allows the targeting of high risk groups of children for intervention programmes aimed at reducing fear and anxiety of hospitals, minimising separation experiences by having parents in residence, focusing on children with repeated hospital admissions and chronic illnesses, and providing information and practical guidance to both parents and children concerning hospital treatments.

But can all life stresses be managed in the same way as hospitalisation? There is no straightforward answer. The major stresses, those of chronic social and family adversity may require a substantially different and more wide-ranging response in policy terms. The population affected is large, the patterning of the stresses difficult to predict and the implementation of policy expensive and time-consuming. It is apparent that a stress programme's information base may result in a decision not to introduce a public policy programme. This can be seen as an important use of adequate and comprehensive information and the prevention of inefficient expenditure.

Processes of stress education and coping programmes

If information is sufficiently comprehensive, decisions concerning the viability, structure and procedures for a stress education programme can be considered.

The aim of such a programme would be to prevent or substantially decrease the risk of distress or disorder as a consequence of information about the effects of such events.

It is important to distinguish between primary and secondary prevention programmes. In primary programmes information will be used to promote to many sections of the public a knowledge base of the undesirable effects of stress such as bereavement and hospitalisation. Particular target groups 'at risk' may be the main focus of such programmes. Secondary prevention programmes aim to prevent, or at least alleviate, the consequences of stressful experiences. Organising intervention programmes for children who have experienced severe trauma, such as disasters, or who have suffered injury following road traffic accidents are such examples.

The major conceptual difference, therefore, is that primary programmes are aimed at minimising the prevalence rates of stressful social factors in the community. Secondary programmes are aimed at minimising the effects of stressful factors that have already occurred in the community.

The relationship, however, between education and coping components in such programmes is unclear. Furthermore, the relative contribution to the effectiveness of these programmes made by information and action is likely to be different for different forms of stress. For example, information given only in education pamphlets, through some active means such as classes or the use of videos, and personal participation through specific involvement of target groups or individuals in tasks and exercises aimed at developing some specific stress alleviating behaviour are three different forms of policy which require different forms of planning and resource.

Information only as a social policy tool

For example, being provided simply with knowledge about stressful factors in children's lives may be both necessary and sufficient in some cases, and providing practical techniques for coping with the effects of such factors may not be necessary. In general, such programmes are likely to be aimed at factors that may affect children's general development and well-being and take the form of parental guidance, advice etc. Warnings about the effects of drug abuse, advice on child-rearing to avoid conflicts in the home, diet and information on child development are all examples of such programmes (Segal, 1983).

Information and action

In other circumstances the ratio of coping to information will need to be revised. In many secondary programmes information about bereavement, divorce and separation will be necessary but insufficient and greater emphasis on 'what to do' components of the programme will become evident.

These differential aspects of public education policy for childhood stress have different resource implications and require different procedures for implementation.

In information based primary prevention, the dissemination of the principles of stress avoidance is the main focus. The use of materials and media are critical features. Thus books, magazines, videos and pamphlets are major sources of primary prevention.

Examples can be found in teaching children, for example, about the risks of assault and molestation through video packages and how to talk to children about death (Sargent, 1979; Lansdown, 1987).

When coping contributions to programmes become greater, the need for resources may rise together with the intensity and contact with affected or potentially affected individuals.

Many psychological treatment strategies are attempting to alleviate the consequences of undesirable events and assist in the prevention of secondary psychological handicaps and maladjustment patterns of behaviour as a consequence of events. For example, crisis intervention techniques following overdose (Caplan, 1961; Bancroft, 1986; Hawton, 1986), suggestions for coping with effects of divorce in children and adolescents (Wallerstein and Kelly, 1980) and how to help children who have been bereaved (Horowitz *et al.*, 1981; Black and Urbanowitz, 1987) represent examples of coping orientated programmes for the sequelae of stressful events.

The coping orientation implies the need to learn skills and techniques to overcome and change for the better or return to the status quo.

Before considering training and treatment programmes in a little more detail we must examine some of the difficulties in implementing a primary or a secondary prevention programme.

Individual differences and public education

Perhaps the most difficult problem for public policy is the importance of individual differences in children's reactions to stressful circumstances. A second problem is the often made assumption that stressful events are related to negative outcomes, and therefore programmes are devised to improve coping in a similar or uniform fashion for all intended recipients. It has been stated that planners and policy makers have wanted to find a set of absolute principles which declare that a particular set of external conditions is inevitably associated with a fixed set of consequences for all children (Kagan, 1979).

The difficulty for planners is that the ultimate consequences of stressful experiences are a result of a complex interaction between personal and situational factors. The necessary assumption of a relative degree of homogeneity is likely to be incorrect in many instances of stressful experiences as there are a wide variety of responses.

In children this poses a significant but not insurmountable dilemma. We have already seen that some effects of life events and experiences in childhood will be influenced by age, sex, temperamental factors, pubertal status, and cognitive abilities, all reflecting personal qualities that public education programmes can and should take into account.

In other words, homogeneous assumptions can be made providing certain conditions are carefully defined. For example, a policy of allowing all parents to stay in hospital with their children in all circumstances may be a laudable but unachievable goal. Research has informed us sufficiently that some groups of children are more at risk than others and therefore it is plausible to plan a target programme for these at-risk groups. Thus pre-school children, children with life-threatening and acute and severe illnesses can become targeted groups under conditions of limited resources.

As well as individual and developmental differences, the effects of stresses may be altered by other social circumstances. The principles again are similar for public education policy. Thus the outcome of divorce is not always undesirable for the child, particularly if it releases him or her from persistent exposure to family violence or persistent arguments in the home. The value of research for public policy is apparent here. Thus the acquisition of knowledge through information poses the opportunity for greater planning on a facility of resources. Clearly, however, these factors are not yet influencing planners.

We have described in Chapters 2 and 8 how variations of response to divorce may occur as a consequence of social and personal factors. Yet the complex variations relating to divorce, its causes and consequences, have rarely been acknowledged in books and pamphlets (Wallerstein and Kelly, 1980; Segal, 1983).

The problems of primary and secondary stress programmes are apparent but relate not just to the difficulties of planning for populations but also to the information base that is provided. It has to be said that there may be circumstances where there is potentially usable information which is not taken up in policy or only partially so to put a particular point of view. Such circumstances take us beyond medicine, psychiatry and psychology and into social and political mechanisms.

HEALTH PROMOTION

A major primary prevention concept has been the promotion of well-being through greater self-awareness and recognition of social stresses. Large-scale programmes designed to avoid stress and/or improve coping skills when stress has been experienced are often referred to as health promotion programmes.

Health promotion programmes were introduced primarily as a tool for target patient groups with problems (i.e. as secondary prevention programmes). In recent years considerable attention has been paid to primary care programmes such as the Stanford Heart Programme, where evidence of behaviour change has been found in individuals as a consequence of a health promotion campaign (Farquhar *et al.*, 1977). This programme demonstrated a significant decrease in mortality from heart disease and was able to attribute this change to a significant degree to its intervention programme.

The Stanford Heart Programme was among the first to meet criteria for a successful promotion programme, i.e.

1. The presentation of an adequate information base about stresses and risk factors.
2. The successful alteration of individuals' knowledge about stress, risk and mortality.
3. The translation of individual knowledge into a behavioural form that adequately minimises or removes such risks.

Furthermore, the Stanford Programme demonstrated that exposure to mass media campaign alone or in conjunction with personal counselling were both significantly more likely to alter risk factor behaviours compared with a non-intervention community control group. In addition, there was little difference between the two interventions.

A comparable study was reported for children from Finland (Puska, 1982; Graham, 1985). This study of 13–15-year-old children was carried out in North Karelia, a region of Finland with very high rates of coronary artery disease. In all schools children were exposed to intensive intervention in which they were given 'health passports', feeding back to them basic data (including information on their own health habits and status). Two comparison schools were identified, one where there was a less intensive mass media campaign and another where there was no interaction.

After 2 years the intensive intervention group showed some significant differences in health-related behaviours compared with the non-intensive group. Thus boys showed a significantly lower rate of an increase in smoking (30 per cent and 13 per cent). Serum cholesterol levels in girls decreased to a significantly greater extent in the intensive intervention group as did their fat intake from milk and butter.

The children did not show increases in unwanted health behaviour, such as hypochondrias, as a consequence of this focus on health. Indeed, children in the follow-up group worried less about their health and had fewer psychosomatic symptoms.

As Graham (1985) has pointed out, this is a particularly important study for two reasons. Firstly, there is a significant association between the prevalence of coronary risk factors in childhood and rates of mortality from coronary disease in adults (Blonde, 1981). Secondly, the interpretation of the Finnish data suggests that the intervention more than other factors produced differences between the groups.

This heart programme is an extremely good example of a primary stress prevention programme and its replication would be extremely worth while.

Health promotion programmes for risks associated with mental disease

Targeting a programme on risk factors for a particular disease that is well defined requires considerable planning expertise. The problems are much greater, however, when the programme attempts to promote or enhance emotional robustness or the nature and benefits of stress management skills in more general terms.

So far no equivalent programme to that of the heart prevention study has been established for the stress of everyday events in preventing psychiatric disorder in childhood and adolescence.

There have, however, been some encouraging signs. Health promotion in school settings, for example, suggests a potential for such programmes. Studies have been carried out which attempted to train children in procedures and skills allowing them to deal with everyday hassles and problems, to manage personal difficulties they may have—such as learning problems—more efficiently, to develop a greater and more efficient range of problem-solving skills and to enhance their ability to select the appropriate strategies for focused problems (Stone, Hindy and Schmidt, 1975; Pellegrini, 1985).

These studies often incorporate a social problem-solving education programme inside the normal school curriculum. Nevertheless, the results are encouraging in that the majority report that children often show gains in their ability to solve problems. In any such study to date, however, methods have been less than satisfactory and the results are open to a number of interpretations.

As a consequence, very useful principles and guidelines are being clarified and put into operation in schools (Zins, Wagner and Maher, 1985). What is needed is a clearer conceptualisation of programmes for stress of life events. It seems unlikely that we will find a global stress-prevention programme. More probably we will need to identify specific life events and high risk groups in the community to be able to incorporate individual differences in response to different stresses.

There may be an important place, however, for life-skills training approaches in both school- and community-based programmes.

Personal involvement in health promotion

Studies to date indicate that programmes will have more success if there is active involvement of the target group. Attempts to persuade individuals to lose weight or stop smoking through advertising and video have often shown poor results because of a lack of personal involvement. Parent support groups and parent education programmes which are numerous for a wide variety of child orientated problems and disorders provide, perhaps, examples of a more personalised stress-management programme.

The techniques have perhaps been best described in work on training and education approaches for families with extremely aggressive youngsters (Patterson, 1982, 1983). These methods involve clear functional analysis of the interrelationships between children's and adults' behaviour by trained observers and a subsequent treatment or training programme aimed at recognising coercive patterns of behaviour between family members, who are assisted in this task by feedback from the observations and provision of strategies for alternative responses to everyday hassles and difficulties.

This interesting and important work was not specifically developed as a health promotion strategy but does demonstrate the importance of involving the subjects experiencing everyday minor events in the training programme.

The role of personal involvement in health promotion has been elucidated further by Graham (1985). He highlights that successful programmes to date seem to share a common concept in using a systematic approach aimed at achieving behaviour change. As Graham points out, this approach could be regarded as a direct, practical application of cognitive-behaviour modification, concerning itself with thought processes to achieve changes in behaviour.

There seems to be, therefore, an important role for cognitive processes in health promotion strategies. Altering thought processes to restructure the way individuals perceive themselves and their illness may be a crucial component in the process of preventing disturbance in individuals as a result of stresses in the community.

For example, in a prevention of smoking programme, techniques which place an emphasis on modelling and behaviour rehearsal were used with 14–16-year-old youngsters to help them cope with certain socially stressful situations. Thus situations in which they were offered cigarettes by friends, teased for being unadventurous and similar minor hassles of everyday life that may predispose to smoking were focused on and alternative strategies to resorting to smoking were suggested (Botvin, Eng and Williams, 1980). The findings demonstrated that experimentally treated youngsters showed only a quarter (4 per cent compared with 16 per cent) the rate of smoking manifested in the untreated control group. The importance of this study was that it concentrated on the hassles and the social context of smoking behaviour, i.e. on managing the internal state of distress ensuing from not accepting cigarettes and therefore not conforming to group behaviour.

The school environment and stress management

Other studies have demonstrated that how children respond to everyday hassles may in part be determined by the attitudes and behaviour of teachers (Bewley, 1979). Indeed, smoking cessation and education programmes may not be able to maintain their ability or effectiveness in schools where smoking is implicitly sanctioned, e.g. through the allowance of smoking by teachers on school premises (Seffrin and Bailey, 1985).

There is also modest evidence that school leavers from a school which has taken a firm line on smoking are less likely to smoke in adult life than those from a school with a permissive approach (Puska, 1982).

These studies emphasise that schools may be particularly important places to focus health promotion strategies to promote primary prevention of undesirable behaviours and mental disorders. They provide an important community focus where the target groups of children are. There is evidence to show that schoolteachers and the policies adopted towards behaviour may influence children's well-being (Rutter et al., 1979).

It is therefore not surprising that psychologists, teachers and others working in school settings have sought to identify techniques of stress management involving cognitive and behavioural approaches that can be usefully applied in the school environment (Forman and O'Mally, 1985).

Overall, the cognitive behavioural approach has been widely adopted in schools and community settings because it can be effectively taught, reasonably efficiently implemented and has been shown to have modest results in decreasing undesirable behaviour such as smoking, substance abuse and cardiovascular disease (Zins, Wagner and Maher, 1985).

The assumptions inherent in all programmes is that everyday stresses have the potential to increase the use of unwanted behaviour which was either previously not present or used infrequently. Children are then in a cumulative undesirable position of not only not having adequate psychological methods of coping with everyday stress but also developing new maladaptive behaviours (smoking etc.) which increase physical and mental morbidity and perhaps mortality.

Everyday hassles are distinctly different from specific life events on a number of parameters. Firstly, they are more frequent, secondly, they may be necessary, for example, in learning the coping skills for stress in later life (Parmalee, 1984), thirdly, in many circumstances they are unavoidable, e.g. sibling rivalry, peer-group disputes. It is also apparent that in many circumstances differences between hassles, difficulties and events may be more apparent than real (Lazarus, 1984). There is a surprising lack of information on such everyday stresses, their qualities and impact on children's lives in general and their relationship to other features of children, such as temperament and past experiences. Clearly we could do with more 'life-style' analysis of such everyday stresses as well as those events and difficulties currently studied.,

For example, everyday hassles can be defined as those social situations that result in making demands on an individual which exceed his or her abilities (Elliot and Eisdorfer, 1982). This rather unsatisfactory definition provides little clarification as to what social situations are being referred to or what constitutes an individual's abilities. It is perhaps not surprising, given the present level of knowledge, that we have limited ideas as to the usefulness of programmes which may improve children's educational and health performance by decreasing everyday hassles.

CHILD CARE AND SOCIAL POLICY

One important example of how research into social adversities has influenced social policy can be found in the alteration of approaches to children in need of care. There are 1600 children's homes in England and Wales, accommodating some 18,000 children, or approximately 20 per cent of all children in public care (Berridge, 1985). Social policy concerning the appropriate placement of children out of the care and control of their parents has often been formulated through ill-informed debate about the best options. In particular, the use of children's homes versus placements with foster families. Thus approximately 41 per cent of the 100,000 children in care in England and Wales are fostered (Hersov, 1985b). In the United States the term 'foster care' includes institutions and family placements so that comparisons between the two systems can be made only when the U.S.A. figures are split into residential and family placements.

Both the U.K. and the U.S.A. derive their social policy from the Elizabethan Poor Law of the seventeenth century. Over the last 200 years public concern with the plight of homeless and abandoned children has changed enormously. Some of these attitudinal changes have been reflected in legislation. For example, the 1834 Poor Law Amendment Act required foster parents to satisfy boarding out committees as to their character and financial status, although the quality of the committee was often inadequate. This may have been because its sole aim was to prevent neglect or ill-treatment of children who were totally deserted or without parents, rather than to foster their development.

The terms foster and adoption were used interchangeably until the 1926 Adoption Act (U.K.), which made an explicit distinction between fostering and adoption. From then on foster parents lacked parity of status as parents. The experiences of evacuated children following the Second World War (see Chapter 4) further increased public awareness of children's needs, and local authority children's departments were set up. Foster care developed rapidly in the 1950s but slowed down in the 1960s because of the large number of failed boarding out placements. This brief overview of policy change in a major area of child welfare demonstrates how public policy changes occur as a *response* to adverse circumstance and difficulties in children's lives. Since the 1960s, substantial research *predicting* children's adjustment has contributed to information about how best to plan and implement public policy.

Longitudinal studies have shown that adults raised in residential care *do not* all have poor adjustment as adults (Quinton and Rutter, 1988). Individual differences in this outcome suggest that a greater focus on the qualities of individual children, their early environment and the type of care resource available may assist in finding the best match between the child's needs and a local authority's available resources.

Whilst these findings indicate that residential care is clearly far from uniformly bad, it is apparent that children are more likely to experience a greater sense of family life if in a foster rather than a residential home. Recent findings have indicated that children in the care of foster parents are more likely to experience a greater range of community neighbourhood contacts, have better physical amenities, have everyday social events managed in a child oriented manner, and have more efficient sanctions on problem-solving strategies demonstrated by foster parents (Colton, 1988).

These results demonstrate the qualitative advantages provided for children by most foster parents. However, one children's home continually showed a 'foster parent home' profile in its dimensions of care, suggesting that the quality of residential homes can converge with foster homes. The criteria for producing this convergence require further investigation.

The policy makers will take these results as confirming the general plan that children should be fostered where possible. However, foster placement breakdown is a major concern in public planning. It is a burden to social resources because of increased work in retrieving children. It increases the risk of poor later social adjustment in adulthood for the children. Follow-up studies in foster placements suggest that perhaps one in four children have poor outcomes (Triseliotis, 1980).

Undoubtedly adoption, with its greater status, legal and familial, for the adoptive parents and child, holds out better hope for later social adjustment (Hersov, 1985b).

The research on fostering and residential care, however, informs us that a blanket policy in favour of family placements for all children is unlikely to meet all needs.

Some children will not adapt and adjust to family life and breakdowns are apparent in both fostering and residential practice. We need to retain some residential care, at least until necessary and sufficient qualities of parent–child relations can be clearly identified and implemented as policy in all circumstances where children are in need of care. The continuing inquiry into these qualities through scientific investigation will provide important information for social policy planning so that child care is not merely a retrospective response only model of legislation but one also able to consider predictions derived from systematic research.

STRESS MANAGEMENT POLICIES—ISSUES AND ETHICS

Encompassing the notion that 'life is stressful' and everyday hassles are potentially harmful to children we make a number of value judgements that may be scientifically incorrect and not gain the widespread acceptance of other individuals or institutions. Closer examination of the argument in favour of stress intervention policies seems worth while.

Firstly, it is apparent that clinicians and researchers have quite rightly found themselves increasingly relating disease and poor health to individuals' lifestyles and habits. 'Behavioural medicine' may be seen as one outcome of such a position. The rationale and strength of the argument lies in the increasing validity of showing a causal (rather than a correlational) connection with people's habits and subsequent mortality and morbidity. It is part of a scientist's responsibility to demonstrate to society that such links exist and cannot be ignored.

It is less clear, however, that society should feel obliged to act on such information. To do so would be to accept wholly, and therefore uncritically, information that is likely to pertain to 'some cases some of the time'. It may also imply that the absolute goal of health is desirable for all, even if not desired by individuals. In other words, the person's right to choose, for example, to smoke, take exercise and avoid everyday hassles would be taken from him in the interests of society at large. The tension between individual and societal rights is hardly new, and a philosophical analysis is beyond the scope of this book (and the abilities of its author!).

It is perhaps worth while pointing out, however, that public education policies for stresses in everyday life do have to consider their precepts and should not confuse stress management as a method of illness prevention, and therefore a part of mental health practice, and stress management as a moral code of practice. There is no justification for mental health specialists concerned with stress management (everyday hassles or events) to view themselves or their methods as responsible for the latter.

It is perhaps surprising how little attention has been paid to the ethics of stress management in relation to children and families (e.g. Graham, 1981). Indeed, rights, morals and position of child and family with each other and within society deserve greater attention from public policy makers, professionals and others concerned with such matters. Public policy should take into account the effects of stressful events and their impact on well-being and intellectual, social and emotional development.

In cases where sufficient information is available to prevent or ameliorate stressful events and difficulties in children's lives there may be at least four reasons why policy implementation is slow or non-existent (Segal, 1983).

1. Politicisation of research data

Should research data on stresses in childhood be at odds with government policies it is unlikely to be implemented unless politically significant. Where research confirms a current political view, implementation may be more likely.

2. The staying power of popular beliefs

Implementation of policies concerning stress in childhood are more likely to succeed if they support a popularly held belief. Research findings have a greater chance of being ignored if they do not. In the latter circumstances the gap between scientific information base and practical implementation is widened. Hospitals are stressful and undesirable, so stress management programmes are likely to meet with general public approval. By contrast, schools may be stressful but desirable and the public may perceive stress in these circumstances as components of achievement and success. Stress management programmes in the school setting will need to take into account the likely priorities they would receive in the general curriculum.

3. Ambiguity of research data

Often crucial issues in a policy debate are matters of interpretation not matters of fact. Paradoxically, useful research on stress is as likely to sharpen areas for disagreement by delineating what we do not know, as much as for agreement through what we have confirmed or discovered.

In an area where multiple stresses of varying nature and quality impact on children, and their relative contributions to a failure of normal development or psychiatric disorder is unclear, it is not surprising that selecting social policy alternatives can prove to be extremely difficult.

4. The lack of central organisation

It will remain difficult to implement any policy aimed at alleviating stress in the best interests of children without an effective government vehicle for so doing.

Children's interests are often subsumed under other government structures (Health, Education, Welfare, etc.).

Rarely are joint initiatives sought or gained by these administrative bodies who may have competing and mutually exclusive responsibilities. Collective initiatives for determining policy on stresses in children's lives are therefore difficult to achieve. The result is that adequate scientific information is inadequately translated from researcher's journals to the legal statute book.

In conclusion, stressful events and difficulties and everyday hassles may have major effects on children's normal development and risk of mental disorder.

Translating these statements into meaningful public policy is a complex procedure. The information base requires continual updating because our knowledge of social events and their consequences is inadequate and incomplete. But we can see that it is extremely difficult, if not impossible, to obtain 'sufficient facts'. There is no single model, not even a complex multivariate one, that can adequately and unambiguously convey a theory of stress and its practical consequences to the level of public policy implementation.

It is apparent that we must focus on specific types of stress, understand its nature and content and its consequences in biological, psychological and social terms. We should determine the prevalence of different types of life events and difficulties in childhood so that policy makers can be persuaded of the importance of adverse social experiences to individuals and society at large. Stress researchers interested in influencing public policy should therefore target their research on stressful events that are likely to persuade policy makers of their application to the benefit of children within society. In other words, some stress research should have a social conscience, be relatively independent of potentially adverse interpretation, not counterintuitive, but believable and politically feasible.

There remains an important role for stress research that seeks to inform without looking to change public opinion. Social and political climates change and with them attitudes to what constitutes important and useful knowledge. We cannot readily predict what will be useful in the future or how present-day research may influence changes in tomorrow's society.

SUMMARY

1. Research into social adversities can and should inform public policy by providing scientific information on the causes and correlates between social factors and health.
2. Information is a necessary but insufficient basis for developing policy for primary or secondary prevention. Plans for action and for getting groups most likely to benefit are also required.
3. Health promotion strategies appear to have the best chance of success when individuals are personally involved, and there is a focus on an alteration of thinking and attitude with a consequential change in behaviour.
4. Blanket policies for stress and child care may fail because they do not take into account subgroups and individual differences in childrens' well being and outcome.
5. Public policy has political, social and moral components and implications. The professional scientific and health community should not view themselves as wholly responsible for these facets of social policy.

References

Abramson, L.Y., Seligman, M.E.P., and Teasdale, J.D. (1978). Learned helplessness in humans: critique and reformulation, *Journal of Abnormal Psychology*, **87**, 49–74.

Ackerman, S.H. (1981). Premature weaning, thermoregulation and the occurrence of gastric pathology. In H. Weiner, M.A. Hafer, and A. Steinkard (eds), *Brain, Behaviour and Bodily Disease*, Raven Press, New York, pp. 67–86.

Adomakoh, C.C. (1973). The pattern of epidemic hysteria in a girls' school in Ghana, *Ghana Medical Journal*, **13**, 407–411.

Ainsworth, M.D.S. (1972). Attachment and dependency: a comparison. In J.L. Gerwitz (ed.), *Attachment and Dependency*, Washington, DC: V.H. Winston.

Ainsworth, M.D.S., Blehar, M.C., Waters, E., and Wall, E. (1978). *Patterns of Attachment: A Psychological Study of the Strange Situation*, Erlbaum, Hillsdale, NJ.

Ainsworth, M.D.S., and Wittig, B.A. (1969). Attachment and exploratory behaviour of one-year-olds in a strange situation. In B. Foss (ed.), *Determinants of Infant Behaviour*, Vol. 4, pp. 111–136, Methuen, London.

Allodi, F. (1980). The psychiatric effects of political persecution and torture on children and families of victims, *Conochan Mental Health*, **28**, 8–10.

Amato, P., and Edgar, D. (1987). *Children in Australian families. The Growth of Competence*, Prentice-Hall, Sydney.

Andrews, G. (1981). A prospective study of life events and psychological symptoms, *Psychological Medicine*, **11**, 795–801.

Andrews, G., Tennant, C., Hewson, D., and Valliant, G. (1978). Life event stress, social support, coping style and risk of psychological impairment, *Journal of Nervous and Mental Disease*, **166**, 307–315.

Anthony, E.J. (1986). Terrorising attacks on children by psychotic parents, *Journal of the American Academy of Child Psychiatry*, **25**, 226–235.

Asher, S.R., and Gottman, J.M. (1981). *The Development of Children's Friendships*, Cambridge University Press, Cambridge.

Aslan, R.F., Raskind, M., Gumbrecht, G., and Halter J. (1982). Stress and age effects on catecholamines in normal subjects, *Journal of Psychosomatic Research*, **25**, 33–41.

Ayalon, O. (1983). Coping with terrorism: the Israeli case. In D. Meichenbaum, and M.E. Joremko (eds), *Stress Reduction and Presentation*, Plenum, New York.

Bailey, D., and Garralda, M.E. (1986). The accuracy of dating childhood life events on a parental questionnaire, *Journal of Psychosomatic Research*, **30**, 655–662.

Bailey, D., and Garralda, M.E. (1987). Children attending primary health care services: a study of recent life events, *Journal of the American Academy of Child and Adolescent Psychiatry*, **6**, 858–864.

Bancroft, J. (1986). Crises intervention. In S. Bloch (ed.), *An Introduction to the Psychotherapies*, Oxford University Press, Oxford.

Bandura, A. (1977). *Social Learning Theory*, Prentice-Hall, Englewood Cliffs, NJ.

Barnes, R.F., Raskind, M., Gumbrecht, G., and Halter J. (1982). The effect of age on plasma catecholamine response to mental stress in man, *Journal of Clinical Endocrinological Metabolism*, **54**, 64–69.

Barnett, L. (1984). Research note—young children's resolution of distress through play, *Journal of Child Psychology and Psychiatry*, **25**, 477–484.

Barrat, J., and Hinde, R.A. (1988). Triadic interactions: Mother–First Born–Second Born. In R.A. Hinde and J. Stevenson-Hinde (eds), *Relations Within Families*, Clarendon Press, Oxford.

Barrett, J.E. (1979). The relationship of life events to onset of neurotic disorders. In J.E. Barrat (ed.), *Stress and Mental Disorder*, Raven Press, New York.

Bartlett, F. (1932). *Remembering: A Study of Experimental and Social Psychology*, Cambridge University Press, Cambridge.

Basham, R. (1978). *Urban anthropology: The Cross-cultural Study of Complex Societies*, Mayfield, Palo Alto, CA.

Bates, J.E. (1987). Temperament in infancy. In J.D. Osofsky (ed.), *Handbook of Infant Development*, Wiley, New York.

Baumrind, D. (1967). Child care practice on teaching 3 patterns of preschool behaviour, *Genetic Psychology Monographs*, **75**, 43–88.

Baumrind, D. (1971). Current patterns of parental authority, *Developmental Psychology Monograph 4*, 1, (Part 1).

Bebbington, P.E. (1985). Three cognitive theories of depression, *Psychological Medicine*, **15**, 759–769.

Bebbington, P.E., Sturt E., Tennant, C., and Hurry, J. (1984). Misfortune and resilience: a community study of women, *Psychological Medicine*, **14**, 347–364.

Beck, A.T. (1970). *Depression, Causes and Treatment*, University of Pennsylvania Press, Philadelphia.

Beck, A.T. (1976). *Cognitive Therapy and Emotional Disorder*, International Universities Press, New York.

Belsky, J., and Pensky, E. (1988). Developmental history, personality and family relationships: towards an emergent family system. In R.A. Hinde and J. Stevenson-Hinde (eds), *Relationships Within Families*, Clarendon Press, Oxford.

Benjamissen, S. (1981). Stressful life events preceding the onset of neurotic depression, *Psychological Medicine*, **11**, 369–378.

Benton, A. (1971). Productivity, distributive justice, and bargaining among children, *Journal of Personality and Social Psychology*, **18**, 68–78.

Bergman, L.R., and Magnusson, D. (1979). Overachievement and catecholamine output in an achievement demanding situation, *Psychosomatic Medicine*, **41**, 181–188.

Berndt, T.J. (1981). The effects of friendship on prosocial intentions and behaviour, *Child Development*, **52**, 636–643.

Berndt, T.J. (1983). Social cognition, social behaviour and children's friendships. In T. Higgins, D. Ruble, and W. Hartup (eds), *Social Cognition and Social Development*, Cambridge University Press, Cambridge.

Berridge, D. (1985). *Children's Homes*, Blackwell, Oxford.

Bewley, B.R. (1979). Teachers Smoking, *British Journal of Preventative and Social Medicine*, **33**, 219–222.

Bifulco, A., Brown, G.W., and Harris, T. (1987). Childhood loss of parent, lack of adequate parental care and adult depression: a replication, *Journal of Affective Disorders*, **12**, 115–118.

Black, D., and Urbanowitz, M.A. (1987). Family intervention with bereaved children, *Journal of Child Psychology and Psychiatry*, **28**, 467–476.

Bloch, S., and Crouch, E., (1985). *Therapeutic Factors in Group Psychotherapy*, Oxford University Press, Oxford.

Block, J., Block, J.H., and Gjerde, P.F. (1988). Parental functioning and home environment in families of divorce: prospective and concurrent analyses, *Journal of the American Academy of Child and Adolescent Psychiatry*, **27**, 207–213.

Block, J.H., Block, J., and Gjerde, P.F. (1986). The personality of children prior to divorce: a prospective study, *Child Development*, **57**, 827–840.

Block, J.H., Block, J., and Morrison A. (1981). Parental agreement–disagreement on child-rearing orientations and gender related personality correlates in children, *Child Development*, **52**, 965–974.

Block Lewis, H. (1986). The role of shame in depression. M. Rutter., C. Izard., and P. Read (eds), *In Depression in Young People*, Guilford Press, London.

Blom, G. (1986). A school disaster—intervention and research aspects, *Journal of the American Academy of Child Psychiatry*, **3**, 336–345.

Blonde, C.V. (1981). Parental history and cardiovascular risk factor variables in children, *Preventive Medicine*, **10**, 25–37.

Bluebond-Langner, M. (1978). *The Private Worlds of Dying Children*, Princeton University Press, Princeton, NJ.

Bontrap, R.W., Luckhurst, E., Lazarus, L., Kiloh, L.G., and Penny, R. (1977). Depressed lymphocyte function after bereavement, *Lancet*, **ii**, 834–836.

Botvin, G.J., Eng, A., and Williams, C.L. (1980). Preventing the onset of cigarette smoking through life skills training, *Preventive Medicine*, **9**, 135–143.

Boucher, J., and Carlsson, G. (1980). Recognition of facial expressions in three cultures, *Journal of Cross-cultural Psychology*, **11**, 263–280.

Bower, G.H., and Cohen, P.R. (1982). Emotional influences in memory and thinking: data and theory. In S. Fishe and M. Clark (eds), *Affect and Social Cognition*, Erlbaum, Hillsdale, NJ.

Bowlby, J. (1969). *Attachment and Loss*. Vol. 1: *Attachment*, Hogarth Press, London.

Bowlby, J. (1973). *Attachment and Loss*. Vol 2: *Separation, Anxiety and Anger*, Hogarth Press, London.

Bowlby, J. (1980). *Attachment and Loss*. Vol. 3: *Loss Sadness and Depression*, Basic Books, New York.

Bowlby, J. (1988). *A Secure Base: Clinical Application of Attachment Theory*, Routledge, London.

Breslau, N. (1985). Psychiatric disorder in children with physical disabilities, *Journal of the American Academy of Child Psychiatry*, **25**, 87–94.

Bretherton, I., and Walters, E. (eds) (1985). *Growing Points of Attachment. Theory and Research*, Monographs of the Society for Research into Child Development, 50.

Breuer, J., and Freud, S. (1893). Studies on hysteria. In J. Strachey (ed.), *Complete Psychological Works of Freud*. Vol. 2. Hogarth Press, London.

Brittain, C.V. (1963). Adolescent choices and parent–peer cross pressures, *American Sociological Review*, **28**, 385–391.

Bronson, W.C. (1981). *Toddlers' Behaviours with Age Mates: Issues of Interaction Cognition, Affect*, Ablex, Norwood, NJ.

Brooks-Gunn, J., and Warren, M.P. (1989). Biological and social contributions to negative affect in young adolescent girls, *Child Development*, **60**, 40–55.

Brown, A.L. (1978). Knowing when, where and how to remember; a problem of meta cognition. In R. Glase (ed.), *Advances in Instructional Psychology*, Vol. 1, Erlbaum, Hillsdale, NJ.

Brown, G.W. (1974). Meaning, measurement and the stress of life events. In B.S. Dohrenwend and B.P. Dohrenwend (eds), *Stressful Life Events: Their Nature and Effects*, Neal Watson Academic Publications, New York.

Brown, G.W. (1988). Early loss of parent and depression in adult life. In S. Fisher and

J. Reason, (eds), *Handbook of Life Stress, Cognition and Health*, Wiley, Chichester.

Brown, G.W., Andrews, B., Harris, T.O., Adler, S., and Bridge, L. (1986). Social support, self-esteem and depression, *Psychological Medicine*, **16**, 813–831.

Brown, G.W., Bifulco, A., and Harris, T. (1987). Life events, vulnerability and onset of depression: some refinements, *British Journal of Psychiatry*, **150**, 30–42.

Brown, G.W, and Birley, T. (1968). Crises and life changes and the onset of schizophrenia, *Journal of Health and Social Behaviour*, **9**, 203–214.

Brown, G.W., and Harris, T. (1978). *The Social Origins of Depression*, Tavistock Press, London.

Brown, G.W., and Harris, T. (1986). Stressor, vulnerability and depression—a question of replication, *Psychological Medicine*, **16**, 739–744.

Brown, G.W., Harris, T., and Bifulco, A. (1986). Long-term effects of early loss of parents. In M. Rutter, C. Izard, and P. Read (eds), *Depression in Young People— Developmental and Clinical Perspectives*, Guilford Press, London.

Brown, G.W., Harris, T., and Peto, J. (1973). Life events and psychiatric disorders: part 2, the nature of the causal link, *Psychological Medicine*, **3**, 159–179.

Brown, M., and Madge, N. (1982). *Despite the Welfare State*, Heinemann Educational, London.

Bruner, J.S. (1975). The ontogenesis of speech acts, *Journal of Child Language*, **2**, 1–19.

Bryant, P. (1974). *Perception and Understanding in Young Children*, Methuen, London.

Bryant, P. (1977). *Piaget: Causes and Alternatives*. In M. Rutter and L. Hersov (eds), *Child Psychiatry, Modern Approaches*, Blackwell, Oxford.

Bullock, K., and Moore, R.Y. (1980). Nucleus ambiguous projections to the thymus gland, *Abstracts of the American Association of Anatomy*, No. **25A**.

Burgess, R.L., and Conger, R.D. (1978). Family interaction in abusive, neglectful and normal families, *Child Development*, **49**, 1163–1173.

Burgess, R.L., and Huston, T.L. (1979). *Social Exchange in Developing Relationships*. Academic Press, New York.

Burgoyne, J., and Clarke, D. (1982). *Making a Go of It*, Routledge and Kegan Paul, London.

Burke, R., and Weir, T. (1978). Sex differences in adolescent life stress, social support and well-being, *Journal of Psychology*, **98**, 227–288.

Butler, S.R., Suskind, M.R., and Schanberg, S.M. (1978). Maternal behaviour as a regulator of polyamine synthesis in the brain and heart of the developing rat pup, *Science*, **199**, 445–446.

Buss, A., and Plomin, R (1984). *Temperament: Early Developing Personality Traits*, Erlbaum, Hillsdale, NJ.

Buzzetti, R., McLoughlin, D., Scavo, D., and Ross, L.H. (1989). A critical assessment of the interactions between the immune system and the hypothalamo–pituitary–adrenal axis, *Journal of Endocrinology*, **120**, 183–187.

Campos, J.J., and Barrett, K.C. (1984). Toward a new understanding of emotions and their development. In C. Izard, J. Kagan, and B. Zajonc (eds), *Emotions, Cognitions and Behaviour*, Cambridge University Press, Cambridge.

Campos, J.L., and Steinberg, G. (1981). Perception and appraisal of emotion: the onset of social referencing. In M. Lamb and L. Sherrod (eds), *Infant and Cognition*, Erlbaum, Hillsdale, NJ.

Cannon, W.B. (1928). The mechanism of emotional disturbance of bodily function, *New England Journal of Medicine*, **198**, 877–892.

Cannon, W.B. (1929). *Bodily Changes in Pain, Hunger, Fear and Rage*, Appleton & Co., New York.

Caplan, G. (1961). *An Approach to Community Mental Health*, Tavistock, London.

Caplan, H.L., Cogill, S.R., Alexandra, H., Mordecai Robson, K., Katz, R., and Kumar, R. (1989). Maternal depression and the emotional development of the child, *British Journal of Psychiatry*, **154**, 818–822.

Carroll, J.J., and Steward, M.S. (1984). The role of cognitive development in children's understanding of their own feelings, *Child Development*, **55**, 1486–1492.

Caspi, A., and Elder, G. (1988). Emergent family patterns—the intergenerational construction of problem behaviour and relationships. In R.A. Hinde, and J. Stevenson-Hinde (eds), *Relationships Within Families*, Clarendon Press, Oxford.

Cederblad, M. (1968). A child psychiatric study on Sudanese Arab children. *Acta Psychiatrica Scandinavica*, supplement No. 200.

Chandler, M.J. (1985). Social structures, and social cognition. In R.A. Hinde, A.N. Perret-Clemont, and J. Stevenson-Hinde (eds), *Social Relations and Cognitive Development*, Clarendon Press, Oxford.

Checkley, S.A., Com, T.H., Glass, I.B., Burton, S.W., and Burke, C.A. (1986). The responsiveness of central alpha adrenoceptors in depression. In J.F.W. Deakin (ed.), *The Biology of Depression*, Gaskell Press, London.

Christensen, N.J. (1986). Is plasma noradrenaline an index of biological age? In N.J. Christensen, O. Henriksen, and N.A Lassen (eds), *The Sympatho-Adrenal System*, Raven Press, New York, pp. 266–272.

Ciaranello, R.D. (1979). Regulation of phenylethanolamine-n-methyltransferase degradation by s-adrenosylmethionine. In E. Usdin, R. Borchardt, and C. Geveling (eds), *Transmethylation*, Elsevier, New York.

Ciaranello, R.D. (1980). Regulation of the synthesis and degradation of phenylethanolamine-n-methyltransferase. In S. Parvez and H. Parvez (eds), *Biogenic Amines and Development*, Elsevier, New York.

Ciaranello, R.D. (1983). Neurochemical aspects of stress. In N. Garmezy, and M. Rutter (eds), *Stress, Coping and Development in Children*, McGraw-Hill, New York.

Clark, M.S., and Isen, A.M. (1982). The relationship between feeling states and social behaviour. In H. Hostorf and A.M. Isen (eds), *Cognitive Social Psychology*, Elsevier, North-Holland, Amsterdam.

Clayton, P.J. (1974). Mortality and morbidity in the 1st year of widowhood, *Archives of General Psychiatry*, **30**, 747–750.

Coddington, D.R. (1972a). The significance of life events as aetiologic factors in diseases of children—I, *Journal of Psychosomatic Research*, **16**, 7–18.

Coddington, D.R., (1972b). The significance of life events as aetiologic factors in diseases of children—II, *Journal of Psychosomatic Research*, **16**, 205–213.

Cogill, S.R., Caplan, H.L., Alexandra, H., Robson, K.M., and Kumar, R. (1986). Impact of maternal postnatal depression on cognitive development of young children, *British Medical Journal*, **292**, 1165–1167.

Cole, P., McMahon, B. (1971). Attributable risk percent in case–control studies, *British Journal of Preventative and Social Medicine*, **25**, 242–244.

Collins, A., Ensroth, P., and Londgren, B.M. (1985). Psychoendocrine stress responses and mood as related to the menstrual cycle, *Psychosomatic Medicine*, **47**, 512–527.

Collins, D.L., Baum, A., and Singer, J.E. (1983). Coping with chronic stress at 3 Mile Island: psychological and biochemical evidence, *Health Psychology*, **2**, 149–166.

Colton, M. (1988). Dimensions of foster and residential care practice, *Journal of Child Psychology and Psychiatry*, **29**, 589–600

Condry, J.C., and Ross, D.F. (1985). Sex and aggression: The influence of gender label on the perception of aggression in children, *Child Development*, **56**, 225–233.

Cooke, D.J., and Hole, D.J. (1983). Aetological importance of stressful life events, *British Journal of Psychiatry*, **143**, 397–400.

Coral, J., and Steward, M. (1984). The role of cognitive development in children's understanding of their own feelings, *Child Development*, **55**, 1486–1492.

Corsario, W.A. (1981). Friendship in the nursery school: social organisation in a peer environment. In S.R. Asher and J.M. Gottman, (eds), *The Development of Children's Friendships*, Cambridge University Press, Cambridge.

Cowen, P.J., and Anderson, I. (1986). 5.H.T. Neuroendocrinology: changes during depressive illness and antidepressant drug treatment. In J.F.W. Deakin (ed.), *The Biology of Depression*, Gaskell Press, London.

Cox, A.D., Puckering, C., Pound A., and Mills, M. (1987). The impact of maternal depression in young children, *Journal of Child Psychology and Psychiatry*, **28**, 917–928.

Cox, T. (1978). *Stress*, Macmillan, London; University Park Press, Baltimore.

Creed, F. (1981). Life events and appendicectomy, *Lancet*, **i**, 1381–1385.

Creed, F., and Pfeffer, J. (1982). *Medicine and Psychiatry: A practical approach*, Pitman Books, London.

Cross, R.J., Brooks, W.H., Royman, T.L., and Markesbery, R. (1982). Hypothalamic-immune interactions. Effects of hypophysectomy on neuroimmuno modulation, *Journal of Neurological Science*, **53**, 557–566.

Cummings, E.M., Zahn-Waxler, C., and Radke-Yarrow, M. (1981). Young people's responses to expressions of anger and affection by others in the family, *Child Development*, **52**, 1274–1282.

Cummings, E.M., Zahn-Waxler, C., and Radke-Yarrow, M. (1984). Developmental changes in children's reactions to anger in the home, *Journal of Child Psychology and Psychiatry*, **25**, 63–74.

Dare, C. (1985). Psychoanalytic theories of development. In M. Rutter and L. Hersov (eds), *Child Psychiatry—Modern Approaches*, Blackwell, Oxford.

Darwin, C. (1872). *The Expression of Emotions im Man and Animals*, John Murray, London.

Deakin, J.F.W. (ed.) (1986). *The Biology of Depression*, Gaskell, London.

Deakin, J.F.W., and Crow, T.J. (1986). Monoamines, rewards and punishments. The anatomy and physiology of the affective disorders. In J.F.W. Deakin (ed.), *The Biology of Depression*, Gaskell, London.

Derryberry, D., and Rothbart, M. (1984). Emotion, attention and temperament. In C. Izard, J. Kagan, and B. Zajonc (eds), *Emotions, Cognitions and Behaviours*, Cambridge University Press, Cambridge.

Despert, J.L. (1942). *Preliminary reporting on children's reactions to war*, New York Hospital and Department of Psychiatry, Cornell University Medical College.

deVries, M.W. (1984). Temperament and infant mortality among the Masai of East Africa, *American Journal of Psychiatry*, **141**, 1189–1194.

Diamond, B., Yelton, D., and Schorff, M.D. (1981). Monoclonal antibodies: a new technology for producing serologic reagents, *New England Journal of Medicine*, **304**, 1344–1348.

Dodge, K.A. (1980). Social cognition and children's aggressive behaviour, *Child Development*, **51**, 162–172.

Dodge, K.A., Murphy, R.R., and Buchsbaum, K. (1984). The assessment of intention and detection skills in children: implications for developmental psychopatholgy, *Child Development*, **55**, 163–173.

Dohrenwend, B.P., and Dohrenwend, B.S. (eds) (1981). *Monographs in Psychosocial Epidemiology*, Prodist, New York.

Dohrenwend, B.P., Dohrenwend, B.S., Worheit, G.J., Bonflett, G.S., Goldstein, K., and Martin, J.L. (1981). Stress in the community: a report on the President's Commission on the accident at Three Mile Island, *Annals of the New York Academy of Science*, **365**, 159–174.

Dohrenwend, B.S., and Dohrenwend, B.P. (1978). Some issues in research on stressful life events, *Journal of Nervous and Mental Diseases*, **16**, 7–16.

Dohrenwend, B.S., Krasnoff, L., Askenasy, A.R., and Dohrenwend, B.P. (1978). Exemplification of a method for scaling life events: the PERI life events scale, *Journal of Health and Social Behaviour*, **19**, 205–229.

Dollinger, S.J., and McGuire, B. (1981). The development of psychological-mindedness: children's understanding of defense mechanisms, *Journal of Clinical Child Psychology*, **10**, 117–121.

Dombush, S.M., Carlsmith, J.M., and Bushwall, S.J. (1985). Single parents, extended households, and the control of adolescents, *Child Development*, **56**, 326–341.

Dorian, B.J., and Garfinkel, P.E. (1987). Stress, immunity and illness—a review, *Psychological Medicine*, **17**, 393–407.

Dorian, B.J., Garfinkel, P.E., Brown, C.M., Shore, A., Gladman, D., and Keystone, E.O. (1982). Aberrations in lymphocyte subpopulations and functions during psychological stress, *Clinical and Experimental Immunology*, **50**, 132–138.

Dorian, B.J., Garfinkel, P.E., Brown, C.M., Shore, A., Gladman, D., Keystone, E.O., and Dorby, P. (1986). Stress, immunity and illness, *Psychosomatic Medicine*, **48**, 304–310.

Douglas, J.W.B. (1975). Early hospital admission and later disturbances of behaviour and learning, *Development Medicine and Child Neurology*, **17**, 456–480.

Douvan, E., and Adelson, J. (1966). *The Adolescent Experience*, Wiley, Chichester.

Dowdney, L., Mrazek, D., Quinton, D., and Rutter, M. (1984). Observation of parent–child interaction with 2 to 3 year olds, *Journal of Child Psychology and Psychiatry*, **25**, 379–407.

Dowdney, L., Skuse, D., Rutter, M., and Mrazek, D. (1985). Parenting qualities: concepts, measures and origins. In J. Stevenson (ed.), *Recent Advances in Developmental Psychopathology*, Pergamon Press, Oxford.

Duck, S.W. (1975). Personality, similarity and friendship choices by adolescents, *European Journal of Social Psychology*, **5**, 351–365.

Duck, S.W. (ed.) (1988). *Handbook of Personal Relationships*, Wiley, Chichester.

Dunn, J. (1983). Sibling relations in early childhood, *Child Development*, **54**, 787–811.

Dunn, J. (1986). Stress, development and family interaction. In M. Rutter, C. Izard, and P. Read (eds), *Depression In Young People*, Guilford Press, London.

Dunn, J. (1988a). Sibling influences on childhood development, *Journal of Child Psychology and Psychiatry*, **29**, 119–127.

Dunn, J. (1988b). Connections between relationships implications of research on mothers and siblings. In R.A. Hinde, and J. Stevenson-Hinde (eds), *Relationships Within Families*, Oxford University Press, Oxford.

Dunn, J., and Dale, N. (1984). I, a Daddy: 2-year-olds collaboration in joint pretend play with sibling and mother. In I. Bretherton (ed.), *Symbolic Play. The Development of Social Understanding*, Academic Press, New York, pp. 131–158.

Dunn, J., and Kendrick, C. (1980a). Studying temperament and parent–child interaction: comparison of interview and direct observation, *Developmental Medicine and Child Neurology*, **4**, 484–486.

Dunn, J., and Kendrick, C. (1980b). The arrival of a sibling: Changes in patterns of interaction between mother and first born child, *Journal of Child Psychology and Psychiatry*, **22**, 1–18.

Dunn, J., and Kendrick, C. (1982). *Sibling: Love, Envy and Understanding*, Harvard University Press, Cambridge, MA.

Dunn, J., and Munn, P. (1986). Siblings and the development of prosocial behaviour, *International Journal of Behavioural Development*, **9**, 265–284.

Dweck, C.S., and Bush, E.S. (1976). Sex differences in learned helplessness. I. Differential debilitation: peer and adult evaluators, *Developmental Psychology*, **12**, 147–156.

Dweck, C.S., Davidson, W., Nelson, S., and Euna, B. (1978). Sex differences in learned helplessness. II. Contingencies of evaluative feed-back in the class room and III. An experimental analysis, *Developmental Psychology*, **14**, 268–276.

Dweck, C.S., and Elliott, E.S. (1983). Achievement Motivation. In P. Mussen and E.M. Hetherington (eds) *Handbook of Child Psychology*. Vol. 4. *Socialisation: Personality and Social Development*, Wiley, New York.

Eagle, M. (1984). *Recent Developments in Psychoanalysis: A Critical Evaluation*, McGraw-Hill, New York.

Earls, F., and Jung, K.G. (1987). Temperament and home environment characteristics as causal factors in the early development of childhood psychopathology, *Journal of the American Academy of Child and Adolescent Psychiatry*, **26**, 491–498.

Earls, F., Smith, E., Reich, W., and Jung, K.G. (1988). Investigating psychopathological consequences of a disaster in children: a pilot study incorporating a structured diagnostic interview, *Journal of the American Academy of Child and Adolescent Psychiatry*, **27**, 90–95.

Easterbrooks, M.A., and Emde, R.N. (1988). Marital and parent–child relationships: the role of affect in the family system. In R.A. Hinde and J. Stevenson-Hinde (eds), *Relationships Within Families*, Clarendon Press, Oxford.

Easterbrooks, M.A., and Lamb, M.E. (1979). The relationship between quality of infant–mother attachment and infant–peer competence in initial encounters with peers, *Child Development*, **50**, 380–387.

Eaton, W. (1978). Life events, social supports and psychiatric symptoms. A re-analysis of New Haven data, *Journal of Health and Social Behaviour*, **19**, 230–234.

Eckerman, C.O., Whatley, J.L., and Kutz, S.L. (1975). The growth of social play with peers during the second year of life, *Developmental Psychology*, **11**, 42–49.

Eckerman, C.O., and Whatley, J.L. (1977). Toys and social interaction between infant peers, *Child Development*, **48**, 1645–1656.

Egeland, B., and Sroufe, L.A. (1981). Attachment and early maltreatment, *Child Development*, **52**, 44–52.

Ekman, P., and Friessen, W. (1972). Constants across cultures in the face of emotion, *Journal of Personality and Social Psychology*, **17**, 124–129.

Ekman, P., and Oster, H. (1979). Facial expressions of emotion, *Annual Review of Psychology*, **30**, 527–544.

Elder, D., and Hallinan, M.T. (1978). Sex differences in children's friendships, *American Sociological Review*, **43**, 237–250.

Elder, G.H. (1974). *Children of the Great Depression*, University of Chicago Press, Chicago.

Elizur, J. (1986). The stress of school entry—parental coping behaviours and children's adjustment to school, *Journal of Child Psychology and Psychiatry*, **29**, 611–624.

Elkins, D. (1958). Some factors related to choice status of ninety-eighth grade children in a school society, *Genetic Psychology Monographs*, **58**, 207–272.

Elliot, G.R., and Eisdorfer, C. (eds) (1982). *Stress and Human Health*, Springer, New York,

Emde, R. (1981). Changing models of infancy and the nature of early development:

remodelling the foundation, *Journal of the American Psychoanalytic Association*, **1**, 179–219.

Emde, R. (1985). Assessment of infancy disorders. In M. Rutter and L. Hersov (eds), *Child and Adolescent Psychiatry: Modern Approaches*, Blackwell, Oxford.

Emde, R., and Harmon, R. (eds) (1984). *Continuities and Discontinuities in Development*, Plenum Press, New York, London.

Emery, R.E., O'Leary, K.D. (1984). Marital discord and child behaviour problems in a non-clinic sample, *Journal of Abnormal Child Psychology*, **12**, 411–420.

Esne, R.F. (1979). Sex differences in childhood psychopathology: a review, *Psychological Bulletin*, **86**, 574–595.

Eth, S., and Pynoos, R. (1985). *Postraumatic Stress Disorder in Children*, American Psychiatric Press, Washington, DC.

Everitt, B.S. (1977). *The Analysis of Contingency Tables*, Chapman and Hall, London.

Everitt, B.S., and Smith, A.M. (1979). Interaction in contingency tables: a brief discussion of alternative definitions, *Psychological Medicine*, **9**, 581–583.

Eysenck, H.J. (ed.) (1981). *A Model for Personality*, Springer-Verlag, New York.

Farquhar, J.W., Maccoby, N., Wood, P.B., Alexander, J.K., Bettrose, H., Brown, B.H. Haskell, W.L., McAllister, A.L., Meyer, A.J., Nash, J.D., and Stern, M.P. (1977). Community Education for Cardiovascular Health, *Lancet*, **i**, 1192–1195.

Ferguson, B.F. (1979). Preparing young children for hospitalization: a comparison of two methods, *Paediatrics*, **64**, 656–664.

Fergusson, D.M., Dimond, M.E., and Horwood, C.J. (1986). Childhood family history and behavioural problems in six-year-old children, *Journal of Child Psychology and Psychiatry*, **27**, 213–226.

Field, T.M. (1984a). Early interactions between infants and their post-partum depressed mothers, *Infant Behaviour and Development*, **7**, 517–522.

Field, T.M. (1984b). Separation stress of young children transferring to new schools, *Developmental Psychology*, **20**, 786–792.

Finer, S.M. (Chairman) (1974). *One Parent Families*, Report of the Committee, Department of Health and Social Security, HMSO, London.

Finkelstein, N.W., Dent, C., Gallagher, K., and Ramey, C.T. (1978). Social behaviour of infants and toddlers in a day-care environment, *Developmental Psychology*, **14**, 257–262.

Finlay-Jones, R., and Brown, G.W. (1981). Types of stressful life event and the onset of anxiety and depressive disorders, *Psychological Medicine*, **11**, 803–815.

Fisher, S. (1986). Homesickness and health in boarding school, *Journal of Environmental Psychology*, **6**, 35–47.

Fisher, S. (1988). Leaving home. In S. Fisher and J. Reason (eds), *Life Stress, Cognition and Health*, Wiley, Chichester.

Fisher, S., Frayer, N., and Murray, K. (1984). The transition from home to boarding school: diary style analysis of the problems and worries of boarding school pupils, *Journal of Environmental Psychology*, **4**, 211–221.

Fisher, S., and Hood, B. (1988). The stress of transition to university: a longitudinal study of vulnerability to psychological disturbance and homesickness, *British Journal of Psychology*, **78**, 425–441.

Fisher, S., Murray, K., and Frayer, N. (1985). Homesickness. Health and efficiency in first year students, *Journal of Environmental Psychology*, **5**, 181–195.

Fisher, S., and Reason, J. (eds) (1988). *Handbook of Life Stress, Cognition and Health*, Wiley, Chichester.

Flavell, J.H. (1982). Structures, stages and sequences in cognitive development. In W.A.

Collins (ed.), *The Concept of Development. The Minnesota Symposia in Child Psychology*, Erlbaum, Hillsdale, NJ.

Flavell, J.H., and Markham, E.M. (1983). Cognitive development. In P. Mussen (ed.), *Handbook of Child Psychology*. Vol. 3, *Cognitive Development*, Wiley, New York.

Flavell, J.H., and Wellman, H. (1977). Metamemory. In R.V. Kail and J. Hagen (eds), *Perspectives on the Development of Memory and Cognition*, Erlbaum, Hillsdale, NJ.

Fleiss, J.L., Williams, J.B., and Dubro, A. (1986). The logistic regression analysis of psychiatric data, *Journal of Psychiatric Research*, **20**, 145–209.

Fogelman, K. (1976). *Britain's 16-year-olds*, National Children's Bureau, London.

Folkman, S., and Lazarus, R. (1984). Personal control and stress and coping processes, *Journal of Personality and Social Psychology*, **46**, 839–852.

Folkman, S., Schaeffer, C., and Lazarus, R.S. (1980). Cognitive processes as mediators of stress and coping. In V. Hamilton and D.M. Warburton (eds), *Human Stress and Cognition: An Information Processing Approach*, Wiley, Chichester.

Foreman, D., and Goodyer, I.M. (1988). Cortisol hypersecretion in juvenile depression, *Journal of Child Psychology and Psychiatry*, **29**, 311–320.

Forman, S., and O'Malley, P. (1985). A school based approach to stress management education of students. In J. Zins, D. Wagner and C. Maher (eds), *Health Promotion in Schools*, Haworth Press, New York.

Forrest, G.C., Standish, E., and Baum, J.D. (1982). Support after perinatal death: a study of support and counselling after perinatal bereavement, *British Medical Journal*, **285**, 1475–1479.

Frankenhauser, M. (1975). Experimental approaches to the study of catecholamines and emotion. In S. Levine and H. Ursin (eds), *Emotions—Their Parameters and Measurements*, Plenum Press, New York.

Frankenhauser M. (1983). Sympathetic-adreno medullary activity, behaviour and the psychosocial environment. In P. Venables and M. Christie (eds), *Research in Psychophysiology*, Wiley, Chichester, pp. 71–94.

Frankenhauser, M., and Johansson, G. (1975) Behaviour and catecholamines in children. In L. Levi (ed.), *Society Stress and Disease*. Vol. 2. *Children and Adolescence*, Oxford University Press, Oxford, pp. 118–126.

Frankenhauser, M., Nordhenen, B., Myrsent, L., and Post, V. (1971). Psychophysiological reactions to under-stimulation and over-stimulation, *Acta Psychiatrica Scandinavica*, **35**, 298–308.

Freeman, H. (ed.) (1984). *Mental Health and the Environment*, Churchill-Livingstone, London.

Freud, A. (1946). *The Ego and the Mechanisms of Defence*, Hogarth Press, London.

Freud, A. (1970). The symptomatology of childhood: a preliminary attempt at a classification, *Psychoanalytic Study of the Child*, **25**, 19–41.

Freud, A., and Dann, S. (1951). An experiment in group upbringing. *The Psychoanalytic Study of the Child*. Vol. 6, International Universities Press, New York.

Freud, S. (1954). *Collected Papers*. Vol. I. Hogarth Press, London.

Friedrich, L.K., and Stein, A.H. (1973). Aggressive and pro-social television programmes and the natural behaviour of pre-school children, *Monographs in Social Research and Child Development*, **38**, Serial No. 151.

Furman, E. (1974). *A Child's Parent Dies: Studies in childhood Bereavment*, Yale University Press, New Haven.

Furman, W., and Buhrmeister, D. (1985). Children's perceptions of the qualities of sibling relationships, *Child Development*, **56**, 448–461.

Gaensbauer, J.J., Harmon, R.J., Cytryn, L., and McKnew, D.H. (1984). Social and affective development in infants with a manic-depressive parent, *American Journal of Psychiatry*, **141**, 223–229.

Galante, R., and Foa, D. (1986). An epidemiological study of psychic trauma and treatment effectiveness for children after a natural disaster, *Journal of the American Academy of Child Psychiatry*, **3**, 357–363.

Gallistel, C.R. (1980). *The Organisation of Action: A New Synthesis*, Erlbaum, Hillsdale, NJ.

Gannon, B., Goodyer, I.M., and Rivlin, E. (1989). The appraisal of life events by adolescents, unpublished manuscript.

Ganong, W.F. (1963). The central nervous system and the synthesis and release of adrenocorticotropic hormone. In A.V. Nalbondor (ed.), *Advances in Neuroendocrinology*, McGraw-Hill, New York.

Garcia-Coll, C., Kagan, J., and Reznick, J.S. (1984). Behavioural inhibition in young children, *Child Development*, **55**, 1005–1019.

Garmezy, N. (1983). Stressors of Childhood. In N. Garmezy and M. Rutter (eds), *Stress Coping and Development*, McGraw-Hill, New York.

Garmezy, N. (1985). Stress-resistant children—the search for protective factors. In J. Stevenson (ed.), *Recent Advances in Developmental Psychopathology*, Pergamon Press, Oxford.

Garmezy, N. (1986). Children under severe stress: critique and commentary. *Journal of the American Academy of Child Psychiatry*, **25**, 384–392.

Garmezy, N., Masten, A.S., and Tellegen, A. (1984). The study of stress and competence in children. A building block for developmental psychopathology, *Child Development*, **55**, 97–111.

Garmezy, N., and Rutter, M. (1985). Acute reactions to stress. In M. Rutter and L. Hersov (eds), *Child Psychiatry. Modern Approaches*, Blackwell, Oxford.

Garralda, M.E., and Bailey, D. (1986). Children with psychiatric disorders in primary care, *Journal of Child Psychology and Psychiatry*, **27**, 611–624.

Garrison, C.Z., Schoenbach, V.J., Schluchter, M.D., and Kaplan, B.H. (1987). Life events in early adolescence, *Journal of the American Academy of Child and Adolescent Psychiatry*, **26**, 865–872.

Gilligan, S., and Bower, G. (1984). Cognitive consequences of emotional arousal. In C. Izard, J. Kagan, and R. Zajonc (eds), *Cognitions, Emotions and Behaviour*, Cambridge University Press, Cambridge.

Gilman, S.C., Schwartz, J.M., Milner, R.J., Bloom, F.E., and Feldman, J.D. (1982). Endorphin enhances lymphocyte proliferation responses, *Proceedings of the National Academy of Sciences, U.S.A.*, **79**, 4226–4230.

Girgus, J.S., and Wolf, J. (1975). Age changes in the ability to encode social class, *Developmental Psychology*, **11**, 118–119.

Giron, L.T., Crutcher, K.A., and Davis, J.N. (1980). Lymph nodes: a possible site for sympathetic neuronal regulation of immune response, *Annals of Neurology*, **8**, 520–555.

Gislason, I.L, and Call, J.D. (1980). Dog bite in infancy. Trauma and personality development, *Journal of the American Academy of Child and Adolescent Psychiatry*, **21**, 203–207.

Gjerde, P.F. (1986). The interpersonal structure of family interaction settings: parent–adolescent relations in dyads and triads, *Developmental Psychology*, **22**, 297–304.

Glaser, R., Kiecolt-Glaser, J.K., Speicher, C., and Holliday, J.E., (1988). Stress, loneliness and changes in herpes virus latency, *Journal of Behavioural Medicine*, **8**, 249–260.

Glass, D.C. (1977). *Behaviour patterns, Stress and Coronary Disease*, Hillsdale, Erlbaum NJ.

Glass, D.C., and Constadd, R.J. (1983). Type A behaviour and catecholamines—a critical review. In C. R. Lake and M. Ziegler (eds), *Norepinephrine: Clinical Aspects*. Academic Press, New York.

Gleser, G.C., Green, B.L., and Winget, C. (1981). *Prolonged Psychosocial Effects of Disaster: A Study of Buffalo Creek*, Academic Press, New York.

Golden, R., and Dohrenwend, B.S. (1981). A path analytic model for testing causal hypotheses about the life stress process. In B. S. Dohrenwend, and B. P. Dohrenwend (eds), *Stressful Life Events and their Contexts*, Neal Watson Academic Publications, New York.

Goldmeier, D., and Johnston, D. (1982). Does psychiatric illness affect the recurrence of genital herpes? *British Journal of Venereal Disease*, **58**, 40–43.

Goodyer, I.M. (1985). Epileptic and pseudoepileptic seizures in childhood and adolescence, *Journal of the American Academy of Child and Adolescent Psychiatry*, **24**, 3–9.

Goodyer, I.M. (1986a). Monosymptomatic hysteria in childhood, family and professional systems involvement, *Journal of Family Therapy*, **8**, 1–13.

Goodyer, I.M. (1986b). Family therapy and the handicapped child. *Developmental Medicine and Child Neurology*, **28**, 247–250.

Goodyer, I.M. (1988). Measurement and methodology in life events research: some recent advances, *Current Opinion in Psychiatry*, **2**, 1–4.

Goodyer, I.M., Kolvin, I., and Gatzanis, S. (1985). Recent undesirable life events and psychiatric disorder in childhood and adolescence, *British Journal of Psychiatry*, **147**, 517–523.

Goodyer, I.M., Kolvin, I., and Gatzanis, S. (1986). The influence of age and sex on the association between recent stressful life events in psychiatric disorders of childhood and adolescence, *Journal of Child Psychology and Psychiatry*, **27**, 681–687.

Goodyer, I.M., Kolvin I., and Gatzanis, S. (1987). The impact of recent life events in psychiatric disorders of childhood and adolescence, *British Journal of Psychiatry*, **151**, 179–185.

Goodyer, I.M., Wright, C., and Altham, P.M.E. (1988). Maternal adversity and recent life events in childhood and adolescence. *Journal of Child Psychology and Psychiatry*, **5**, 651–669.

Goodyer, I.M., Wright, C., and Altham, P.M.E. (1989a). Recent friendships in anxious and depressed school-age children, *Psychological Medicine*, **19**, 165–174.

Goodyer, I.M., Wright, C., and Altham, P.M.E. (1989b). Recent life events and friendship difficulties in anxious and depressed school-age children, *British Journal of Psychiatry* (in press).

Goodyer, I.M., Wright, C., and Altham, P.M.E. (1989c). Recent adversity and achievements in anxious and depressed school-age children, *Journal of Child Psychology and Psychiatry*, (in press).

Gordon, F.R., and Flavell, J.H. (1977). The development of intuitions about cognitive cueing, *Child Development*, **48**, 1027–1033.

Gordon, I. (1942). Allergy, enuresis and stammering, *British Medical Journal*, **1**, 357–358.

Graham, D.T., and Stevenson, J. (1963). Disease as a response to life stress. In H. Lief, V. Lief and N. Lief (eds), *The Psychological Basis of Medical Practice*, Harper Row, New York.

Graham, P. (1981). Ethics in child psychiatry. In S. Bloch and P. Chodoff (eds), *Psychiatric Ethics*, Oxford University Press, Oxford.

Graham, P. (1985). Psychology and the health of children, *Journal of Child Psychology and Psychiatry*, **26**, 333–348.

Graham, P., Rutter, M., and George, S. (1973). Temperamental characteristics as predictors of behaviour disorders in children, *American Journal of Orthopsychiatry*, **3**, 328–339.

Graham, P., and Stevenson, J. (1985). A twin study of genetic influences on behavioural deviance, *Journal of the American Academy of Child and Adolescent Psychiatry*, **24**, 33–41.

Graham, P., and Stevenson, J. (1987). Temperament and psychiatric disorder. The genetic contribution to behaviour in childhood. *Australian and New Zealand Journal of Psychiatry*, **21**, 267–274.

Grant, I., Sweetwood, H., Yager, J., and Gerst, M. (1981). Quality of life events in relation to psychiatric symptoms, *Archives of General Psychiatry*, **38**, 335–339.

Gray, J.A. (1982). *The Neuropsychology of Anxiety*, Oxford University Press, Oxford.

Greene, W.A., and Miller, G. (1958). Psychological factors and reticulo-endothelial disease—IV, *Psychosomatic Medicine*, **20**, 124–127.

Greer, S. (1983). Cancer and the mind, *British Journal of Psychiatry*, **143**, 535–543.

Halsey, A.H. (1986). *Change in British Society*, Oxford University Press, Oxford.

Handford, H.A., Mayes, S.D., Mattison, R.E., Humphrey, F.J., Bagnata, S., Bixler, E.O., and Kales, J.D. (1986). Three Mile Island nuclear accident: a disaster study of child and parent reaction, *Journal of the American Academy of Child Psychiatry*, **25**, 346–356.

Harbison, J., and Harbison, J. (1980). *Society Under Stress: Children and Young People in Northern Ireland*, Open Books, Somerset.

Harlow, H.F. (1959). The development of learning in rhesus monkeys, *American Scientist*, **47**, 459–479.

Harre, R. (1984). Social elements as mind, *British Journal of Medical Psychology*, **57**, 127–135.

Harris, F.R., Wolf, M.M., and Bauer, D.M. (1967). Effects of adult social reinforcement on child behaviour. In F.R. Harris, M.M. Wolf, and D.M. Bauer (eds), *The Young Child*, Plenum Press, New York.

Harris, P. (1989). *Children and Emotion*, Blackwell, Oxford.

Harris, P.L., Olthof, T., and Terwogt, M. (1981). Children's knowledge of emotion, *Journal of Child Psychology and Psychiatry*, **22**, 247–261.

Harris, T.O., Brown, G.W., and Bifulco, A. (1986). Loss of parent in childhood and adult psychiatric disorder: The Walthamstow Study. 1. The role of lack of adequate parental care. *Psychological Medicine*, **16**, 641–659.

Harter, S. (1983). Developmental perspective on the self-system. In P. Mussen and E.M. Hetherington (eds), *Handbook of Child Psychology*. Vol. 4. *Social and Personality Development*, Wiley, New York.

Harter, S. (1986). Cognitive developmental processes in the integration of concepts about emotions and the self, *Social Cognition*, **4**, 119–151.

Hartup, W. (1974). Aggression in childhood: developmental perspectives, *American Psychologist*, **29**, 336–341.

Hartup, W. (1980). Peer relations and family relations: two social worlds. In M. Rutter (ed.), *Developmental Psychiatry*, Heinmann, London.

Hartup, W. (1983). Peer relations. In P. Mussen and M. Hetherington (eds), *Handbook of Child Psychology*. Vol. 4. *Social and Personality Development*, Wiley, New York.

Hartup, W., Brady, J., and Newcomb, A. (1985). Social cognition and social interaction in childhood. In E. Higgins, D. Ruble, and W. Hartup (eds), *Social Cognition and Social Development*, Cambridge University Press, Cambridge.

Hawk, E. (1982). The killings of Cambodia, *New Republic*, **198**, 17–21.
Hawton, K. (1982). Attempted suicide in children and adolescents, *Journal of Child Psychology and Psychiatry*, **23**, 497–504.
Hawton, K. (1986). Attempted Suicide in children and adolescents. In A. Kazdin (ed.), *Recent advances in Psychopathology*, Sage Publications, New York.
Hebb, D.O. (1955). Drives and the central nervous system, *Psychological Review*, **62**, 243–255.
Heisel, J.S., Ream, S., Raitz, R., Rappaport, M., and Coddington, D. (1973). The significance of life events as contributing factors in the disease of children: III, a study of paediatric patients, *Journal of Paediatrics*, **83**, 119–123.
Helsing, K.J., and Szklo, M. (1981). Mortality after bereavement, *American Journal of Epidemiology*, **114**, 41–52.
Henderson, S. (1977). The social network, support and neurosis, *British Journal of Psychiatry*, **131**, 15–20.
Henderson, S., Byrne, D.G., and Duncan-Jones, P. (1981). *Neurosis and the Social Environment*, Academic Press, London.
Henry, J.P. (1980). *Present Concepts of Stress Today*. In E. Usdin, R. Kvetnansky, and I. Kopin (eds), *Catecholamines and Stress: Recent Advances*, Elsevier, New York.
Herbert, J. (1987). Neuroendocrine response to social stress, *Bailliere's Clinical Endocrinology and Metabolism*, **1**, 467–490.
Hersov, L. (1985a). Emotional disorders. In M. Rutter and L. Hersov (eds), *Child Psychiatry—Modern Approaches*, Blackwell, Oxford.
Hersov, L. (1985b). Adoption and Fostering. In M. Rutter and L. Hersov (eds), *Child Psychiatry—Modern Approaches*, Blackwell, Oxford.
Hersov, L., and Berg, I. (eds). (1980). *Out of School*, Wiley, Chichester.
Hetherington, E.M. (1988). Parents, children and siblings: six years after divorce. In R.A. Hinde and J. Stevenson-Hinde (eds), *Relations Within Families*, Clarendon Press, Oxford.
Hetherington, E.M. (1989). Coping with family transitions: winners, losers and survivors, *Child Development*, **60**, 1–14.
Hetherington, E.M., Cox, M., and Cox, R. (1978). The aftermath of divorce. In *Mother–Child Relations*, National Association for the Education of Young Children, Washington, DC.
Hetherington, E.M., Cox, M., and Cox, R. (1979). Family interaction and the social, emotional and cognitive development of children following divorce. In V. Vaughn and T. Brazelton (eds), *The Family: Setting Priorities*, Science and Medicine, New York.
Hetherington, E.M., Cox, M., and Cox, R. (1982). Effects of Divorce on parents and children. In M.E. Lamb (ed.), *Non-traditional Families: Parenting and Child Development*, Erlbaum, Hillsdale, NJ.
Hetherington, E.M., Cox, M., and Cox, R. (1985). Long-term effects of divorce and re-marriage on the adjustment of children, *Journal of the American Academy of Psychology*, **25**, 518–530.
Higley, J.D., and Suomi, S.J. (1986). Parental behaviour in non-human primates. In R.W. Sluck and M. Herbert (eds), *Parental Behaviour*, Blackwell, Oxford.
Hill, C.W., Greer, W.E., and Felsenfeld, O. (1967). Psychological stress, early response to foreign protein and blood cortisol in vervets, *Psychosomatic Medicine*, **29**, 279–283.
Hinde, R.A. (1979). *Towards Understanding Relationships*, Academic Press, London.
Hinde, R.A. (ed.) (1983). *Primate Social Relationships*, Blackwell, Oxford.
Hinde, R.A. (1987). *Individuals, Relationships and Culture*, Cambridge University Press, Cambridge.
Hinde, R.A., and Bateson, P. (1984). Discontinuities versus continuities in behavioural

development and the neglect of the process, *International Journal of Behavioural Development*, **7**, 129–143.

Hinde, R.A., Perret-Clermont, A.N., and Stevenson-Hinde, J. (1985). *Social Relationships and Cognitive Development*, Clarendon Press, Oxford.

Hinde, R.A., and Stevenson-Hinde, J. (eds) (1988). *Relationships Within Families*, Clarendon Press, Oxford.

Hinkle, L.E. (1974). The effect of exposure to culture change, social change and changes in interpersonal relationships on health. In B.S. Dohrenwend and B.P. Dohrenwend (eds), *Stressful Life Events, Their Nature and Effects*, Wiley, New York.

Hirata-Hibi, M. (1967). Plasma cell reaction and thymic germinal centres after a chronic form of electric stress, *Journal of the Reticuloendothelial Society*, **4**, 370–389.

Hoare, P. (1984). The development of psychiatric disorder in school-children with epilepsy, *Developmental Medicine and Child Neurology*, **26**, 3–13.

Hoare, P. (1987). Children with epilepsy and their families, *Journal of Child Psychology and Psychiatry*, **28**, 651–656.

Hobson, P. (1985). Piaget: on ways of knowing in childhood. In M. Rutter and L. Hersov (eds), *Child Psychiatry. Modern Approaches*, Blackwell, Oxford.

Holmes, T., and Rahe, R. (1967). The social readjustment rating scale, *Journal of Psychosomatic Research*, **11**, 213–218.

Hormuth, S. (1984). Transitions in commitments to roles and self-concept change: relocation as a paradigm. In V.L. Allan and E. Van de Vlient (eds), *Role Transitions, Explorations and Explanations*. Plenum Press, New York.

Horowitz, M.J., Krupnick, J., Kaltreider, N., Leong, A., and Marman, C. (1981). Initial psychological response to parental death, *Archives of General Psychiatry*, **38**, 316–323.

Hultsch, D.F., and Plemons, J.K. (1979). Life events and life span development. In P.B. Baltes and O.G. Brim (eds), *Life Span Development and Behaviour*. Vol. 2, Academic Press, New York.

Isaacs, S. (1941). *Cambridge Education Survey: A Wartime Study in Social Welfare and Education*, Methuen, London.

Izard, C. (1977). *Human Emotions*, Plenum Press, New York.

Izard, C. (ed.) (1982). *Measuring Emotions in Infants and Children*, Cambridge University Press, Cambridge.

Izard, C. (1984). Emotion–Cognition relationships and human development. In C. Izard, J. Kagan, and R.B. Zajonc (eds), *Emotions, Cognitions and Behaviour*, Cambridge University Press, Cambridge.

Izard, C., Kagan, J., and Zajonc, R.B. (1984). *Emotions, Cognition and Behaviour*, Cambridge University Press, Cambridge.

Jemmott, J.B., III, Borysenki, J., Borysenko, M., McClelland, D., Chapman, R., Meyer, D., and Benson, H. (1983). Academic stress, power motivation and decrease in secretion rate of salivary secretory immunoglobulin A, *Lancet*, **i**, 1400–1402.

Joaso, A., and McKenzie, J. (1976). Stress and immune response in rats, *International Archives of Allergy and Applied Immunology*, **50**, 659–663.

Justice, A. (1985). Review of the effects of stress on cancer in laboratory animals: importance of time of stress application and type of tumour, *Psychological Bulletin*, **98**, 108–138.

Kagan, J. (1979). Family experience and the child's development, *American Psychologist*, **34**, 886–891.

Kagan, J. (1980). The emergence of self, *Journal of Child Psychology and Psychiatry*, **23**, 363–381.

Kagan, J. (1984). The idea of emotion in human development. In C. Izard, J. Kagan, and R.B. Zajonc (eds), *Emotions, Cognitions and Behaviour*, Cambridge University Press, Cambridge.

Kagan, J., Reznick, J.S., and Snidman, N. (1987). The physiology and psychology of behavioural inhibition in children, *Child Development*, **58**, 1459–1473.

Kagwa, B.H. (1964). The problem of mass hysteria in East Africa, *East African Medical Journal*, **41**, 560–566.

Kaplan, A. (1964). *The Conduct of Inquiry*, Crowell, New York.

Karasek, R.A. (1979). Job demands, job decision, latitude and mental strain: implications for job re-design, *Administrative Science Quarterly*, **24**, 43–48.

Kashani, J., Hodges, K., Simonds, J., and Hilderbrand, S. (1981). Life events and hospitalisation in children: a comparison with a general population, *British Journal of Psychiatry*, **139**, 221–225.

Kasl, S.V., Evans, A.S., and Weiderman, J.C. (1979). Psychosocial risk factors in the development of infectious mononucleosis, *Psychosomatic Medicine*, **41**, 445–466.

Kauffman, M., and Elizur, J. (1983). Bereavement responses of Kibbutz and non-Kibbutz children following the death of the father, *Journal of Child Psychology and Psychiatry*, **24**, 435–443.

Keller, S.E., Schleifer, S.J., Sherman, J., Camerino, M.S., Smith, H., and Stein, M. (1981). Comparison of a simplified whole blood and isolated lymphocyte stimulation technique, *Immunology Communications*, **10**, 417–431.

Keller, S.E., Stein, M., Camerino, M.S., Schleifer, S.J., and Sherman, J. (1980). Suppression of lymphocyte stimulation by anterior hypothalamic lesions in the guinea pig, *Cellular Immunology*, **52**, 334–340.

Keller, S.E., Weiss, J., Schleifer, S.J., Miller, N.E., and Stein, M. (1983). Stress induced suppression of immunity in adrenalectomised rats, *Science*, **221**, 1301–1304.

Kelly, H.H. (1979). *Personal Relationships Their Structures and Processes*, Halstead Press, New York.

Kendal, D. (1978). Homophily, selection and socialisation in adolescent friendships, *American Journal of Sociology*, **84**, 427–436.

Kendall, P., and Bronswell, P. (1984). *Cognitive Behavioural Therapy of Impulsive Children*, Guilford Press, New York.

Kendel, D.B., and Lesser, G. (1972). *Youth in Two worlds*, Josey Bass, San Francisco.

Kenney, M., Mason, W., and Hill, S. (1979). The effects of age, objects, and visual experience on affective responses of rhesus monkeys to strangers, *Developmental Psychology*, **15**, 176–184.

Kenny, S., Thompson, R., Stancer, H.C., Roy, A., and Persad, E. (1983). Life events precipitating mania, *British Journal of Psychiatry*, **142**, 398–403.

Keogh, B.K. (1982). Temperament: an individual difference of importance in intervention programmes, *Topics in Early Childhood Special Education*, **2**, 25–31.

Keverne, E. (1988). Central mechanisms underlying the neural and neuroendocrine determinants of maternal behaviour, *Psychoneuroendocrinology*, **13**, 127–141.

Kiecolt-Glaser, J.K., Fisher, L., Ogrocki, P., Stout, J.C., Speicher, C.E., and Glaser, R. (1987). Marital quality, marital disruption and immune function, *Psychosomatic Medicine*, **10**, 21–30.

Kiecolt-Glaser, J.K., Speicher, C.E., Holliday, J.E., and Glaser, R. (1984). Stress and the transformation of lymphocytes by Epstein–Barr virus, *Journal of Behavioural Medicine*, **7**, 1–12.

Killen, J.D. (1985). Prevention of adolescent tobacco smoking; the social pressure resistance training approach, *Journal of Child Psychology and Psychiatry*, **26**, 7–16.

Kinston, W., and Rosser, R. (1974). Disaster effects on mental and physical state, *Journal of Psychosomatic Research*, **18**, 437–456.

Kinzie, J.D., Frederick, M.R., and Ruth, B. (1984). Post-traumatic stress disorder among survivors of Cambodian concentration camps, *American Journal of Psychiatry*, **141**, 645–650.

Kinzie, J.D., Sock, W., Angell, M., Marson, S., and Ruth, B. (1986). The psychiatric effects of massive trauma on Cambodian children. 1—The Children, *Journal of the American Academy of Child Psychiatry*, **25**, 370–376.

Kohlberg, L. (1969). Stage and sequence: the cognitive–developmental approach to socialization. In D. Goslin (ed.), *Handbook of Socialization Theory and Research*, Rand-McNally, Chicago.

Kohnstamm, G. (ed.) (1986). *Temperament Discussed*, Swets North America Inc, Berwyn.

Kolvin, I., Garside, R.F., Nicol, R.F., MacMillan, A., Wolstenholme, F., and Leitch, I.M. (1981). *Help Starts Here: The Maladjusted Child in Ordinary School*, Tavistock Press, London.

Kolvin, I., Miller, F.W., Garside, R.F., Wolstenholme, F., and Gatzanis, S. (1983). A longitudinal study of deprivation: life cycle changes in one generation—implications for the next generation. In M.H. Schmidt and H. Remschmidt (eds), *Epidemiological Approaches to Child Psychiatry*, Vol. 2, 21–30, George Thieme, Stuttgart and New York.

Koocher, G.P., and O'Malley, J.E. (1981). *The Damocles Syndrome*, McGraw-Hill, New York.

Kuhn, C.M., Buttier, S.R., and Schorberg, S.M. (1978). Selective depression of serum growth hormone during maternal deprivation in rat pups, *Science*, **201**, 1034–1036.

Lamb, M.E. (1977). Father–Infant and Mother–Infant interaction in the first year of life, *Child Development*, **48**, 167–181.

Lamb, M.E., Frodi, A.M., Hwang, C.P., Frodi, M., and Steinberg, M. (1982). Mother and father–infant interaction involving play and holding in traditional and non-traditional Swedish families, *Developmental psychology*, **18**, 215–221.

Lambert, L., and Streather, J. (1980). *Children in Changing families: A study of adoption and illegitimacy*. MacMillan Press, London.

Langmeier, J., and Matejeck, Z. (1975). *Psychological Deprivation in Childhood*, Halstead Press, New York.

Lansdown, R. (1987). The development of the concept of death and its relationship to communicating with dying children. In E. Koras (ed.). *Current Issues in Clinical Psychology*, Plenum Press, London.

Lansdown, R., and Benjamin, G. (1985). The development of the concept of death in children aged 5–9 years. *Child Care, Health and Development*, **11**, 13–20.

Lansdown, R., and Goldman, A. (1988). The psychological care of children with malignant disease, *Journal of Child Psychology and Psychiatry*, **5**, 555–567.

Lask, B., and Matthew, D. (1979). Childhood asthma: a controlled trial of family psychotherapy, *Archives of Diseases of Childhood*, **54**, 116–119.

Laudenslager, M.L., Capitanio., J.P., and Reite, M. (1985). Possible effects of early separation experiences on subsequent immune function in isolated macaque monkeys, *American Journal of Psychiatry*, **142**, 862–864.

Lavik, N. (1977). Urban–rural differences in rates of disorder. In P.J. Graham (ed.), *Epidemiological Approaches in Child Psychiatry*, Academic Press, London.

Lazarus, R.S. (1984). Puzzles in the study of daily hassles, *Journal of Behaviour Medicine*, **7**, 375–389.

Lazarus, R.S., and Folkman, S. (1984). *Stress, Appraisal and Coping*, Springer, New York.

Lee, C.J., and Bates, J.E. (1985). Mother–child interaction at age 2 years and perceived difficult temperament, *Child Development*, **56**, 1314–1325.

Lentz, K. (1985). Fears and worries of young children expressed in a contextual play setting, *Journal of Child Psychology and Psychiatry*, **3**, 467–476.

Leon, G.R., Butcher, J.N., Kleinman, M., Goldberg, A., and Alnagor, M. (1981). Survivors of the Holocaust and their children: current status and adjustment, *Journal of Personality and Social Psychology*, **41**, 503–516.

Levine, R.J., Sexton, D.J., Romm, F.J., Wood, B.T., and Kaiser, J. (1974). Outbreak of psychosomatic illness at a rural elementary school, *Lancet*, **ii**, 1500–1503.

Levine, S. (1983). A Psychobiological approach to the ontogeny of coping. In N. Garmezy and M. Rutter (eds), *Stress, Coping and Development in Children*, McGraw-Hill, New York.

Lewis, C. (1986). The role of the father in the human family. In W. Sluckin and M. Herbert (eds), *Parental Behaviour*, Blackwell, Oxford.

Lifton, R.J. (1980). The concept of the survivor. In J.E. Dimsdale (ed.), *Survivors, Victims and Perpetrators: Essays on the Nazi Holocaust*, Hemisphere Publishing Corporation, Washington.

Lilienfield, A.M., and Lilienfield, D.G. (1980). *Foundations of Epidemiology*, Oxford University Press, Oxford.

Linn, B.S., Linn, M.W., and Jersen, J. (1982). Degree of depression and immune responsiveness, *Psychosomatic Medicine*, **44**, 128–129.

Lipsitt, L. (1983). Towards understanding the origins of coping behaviour. In N. Garmezy and M. Rutter (eds), *Stress, Coping and Development*, McGraw-Hill, New York.

Lister, E.D. (1982). Forced silence: a neglected dimension of trauma, *American Journal of Psychiatry*, **139**, 872–876.

Lloyd, C. (1980a). Life events and depressive disorder reviewed, I. Events as predisposing factors, *Archives of General Psychiatry*, **37**, 529–535.

Lloyd, C. (1980b). Life events and depressive disorder reviewed, II. Events as precipitating factors, *Archives of General Psychiatry*, **37**, 541–548.

Locke, S.E., Kraus, L., Leserman, J.M., Hurst, M.W., Heisel, S., and Williams, R.M. (1984). Life change stress, psychiatric symptoms and natural killer cell activity. *Psychosomatic Medicine*, **45**, 441–453.

Loney, M. (ed.) (1987). *The State on the Market*, Sage Publications, London.

Long, C.G., and Moore, J.R. (1979). Parental expectations for their epileptic children, *Journal of Child Psychology and Psychiatry*, **20**, 299–312.

Luborsky, L., Mintz, J., Brightman, V., and Katcher, A.H. (1976). Herpes simplex virus and moods: a longitudinal study, *Journal of Psychosomatic Research*, **20**, 543–548.

Lundeberg, U. (1983a). Note on type A behaviour and cardiovascular response to challenge in 3–6-year-old children, *Journal of Psychosomatic Research*, **27**, 39–42.

Lundeberg, U. (1983b). Sex differences in behaviour pattern and catecholamines and cortisol excretion in 3–6-year-old day-care children, *Biological Psychiatry*, **16**, 503–512.

Lundeberg, U. (1986). Stress and type A behaviour in children, *Journal of the American Academy of Child and Adolescent Psychiatry*, **6**, 771–778.

Lundeberg, U., and Frankenhauser, M. (1980). Pituitary–adrenal and sympathetic-adrenal correlates of distress and effort, *Journal of Psychosomatic Research*, **24**, 125–130.

Lutkenhaus, P., Grossman, K.E., and Grossman, K. (1985). Infant–mother attachment at 12 months and style of interaction with a stranger at age 3 years, *Child Development*, **56**, 1535–1542.

Lynn, L.E. (ed.) (1978). *Knowledge and Policy: the Uncertain Connection*, National Academy of Sciences, Washington, DC.

Maccoby, R., and Jacklin, E. (1978). *The Psychology of Sex Differences*, Stanford University Press, Stanford, CA.

Maccoby, R., and Jacklin, E. (1980). Psychological sex differences. In M. Rutter (ed.), *Scientific Foundations of Developmental Psychiatry*, Heinemann Medical, London.

Macintyre, A. (1976). *A Short History of Ethics*, Routlege & Keegan Paul, London.

Madge, N. (ed.) (1983). *Families at Risk*, Heinmann, London.

Main, M., Kaplan, N., and Cassidy, J. (1985). Security in infancy, childhood and adulthood. In I. Bretherton and E. Waters (eds), *Growing Points of Attachment Theory and Research*, Monographs for the Society for Research into Child Development, **50**.

Main, M., and Weston, D. (1981). The quality of the toddler's relationship to mother and father, *Child Development*, **52**, 932–940.

Malan, D.H. (1979). *Individual Psychotherapy and the Science of Psychodynamics*, Butterworths, London.

Malmquist, C.P. (1986). Children who witness parental murder: post traumatic aspects, *Journal of the American Academy of Child Psychiatry*, **25**, 320–325.

Mandler, G. (1975). *Mind and Emotion*, Wiley, New York.

Markus, H. (1977). Self-schemata and processing information about the self, *Journal of Personality and Social Psychology*, **35**, 63–78.

Marteau, T.M., Bloch, S., and Baum, J.D. (1987). Family life and diabetic control, *Journal of Child Psychology and Psychiatry*, **28**, 823–835.

Mason, J.W. (1975). A historical view of the stress field, part I, *Journal of Human Stress*, **1**, 6–12.

Mason, W.A. (1979). Ontogeny of social behaviour. In P. Monler, and G. Vandebergh (eds), *Handbook of Behavioural Neurobiology*. No. 3: *Social Behaviour and Communication*, Plenum Press, New York.

Masten, A.S., and Garmezy, N. (1985). Risk, Vulnerability, and protective factors in developmental psychopathology. In B. Lahey and K. Kaden (eds), *Advances in Clinical Child Psychology* Vol. 8, Plenum Press, New York.

Masten, A.S., Garmezy, N., Tellegen, A., Pellegrini, D., Larkin, K., and Larsen, A. (1988). Competence and stress in school children: the moderating effects of individual and family qualities. *Journal of Child Psychology and Psychiatry*, **6**, 745–764.

Masuda, M., and Holmes, T. (1967). Magnitude estimations of social readjustments, *Journal of Psychosomatic Research*, **11**, 219–228.

Matas, L., Arend, R.A., and Sroufe, L.A. (1978). Continuity and adaptation in the second year: the relationship between quality of attachment and later competence, *Child Development*, **49**, 547–556.

Mattson, A., Gross, S., and Hall, T.W. (1971). Psychoendocrine study of adaptation in young haemophiliacs, *Psychosomatic Medicine*, **33**, 215–225.

Maughan, B., and Rutter, M. (1986). Black pupils progress in secondary schools—II. examination attainments, *British Journal of Developmental Psychology*, **4**, 19–29.

Mawson, D., Marks, I.M., Ramm, L., and Stern, R.S. (1981). Guided mourning for morbid grief: a controlled study, *British Journal of Psychiatry*, **138**, 185–193.

McCall, R.B. (1981). Nature–nurture and 2 realms of development: a proposed integration with respect to mental development, *Child Development*, **52**, 1–12.

McCarthy, D., and Saegart, S. (1976). Residential density social control and social withdrawal, *Human Ecology*, **6**, 253–272.

McFarlane, A.C. (1987). Life events and psychiatric disorder: the role of natural disaster, *British Journal of Psychiatry*, **151**, 362–367.

McFarlane, A.C. (1988). Recent life events and psychiatric disorder in children: the interaction with preceding extreme adversity, *Journal of Child Psychology and Psychiatry*, **29**, 677–691.

McFarlane, A.C., Policansy, S.K., and Irwin, C. (1987). A longitudinal study of the psychological morbidity in children due to natural disaster, *Psychological Medicine*, **17**, 727–738.

McGee, R., Williams, S., and Silva, P.A. (1985). An evaluation of the malaise inventory, *Journal of Psychosomatic Research*, **30**, 147–152.

McMahon, B., and Pugh, T.F. (1970). *Epidemiological Principles and Methods*, Little, Brown & Co., Boston.

McWhirter, L., and Trew, K. (1981). Social awareness in Northern Ireland, *Bulletin of the British Psychological Society*, **34**, 308–311.

Meade, G.H. (1934). *Mind, Self and Society*, University of Chicago Press, Chicago.

Medrich, E.A., Rosen, J., Rubin V., and Buckley, S. (1982). *The Serious Business of Growing Up*, University of California Press, Berkeley.

Meichenbaum, D. (1967). *Cognitive-Behaviour Modification, an Integrative Approach*, Plenum, Press, New York.

Meichenbaum, D., and Cameron, R. (1983). Stress inoculation training: toward a general paradigm for training coping skills. In D. Meichenbaum and P. Jaremko (eds), *Stress Reduction and Prevention*, Plenum Press, New York.

Meichenbaum, P., and Novaco, R. (1978). Stress Inoculation: a preventative approach. In C.D. Spielberger and I.G. Sarason (eds), *Stress and Anxiety*. Vol. 5, Wiley, New York.

Mendelson, M., Haith, M., and Goldman-Rakic, P. (1982). Face scanning and responsiveness to social cues in infant rhesus monkeys, *Developmental Psychology*, **18**, 222–228.

Meyer, A. (1951). The life chart and the obligation of specifying positive data in psychopathological diagnosis. In E.E. Winters (ed.), *The Collected Papers of Adolf Meyer Vol. III*, Johns Hopkins Press, Baltimore.

Meyer, R., and Haggerty, R. (1962). Streptococcal infections in families, *Paediatrics*, **29**, 539–549.

Migeon, C. (1980). Physiology and pathology of adrenocortical function in infancy and childhood. In R. Collu, P. Duchamy, and A. Guydon (eds), *Paediatric Endocrinology*, Raven Press, New York, pp. 465–522.

Milgram, S. (1970). The experiences of living in cities, *Science*, **167**, 1461–1468.

Miller, F.J.W., Kolvin, I., and Fells, H. (1985). Becoming deprived: a cross-generation study based upon the Newcastle-Upon-Tyne 1000 family study. In A.R. Nicol (ed.), *Longitudinal Studies in Child Psychology and Psychiatry*, Wiley, Chichester.

Miller, P.McC., and Ingham, J.G. (1983). Dimensions of experience, *Psychological Medicine*, **13**, 417–429.

Miller, P.McC., Ingham, J.G., Kreitman, N.B., Surtees, P.G., and Sashidharan, S.P. (1987). Life events and other factors implicated in the onset and remission of psychiatric illness in women, *Journal of Affective Disorders*, **12**, 73–88.

Mills, M., Puckering, C., Pound, A., and Cox, A. (1985). What is it about depressed mothers that influences their children's functioning. In J. Stevenson (ed.), *Recent Advances in Developmental Psychopathology*, Pergamon Press, Oxford.

Minde, K.K., Minde, R., and Musici, L. (1982). Some aspects of disruption of the attachment system in young children: a transcultural perspective. In J. Anthony and C. Chiland (eds), *The Children in His Family—Children in Turmoil: Tomorrow's Parents* Vol. 7, Wiley Interscience, New York.

Miscione, J.L., Marvin, R.S., O'Brien, R.G., and Greenberg, M.T. (1978). A developmental study of pre-school children's understanding of the words 'know' and 'guess', *Child Development*, **49**, 1107–1113.

Monaghan, J., Robinson, J., and Dodge, J. (1979). The children's life event inventory, *Journal of Psychosomatic Research*, **23**, 63–68.

Monck, E., and Dobbs, R. (1985). Measuring life events in an adolescent population: methodological issues and related findings, *Psychological Medicine*, **15**, 841–850.

Moore, B., Underwood, B., and Rosenhan, D.L. (1984). Emotion, self and others. In C. Izard, J. Kagan, and R.B. Zajonc (eds), *Emotions, Cognitions and Behaviour*, Cambridge University Press, Cambridge.

Morris-Jones, P.H. (1987). Advances in managing children transferring to new schools. *Developmental Psychology*, **20**, 786–792.

Moskovitz, S. (1983). *Love Despite Hate: Child Survivors of the Holocaust and Their Adult Lives* Schocken Books, New York.

Moss, P.D., and McEvedy, P. (1966). An epidemic of overbreathing amongst schoolgirls, *British Medical Journal*, **2**, 1295–1300.

Mueller, E. (1972). The maintenance of verbal exchanges between young children, *Child Development*, **43**, 930–938.

Mueller, E., and Bremner, J. (1977). The origins of social skills and interaction among playgroup toddlers, *Child Development*, **48**, 854–861.

Mueller, E., and Rich, A. (1976). Clustering and socially directed behaviours in a play-group of 1-year-old boys, *Journal of Child Psychology and Psychiatry*, **17**, 315–322.

Murray, L. (1988). Effects of post-natal depression on infant development: direct studies of early mother–infant interactions. In R. Kumar and I.F. Brockington (eds), *Motherhood and Mental Illness*, Wright, London.

Murray, L., and Trevarthen, C.B. (1986). The infant's role in mother–infant communication, *Journal of Child Language*, **13**, 15–29.

Murray-Parkes, C., and Stevenson-Hinde, J. (eds) (1982). *The Place of Attachment in Human Behaviour*, Tavistock, London.

Nelson, R.R., and Skidmore, F. (eds) (1983). *American Families and the Economy*, National Academy Press, Washington DC.

Newcombe, A.F., and Brady, J.E. (1982). Mutuality in boys' friendship relations, *Child Development*, **53**, 392–395.

Newman, O. (1973). *Defensible space*, Architectural Press, London.

Nicol, A.R. (1987). Psychotherapy and the school—an update, *Journal of Child Psychology and Psychiatry*, **28**, 657–665.

Osborn, S.G. (1980). Moving home, leaving London and delinquent trends, *British Journal of Criminology*, **20**, 54–61.

Ouston, J., Maughan, B., and Mortimore, P. (1980). School influences. In M. Rutter (ed.) *Scientific Foundations of Developmental Psychiatry*, Heinemann Medical, London.

Packman, J. (1986). *Who Needs Care*, Blackwell Scientific, Oxford.

Parker, G. (1979). Parental characteristics in relation to depressive disorders, *British Journal of Psychiatry*, **134**, 138–147.

Parker, G. (1981). Parental representations of patients with anxiety neurosis, *Acta Psychiatrica Scandinavica*, **65**, 33–36.

Parker, G. (1983). Parental affectionless control as an antecedent to adult depression, *Archives of General Psychiatry*, **40**, 956–960.

Parkes, C.M. (1985). Bereavement, *British Journal of Psychiatry*, **146**, 11–17.

Parmalee, A.H., Jr (1984). Children's illnesses: their beneficial effect on behavioural development, *Child Development*, **57**, 1–10.

Parry, G., and Shapiro, D.A. (1986). Social support and life events in working class women, *Archives of General Psychiatry*, **43**, 313–320.
Parry-Jones, W. (1985). Adolescent disturbance. In M. Rutter and L. Hersov (eds), *Child Psychiatry—Modern Approaches*, Blackwell, Oxford.
Patterson, G.R. (1982). *Coercive Family Process. A Social Learning Approach*. Vol. 3, Castalia, Eugene, OR.
Patterson, G.R. (1983). Stress: a change agent for family process. In N. Garmezy and M. Rutter (eds), *Stress, Coping and Development*, McGraw-Hill, New York.
Patterson, G.R. (1984). Siblings: fellow travellers in coercive family processes, *Advances in the Study of Aggression*, **1**, 173–214.
Patterson, G.R. (1986a). The contribution of siblings to train for fighting. A microsocial analysis. In D. Olweus, J. Block, and M. Radke-Yarrow (eds), *Development of Antisocial and Prosocial Behaviour. Research Theories and Issues*, Academic Press, New York, pp. 235–261.
Patterson, G.R. (1986b). Performance models for antisocial boys, *American Psychologist*, **41**, 432–444.
Patterson, G.R., and Dishion, T.J. (1988). Multilevel family process models: traits, interactions and relationships. In R.A. Hinde and J. Stevenson-Hinde (eds), *Relationships Within Families*, Clarendon Press, Oxford.
Paykel, E.S. (1974). Life stress and psychiatric disorder. In B.S. Dohrenwend and B.P. Dohrenwend (eds), *Stressful Life Events: Their Nature and Effects*, Wiley, New York.
Paykel, E.S. (1978). The contribution of life events to causation of psychiatric illness, *Psychological Medicine*, **8**, 245–253.
Paykel, E.S. (1983). Methodological aspects of life events research, *Journal of Psychosomatic Research*, **27**, 341–352.
Paykel, E.S., Emms, E.M., Fletcher, J., and Rassaby, E.S. (1980). Life events and social support in puerperal depression, *British Journal of Psychiatry*, **139**, 339–346.
Paykel, E.S., Myers, J., Dienelt, M., Klerman, G., Lindethal, J., and Pepper, P. (1969). Life events and depression, *Archives of General Psychiatry*, **5**, 340–347.
Paykel, E.S., and Rowan, P. (1979). Affective disorders. In K. Granville-Grossman (ed.), *Recent Advances in Clinical Psychiatry*, Churchill-Livingstone, Edinburgh.
Pearlin, L.I., and Schooler, C. (1978). The structure of coping, *Journal of Health and Social Behaviour*, **19**, 2–21.
Pellegrini, D. (1985). Social cognition and competence in middle childhood, *Child Development*, **56**, 253–264.
Pellegrini, D. (1985). Training in social problem solving. In M. Rutter and L. Hersov (eds), *Child and Adolescent Psychiatry: Modern Approaches*, Blackwell Scientific, Oxford.
Pellegrini, D.S., and Urbain, E.S. (1985). An evaluation of interpersonal cognitive problem solving training with children, *Journal of Child Psychology and Psychiatry*, **26**, 17–42.
Pettit, S.G., Dodge, K.A., and Brown, M.M. (1988). Early family experience, and social competence, *Child Development*, **59**, 107–120.
Piaget, J. (1970). *Genetic Epistemology* (translated by E. Duckworth), Columbia University Press, New York.
Plomin, R., and Dunn, J. (eds) (1986). *The Study of Temperament: Changes, Continuities and Challenges*, Erlbaum, Hillsdale, NJ.
Popper, K. (1962). *Conjectures and Refutations*, Academic Press, New York.
Porter, A. (1982). Disciplinary attitudes and cigarette smoking: comparison of two schools, *British Medical Journal*, **285**, 1725–1726.

Posner, M.I., and Snyder, C.R. (1975). Attention and cognitive control. In *Information Processing and Cognition: The Loyola Symposium*, Erlbaum, Hillsdale, NJ.

Puig-Antich, J. (1986). Psychobiological markers: effects of age and puberty. In M. Rutter, C. Izard, and P. Read (eds), *Depression in Young People—Developmental and Clinical Perspectives*, Guilford Press, London.

Puska, P. (1982). The North Karelia Youth Project: evaluation of 2 years' intervention in health behaviour and CVD risk factors among 13–15-year-old children, *Preventive Medicine*, **11**, 550–570.

Pynoos, R., and Eth, S. (1984). The child as witness to homicide, *Journal of Social Issues*, **40**, 87–108.

Pynoos, R., and Eth, S. (1986). Witness to violence: the child interview, *Journal of the American Academy of Child and Adolescent Psychiatry*, **3**, 306–319.

Quinton, D. (1980). Cultural and community influences. In M. Rutter (ed.), *Scientific Foundations of Developmental Psychiatry*, Heinemann Medical, London.

Quinton, D. (1988). Urbanism and child mental health. *Journal of Child Psychology and Psychiatry*, **29**, 11–20.

Quinton, D., and Rutter, M. (1976). Early hospital admissions and later disturbances of behaviour: an attempted replication of Douglas's finding, *Developmental Medicine and Child Neurology*, **18**, 447–459.

Quinton, D., and Rutter, M. (1985a). Family pathology and child psychiatric disorder: a four year prospective study. In A.R. Nicol (ed.), *Longitudinal Studies in Child Psychology and Psychiatry*, Wiley, Chichester.

Quinton, D., and Rutter, M. (1985b). Parenting behaviour of mothers raised in care. In A.R. Nicol (ed.), *Longitudinal Studies in Child Psychology and Psychiatry*, Wiley, Chichester.

Quinton, D., and Rutter, M. (1988). *Parental Breakdown: The Making and Breaking of Intergenerational Links*. Gower, Aldershot.

Radke-Yarrow, M., and Sherman, T. (1985). Interaction of Cognition and Emotion in Development. In R.A. Hinde, A.N. Perret-Clermont, and J. Stevenson-Hinde (eds), *Social Relationships and Cognitive Development*, Oxford University Press, Oxford.

Radke-Yarrow, M., and Zahn-Waxler, C. (1984). Roots, motives and patterning in children's prosocial behaviour. In E. Staub, D. Bar-Tal, J. Karylowski, and J. Reykowski (eds), *The Development and Maintenance of Pro-Social Behaviour: An International Perspective on Positive Morality*, Plenum Press, New York.

Rahe, R., and Holmes, T. (1965). Social, psychological and psychophysiological aspects of inguinal hernia, *Journal of Psychosomatic Research*, **8**, 487–492.

Rahim, S.I., and Cederblad, M. (1984). Effects of rapid urbanisation on child behaviour and health in a part of Khartoum, Sudan, *Journal of Child Psychology and Psychiatry*, **25**, 625–642.

Raphael, B. (1982). The young child and the death of a parent. In C. Murray-Parkes and J. Stevenson-Hinde (eds), *The Place of Attachment in Human Behaviour*, Wiley, Chichester.

Raphael, B. (1986). *When Disaster Strikes: A Handbook for the caring professions*, Hutchinson, London.

Ravi, A., and Klingman, A. (1983). Children under Stress. In S. Bregnity (ed.), *Stress in Israel*, Van Nostrand Reinhold, New York.

Reite, M., and Field, T. (eds) (1985). *The Psychobiology of Attachment and Separation*, Academic Press, London.

Reite, M., Horbeck, R., and Hoffman, A. (1981). Altered cellular immune response following peer separation, *Life Science*, **29**, 1133–1135.

Rest, J., Davison, M.L., and Robbins, S. (1978). Age trends in judging moral issues:

a review of cross-sectional, longitudinal and sequential studies of the Defining Issues test, *Child Development*, **49**, 263–279.

Richards, M.P.M. (1988). Parental divorce and children. In G. Burrows (ed.), *Handbook of Studies in Child Psychiatry*, Elsevier, Amsterdam.

Richman, N. (1977). Behaviour problems in pre-school children, *British Journal of Psychiatry*, **131**, 523–527.

Richman, N. (1985). Disorders of pre-school children. In M. Rutter and L. Hersov (eds), *Child and Adolescent Psychiatry—Modern Approaches*, Blackwell, Oxford.

Richman, N., Stevenson, J., and Graham, P. (1982). *Pre-school to School: A Behavioural Study*, Academic Press, London.

Ricks, M. (1985). The social transmission of parental behaviour: attachment across generations. In I. Bretherton and E. Walters (eds), *Growing Points of Attachment. Theory and Research*, Monographs of the Society for Research on Child Development, 50.

Riley, V. (1981). Psychoneuroendocrine influences in immune competence and neoplasia, *Science*, **212**, 1100–1109.

Ritchie, K. (1981). Research note—Interaction in the families of epileptic children, *Journal of Child Psychology and Psychiatry*, **22**, 65–71.

Robertson, J., and Robertson J. (1971). Young children in brief separation: a fresh look, *Psychoanalytic Study of the Child*, **26**, 264–315.

Rogers, M., Dubey, M., and Reich, P. (1979). The influence of the psyche and the brain on immunity and disease susceptibility: a critical review, *Psychosomatic Medicine*, **41**, 147–164.

Rose, N. (1973). *10 Therapeutic Playgroups*, NSPCC, London.

Rose, R.M. (1980). Endocrine responses to stressful psychological events, *Psychiatric Clinics of North America*, **2**, 53–71.

Rose, R.M. (1984). Overview of the endocrinology of stress. In G.M. Brown, S.H. Kaslow, and S. Reichlin (eds), *Neuroendocrinology and Psychiatric Disorder*, Academic Press, New York.

Ross, H.S., and Goldman, B.M. (1976). Establishing new social relations in infancy, *Advances in Communication and Affect*. Vol. 4, Plenum Press, New York.

Rubenstein, J., and Howes, C. (1976). The effects of peers on toddler interaction with mothers and toys, *Child Development*, **47**, 597–605.

Rubin, K.H. (1980). *Children's Friendships*, Harvard University Press, Cambridge.

Rubin, K.H., and Krasnor, L.R. (1980). Changes in the play behaviours of pre-schoolers: a short-term longitudinal investigation, *Canadian Journal of Behavioural Science*, **12**, 278–282.

Rubin, K.H., Maioris, T.L., and Homung, M. (1976). Free play behaviour in middle and lower class preschoolers: Partgen and Piaget revisited, *Child Development*, **47**, 414–419.

Rubin, K.H., Watson, K.S., and Jambor, T.W. (1978). Freeplay behaviours in preschool and kindergarten children, *Child Development*, **49**, 534–536.

Rump, E., and Court, J. (1971). The Eyesenck personality inventory and social desirability response set with student and clinical groups, *British Journal of Social and Clinical Psychology*, **10**, 42–54.

Rutter, M. (1966). *Children of Sick Parents: An Environmental Approach and Psychiatric Study*, Maudsley Monograph No.16, Institute of Psychiatry, London, Oxford University Press, Oxford.

Rutter, M. (1972). *Maternal Deprivation Re-assessed*, Penguin, Harmondsworth.

Rutter, M. (1973). Why are London children so disturbed? *Proceedings of the Royal Society of Medicine*, **66**, 1221–1225.

Rutter, M. (1979). Protective factors in children's response to stress and disadvantage. In M.W. Kent and J.E. Rolfe (eds), *Primary Prevention of Psychopathology: Social Competence in Children*. Vol. 3, Hanover Press, University of New England.

Rutter, M. (1980). Socio-emotional development. In M. Rutter (ed.), *Developmental Psychiatry*, Heinemann, London.

Rutter, M. (1981a). The city and the child, *American Journal of Orthopsychiatry*, **51**, 610–625.

Rutter, M. (1981b). Stress, coping and development—some issues and some questions, *Journal of Child Psychology and Psychiatry*, **22**, 323–356.

Rutter, M. (1982). Epidemiological longitudinal approaches to the study of development. In W.A. Collins (ed.), *The Concept of Development. Minnesota Symposium On Child Psychology*, Vol. 15, Hillsdale, NJ.

Rutter, M. (1983a). Statistical and personal interactions: facets and perspectives. In D. Magnuson and V. Allen (eds), *Human Development: An Interactional Perspective*, Academic Press, New York.

Rutter, M., (1983b). Stress, Coping and Development. Some issues and some questions. In N. Garmezy and M. Rutter (eds), *Stress, coping and Development*, McGraw-Hill, New York.

Rutter, M. (1985a). Family and school influences on behavioural development, *Journal of Child Psychology and Psychiatry*, **3**, 349–368.

Rutter, M. (1985b). Family and school influences. Meanings, mechanisms and implications. In A.R. Nicol (ed.), *Longitudinal Studies in Child Psychology and Psychiatry*, Wiley, Chichester.

Rutter, M. (1985c). Family and school influences on cognitive development. In R.A. Hinde, A.N. Perret-Clermont, and J. Stevenson-Hinde (eds), *Social Relationships and Cognitive Development*, Clarendon Press, Oxford.

Rutter, M. (1985d). Resilience in the face of adversity: protective factors and resistance to psychiatric disorder, *British Journal of Psychiatry*, **147**, 598–611.

Rutter, M. (1986a). The developmental psychopathology of depression. In M. Rutter, C. Izard, and P. Read (eds), *Depression in Young People—Developmental and Clinical Perspectives*, Guilford Press, New York.

Rutter, M. (1986b). Psychosocial resilience and protective mechanisms. In D. Cicchetti, K. Neuchterlein, and S. Weintraub (eds), *Risk and Protective Factors in the Development of Psychopathology*, Cambridge University Press, Cambridge.

Rutter, M. (1987a). The role of cognition in child development and disorder, *British Journal of Medical Psychology*, **60**, 1–16.

Rutter, M. (1987b). Psychosocial resilience and protective mechanisms, *American Journal of Orthopsychiatry*, **57**, 317–331.

Rutter, M. (1987c). Temperament, personality and personality disorder. *British Journal of Psychiatry*, **150**, 443–458.

Rutter, M. (1988a). Functions and consequences of relationships: some psychopathological considerations. In R.A. Hinde and J. Stevenson-Hinde (eds), *Relationships Within Families*, Clarendon Press, Oxford.

Rutter, M. (1988b). Psychiatric disorder in parents as a risk factor for children, *Journal of the American Academy of Child and Adolescent Psychiatry* (in press).

Rutter, M. (1989). Pathways from childhood to adult life, *Journal of Child Psychology and Psychiatry*, **30**, 23–53.

Rutter, M., and Giller, H. (1983). *Juvenile Delinquency Trends and Perspectives*, Penguin, Hardmondsworth, and Guilford Press, New York.

Rutter, M., Graham, P., Chadwick, O., and Yule, W. (1976). Adolescent turmoil fact or fiction? *Journal of Child Psychology and Psychiatry*, **17**, 35–36.

Rutter, M., Graham, P., and Yule, W. (1970). *A Neuropsychiatric Study in Childhood, Clinics in Developmental Medicine*, Nos. 35/36, Heinemann/Spastics International Medical Publications, London.

Rutter, M., and Hersov, L. (1985). *Child Psychiatry—Modern Approaches*, Blackwell, Oxford.

Rutter, M., Maughan, B., Mortimore, P., Ouston, J., and Smith, A. (1979). *Fifteen Thousand Hours: Secondary Schools and Their Effects on Children*, Open books London, and Harvard University Press, Massachusetts.

Rutter, M., Tizard, J., and Whitmore, K. (1970). *Health Education and Behaviour*, Longmans, London.

Rutter, M., Cox, A., Tupling, C., Berger, M., and Yule, W. (1975a). Attainment and adjustment in 2 geographical areas—I. The prevalence of psychiatric disorder, *British Journal of Psychiatry*, **126**, 493–509.

Rutter, M., Yule, B., Quinton, D., Rowlands, O., Yule, W., and Berger, M. (1975b). Attainment and Adjustment in 2 Geographical areas—II Some factors accounting for area differences, *British Journal of Psychiatry*, **126**, 520–533.

Sack, W.H., Angell, R., Kinzie, J.D., and Rath, B. (1986). The psychiatric effects of massive trauma on Cambodian children: II, the family, the home and school, *Journal of the American Academy of Child Psychiatry*, **25**, 377–383.

Sargent, M. (1979). Caring about kids: talking to children about death, quoted by J. Segal in N. Garmezy and M. Rutter (eds) (1983), *Stress Coping and Development*, p. 340. McGraw-Hill, New York.

Savin-Williams, R.C. (1980). Social interactions of adolescent females in natural groups. In H.C. Foot, A.R. Chapman, and J.R. Smith (eds), *Friendships and Social Relationships in Children*, Wiley, New York.

Schachter, S., and Singer, J. (1962). Cognitive, social and physiological determinants of emotional state, *Psychological Review*, **69**, 379–399.

Schaffer, H.R. (1966). Activity level as a constitutional determinant of infantile reaction to deprivation, *Child Development*, **37**, 595–602.

Schleiffer, S.J., Keller, S.E., Carnerino, M., Thornton, J.C., and Stein, M.D. (1983). Suppression of lymphocyte stimulation following bereavement, *Journal of the American Medical Association*, **250**, 374–377.

Schleiffer, S.J., Keller, S.E., Siris, S.G., Davis, K.L., and Stein, M.D. (1985). Depression and immunity. Lymphocyte function in ambulatory depressed patients, hospitalised schizophrenic patients and patients hospitalised for herniorrhaphy, *Archives of General Psychiatry*, **42**, 129–133.

Schleiffer, S.J., Scott, B., Stein, M.D., and Keller, S.E. (1986). Behavioural and developmental aspects of immunity, *Journal of the American Academy of Child and Adolescent Psychiatry*, **25**, 751–763.

Seffrin, J., and Bailey, W. (1985). Approaches to adolescent smoking cessation and education. In J. Zins, D. Wagner, and C. Maker (eds), *Health Promotion in Schools*, Haworth Press, New York.

Segal, J. (1975). Research in the service of mental health, report of the research task force of the National Institute of Mental Health, quoted in Segal (1983) p. 340.

Segal, J. (1983). Utilisation of stress and coping. In N. Garmezy and M. Rutter (eds), *Stress, Coping and Development*, McGraw-Hill, New York.

Seligman, M.E.P., Abramson, L.Y., and Semmel, A. van Boeyer (1979). Depressive attributional style, *Journal of Abnormal Psychology*, **88**, 242–247.

Selman, R.L. (1980). *The Growth of Interpersonal Understanding*, Academic Press, London.

Selman, R.L. (1981). The child as a friendship philosopher: a case study in the growth of interpersonal understanding. In S. Asher and J.M. Gottman (eds), *The Development of Children's Friendships*, Cambridge University Press, Cambridge.

Selman, R.L., and Jaquette, D. (1977). The development of interpersonal awareness: Howard-Judge Baker social reasoning project, quoted in Berndt (1983) p. 163.

Selye, H. (1956). *The Stress of Life*. McGraw-Hill, New York.

Sharit, Y., Lewis, J.W., Terman, G.W., Gale, R.P., and Lilbeskind, J.C. (1984). Opioide peptides mediate the suppressive effect of stress on natural killer cell cytotoxicity, *Science*, **223**, 188–190.

Shaw, D., and Emery, R. (1988). Chronic family adversity and school-age children's adjustment, *Journal of the American Academy of Child and Adolescent Psychiatry*, **2**, 200–206.

Simmons, R.G., and Blyth, D. (1987). *Moving into Adolescence*, Aldine De Gruyter, New York.

Simon, H.A. (1979). Information processing models of cognition. In M. Rosenweig, and L. Ponter (eds), *Annual Review of Psychology*, **30**, 363–396.

Sjoback, H. (1973). *The Psychoanalytic Theory of Defensive Process*, Wiley, New York.

Skinner, B.F. (1953). *Science and Human Behaviour*, Free Press, Glencoe, Illinois.

Skuse, D. (1984). Extreme deprivation in early childhood—II. theoretical issues and a comparative review, *Journal of Child Psychology and Psychiatry*, **25**, 543–572.

Skuse, D., and Cox, A. (1985). Parenting the pre-school child: clinical and social implications of research into past and current disadvantage. In J. Stevenson (ed.), *Recent Advances in Developmental Psychopathology*, Pergamon Press, Oxford.

Skynner, R. (1974). School phobia: a reappraisal, *British Journal of Medical Psychology*, **47**, 1–16.

Smith, E.M., Meyer, W.J., and Blalock, J.E. (1982). Virus induced corticosterone in hypophysectomised mice: a possible lymphoid adrenal axis, *Science*, **218**, 1311–1312.

Smith, H.W. (1973). Some developmental interpersonal dynamics through childhood, *American Sociological Review*, **38**, 345–352.

Smith, P.K., and Connolly, K. (1972). Patterns of play and social interaction in pre-school children. In N. Blurton-Jones (ed.), *Ethological Studies of Child Behaviour*, Cambridge University Press, Cambridge.

Smith, W., and Rossman, R.B. (1986). Developmental changes in trait and situational denial under stress during childhood, *Journal of Child Psychology and Psychiatry*, **27**, 227–235.

Solomen, S., and Bromet E. (1982). The role of social factors in affective disorder: an assessment of the vulnerability model of Brown and his colleagues, *Psychological Medicine*, **12**, 123–130.

Solomon, G.F., and Amkraut, A.A. (1981). Psychologic and central nervous system influences on immune mechanisms, *Annual Review of Microbiology*, **35**, 155–184.

Spence, J.T., and Helmreich, R. (1978). *Masculinity and Femininity: Their Psychological Dimensions Correlates and Antecedents*, University of Texas Press, Austin.

Spitz, R. (1946). Analytic depression, *Psychoanalytic Study of the Child*, **2**, 313–342.

Spivack, G., and Shure, M.B., (1974). *Social Adjustment of Young Children*, Josey-Bass, San Francisco.

Sroufe, L.A. (1979a). Socioemotional development. In J. Osofsky (ed.), *Handbook of Infant Development*, Wiley, New York.

Sroufe, L.A. (1979b). The coherence of individual development, *American Psychologist*, **34**, 834–841.

Sroufe, L.A. (1985). Attachment classification from the perspective of infant–caregiver relationships and infant temperament, *Child Development*, **56**, 1–14.

Sroufe, L.A., and Fleeson. J. (1988). The coherence of family relationships. In R.A.

Hinde and J. Stevenson-Hinde (eds), *Relationships Within Families*, Oxford University Press, Oxford.

Stein, M., Keller, S., and Schleifer, S. (1981). The hypothalamus and the immune response. In H. Weiner, M. Hoffer, and A.J. Stunkard (eds), *Brain, Behaviour and Bodily Disease*, Raven Press, New York.

Stein, M., Schleifer, S., and Keller, S. (1982). The role of the brain and neuroendocrine system in immune regulation: potential links to neoplastic disease. In S. Levy (ed.), *Biological Mediators of Behaviour and Disease*, Elsevier, New York, pp. 147–168.

Steinhausen, H.C., and Radtke, B. (1986). Life events and child psychiatric disorders, *Journal of the American Academy of Child and Adolescent Psychiatry*, **1**, 125–129.

Steptoe, A. (1986). Research programme on breakdown in human adaptation of stress, *Stress Medicine*, **2**, 235–257.

Steptoe, A. (1987). The assessment of sympathetic nervous function in human stress research, *Journal of Psychosomatic Research*, **31**, 141–152.

Stern, D.N. (1977). *The First Relationships: Infant and Mother*, Harvard University Press, Cambridge, MA.

Stern, D.N. (1985). *The Interpersonal World of the Infant. A View from Psychoanalysis and Developmental Psychology*. Basic Books, New York.

Stevenson-Hinde, J. (1988). Individuals in relationships. In R.A. Hinde and J. Stevenson-Hinde (eds), *Relationships Within Families*. Clarendon Press, Oxford.

Stone, G., Hindy, W.C., and Schmidt, G.W. (1975). Teaching Mental Health Behaviours to Elementary School Children. *Professional Psychology*, **6**, 34–40.

Sullivan, H.S. (1953). *The Interpersonal Theory of Psychiatry*, Norton, New York.

Suomi, S.J., Kraemer, G.W., Baysinger, C.M., and Delizio, R.D. (1981). Inherited and experiential factors associated with individual differences in anxious behaviour displayed by rhesus monkeys. In D.F. Klein and J. Rabkin (eds), *Anxiety: New Research and Changing Concepts*, Raven Press, New York.

Sylvester-Bradley, B. (1981). Negativity in early infant and adult exchanges and its developmental significance. In P. Robinson (ed.), *Communication and Development*, Academic Press, London.

Taylor, D.C. (1985). Psychological aspects of chronic sickness, In M. Rutter and L. Hersov (eds), *Child and Adolescent Psychiatry: Modern Approaches*, Blackwell, Oxford.

Taylor, M.C., and Hall, J.A. (1982). Psychological androgyny: a review and reformulation of theories, methods and conclusions, *Psychological Bulletin*, **92**, 347–366.

Teasdale, J.D. (1983). Changes in cognition during depression: psychopathological implications, *Journal of the Royal Society of Medicine*, **76**, 1038–1043.

Tennant, C. (1985). Female vulnerability to depression, *Psychological Medicine*, **15**, 733–737.

Tennant, C., and Andrews, G. (1977). A scale to measure the stress of life events, *Australian and New Zealand Journal of Psychiatry*, **10**, 27–33.

Tennant, C., and Andrews, G. (1978). The pathogenic quality of life-event stress in neurotic impairment, *Archives of General Psychiatry*, **35**, 859–863.

Tennant, C., and Bebbington, P. (1978). The social causation of depression: a critique of the work of Brown and his colleagues, *Psychological Medicine*, **8**, 565–575.

Tennant, C., Bebbington, P., and Hurry, J. (1981). The role of life events in depressive illness. Is there a substantial causal relation? *Psychological Medicine*, **11**, 379–389.

Tennant, C., Hurry, J., and Bebbington, P. (1982). The relation of childhood separation experiences to adult depression and anxiety states, *British Journal of Psychiatry*, **141**, 475–482.

Tennes, K., and Kreye, M. (1985). Children's adrenocortical responses to classroom activities and tests in elementary school children, *Psychosomatic Medicine*, **47**, 451–460.

Tennes, K., Kreye, M., Avitable, N., and Wells, R., (1986). Behavioural correlates of excreted catecholamines and cortisol in second-grade children, *Journal of the American Academy of Child Psychiatry*, **25**, 764–770.

Terr, L.C. (1979). Children of Chowchilla—a study of Psychic Trauma, *Psychoanalytic Study of the Child*, **34**, 552–623.

Terr, L.C. (1981). Psychic trauma in children: observations following the Chowchilla school bus kidnapping, *American Journal of Psychiatry*, **138**, 14–19.

Terr, L.C. (1983). Chowchilla revisited: the effects of psychic trauma four years after a school bus kidnapping, *American Journal of Psychiatry*, **140**, 1543–1550.

Tesser, A., and Smith, J. (1980). Some effects of task relevance and friendship on helping: you don't always help the one you like, *Journal of Experimental and Social Psychology*, **16**, 582–590.

Thomas, A., and Chess, S. (1977). *Temperament and Development*, Brunner/Mazel, New York.

Tizard, B., and Hodges, J. (1978). The effect of early institutional rearing on the development of 8-year-old children, *Journal of Child Psychology and Psychiatry*, **19**, 99–118.

Trevarthen, C.B. (1985). Facial expressions of emotion in mother–infant dyads, *Human Neurobiology*, **4**, 21–32.

Triseliotis, J. (1980). Growing up in foster care and after. In J. Triseliotis (ed.), *New Developments in Foster Care and Adoption*, Routledge & Kegan Paul, London.

Uhlenhuth, E.H., and Paykel, E.S. (1973). Symptom configuration and life events, *Archives of General Psychiatry*, **28**, 744–748.

Ursin, H., Baade, E., and Levine, S.N. (eds) (1978). *Psychobiology of Stress: A Study of Coping Men*, Academic Press, New York.

Vandell, D.L. (1980). Sociability with peer and mother during the first year, *Developmental Psychology*, **16**, 355–361.

Van Eerdewegh, M., Bieri, M., Parilla, R., and Clayton, P. (1982). The bereaved child, *British Journal of Psychiatry*, **140**, 23–29.

Vaughn, B., Egeland, B., Sroufe, L.A., and Waters, E. (1979). Individual differences in infant–mother attachment at 12 and 18 months: stability and change in families under stress, *Child Development*, **50**, 971–975.

Venkatamiah, S.R., and Bosathi, K.K. (1977). Socio-psychological analysis of children's quarrels. Empirical investigation—results and discussion, *Child Psychiatry Quarterly*, **10**, 1–7.

Vieil, H.O. (1985). Dimensions of social support: a conceptual framework for research, *Social Psychiatry*, **20**, 156–162.

Vygotsky, L.S. (1934). *Thought and Language*, MIT Press, Cambridge MA.

Waldrop, M.F., and Halverson, C. (1975). Intensive and extensive peer behaviour: longitudinal and cross-sectional analysis, *Child Development*, **46**, 19–28.

Waller, L., and Okihiro, N. (1978). *Burglary: The Victim and the Public*, University of Toronto Press, Toronto.

Wallerstein, J. (1983). Children of divorce—stress and developmental tasks. In N. Garmezy and M. Rutter (eds), *Stress Coping and Development*, McGraw-Hill, New York.

Wallerstein, J., and Kelly, J. (1980). *Surviving the break-up. How Children and Parents Cope with Divorce*, New York, Basic Books.

Warheit, G.J. (1979). Life events, coping, stress and depressive symptomatology, *American Journal of Psychiatry*, **136**, 502–507.

Wasserman, G.A. (1986). Affective expression in normal and physically handicapped infants: situational and developmental effects, *Journal of the American Academy of Child Psychiatry*, **3**, 393–399.

Wasserman, G.A., and Allen, R. (1985). Maternal withdrawal from handicapped toddlers, *Journal of Child Psychology and Psychiatry*, **26**, 381–387.

Waters, E. (1978). The reliability and stability of individual differences in infant–mother attachment, *Child Development*, **49**, 483–494.

Waters, E., Wippman, J., and Sroufe, L.A. (1979). Attachment, positive affect and competence in the peer group: two studies in construct validation, *Child Development*, **50**, 821–829.

Weiss, E., Olin, B., Rollin, H.R., Fischer, H.B., and Bepler, C. (1957). Emotional factors in coronary occlusion, *Archives of Internal Medicine*, **99**, 628–634.

Weissman, M.W., Gammon, D., John, K., Merikangas, R., Warner, V., Prusoff, B., and Sholomska, D. (1987). Children of depressed parents, *Archives of General Psychiatry*, **44**, 847–853.

Wellman, H.M., and Johnson, C.N. (1979a). Understanding mental processes: a developmental study of 'remember' and 'forget', *Child Development*, **50**, 79–88.

Wellman, H.M., and Johnson, C.N. (1979b). Understanding of mental process: a developmental study of 'know' and 'guess', *Child Development*, **49**, 1107–1113.

Werner, E., and Smith, R.S. (1982). *Vulnerable but Invincible. A Study of Resilient Children*, McGraw-Hill, New York.

West, D.J. (1982). *Delinquency, its Roots, Careers and Prospects*, Heinemann Educational, London.

Whitehead, L. (1979). Sex differences in children's responses to family stress: a reevaluation, *Journal of Child Psychology and Psychiatry*, **20**, 246–254.

Williams, L., and Westermeyer (1983). Psychiatric problems among adolescent southeast Asian refugees, *Journal of Nervous and Mental Disease*, **171**, 79–85.

Wilson, R., and Cairns, E. (1988). Sex-role attributes, perceived competence and the development of depression in adolescence, *Journal of Child Psychology and Psychiatry*, **29**, 635–650.

Wilson, S. (1978). Vandalism and 'defensible space' on London housing estates. In R. Clarke (ed.), *Tackling Vandalism. Home Office Research Study*, HMSO, London.

Wing, J.K., Mann, S., Leff, J., and Nixon, J. (1978). The concept of a case in psychiatric population surveys, *Psychological Medicine*, **8**, 203–217.

Winnicott, D. (1968). *Through Paediatrics to Psychoanalysis*, pp. 204–218. Hayworth Press, London.

Wisley, D.W., Mascer, F.T., and Morgan S.B. (1983). Psychological aspects of severe burn injuries in children, *Health Psychology*, **2**, 45–72.

Wolff, H.G., Wolf, S., and Hare, C. (eds) (1950). *Life Stress and Bodily Disease*, Williams and Wilkins, Baltimore.

Wolkind, S., and Kruk, S. (1985). From child to parent: early separation and the adaptation to motherhood. In A.R. Nicol (ed.), *Longitudinal Studies in Child Psychology and Psychiatry*, Wiley, Chichester.

Wolkind, S., and Rutter, M. (1985a). Separation, loss and family relationships. In M. Rutter and L. Hersov (eds), *Child Psychiatry—Modern Approaches*, Blackwell, Oxford.

Wolkind, S., and Rutter, M.(1985b). Socio-cultural factors. In M. Rutter and L. Hersov (eds), *Child Psychiatry—Modern Approaches*, Blackwell, Oxford.

Wolkind, S.N., Vyas, I., and Haris, R. (1982). Families and children—child psychiatric contributions in the general hospital. In F. Creed and J. Pfeffer (eds), *Medicine and Psychiatry. A Practical Approach*, Pitman, London.

Woodward, S., Pope, A., Robson, W.J., and Hogan, O. (1985). Bereavement counselling after sudden infant death, *British Medical Journal*, **290**, 363–365.

Wright, B.A. (1942). Altruism in children and the perceived conduct of others, *Journal of Abnormal and Social Psychology*, **37**, 218–223.

Yamamoto, K., Soliman, A., Parsons, J., and Davis, O.C., Jr (1987). Voices in unison: stressful events in the lives of children in 6 countries, *Journal of Child Psychology and Psychiatry*, **6**, 855–864.

Younnis, J. (1980). *Parents and Peers in Social Development: A Sullivan–Piaget Perspective*, University of Chicago Press, Chicago.

Yule, W., and Williams, R. (1988). Post-traumatic stress reactions in children. Paper read at the first European Conference on Traumatic Stress Research (August) and the World Congress of Behaviour Therapy (September).

Zahn-Waxler, C., Chapman, M., and Cummings, E.M. (1986). Cognitive and social development in infants and toddlers with a bipolar parent, *Child Psychiatry and Human Development*, **15**, 75–85.

Zahn-Waxler, C., and Radke-Yarrow, M. (1982). The development of altruism: alternative research strategies. In N. Eisenberg (ed.), *Development of Prosocial Behaviour*, Academic Press, New York.

Zahn-Waxler, C., Cummings, E.M., McKnew, D.H., and Radke-Yarrow, M. (1984a). Altruism, aggression and social interactions in young children with a manic-depressive parent, *Child Development*, **55**, 112–122.

Zahn-Waxler, C., McKnew, D.H., Cummings, E.M., Davenport, Y.B., and Radke-Yarrow, M. (1984b). Problem behaviours and peer interactions of young children with a manic-depressive parent, *American Journal of Psychiatry*, **141**, 236–240.

Zajonc, R.B., and Markus, H. (1984). Affect and cognition: the hard interface. In C. Izard, J. Kagan, and R.B. Zajonc (eds), *Emotions, Cognitions and Behaviours*, Cambridge University Press, Cambridge.

Zins, J., Wagner, D., and Maher, C. (eds) (1985). *Health Promotion in Schools*, Haworth Press, New York.

Zuckerman, M. (1979). *Sensation Seeking: Beyond the Optimal Level of Arousal*, Erlbaum, Hillsdale, NJ.

INDEX